Torah MiEtzion
New Readings in Tanach
Volume 1: Bereshit

TORAH MIETZION
New Readings in Tanach
BERESHIT

EDITORS

Rav Ezra Bick &
Rav Yaakov Beasley

Maggid Books
Yeshivat Har Etzion

Torah MiEtzion
New Readings in Tanach
Volume 1: Bereshit

First Edition, 2011

Maggid Books
A division of Koren Publishers Jerusalem Ltd.

POB 8531, New Milford, CT 06776-8531, USA
& POB 4044, Jerusalem 91040, Israel

www.korenpub.com

© Yeshivat Har Etzion 2011

ISBN 978 161 329 0064, *hardcover original*

A CIP catalogue record for this title is
available from the British Library

Printed and bound in USA

כִּי יְדַעְתִּיו לְמַעַן אֲשֶׁר יְצַוֶּה אֶת בָּנָיו וְאֶת בֵּיתוֹ אַחֲרָיו
וְשָׁמְרוּ דֶּרֶךְ ה' לַעֲשׂוֹת צְדָקָה וּמִשְׁפָּט
(בראשית יח, יט)

Dedicated in loving memory of
Dr. William Major *z"l*
אברהם זאב בן יהודה ז"ל

A Holocaust survivor and devoted psychiatrist, Dr. Major was animated by a deep love of Torah, Israel and the Jewish People. Through his personal example of quiet dignity and deep commitment to ḥesed and Torah study, he conveyed these values to his family and made an indelible impression on those who were privileged to know him.

Dr. Major cherished Yeshivat Har Etzion, which in his eyes embodied his loves and commitments, and was deeply grateful for all that his children gained there. It is therefore a singularly fitting tribute that this series – which brings the profound and innovative Torah of Yeshivat Har Etzion to the broader public – is dedicated to his memory.

תהא נשמתו צרורה בצרור החיים

Contents

Contributors

Preface

The present volume, the first in a five volume series, presents a selection of *shiurim* given on the *parasha* by different lecturers, all of whom are connected in one way or another with Yeshivat Har Etzion. Most of them originally appeared as part of the Parsha series of the Israel Koschitzky Virtual Beit Midrash, which has been appearing for the last fifteen years and is disseminated over the Internet. But the impetus for publication is not merely a desire to repackage a successful and interesting series of *shiurim*. The VBM series has managed to be itself the catalyst for the written expression of a body of work, from different authors, which represents a distinct approach to *parshanut HaTorah* – one which has been developing over the last forty years in the yeshiva and its affiliated Herzog Teacher's College, and which today is the most vibrant and influential school of modern commentary and interpretation of the biblical text within the Torah world.

One of the unique characteristics of Yeshivat Har Etzion was the inclusion of serious study of Tanach in the curriculum from the outset of the yeshiva. Years before the establishment of an academic affiliate – Herzog Teacher's College – the yeshiva held regular *shiurim* on Tanach alongside the traditional *shiurim* in Gemara which occupied the yeshiva's core. Rav Amital *zt"l*, the yeshiva's founder, explained that this was essential to his vision of the yeshiva, to foster an organic understanding of Torah and Torah philosophy, for which it was obvious to him that Tanach was part of the foundation. When, a few years later, the yeshiva established a teacher's college, the Tanach department was one of the two main divisions of the college. It naturally attracted scholars and students, eventually adding to its staff young teachers who had themselves been educated in the yeshiva. Today, aside from the ongoing study of Tanach in the yeshiva itself, and the scheduled curriculum of Tanach studies in Herzog College, the college also sponsors a yearly conference on Tanach (*yemei iyun beTanach*), which attracts dozens of scholars and thousands of teachers and students from all over Israel for a week of *shiurim* on all aspects and books of Tanach, and publishes a scholarly journal of Tanach studies (*Megadim*).

The combined influence of all these related activities has resulted in what some have called a "revolution in the study of Tanach." The accuracy of that description is supported by the controversy that erupted a few years back, when a prominent Rosh Yeshiva distributed a pamphlet dedicated solely to attacking it. For many, on the other hand, the controversy was rather mystifying, as the principles behind the "revolution" were the way they had always assumed one should approach the study of Tanach, precisely because it was *"divrei Elokim Ḥayyim,"* the word of the Living God.

What are the salient features of this approach, as exemplified in the essays in this volume? I am sure that many readers will not find any of these features particularly revolutionary, as they will be familiar from many contemporary commentaries. Indeed, these principles are not at all exclusive to Yeshivat Har Etzion, partly because of the success in disseminating them, and partly because the roots of the approach are found in the wider field of Jewish studies. Nonetheless, the yeshiva is the clear center of this kind of study, and is perhaps the only institution where Tanach studies are focused on producing original insights and deeper meanings in this manner. I would like to highlight four features.

1. UNDERSTANDING TANACH THROUGH TANACH

First and foremost is the belief that Tanach is meant to be read and understood by the reader, without the absolute necessity of outside interlocutors. The keys to understanding Tanach are found within Tanach itself. This does not mean that *Torah shebe'al peh*, for instance, is not necessary for understanding halakha, or is not an additional part of the meaning of a verse. It does mean that there is a *peshat*, a plain meaning, which is accessible and which is **meant** to be understood by the reader.

This should not be understood as a license, but rather as an obligation and a challenge. It does not lighten the load of interpretation, but rather imposes a burden – the meaning of the text is found in the text, and your job is to find it. The Torah was not written in order to mystify you or lead you down blind alleys; the meaning and the message are there, perhaps easily seen, perhaps uncovered by diligent exertion, but nonetheless there to be found. Hence, the most important tool in interpretation is to read well, sensitively and openly, listening carefully to every word, and asking oneself what the text is saying.

It has sometimes been claimed that this leads to disregard of the classical commentators. Factually, this claim is false, as can be seen in the essays in this volume. Most of the discussions here use, reflect, and sometimes disagree with, classical and later commentators, even as they seek to go beyond them. However, it is true that the use of commentators is different than in some other schools. The study of Tanach exemplified in this volume is not the study of the commentators. It is the study of Tanach. In other words, the pioneering work of Rashi and Ramban, Radak and Abarbanel, the Netziv and Rav Hirsch, are aids, not the subject itself. In many schools today, it would be fair to say that the subject is "Ḥumash im Rashi." The subject of this volume is "Ḥumash." This is not a belittlement of Rashi. It does reflect a belief that the Torah is accessible, even without Rashi. Rashi clarifies the meaning of the text for me – and sometimes, perhaps, obscures it. The challenge is to use Rashi without being so dependent on him that I cannot approach the text afresh.

In Orthodox academic study of Tanach today, in many places the majority of what is taught is *parshanut*, how the great commentators approached the text, and not the text itself. This trend was undoubtedly strengthened by the extraordinary work of Nechama Leibowitz, who taught an entire generation how to understand Rashi, to ask what was bothering Rashi, to compare the different commentaries and evaluate their different approaches. One result of this massive undertaking was to encourage the shift of focus from the biblical text to the classical commentaries as a field unto itself. But accompanying this trend is undoubtedly a fear of approaching the text directly, whether from modesty or prudence. In that sense, the studies in this volume are revolutionary in the confidence they express that one can – and indeed must – approach the text directly.

Revolution is undoubtedly a relative word. Rashbam quotes his grandfather, Rashi, as encouraging him to engage in the search for the "interpretations (*peshatim*) which arise anew every day." The Middle Ages were a time where the search for a deeper understanding of the text, based on reading and examining it directly, were the basis for nearly all the great achievements in *parshanut*. The approach here is no more than first and foremost a return to that great imperative.

Two results follow directly from this initial premise.

2. LITERARY TOOLS

If we are reading the text directly, then we are reading it as a text is meant to be read, and this introduces the need to read using the tools of literary analysis. Of course, if the Torah is not a book, but a code or a mystery, it would be illegitimate to read it with the same eyes and mind that one reads literature. For this we have the oft-repeated principle, *dibra Torah belashon benei adam*. The Torah is literature, divine literature, written not in a special divine language but in the language and the style of man.

This exhibits itself in many ways. The most important is in being open to a close and sensitive reading of the text, to the choice of every word, to trying to determine the influence of the choice of a particular phrase or the order of a sentence. Every essay in this volume exhibits a heightened sensitivity to what the text is trying to say. The ear of the reader is exhorted to press itself as close as possible, to hear even the hint of an echo of an idea, to notice the change of inflection in one telling or another, to consider the import of one word as opposed to its synonym, and in general to listen, to listen and to be willing to infer. Here, too, I think it is obvious that this not really as revolutionary as it might sound. Is this not the main emphasis of the Midrash – a careful emphasis on the particular word used and a search for what that particular word or phrase might be hinting? If one would accuse the authors of this work of engaging in *drush*, the accusation would be accepted, I think, with pride. It might indeed be said that a literary sensitivity obscures the fence between *drush* and *peshat*, or, to put it another way, it presents *drush* as *peshat* on another level, a second layer of *peshat*.

There is, in fact, a divide among the authors of this volume between those who avoid Midrash and those who consciously use it. I think both are engaged in a form of Midrash, in the finest sense of the word. Some of my colleagues, in my own opinion unnecessarily, fear the authority of Midrash and its effects on their own ability to read the text afresh. But, in any event, the methodology used here is a return to *drush*, not as homiletics, and not as free imagination to supplement the fact of the biblical narrative, but as the reading of the text itself, closely, imaginatively, and sensitively.

Different authors use different literary tools, aside from the shared commitment to listening to every word. You will find here structural analysis (Samet, Grossman), terminology analysis, such as the discovery of a "leading term" (Bazak, Waxman), textual comparison (just about everyone), plot analysis (Rimon, Medan), character analysis (Bick, Lichtenstein, Granot), and more. There are, naturally, major disagreements among the different authors, not only on particular points, but also in approach. There are also differences in approach which reflect on different areas of interest – psychology, philosophy, literature. (In some cases, not surprisingly, this is a reflection of which secular field was studied by the author.) Because the understanding of a literary work necessarily requires understanding of external factors in its writing, the studies will incorporate findings from history, archeology, Semitics, and not only literature per se. This is not a monolithic work in terms of its specific content, but it does express a fairly consistent approach on what the reader and interpreter is looking for.

3. PARASHA, SEFER, TANACH

Another result of the above is that the field of interest is not focused on the single verse, but on the story, the entire narrative, and in some cases, the whole Tanach. To a great extent, classical commentary was verse- or even word-oriented. We could not begin to operate today without the great achievements in explaining the meaning of every word, phrase and sentence in Tanach. Today, because we are listening to the narrative as literature, the focus is widened: what is the story about? What is the meaning of the larger picture? Where are we going, and toward what are we being led? Among the great commentators of the Middle Ages, Ramban occasionally looks at the wider picture. Abarbanel is probably the most prominent example of the approach that begins with the *parasha* rather than the verse, as is clear from the structure of his commentary. But most medieval commentary is directed immediately at one verse at a time. The essays in this volume are all about explaining an entire story, or at least an episode, and, in some cases, cast even a wider net, explaining the entire *sefer*. This influences method as well. One of the common devices used in all of the essays of the book is comparison with other sections of Tanach, not just to discover the meaning of an obscure Hebrew word, but to understand the meaning of a narrative by comparing literary themes, expressions, allusions and parallelisms throughout Tanach. (This too is an obvious return to the method of rabbinic Midrash.)

4. SIGNIFICANCE

Finally, a crucial feature of the school of interpretation presented here is the search for significance and meaning. This is important not in relation to more traditional schools, such as the yeshiva world or synagogue, where the search for spiritual meaning overshadows the need for textual interpretation. However, given that we are dealing in genuine textual commentary, it is necessary to emphasize the deeply held belief that the text is a divine text, with a meaning and a message, and that purpose is itself part of the method of interpretation. It is not just that one would like, as an added bonus, to find some positive message in a biblical text. It is a principle of interpretation that the text has a purpose, consistent with the purpose of the Torah as a whole. In other words, it is a fair question to ask, at the outset of the exploration of interpretation, what is the significance and purpose of a story, text, or narrative. All traditional commentators do this occasionally, prominently Ramban, and none more explicitly than Ralbag, but many modern commentators, especially those committed to "Tanach as literature," have shied away from doing so – even when they are personally committed to Tanach as a holy text. The essays in this book are suffused with the quest for meaning and significance, often explicitly, and universally implicitly. There are undoubtedly places which might view this as a fault. One of the authors in this book, a lecturer at Herzog College as well as at a university in Israel, told me how he once wrote an article for an academic journal, which he divided into two parts. The first solved a particular textual problem in *Trei Asar*, and the second addressed the significance (in light of the textual interpretation) of the passage. The reviewer told the author that the first part was very good, but in the second part he was writing "Herzog College." (He approved the article anyway.) Naturally, the author accepted the comment as a compliment, even if it was not so intended.

Commentary on Tanach was once a great rabbinic occupation. We need only remember that the two greatest Talmudic figures of medieval France and Spain, Rashi and Ramban, were both great biblical commentators, upon whose works all subsequent commentaries are built. Gradually, rabbinic attention became more segmented. I doubt that anything sinister was taking place here, at least at first – the thrust towards specialization occurs in Torah studies just as it does in other fields. While the greatest figures in the earlier Middle Ages were often polymaths, combining halakha, Bible, and philosophy – figures like Rabbi Sa'adia Gaon and Rambam spring to mind – and Ramban could warn his students of Kabbala to not pay attention to any kabbalist who was not a master of halakha, over the years the divide between the different areas of traditional scholarship became more pronounced. In the modern yeshiva world, most yeshivot view *parashat hashavua* as a rote ritual to cover Ḥumash veRashi weekly, and perhaps as a source for homiletics of weekly discourses, whether of a *musar* nature or general ideological *drush*. While Talmud is learned in order to plumb its depths and uncover new interpretations and nuances, the study of Tanach is viewed at best as a religious obligation to familiarize oneself with classic texts. In fact, in large sections of the yeshiva world, it is basically ignored altogether. I suspect very strongly that the major factor behind the kind of Tanach commentary in this work and in the Etzion school in general is the return of the study of Tanach to the *beit midrash*, to the world shared with Talmudic learning. The true common denominator of all of the authors in this volume is their roots in the *beit midrash* and their perception of the study of Tanach as a continuation of Talmud. This has a direct influence – as I tried to indicate above in the comparison with the method of Midrash – as well as in a more indirect influence in the method of Talmudic explanation in a modern yeshiva, obviously not in the details, but in the kind of search for underlying meaning and conceptual analysis – a kind of biblical *lomdus*, if you will. The reason why there is such a concentration of this kind of analysis in Yeshivat Har Etzion is because of the integration of Tanach into the *beit midrash* that exists there, and wherever a similar approach is found today – and it is indeed found elsewhere – it is because the individual has refused to allow his education to become bifurcated between Talmud and Tanach. If there are great institutions of Torah learning where Tanach is studied, but nonetheless do not engage in the sort of analysis done here, it is because the "Tanach department" there is divorced from the "Talmud department." The consequence is that the Talmudists, when they turn to Tanach, engage in homiletics, and the "Tanachists" engage in the history of commentary, or limit themselves to the details of philology and grammar. The greatest exception to this division in the modern yeshiva world is Rav Naftali Tzvi Yehuda Berlin, the Netziv. He and his commentary, the *Ha'amek Davar*, may indeed be considered the grandfather of the movement exemplified by these volumes.

The importance of these volumes is not so much in introducing a new method, for I am sure that most readers have had some exposure to it, either directly through reading or hearing one of the authors, or through other similar authors. The importance is in the concentration in one place, demonstrating the power and consistency in reading the entire Torah this way. It is not a method of producing a *hiddush*, or of solving some particular hitherto unexplained problem, but of reading Tanach as a whole. The book is a recommendation that everyone should read every *parasha* in this way – reading, or perhaps rereading, and then rereading again, and thereby understanding the message and the meaning.

* * *

The majority of the essays in this book were originally published in the Parsha series of the Israel Koschitzky Virtual Beit Midrash (www.vbm-torah.org). The VBM is an ongoing project of multiple weekly *shiurim* in all aspects of Torah learning, and this is therefore the place to express our thanks to the Israel Koschitzky Family Charitable Foundation for its generous support which both enabled the work presented in this volume and maintains the continued worldwide dissemination of Torah through the VBM. Those articles have been read, in their original form, by thousands of readers. In some cases, they have been shortened for publication in this book. The archives of the VBM have between ten and fifteen excellent articles on each *parasha*. The originals of the articles published here, as well as all of the others, can be accessed on the VBM website.

The article of Rav Breuer *zt"l* is translated from his book *Pirkei Bereshit* (Tevunot 1999). *The Land and the Land of Canaan* by Rav Yoel Bin-Nun was provided by the author. The article of Rav Aharon Lichtenstein was adapted and translated from a lecture given at the *yemei iyun beTanach* in 2006.

Many more studies in all aspects of Tanach can be found in the 50 volumes of *Megadim*, the Tanach journal of Herzog College.

Those articles originally written in Hebrew were ably and elegantly translated by Kaeren Fish, David Silverberg, and David Strauss.

In the name of all of the authors, I invite the readers to comment and contribute to the ongoing endeavor *lehagdil Torah uleha'adira*.

Virtual Beit Midrash: http://www.vbm-torah.org
VBM Parsha archives: http://www.vbm-torah.org/parsha.htm
Correspondence: office@etzion.org.il

Ezra Bick
Erev Ḥag Matan Torah, 5771

Parashat Bereshit

"And God Saw that It Was Good"

by Rav Chanoch Waxman

I.

Parashat Bereshit begins with a bang. "In the beginning, God created the heaven and the earth" (Gen. 1:1). In a striking passage, the Torah teaches the crucial philosophical and theological truth that it was God who created the world. From a certain perspective, one might say that the rest of the Torah, or at least the remainder of the creation story presented in chapter one, constitutes mere detailing and development of this fundamental theme.

However, this is not the only fundamental truth chapter one aims to teach. Throughout the chapter the Torah emphasizes not just God's creative act, but also the quality of the created objects. After the introductory verses (1:1–2), God orders the existence of light (1:3). The immediate accomplishment of this directive is closely followed by God's observation that His work is good: "And God saw that the light was good…" (1:4). From this point on, the staccato phrase, "And God saw that it was good," appears repeatedly throughout the chapter (1:10, 12, 18, 21, 25). Taken together, these six appearances of the term "good" more or less follow a pattern and define a general creation formula. God speaks and creates. Following on the heels of God's creation of a particular object or entity, God notes that His work is good.

3

In addition, the chapter closes with the phrase, "And God saw everything that he had made, and, behold, it was very good" (1:31). The placement of the term "good" at the end of the chapter, the modification of the stock phrase to include the modifier "very" (טוב מאוד) and the expansion of God's vision to include "everything that He had made" all serve to emphasize the point made above. God's world and the things He has made are good.

Finally, the term "good" modifies God's work seven times throughout the chapter, highlighting this as a key term and generating a parallel between the seven "goods" and the seven days of the creation process. No more need be said. Chapter one of Sefer Bereshit teaches not just of God the creator, but also of the good things He has made, the "good world."

II.

The making of mankind constitutes the crescendo of the creation narrative of chapter one. God creates man last, at the conclusion of six days of labor, an entire world of warm-up. This seems to signal that man represents God's crowning achievement in creating the "good world." Let us take a look at the text.

> And God said, Let Us make mankind in Our image and likeness and they will have dominion over the fish of the sea, the birds of the air, the cattle and over all the earth and every creeping thing that creeps on the earth. So God created mankind in His own image, in the image of God He created him; male and female He created them. And God blessed them... (1:26–28)

Strikingly, the term "good" is completely absent from *parashat adam*, the creation of mankind. The key word of Chapter One is missing! Furthermore, the creation of man deviates from the standard creation formula. While in the standard formula, creation is always followed by vision, i.e. God's observation of goodness, here God makes no observation as to the goodness of His handiwork. It is not the case that God created man and then "saw that it was good." We are left with the apparent conclusion that while all else in God's world is good, man is apparently not "good."

This seems a bit hard to accept (see *Bereshit Raba* 9:14 and Abarbanel on our topic). A short detour to the end of *Parashat Bereshit* should help explain this intuition. There, the Torah depicts God as regretting the creation of man: "And God repented that He had made man..." (6:5). This regret results from the evil (*ra*) of man's thoughts, heart and actions: "And God **saw** (וירא) that the wickedness (רעת) of man was great in the earth, and that all the impulse of the thoughts of his heart was only evil (רע) continually" (6:5). The text implicitly contrasts the "*ra*" (רע) of man in Chapter Six with the "*tov*" (טוב) of the world of Chapter One through the obvious "bad-good" linguistic dichotomy.

This contrast is further highlighted by the texts' utilizing the phrase, "And God saw" (וירא), part of the stock good-world formula of Chapter One. When God observes man, he sees "bad." This seems to constitute a result of the events of *Parashat Bereshit*: rebellion, murder, etc. Of course mankind deserves the accolade "bad" by the time we reach Chapter Six. However, in Chapter One, we stand at the very inception of man's existence, before mankind's sad history of disobedience and sin. Is it truly the case that man is already "not good" from the very start? Can it really be that from his very beginnings he constitutes the proverbial "bad apple" in an otherwise good world?

III.

Often in Torah study, a new question can help answer an old question. In this spirit, let us plunge a little deeper into the role of the term "good" in Chapter One. Earlier, I argued that the term should be viewed as part of a creation formula in which God first creates a particular thing and then immediately observes that it is good. Furthermore, I claimed that the seven appearances of the term in the chapter parallel the seven days of the entire creation process. Finally, I maintained that the last appearance of the term, the "very good" of 1:31, constitutes a deliberate variation on the stock phrase meant to summarize and modify the entire creation of Chapter One.

Two conclusions, or perhaps expectations, emerge naturally from this line of thinking. First, every object created should be followed by the observation of its goodness. Second, the six appearances of the stock phrase, "And God saw that it was good," parallel the six days of active creation and should be apportioned one to each day. A quick glance at Chapter One should be enough to demonstrate that this structure more or less holds up (see Days One, Four, Five and Six). However, the creation of man (1:27) is not the only problem. Let us take a careful look at the making of the "firmament" (רקיע) on Day Two.

> And God said, Let there be a firmament in the midst of the waters, and let it divide water from water. And God made the firmament, and divided the waters which were under the firmament from the waters which were above the firmament: and it was so. And God called the firmament Heaven. And there was evening and there was morning, a second day. (1:6–8)

God makes the firmament and yet does not note its goodness. Does this mean that the sky, like man, is not good? Is Day Two not a good day? Quite clearly, something in our thinking must be modified.

Reading the Day Three story and a bit of thought about the making of the firmament should provide the necessary clarification. The story of Day Three (1:9–12) divides into two subsections. In the first, God causes the waters under the firmament, now called heaven, to gather and move aside, thereby creating the dry land and the seas. God then sees that "it was good" (1:9–10). In the second subsection, God decrees the existence of grasses and trees. As usual, upon realization of His decree, God observes that "it was good" (1:11–12). It appears that the missing "good" of the firmament and Day Two has made its way to Day Three.

This is no accident, as an organic connection exists between the creation of the firmament on Day Two and the creation of the dry land and seas on Day Three. In Chapter One, the structure of the world around us consists of dry land, seas, sky and waters above the sky – all formed out of the watery chaos (1:2). Day Two (1:6–8) and the first subsection of Day Three (1:9–10) describe the process by which this occurs. First, God limits the waters by creating the firmament, placing some water above the sky and some beneath. Second, in the next stage of the limitation, God causes the waters to gather together, thereby revealing the dry land. The creation of the firmament, dry land and seas in fact constitutes one unit that may be termed "the limitation of the waters."

This should help explain why the term "good" fails to appear on Day Two in reference to the firmament. In fact, it does appear in reference to the firmament – but only in verse ten, at the end of the process of "the limitation of the waters," a process in which the creation of the firmament constitutes merely a preliminary stage. Only after the waters have found their **final place**, only after the creation of the sea-land-sky system is **complete**, does the word "good" appear. Only that which is complete and "in place" can be termed good in God's eyes.

As signaled above, I believe that the problem of the firmament and Day Two provides crucial insight into the meaning of the term "good" in Chapter One. Only that which has found its proper place, which is complete and which plays its role as part of a well-ordered world, can be termed "good." However, to resolve the problem of the creation of man, we must take another step and figure out in what sense mankind at the moment of its creation has not yet found its "proper place."

IV.

The difficult phrase and concept "*tzelem Elokim*," image of God, constitutes part of the core of *parashat adam*, the creation narrative of mankind. The term or a variation on its root appears once in the planning stage: "Let Us make mankind in Our image (1:26) "... (צלמנו), and twice in the action stage: "So God created mankind in His own image (בצלמו), in the image of God (בצלם אלקים) He created them..." (1:27). But what does it mean?

The options suggested by Jewish exegetes span the gamut from the actual form of God (Rashi 1:27), to divine soul (Ramban), to rational intellect (Rambam, Guide for the Perplexed I:1). In my opinion, an additional interpretation of the concept of *tzelem Elokim* can be formulated in light of the actions of Elokim in Chapter One.

While God does indeed create the world out of nothing at the outset of the chapter, creation out of nothing is not His primary occupation in Chapter One. Rather, most of God's activity in the chapter is dedicated to the process of fashioning the primordial chaos into a well-ordered and inhabited world (see Ramban 1:1). A quick reference to the text should help confirm this claim. At the start of the narrative, the world is "without form and void" (1:2); it is shapeless and empty of recognizable entities – but it is not completely empty. There are "depths," "water" and "darkness" (1:2) – an altogether frightening and dreary picture, but all is not lost. The very same verse also refers to "the wind of God" (רוח אלקים), a symbol of God's presence. Elokim subsequently creates light, the antithesis of the dark of 1:2. On Day Two, God creates the firmament, the beginning of the process of "the limitation of the waters," thereby eventually yielding the sky-land-seas structure, the antidote to the shapeless encompassing wateriness of 1:2. By the middle of Day Three, God moves on to the problem of "void" and in the remainder of the six days of active work fills the land with grasses, trees, animals and people; the heavens with birds, sun, moon and stars; and the seas with fish. Elokim of Chapter One is not so much God the creator but perhaps more accurately God the constructor, the shaper, the molder, the conqueror of chaos, who through various means arranges a well-ordered and inhabited world.

The internal structure and interrelationship of the six days of creation support this interpretation. The days and their creation contents may be charted as follows:

# Day	Creation contents	# Day	Creation contents
One	*Light*	Four	*Sun, Moon, and Stars*
Two	*Sky*	Five	*Birds and Fish*
Three	*Land, Grass and Trees*	Six	*Animals and People*

We may well think of column two, the items created on Days One through Three, as resources. If so, the items listed in column four, created on Days Four through Six, constitute the utilizers of these resources. The heavenly bodies "utilize" light, the birds utilize and fill the sky and the animals and people utilize the land, grass and trees. While some details remain to be ironed out (see questions for further study), the basic idea should be clear. Elokim, the conqueror of chaos, structures a well-ordered, balanced and full world.

This brings us full circle to the concept of *tzelem Elokim*, the making of mankind in God's image in Chapter One. Let us return to *parashat adam*.

Let Us make mankind in Our image and likeness and they will have dominion over the fish of the sea, the birds of the air, the cattle and over all the earth and every creeping thing that creeps on the earth. So God created mankind in His own image, in the image of God He created them. And God blessed them, and God said to them: Be fruitful and multiply, fill the earth and subdue it; and have dominion over the fish of the sea, and over the birds of the air and over every living thing that moves on the earth. (1:26–28)

Elokim plans and executes the making of a creature in His own image – a creature with the capacity for conquering chaos, for structuring a well-ordered, balanced, full and good world. God charges this being with filling the world and ruling over it. In fact, He charges this being to realize the meaning and potential of its own *tzelem Elokim*, its own built in divine-like potential – to fashion and maintain a good world.

All of this should help us finally tackle the problem of the lack of "And God saw that it was good" in *parashat adam*, a problem we reformulated as the question of mankind's "place" and "completeness." The analysis until this point should make us realize that mankind of Chapter One has no particular "place." Rather, its place in the scheme of things is in the fulfilling of its mission, a mission that involves moving over the world, filling it, ruling it, and when necessary reinforcing, ensuring and remaking the good world wrought by God. Man remains incomplete and out of "place" as long as he has not yet fulfilled his mission.

If so, we realize that mankind is not bad from the very start, nor even "not good." Rather, as *tzelem Elokim* whose good lies external to him, in the challenge of his mission in the world, man is **not yet good**. Only the crucible of history and the fulfillment of his mission will deliver the verdict.

v.

Before closing, I would like to explore another aspect of mankind as *tzelem Elokim*, graced with potential, confronted with challenge, and as yet "good." Much has been said in Jewish thought and exegesis equating man and the world. For example, both the famed Mishnaic statement valuing the life of a single individual as equal to the world (Mishna *Sanhedrin* 4:3), and the kabbalistic doctrine of man as a microcosm (*olam katan*) make this fundamental equation. In point of fact, this equation has its roots in the language of the Bible. Let us return to the language of Chapter One.

> In the beginning God created (ברא) the Heaven and the Earth. And the earth was without form and void; and darkness was on the face of the deep; and a wind from God moved over the surface of the waters. (1:1–2)

Previously, I have implicitly argued that these two verses should be viewed as a kind of preface to the primary description of world-making, or more properly world-structuring, of Chapter One. To elaborate, verse two should be read as a description of the state of the world in its embryonic stage, at the beginning the process, before the ordering of the six days of creation. Verse one constitutes a kind of preface to the preface. The terms "Heaven" and "Earth" are not references to the specific objects of sky and ground – after all, they are made on Days Two and Three respectively. Rather, they constitute a biblical colloquialism for "everything," a way to say "the world" (see 2:1; 14:19; Ex. 31:17; Deut. 3:24). As such, the verses teach 1. God's creation of the world, and 2. the initial state of the created world, chaotic void, darkness and depths. (See Rashi on 1:1, Ramban on 1:1, *Bereshit Raba* 1:19.)

From this point on, the term *"bara"* (ברא), normally translated as "created," all but disappears from Chapter One. While God speaks (ויאמר), and makes (ויעש), the word *"bara"* (ברא) is almost completely absent from the ensuing chapter. This is not surprising. It is a word utilized to describe the creation of "the world" and primordial chaos. The remainder of the chapter describes the countering, limitation and structuring of this initial state. Consequently, the term *"bara"* is banished from the text, its place taken by speaking and making.

All of this changes when we arrive at the making of mankind. By now, the verses should be familiar:

> And God said, Let Us make (נעשה) mankind…So God created (ויברא) mankind in his own image, in the image of God

He created (ברא) him; male and female He created (ברא) them. (1:26–27)

In place of the standard terminology of Chapter One – "speaking" and "making" – the Torah reverts to the term "bara" (ברא) to describe the making of mankind and utilizes this verb three times within one verse. Moreover, the planning stage (1:26) utilizes the standard language to plan the forming of man. However, as we move to execution (1:27), the standard language is deliberately supplanted by the non-standard terminology previously used to describe the creation of the whole world – the term "bara." No wonder Jewish thought and exegesis have consistently equated man and the world.

All of this is meant to force upon us the following conclusion. If mankind stands in parallel to the world, if the creation process of mankind parallels and resembles that of the world, then just as the world is created in an initial state, so too mankind is created in an initial state. If the world begins its way possessed by the void, empty, dark and deep, so too mankind begins its way possessing void, emptiness, darkness and depths. If the positive element in the world at the beginning of its making is the wind, spirit or presence of Elokim (1:2), then so too the positive in mankind at its beginnings is its "tzelem Elokim." Just as Elokim of Chapter One counters the darkness and chaos and forms a well-ordered and good world, so too must tzelem Elokim counter his own internal dark chaos and form a well-ordered and good world.

In fact, the text of parashat adam utilizes both the verb "bara" and the noun "tzelem" three times, implicitly balancing them off one against the other and placing them in tension. The entire parallel implicitly provides another challenge to mankind, another mission: the task of self-making. Hence we have stumbled upon another sense in which man is **not yet** complete, **not yet** good. Mankind has yet to imitate the labor of Elokim, not just in the external realm of the world, but also in the internal realm of man's self.

While this all sounds quite nice and literary, a sharper formulation of the supposed darkness, depths and chaos of man's initial state seems in order. Without overstressing the point, the terms of 1:2, "tohu vavohu" (best translated as some sort of combination of emptiness, formlessness, and chaos), *"ḥoshekh"* (darkness), and finally *"tehom"* (depths), strike a dreary image in and of themselves. Furthermore, they comprise the state of the world **before** the initiation of God's action during the six days, the establishment of "good" in the world. Apparently, they are symbolic of a state prior to "good" or other than "good." They symbolize what we normally call "evil," or at least the potential for something other than good that lurks within the world. It is no accident that these terms become transformed into symbols of destruction, death and evil throughout Tanach (see I Sam. 12:21; Jer. 4:22–27; Is. 5:20; 9:1; 34:8–12; 49:9; Job 10:20–22).

Does mankind possess a dark side? Can man's very self pulsate with chaotic and often destructive desires? Does he contain within himself the potential for evil? These are, of course, rhetorical questions. Of course mankind possesses a dual nature, potential for both good and evil. Self-discipline and the creation of a good self constitute an almost unceasing challenge for mankind (see Ramban 1:26 and *Bereshit Raba* 9:9 for the classic rabbinic formulations of man's dual nature). Consequently, the possibility of man's goodness is intimately tied up with the darkness that resides within. Meeting the challenge comprises the very essence of man's goodness.

VI.

By the end of *Parashat Bereshit*, the Torah states that God saw "that the wickedness (רָעַת) of man was great in the earth, and that all the impulse of the thoughts of his heart was only evil (רַע) continually" (6:5). The first generations of mankind failed in their task and were subsequently destroyed. But the story does not end there. The task remained, and yet remains in front of each successive generation of mankind, waiting to be successfully met.

Religious Sin, Ethical Sin and the Punishment of Exile

by Rav Yonatan Grossman

T his week, I wish to discuss the beginning of sin – the beginning of man's rebellion against his God. In the *parasha*, two sins are found, committed by the first two generations on earth: Adam's sin in Eden and Cain's murder of his brother Abel. It seems that the Torah is attempting to draw a parallel between these two sins. This is expressed through the internal development in the two stories and through similar phraseology used in both narratives. Let us list the central similarities:

A. God turns to the sinner with a rhetorical question. The two questions are connected to the geographical location of the person for whom God is searching:
    1. To Adam: "The Lord God called out to the man and said to him: Where are you?" (3:9)
    2. To Cain: "The Lord said to Cain: Where is your brother Abel?" (4:9)
B. The initial reaction of the sinner upon hearing the divine search is to avoid an honest answer. Here too, the Torah records a similar

response from both sinners – "*Anokhi*" ("I" – an unusual, more archaic form, as opposed to "*Ani*"):

1. In Adam's words: "He replied: 'I heard the sound of You in the garden and I was afraid because I (*anokhi*) was naked, so I hid.'" (3:10)
2. In Cain's words: "And he said: I do not know, am I (*anokhi*) my brother's keeper?" (4:9)

C. The two sinners mention hiding from God, albeit in different contexts:

1. Adam claims (see above) that he was hiding because of his nakedness.
2. Cain says: "I must hide from Your face" (4:14)

D. God's rebuke of the sinners opens with a similar expression:

1. God said to Eve: "What is this you have done?!" (3:13)
2. To Cain, He says: "What have you done?" (4:10)

E. The punishment inflicted upon the sinner is connected to the fertility of the land and to the produce which it produces:

1. The punishment of Adam: "To Adam He said: 'By toil shall you eat of it, all the days of your life. Thorns and thistles shall sprout for you, but your food shall be the grasses of the field'" (3: 17–18)
2. The punishment of Cain: "If you till the soil, it shall no longer yield its strength to you" (4:12)

F. Beyond the specific punishment, in both places we find a curse which God addresses to each of the sinners.

1. In Eden, God says to the serpent: "More cursed shall you be than all cattle and all the wild beasts" (3:14)
2. To Cain, God says: "Therefore you shall be more cursed than the ground" (4:11)

G. The motif of death hanging over the head of the sinner is found in the two stories.

1. Adam: "Until you return to the ground, for from it you were taken. For dust you are and to dust you shall return" (3:19)
2. Cain also complains that he is in mortal danger: "…anyone who meets me may kill me" (4:14)

H. Even the continuation of the stories is similar.

1. Immediately after Adam's sin and punishment, we read, "And Adam knew his wife Eve and she conceived and bore Cain" (4:1)
2. Immediately after Cain's sin and punishment, we read, "Cain knew his wife and she conceived and bore Enoch" (4:17)

I. Moreover, there is a striking, singular expression which appears exclusively in these two stories.
   1. When God turns to woman, he says to her: "Yet your desire shall be for your husband and he shall rule over you" (3:16)
   2. When He turns to Cain, after refusing his offering, He uses an identical phrase: "Its desire is towards you, yet you can rule over it" (4:7)

Though the context is different in the two stories, from a literary perspective, the placement of such an irregular phrase in two consecutive stories clearly creates a link between them, and beyond this specific phrase, the two plots are woven in a very similar fashion.

What is the Torah's purpose in comparing these two sins of the first two generations of man? It seems to me that one must answer this question on two different levels. First, it seems that the Torah is trying to compare a religious sin and an ethical sin. In analyzing the exact sin of Adam and his wife in the Garden of Eden, we are faced with many difficulties. The nature of the sin is not at all clear, because we do not understand what that Tree of Knowledge was. It is difficult to assume that it is a tree which imparts wisdom to man, and that man was devoid of intellectual ability before the eating (see Guide for the Perplexed, 1:2). Other suggestions in the commentators are speculative and it is therefore difficult to decide between them. It would seem that the Torah is deliberately obscuring the exact particulars of the sin. This is crucial to the story, and its message is that man should have refrained from eating from the tree of knowledge simply because of God's command. This is the basic model of religious commandment and religious sin. There is a certain commandment to which man must acquiesce. Whether or not the reason for the commandment is clear, he has to subject his will to God's command.

In contrast to religious sin, Cain's sin is of a different nature.

Cain has an excellent claim in his defense, which he does not use. He can argue that he was never commanded about murder. How could he have known that killing is prohibited?! This is not only a good claim for Cain, but a question for God – how is it that He punishes Cain without prior warning and without revealing to him that murder is prohibited? The answer to both of these questions is clear. There is no need for an explicit divine commandment to prohibit murder, and thus Cain cannot advance this defense. Every person understands instinctively that he may not take the life of his fellow. This is a cornerstone of the moral world, and it does not require an external commandment to confirm it and give it validity. The moral, ethical world obligates itself, because it is true. Man is obligated to behave morally because his conscience and natural ethics obligate him to behave this way. If he transgresses this natural law, God will demand an accounting from him.

We can now return to the comparison between the sin of Adam and the sin of Cain. The sin of Adam is the archetype of religious sin (based on an explicit divine command), whereas the sin of Cain is the archetype of **the** moral sin: **murder**. By comparing these two sins, the Torah emphasizes the innovation of Judaism – ethical sin is equal to religious sin! Not only does one who transgresses religious laws harm his relation with God, but so does one who does not treat his fellow with morality and goodness. This does not require a commandment, but nevertheless stands parallel to absolute religious commandment.

This entire discussion was based on the fact that the similar phrases which appear in both stories hint to us that we should compare the two. However, it is possible that the Torah is hinting to us that we should read the one against the background of the other – not specifically as a parallel, but as a continuance of the process. Let us first turn to the words of Ramban at the beginning of *Parashat Bereshit*. He attempts to understand why the Torah opens with the book of Genesis and not with Exodus:

> And Rabbi Yitzḥak gave a reason for this. The Torah began with 'In the beginning,' and the story of creation until the creation of man and that He made man rule over all of His handiwork and He set everything under his feet, and the garden of Eden which is

the choicest of places which were created on this earth was set as his place of dwelling, until man's sin expelled him from there, and the people of the generation of the flood who by their sin were expelled from the world entire, and only the righteous amongst them and his children were saved, and their children's sin caused them to be scattered in places and distributed in lands.... If so, it is suitable when a nation sins exceedingly, that it will lose its place and another nation will come to inherit its land, because this is God's verdict in the land, since the beginning.

According to Ramban, Genesis comes to teach us that exile is a punishment of sin. This, Ramban claims, is active in the land of Israel, and thus the land expelled the seven nations. Even the nation of Israel is constantly under the threat of exile should it sin, God forbid.

If we return to the comparison of the two sins in our *parasha*, we find an additional parallel to which we did not pay attention before. In both places, the result of sin is exile, and in both instances, the exile is eastward. It is worth noting that in both cases the exile is not presented as part of the direct punishment of God, but rather as a necessary consequence of the sin, beyond the specific punishment.

By Adam we read, after the conclusion of the section dealing with the punishment:

> So God banished him from the Garden of Eden to till the soil from which he was taken. He drove man out, and placed east of the Garden of Eden the cherubim and the fiery ever-turning sword... (3:23–24)

Similarly we read about Cain (again after the detailing of the punishment):

> Cain left the presence of God and settled in the land of Nod, east of Eden. (4:16)

In light of Ramban's words, it seems to me that we should pay attention specifically to this last comparison. Possibly, the entire parallel created by the Torah between the two stories is designed to reach this conclusion. The punishment of exile continues from one story to the next.

I would like to suggest that the message hidden in this link, created by the Torah between the two stories, is the continuous process of exile. In its later, "Jewish" version, this message states that there is land in which the Divine Presence dwells and from which the sinner is driven away automatically. This holy land cannot suffer a sinner living on it and it expels him.

According to this criterion, we note that the Land of Israel becomes the Garden of Eden:

> Do not defile yourselves in any of those ways, for it is by such that the nations which I am casting out before you defiled themselves. Thus the land became defiled; and I called it to account for its iniquity and the land spewed out its inhabitants … for all those abhorrent things were done by the people who were in the land before you, and the land became defiled. So let not the land spew you out for defiling it as it spewed out the nation that came before you. (Lev. 18:24–28)

This applies not only in religious sins, as noted in Leviticus. With murder as well, we read that the land itself becomes defiled, and this results from the dwelling of the Divine Presence within the place (as in the sin of Cain):

> You shall not pollute the land in which you live; for blood pollutes the land, and the land can have no expiation for blood that is shed on it, except by the blood of him who shed it. You shall not defile the land in which you live, in which I myself abide, for I, the Lord, abide among the Israelite people. (Num. 35:33–34)

God demands of man both religious perfection and moral perfection. One who wishes to dwell beside the Divine Presence must perfect himself in both areas. Failure within either the religious sphere or within the moral sphere expels man from the presence of God.

Why Did God Not Accept Cain's Offering?

by Rav Elchanan Samet

I. INTRODUCTION

In his article "The Concept of Property and Acquisition in the Holy Scriptures," Hillel Zeitlin *hy"d*[1] asks the following: "For a long time the story of Cain and Abel has distressed me: Why did God 'accept Abel and his offering' but not Cain and his?" He continues:

> I have examined the commentaries on this matter and have not found a satisfying explanation. To the early commentators it was clear that Cain brought unfit produce (see Rashi on 4:3, quoting *Bereshit Raba* 22:5). This may be true, but a literal reading of the text – "And after some time Cain brought of the fruit of the ground an offering to God" – in no way suggests that his offering was of inferior quality.

Considering this last point, we note that while verse 3 (quoted by Zeitlin) does not explicitly describe Cain's offering as poor quality, this explanation is based on a comparison between verse 3 and verse 4. Two qualities of Abel's sacrifice are lacking in that of Cain: the double emphasis on the

---

1. An important thinker who perished in the Warsaw Ghetto.

finest quality – Abel brings "the firstlings of his flock" ("בכורות צאנו")
and "the fatlings among them" (Rabbi Sa'adia Gaon's understanding of
the term "ומחלבהן"), and the fact that Abel brings the finest of "**his** flock,"
emphasizing the personal aspect of his sacrifice.

Still, the conclusion that Cain brought a sacrifice of inferior quality is not necessarily inevitable. An accurate examination of the verses
tells us only that Cain did not invest the same effort in his offering as Abel
did; he simply brought what he had on hand. We may even comment in
Cain's favor that he brings his offering first. Should this fact not balance
somewhat the qualitative advantage of Abel's offering? R. Avraham Sava
raises this suggestion in his commentary *Tzror HaMor*:

It appears that Abel followed his brother's example. Since Cain
had brought an offering, he did too – it was not his own initiative.

This troublesome question concerns more than just one difficult
aspect of the story. The question concerns the principal event which is
being narrated: fratricide. The simultaneous acceptance of Abel's offering and rejection of Cain's leads to murder. Cain's terrible psychological
reaction expresses anger against God and jealousy of his brother.[2] God's
words of appeasement to him do not find their way into his stormy
and angry heart. It appears that the rebuke and warning not only fail
to achieve their purpose, but they become an impetus in his decision
to kill his brother.

II. PRINCIPLES IN SEEKING AN EXPLANATION

Clearly, Cain's action is not a sudden and unexpected sinful outburst,
but rather the final deterioration in a process that began long before.
This becomes apparent from God's words of rebuke and support to him
in verse 7. Although the details are unknown to us, they indicate that
there is some sin relating to Cain that goes back to the beginning of the
story, and that there is some possibility that Cain will "improve." Is the

---

2. According to *Midrash Tanḥuma* (Genesis 9), following Abel's murder when God
asks, 'Where is Abel your brother?' Cain responds, "...It is You who killed him...
for had You accepted my offering as You did his, I would not have been jealous of
him."

Torah trying to hide Cain's first sin? This does not seem to be the case, for then the story becomes rather disjointed and opaque.

It would seem, then, that the Torah is explaining – or at least hinting at – the reason for the criticism of Cain. The key must lie somewhere between verses 1–4 of chapter four, because verse 5 already contains the result of his sin: "And Cain and his offering God did not accept, and Cain was very angry…" The continuation of the story is also significant for a clarification of the mystery: God's words to Cain in verse 7 not only confirm the existence of his earlier sin (as explained above), but perhaps also contain some hint of the actual nature of the sin. The second half of the story (verses 9–16), dealing with his punishment, may be meant to teach us about the root of his sin.

III. EXAMINING VERSES 1–5

Let us first examine verses 1–5 and see what we may discover from them. The description of the bringing of the offerings by the two brothers in verses 3–4 has already been discussed, and we concluded that this account does not provide sufficient reason for the rejection of Cain's offering. The description of the birth of the brothers and their names, in verses 1–2, likewise fails to provide us with a reason – for surely their birth and their names cannot burden one of them with moral culpability. Thus, by a process of elimination, we are left only with the single characteristic of each brother as described in the text: "And Abel was a keeper of sheep, and Cain was a tiller of the ground" (4:2). The choice of a profession, and the lifestyle which it entails, is made when a person reaches maturity, and it teaches us something about his moral tendencies. And thus we find here the key to the mystery of our story.

Close scrutiny of verses 1–5 confirms this. These verses contain, in quick succession, four symmetrical contrasts between the two brothers. Let us study these and their structure:

A. "…and she gave birth to Cain, and she said: 'I have acquired a man from God.'
vs.
"And again she gave birth, to his brother Abel."
B. "And Abel was a keeper of sheep"

vs.

"and Cain was a tiller of the ground."

C. "And it happened after some days that Cain brought of the fruit of the ground an offering to God"

vs.

"And Abel also brought of the firstlings of his flock and from the fatlings among them."

D. "And God accepted Abel and his offering"

vs.

"but Cain and his offering He did not accept (and Cain was very angry and his face fell)."

The parallels contrast between the brothers in four areas: A. their birth and names, B. their professions, C. their offerings, and D. the divine reaction to these offerings. The most noticeable phenomenon here is the way in which the brothers are presented in alternating order: A. Cain-Abel, B. Abel-Cain, C. Cain-Abel, D. Abel-Cain. Is this simply an artistic device, or does it also bear some significance with regard to the content and message of the story? We suggest that the Torah seeks to emphasize that in each area in which they are compared, one brother has an advantage over the other, and the Torah lists this brother first in that area. This structure hints at the comparison and inner connection between areas A and C, in which Cain has the advantage, and areas B and D where Abel has the advantage. Let us explain this in more detail.

Area A:

The emphasis on the fact that Cain is the firstborn of Adam and *Eve* is obvious. Abel's secondary status in this regard finds expression in several ways:

1. The introduction to Cain's birth, "And Adam knew Eve his wife and she conceived," is lacking with regard to Abel.
2. Before stating the fact of Abel's birth, the Torah adds "again" (*vatasaf*), hinting at the fact that Abel's birth was an "addition" (*tosefet*) to Cain's birth – an event of secondary significance.
3. The baby is called "...his brother, Abel" – implying that his own

name is not as important as the fact of his being the brother of the firstborn.

4. In contrast to the reason supplied by the mother for the choice of Cain's name, no reason is given for the choice of Abel's name.

5. The literal meaning of the two names chosen also hints at Cain's advantage over Abel.

All of these points emphasize the preferential status of Cain, the firstborn, in contrast with the inferior status of Abel, "his brother."

Area B:

"And Abel was a keeper of sheep, and Cain was a tiller of the ground." The parallel – "And Abel was...and Cain was..." hints at the disparity between these two occupations. They involve opposite lifestyles: the tiller of the ground remains close to the ground and lives in a house. The keeper of sheep wanders with his flock over great distances; he lives in a tent. The tiller of the ground is nourished by the ground's produce; the keeper of sheep enjoys their meat and wool.

But the contrast between them is also socio-historical in nature: human society in ancient times was divided between landed tribes (or nations which worked the earth) and wandering tribes (or nations which made their living from shepherding). There was constant tension between them, arising not only from the obvious conflict of interests but also from the conflict of mentalities between these two lifestyles. All these differences – in lifestyle, social culture and economic interests – already find expression in the division between these first two brothers, Cain and Abel.

What, then, is the significance of Abel's advantage in this area? Is this because this younger son was the first to choose his occupation? This does not seem likely. On the contrary, it appears that areas A and B are connected with a causal link: Cain, because he is the elder, is given land and becomes a tiller of the ground. Abel, since he is the younger, becomes a shepherd. (Similar causal links also exist between areas B and C, and areas C and D)

Why, then, is Abel mentioned first? Let us leave this question for later.

Area C:

Cain brings some of the fruit of the ground, which he has been tilling, while Abel brings some of his sheep, since he is a shepherd. We had already discussed the difference in quality between their respective offerings. But if the juxtaposition here hints at the superiority of Abel's offering, why is Cain mentioned first?

The answer is that Cain brought his offering first. His advantage is in the dimension of time. This is hinted at in the words, "And Abel brought, **also he**." Hence, area C resembles area A not only in that Cain is mentioned first, but also because of the common reason for this: his being first chronologically. Earlier we read, "And **again** she gave birth"; here we read, "and Abel brought, **also he**." Here we find the solution to the paradox presented by Cain's offering coming first chronologically while Abel's offering is qualitatively better: Cain brings his offering first because he is the firstborn. The right of the firstborn is due to him not only in his status in the family (including both the choice of profession and his inheritance of the land), but also in the area of the annual religious ceremony.

Area D:

"And God accepted Abel and his offering, but Cain and his offering He did not accept." The intention here behind mentioning Abel first is obvious: God prefers Abel and his offering; this implies that God ignores Cain and his offering, and hence we deduce that they are not desired by God. The contrasting structure – "And He accepted…He did not accept" creates a dramatic and surprising climax, concluding the four juxtapositions between the brothers. From here on, the narrative focuses on a discussion of Cain's reaction to his "deprivation" and God's words of appeasement and rebuke to him.

Having noted that area C is parallel to area A, echoing and propagating Cain's precedence owing to his status as eldest, we may assume that area D – parallel to area B in that both mention Abel first – will likewise continue the theme of B. In other words, God accepted Abel, the younger and secondary son, **because** he was a shepherd, but did not accept Cain **because** he was a tiller of the ground. For this very reason, the Torah mentioned Abel first in area B: because a shepherd is preferable, spiritually and morally, and his lifestyle is more acceptable to God, while the lifestyle of the tiller of the ground is fundamentally flawed.

Thus, areas A and C highlighted the **social** superiority of the first-born and his rights of preference concerning those matters related to his firstborn status, while B and D reveal the **spiritual** superiority of the younger – chosen – brother, owing to his positive qualities and characteristics. God is not "impressed" by the firstborn, and the preferential treatment that Cain receives as the firstborn from his parents (and society), as well as his personal economic and cultural power as expressed in his name and his choice to be a "tiller of the ground," do not influence God's view of him. Even Cain's right to be the first participant in the religious ceremony (also an expression of social superiority) is not regarded by God as important.

God chooses specifically the younger brother, the weaker and secondary, who enjoys neither social respect nor real estate power but rather runs his life modestly and with a genuine seeking of God. And indeed, this superiority of Abel is even hinted at in the two areas in which Cain is mentioned first. In area A, Abel's name implies modesty and self-deprecation, almost the direct opposite of the perspective implied by Cain's name. In area C, his personal effort is emphasized when describing the offering he brings to God, appearing to cancel out the pride of Cain's place as the first of those bringing offerings owing to his status as firstborn.

IV. "GROUND" AS A THEME IN THE STORY

The word "ground" (אדמה) appears six times during the course of the story, and once the word "field" is used instead (referring to the specific land, owned and worked by Cain, where the murder takes place). The ground is not merely Cain's place of work and the source of his income – it is also the scene of the murder. The first half of the story (verses 1–8) mentions the word "ground" three times, in its description of Cain's connection with the ground (his tilling of it, his bringing its fruits as an offering, and his murder of Abel upon it). The next three instances of the word in the second half of the story (verses 9–16), in God's words to Cain, parallel the first three in the inverse order:

4–3 In light of the murder of Abel in the field (it also appears that his blood and corpse were buried there), God says to Cain, "Your brother's blood calls to Me from the ground." In other words, you cannot hide your deed; the ground will not cooperate in this venture.

5–2 In the past, the ground offered Cain its fruits (compare further on, verse 12: "it will no longer yield its strength to you"), and Cain made use of them for the purpose of bringing an offering to God. Now, in light of the murder, the ground has "opened its mouth **to accept (take)** your brother's blood from your hand." The ground will henceforth no longer be a source of divine gifts and blessing; it will now become the source of Cain's curse: "You are cursed **from the ground**."

6–1 Cain, who chose to be a "tiller of the ground," will now cut himself off from it. And the ground will no longer respond to his working of it: "When **you till the ground** it will no longer yield its strength to you." As a result, "You will be a wanderer and a vagabond upon the earth" – Cain will be forced to adapt himself to the lifestyle of Abel, who, as a shepherd, would wander upon the earth in search of pasture for his flocks.

In the seventh and final mention of the word, we hear from Cain himself the significance of his punishment: "Behold, You have driven me out today from upon the ground, and I shall be hidden from Your face."

Thus we learn that the tilling of the ground and the relationship between man and ground are at the heart of the story, and they join all of its stages. Both the sin and its punishment are connected with this cultivated ground. The story comes to teach us that the ground cannot tolerate a person who uses it for a negative purpose, and it vomits him out from upon it. This is the relationship that God has set out since the beginning of days to exist between man and ground.

V. THE DISADVANTAGE OF LABOR ON THE GROUND

What is this danger, this moral disadvantage, related to the working of the ground to which our story hints? Two personalities both felt, in light of our narrative, that the biblical attitude towards labor on the land is ambivalent, while its attitude to shepherding is positive. One is Hillel

Zeitlin, already quoted at the beginning; the other, preceding him, is Rav Hirsch, in his commentary to this biblical text. Their commentaries are similar in many ways, but each of them has a slightly different perspective. Rav Hirsch says (with some omissions):

> Agriculture demands all of a person's physical strength...he needs to devote his whole life to his bodily existence. The concept of "Cain," i.e. *"kana"* [acquisition] – self-recognition and the pride associated with acquiring – are most evident in the farmer. By the sweat of his brow he has made his ground bear fruit, and it becomes something of ultimate value for him – it becomes part of his personality, he holds onto it and settles...Once he has placed the yoke of pursuit of acquisition upon his neck, his spirit also becomes subservient...This leads to slavery...Moreover, he will easily be brought to admiration of the forces of nature, upon whose influences the success of his field depends. Faith in God and in the superiority of man was first lost among the agricultural nations. There idol worship first developed.
>
> In contrast, the life of the shepherd is most elevated. He is concerned principally with living things. His care of them arouses within him humane feelings and sympathy for suffering. His acquisitions are portable. The flock needs the shepherd's care, but their existence is not in his hands. Thus, the shepherd is protected from the danger of overestimating his own value and that of his property...For this reason our forefathers were shepherds, and Moses and David also shepherded flocks...Egyptian culture was based on agriculture. This found expression in paganism on one hand and enslavement of people on the other. Faith in God, human freedom and the divine image existed only in the hearts of our shepherd forefathers...

Zeitlin states as follows (also with some omissions):

> The Holy Scriptures almost always prefer a shepherd to a tiller of the soil...But why [does the Torah prefer shepherds to tillers of

the ground]? Did God not place Adam in the Garden of Eden in order "to work it and to guard it"? Is it not true that God "did not create it [the world] a wasteland" [Is. 45:18]?

The key to understanding this lies…in the socio-moral reasons…Working the land involves the concept of private ownership…and the Holy Scriptures do not recognize a private individual's rights over land, except under the known conditions and limitations.

Both Rav Hirsch and Zeitlin sensed the inherent problem in what they were saying. In the words of Rav Hirsch,

Man's natural labor was agriculture. Man needed to "work the land" in order to provide himself with food for sustenance…This is also Israel's destiny, according to the Torah.

But most of the examples of great men who were shepherds are taken from the period preceding Israel's settlement of the land. Rav Hirsch's response is as follows:

The Torah anticipates the chronic dangers inherent in agriculture and prescribes the remedy, legislating against deification of property. Shabbat and *shemitta* [the sabbatical year] forever testify that the earth belongs to God, and man is His servant. The agricultural laws, such as the prohibitions of *kilayim* [mixing seeds] and *orla* [fruit of young trees] on one hand and the positive injunctions of *leket*, *shikheha* and *pe'ah* [leftover produce for the poor] on the other, remind man of God's presence, cautioning him to maintain brotherly and neighborly love. Thus the Torah solves the moral problem of agriculture; in this way a society of God-fearing farmers is created, all sharing brotherly love and equality. But outside of the Torah framework a danger is presented to faith in God and to the freedom and equality of all men.

According to both of these commentators, Cain is therefore the representative and founder of the culture of tillers of the earth, before this culture became sweetened and refined by the mitzvot of the Torah. For this reason, Cain's very choice of this negative lifestyle – as well as its influence on his character – are what caused God not to accept his offering, and they are the root of the deterioration to the point of fratricide.

Cain and Abel

by Rav Ezra Bick

I.

The story of Cain and Abel is one that is easily skipped over lightly when we think of the great themes of the early *parashot* of the Torah. The first part of *Bereshit* is first and foremost about God's relationship to the natural world as Creator, an obviously important point for the foundations of religious belief. The story of man in the Garden of Eden is about obedience and sin, about the relationship of man and woman, about innocence and knowledge, and we are naturally led to ponder its significance. Next week's *parasha*, describing two societies and their sins and punishments, is crucial to understanding human society; and the figure of Noaḥ, in all its complexities, serves as a launching point for understanding how the righteous man relates to a sinful world. The story of Cain and Abel, though, poses what seems to be no particular lesson. I think that most of us quickly summarize it in our minds as about murder – with the moral being that murder is bad. But since this is the Torah's third story, such a cursory treatment of this *parasha* is clearly unjustified. Our task, then, is to determine the real significance of this story and why it is here. To do this, we first have to understand the character of the "hero," Cain.

31

II.

Our first inclination is to catalogue Cain as a villain. After all, he is a murderer, and is cursed by God. The corollary conclusion is that Abel must be a saint. The latter conclusion is based on an aesthetic desire for balance, especially in a story with two brothers (remember Isaac and Ishmael, Jacob and Esau), but is also supported by the fact that God accepts his sacrifice while refusing that of Cain.

This position, at least the first half of it, is forwarded by Rashi (based on midrashim), who states that Cain's offering was inferior in quality, indicating his irreligiosity (4:3), and that he deliberately set out to kill Abel (4:8). Furthermore, Rashi interprets verse 15 to mean that God decreed that Cain would be killed after seven generations as a **punishment** (*nekama*, "vengeance," in the language of the verse) for murder. By this, I believe Rashi is answering the question of how a tale of murder could not end with the proper divine punishment – death. Exile is not the appropriate punishment, especially if the main moral of the story is that murder is a sin which will not go unpunished. Rashi's answer is that Cain indeed suffers the death penalty, even if it is delayed.

However, the simple order of the verses indicates that the actual punishment for Cain's crime is exile and wandering (4:11–12). Only after Cain complains that this will leave him open to being killed does God give him a mark to protect him, adding that *"kol horeg Kayin shivatayim yukam"* (4:15). Even if this does predict that Cain will be killed (which is **not** the simple reading of the verse), it is not necessarily projected as the punishment for the crime.

But the real difficulty with the position taken by Rashi is in the hints that the Torah gives us concerning the personalities of Cain and Abel.

> Adam was intimate with *Eve* his wife, and she conceived and gave birth to Cain, and she said, "I have made [*kaniti*] a man with God." And she continued to give birth to his brother, to Abel; and Abel was a shepherd, while Cain worked with the land. After many days, Cain brought an offering to God from the fruit of the land. And Abel, he also brought from the first-born of his sheep and from their fat – and God turned to Abel and to his offering, But

He did not turn to Cain and to his offering; and Cain was very
troubled and his face fell. (4:1–5)

Our first point of interest is the Torah's description of the births of the
two brothers. The birth of Cain is described as a momentous occasion,
giving rise to *Eve's* exclamation, "I have made a man with God." While
this is obviously due to the fact that he is the first-born, not only to his
happy parents, but to human history, it stands in stark contrast to the
birth of his brother, whose birth is described as an afterthought, and
who does not even merit an explanation of his name. Compare this with
other cases of the births of brothers in the Torah, such as Esau and Jacob
(25:25–26), or the list of births of Jacob's wife Leah (29:32–35), where
each son is accorded an explanation for his name. It is safe to say that
a character whose name is not explained in the Torah, especially when
juxtaposed next to one whose name is explained, is a non-important
character. If Abel is the first individual to bring a proper sacrifice to God –
in effect, the man who invented formal religion – we would expect more.

The comparison between the births and the names merely highlights the extremely problematic nature of Abel's name. "*Hevel*" means
"nothing, vanity, wind, vapor." Of the nearly sixty appearances of this
word in Tanach, not one is in a positive context. The word is always used
to describe something of no consequence, mere wind, vanity, or foolish-
ness. Since names are descriptive in Tanach, especially for a symbolic
character, this would seem to indicate that we should not be viewing
Abel as a paradigm of virtue or human accomplishment. In fact, Cain's
name could well be translated as "accomplishment," while Abel's name
means the opposite.

One could argue that this does not indicate anything about the
Torah's attitude towards Cain and Abel, but only about the attitude of
their parents, who were excited about the birth of the first and more
or less ignored the second. This "psychological" reading of the *parasha*
would result in a picture of Cain as the favored first son, and Abel as the
ignored, belittled brother. Perhaps Eve was surprised to discover that
she was bearing a second child (assuming that they were twins, as would
appear from the fact that a second pregnancy is not mentioned), and perhaps she assumed that a second child was unnecessary, an insignificant

addition – in other words, *hevel*. This perception of the psychological difficulties of Cain and Abel could then be used to understand the strained relationship between them, and Abel's "overachieving" would be seen as an attempt to gain his parents' – and perhaps God's – approval.

This would be an interesting approach, but I have a basic methodological problem with it. If it is correct, then the moral of the story will revolve around the problems of parenting, rather than the sin of murder. I have nothing against using psychological insights to understand a *parasha* in the Torah, but in this case, the psychological insights, the central point of the story, is barely hinted at in the text. It does not appear to be logical to assume that the central message of a given *parasha* is buried in hints and inferences. Perhaps these insights can help us understand how these two individuals related to themselves and each other, but I do not think that they answer our question of the relative evaluation of Cain and Abel.

But there is also a further textual indication about the personalities of Cain and Abel, and that is in the actual bringing of the offerings (verses 3–4). The initiative to bring an offering to God is Cain's. The verse stresses that "Abel, he too, brought an offering." Abel is copying Cain, following along in the initiative of his older brother. Just as his birth appears an afterthought to that of Cain, so too his offering to God is apparently following the footsteps of Cain. Cain is the originator of the idea of sacrifice; he was the first to understand that if your work succeeds, it is only because God has blessed it and therefore one must show that one understands from where all blessing comes by giving a portion to the true owner and creator of all. Abel merely imitates his brother. Cain is an *"ish"* (verse 1), an individual, a unique personality; Abel is a *"gam hu"* (verse 4), an "also he" person. He is a *"nochshlepper"* – I wish I knew how to say that in English! But I hope those of you who are not familiar with the word can guess its meaning – an "also-shlepper-along."

III.

I think it is safe to say that Cain was the more serious individual, more creative and more substantive. This immediately brings us to the question why his offering was not accepted by God, while that of his unoriginal brother was.

The answer to this question is found in verse 7. Unfortunately, verse 7 is among the most difficult in the Torah. It appears to be deliberately cryptic, and is therefore impossible to translate neutrally; that is, the translation depends on which among the many available interpretations is adopted.

For the time being, I propose to skip this question and move on to the murder itself. My attempt to somehow rehabilitate the character of Cain will surely founder on the incontrovertible fact that he was a murderer, who killed his only brother (as well as a quarter of the world's population).

Cain said to Abel his brother; and while they were in the field, Cain rose up on Abel his brother, and killed him. (4:8)

The first half of the verse is obviously incomplete. It is not only that we would want to know what Cain said, while the verse does not inform us. Grammatically, the verb *"amar"* (said) requires a direct object, unlike the verb *"diber"* (spoke) which could be used without one. It is possible to describe someone as "speaking," without specifying what he said; but it is technically incomplete to say of someone that he is "saying," without adding an object. All of the commentators and midrashim suggest different contents for what Cain said, but it seems to me that the Torah's omission here indicates that it is not important to know what specifically what was said, but only that speech preceded the act of violence. Apparently, Cain did not approach Abel with the intention of killing him. Instead, words led to an argument, which eventually led to Abel being killed. This is what is known legally as manslaughter rather than premeditated murder.

This impression is reinforced by the repeated reference to Abel as "Abel his brother." If this had appeared only in reference to the murder itself, I would be inclined to interpret it ironically, as emphasizing the enormity of the crime. But as it appears not in the description of the murder itself, but in the previous two phrases – "saying" and "rising up" – it seems to me to indicate the opposite; namely, that at every stage up to the actual murder, Cain still related to Abel as a brother. Following this lead, I remind you of the midrash which describes how Cain did not know how to kill. Expanding this somewhat, perhaps Cain did not even realize that he was killing Abel until it was too late. One must remember that no one had even died yet in human history. Cain "rose up against Abel," and suddenly, he had killed him.

This would explain his punishment – which is akin to *galut*, exile, the punishment in the Torah for inadvertent manslaughter rather than for murder. Of course there is no city of refuge to which Cain can be sent, but his lot is similar to that of the accidental murderer of the Torah, who is uprooted from his home and sent away (see Num. ch. 35).

So, what is the picture that emerges? Cain, the more talented and religiously more sophisticated elder son, is haunted by the success of his younger brother, and quarrels with him until, either accidentally or at least without premeditation, he kills him. Have I managed to rescue the reputation of Cain? Is he to be considered a *Tzaddik*? Of course not! But neither is he to be considered a symbol of a *rasha*, of evil personified. He should not be added to the list of great villains in the Torah, such as Nimrod, Esau, or Pharaoh. Rather, he is an example of a tragic figure.

IV.

If this story is not about murder and its deserved punishment, then what is it about? I think the answer is that it is about brotherhood, jealousy, competition, and the roots of strife. The message may appear extremely pessimistic and depressing, but the Torah is telling us that strife, and even murder, are rooted deeply in human nature. To put it another way, human strife is primordial, a direct result of the fact that there are at least two human beings. The very first two humans quarreled, and the result was murder. They quarreled not because they were somehow a danger to each other, but because they were in competition – one was a farmer and one a shepherd. Automatically, instead of cooperating, they entered different occupations and competed – economically and eventually religiously. The root of great evils does not necessarily lie in an evil personality, nor is it some terrible decadence from a naturally pure state. It is important to realize that Cain was a positive character, caught up in natural human impulses and emotions. The root of what happened here is not the corrupt nature of Cain, but the human family and human society. Man, in his desire to succeed and progress, is led to compete, and from this the road to strife is very short. Had we met the two brothers before the terrible end, we may well have sympathized more with Cain, rather than with his "worthless" (*hevel*) brother. But in the end, that makes no difference, because fine qualities are no guarantee against an upsurge of emotions.

There is a recurring theme in some western philosophies that the natural state of man is simple morality, and evil results from some decadent process of progress and social complexity. The Torah is warning us of the opposite. There is nothing particularly pure in the noble savage, in primitive social structures. The seeds of evil are found in the simplest social structure of all, a simple family. Morality is not natural, instincts should not be trusted, and "just being yourself" is a recipe for trouble. On the contrary, morality is the product of a highly structured and difficult course of training and restraint – namely, the Torah. Human history begins in competition leading to strife and murder; it takes a great effort on the part of an individual, and all of history on the part of mankind, to reach a state of cooperation, with true moral peace and genuine brotherhood.

V.

Now we can analyze God's response to Cain's despair at not being favored when bringing his offering. First, we note that God precedes his response with an exclamation of surprise – "Why are you disturbed and why has your face fallen?" This would appear to be a strange question – after all, Cain has just had his offering rejected! Is that not a good enough reason to be disturbed? The answer is that Cain is not disturbed by the nature of his relationship with God, but by his relative standing in the competition with Abel. Indeed, we do not know that Cain has been rejected. All the Torah says is that some special sign of favor (the midrash suggests that fire came down from heaven to devour the offering) which was accorded to Abel was absent in Cain's case. This does not mean that God is angry at Cain, only that, for some reason which we do not know, He chose to give a special sign to Abel. Speculating, perhaps Abel is depressed by the fact that he is engaged in a relatively less valuable field of occupation. Adam's family (according to the sages) is not permitted to eat meat, and has only a limited need for wool. (See the Netziv who considers Abel's occupation with things that are only luxuries rather than staples to be the source of his name as *Hevel* – "vanity.") But the reason is not really important – the Torah does not even hint at it. What is important is Cain's response, a response of jealousy derived from his choosing to measure his own value as a function of his success in competition.

God's answer is: "If you do well, you succeed, but if you do not do well, it will lurk on the door of sin." I would like to suggest that this means that Cain should be concerned only with one thing – is he doing well, doing good, intrinsically – and be unconcerned with the competition with Abel. If you are doing well, then that is what matters. If you are not doing good things, then your desire to succeed will be the seed of sin. The desire to produce, even to produce religious expression (i.e. bringing the first offering in history), is on the one hand the secret of man's greatness, but if expressed for the sake of competition, is on the other hand the source of sin. Rebellion against God is the first source of sin. Not realizing one's intrinsic worth, and trying to find value by surpassing others, is the second source. In some ways it is the more invidious, and definitely is the more common.

Cain fails this test, and his competitiveness and lack of self-worth lead him to fratricide. Having failed to find his value in the land he toils, he is removed from it and condemned to a life of wandering. Feeling that his life is worthless now (a life of *hevel*), he fears that any who meet him will kill him, as one would squash a worthless creature. But the message of God still holds – if he produces, if he does good, then his life has value. God gives him a sign to protect him. Cain's potential still holds true.

Parashat Noaḥ

Consolation for the Land

by Rav Yehuda Rock

As often happens, this week's *parasha* – Noaḥ – starts in the middle of a story. The last four verses of *Parashat Bereshit* are unquestionably an introduction to the story of the Flood:

> And God saw that the wickedness of man was great in the land … and God repented for having made man in the land … And God said: I shall wipe out man whom I have created from the face of the earth … but found favor in God's eyes.

However, it seems that the story of Noaḥ begins even earlier. When Noaḥ is born to Lemekh, a descendant of Shet, we read (5:29):

> He called his name Noaḥ, saying: This one shall **comfort us** [*yenaḥamenu*] for our work and the toil of our hands caused by **the ground**, which God has cursed. (5:29)

It seems clear that Lemekh refers here to the curse dating back to the sin of Adam (3:17–19):

And to Adam He said: Since you listened to your wife and ate from the tree concerning which I commanded you, saying, You shall not eat from it, Cursed **is the ground** for your sake. **In sorrow** shall you eat of it all the days of your life, and it shall bring forth thorns and thistles for you, and you shall eat the herb of the field. By the sweat of your brow shall you eat bread until you return to **the ground**, for from it you were taken; for you are dust, and you shall return to dust.

Indeed, during Noaḥ's lifetime the curse of the ground is nullified (8:21):

God smelled the sweet savor, and God said in His heart: I shall not again **curse** the **ground** for **man's** sake, for the inclination of man's heart is evil from his youth; nor shall I again smite all life, as I have done…

Thus, God's promise here, in the wake of the sacrifices that Noaḥ offers after leaving the ark, represents the realization of Lemekh's hopes in naming his son "Noaḥ."

However, upon closer inspection, the connection turns out to be less simple. There are actually two separate curses. The curse of the land, imposed at the time of Adam, concerned agricultural labor. It meant that growing produce would involve great effort and difficulty, and that the ground would yield "thorns and thistles." The curse that was revoked following Noaḥ's departure from the ark, on the other hand, concerns the annihilation of man from the face of the earth. To which of these two curses was Lemekh referring? If Lemekh is referring to the curse from the time of Adam, why does the Torah describe the revoking of the curse, when Noaḥ leaves the ark, in language that recalls Lemekh's declaration? Furthermore, we would expect some continuation of this story: either a fulfillment of Lemekh's words with the cancellation of the curse of the land imposed at the time of Adam, by means of some sort of agricultural progress, or some explanation as to why his words were not fulfilled. However, the Torah goes on to devote no attention at all to the cancellation of the curse, "In sorrow you shall eat of it all the days of your life." Thus Lemekh's words seem to represent no more than a wish, with no implications or connection to the rest of the story, and it is not clear why the Torah records them at all.

Rashi understands Lemekh's declaration as referring to the curse of Adam, and he views it as a sort of prophecy which comes to be realized. Basing his explanation on the Midrash (*Midrash Tanḥuma, Bereshit* 11), Rashi (commenting on 5:29) "fills in" that which the text omits in the story of the realization of Lemekh's words by supplying the agricultural enhancement:

> Until Noaḥ's time, people had no plowing instrument, and he made one for them. The land (until then) had produced thorns and thistles when sowed with wheat, because of Adam's curse, but in the days of Noaḥ the land was comforted.

The plain text, however, contains no hint of this development.

Some of the later commentators have gone even further and located the fulfillment of Lemekh's words in the story of Noaḥ, a man of the ground, planting the vineyard (8:20). According to this view, "wine makes man's heart glad," and this gladness is the comfort for the sorrow of toiling over the ground. In Proverbs (31:6–7) we read: "Give strong drink to one who is about to die, and wine to those of bitter spirit; let him drink and forget his poverty, and remember his toil no more." Similarly, in Jeremiah (16:7) we find the concept of the "cup of consolation."

However, none of this answers the question of why the Torah chooses to describe the revoking of the curse, after Noaḥ leaves the ark, in language that is reminiscent of Lemekh's declaration.

On the other hand, if we propose that Lemekh's words are realized in God's promise not to annihilate man ever again, we must ask why such a scenario would have occurred to Lemekh at all, prior to the Flood. And what sort of consolation would Noaḥ then have brought, relative to the situation at the time of his birth, when the idea of the Flood had not yet arisen? Furthermore, how do we then explain the significance of the linguistic parallels to the curse of Adam?

Ibn Ezra ignores the linguistic parallels and asserts that Lemekh's words are realized in the fact that it is Noaḥ who gives life to the land by reviving the world after the Flood. To Ibn Ezra's view, the reference to Noaḥ as a "man of the ground" is connected to this idea. In order to answer the question of how Lemekh would relate to this possibility, Ibn Ezra proposes that this was a real prophecy, conveyed by a real prophet (Adam) to Lemekh, or derived himself "through wisdom" (apparently, he refers here to astrology). However, all of this supporting theory is likewise absent from the text. Furthermore, while it addresses the technical question of how Lemekh could have known what would happen during Noaḥ's life, it does not explain how this "prophecy" was relevant during Lemekh's time.

It seems that Lemekh must have been referring to the curse of the land from the time of Adam. From a literary perspective, the reader – at this stage of the narrative – is aware only of that original curse; hence, the meaning of Lemekh's words, viewed in context, is the expression of a wish or prayer that his son Noaḥ would somehow bring about some comfort from the curse upon the land from the time of Adam. We must therefore seek the significance of the linguistic connection further on, after Noaḥ leaves the ark, and also explore the fate of Lemekh's wish.

Before addressing these questions, however, let us first examine the brief unit that is located in between Lemekh's wish and the continuation of the story of Noaḥ – the story of the "distinguished men" (*benei haelohim*, literally "children of gods" or "children of judges") and the daughters of man.

The verses read as follows (6:1–4):

> And it was, when man began to multiply upon the face of the earth, and daughters were born to them, that the distinguished men saw that the daughters of man were beautiful, and they took wives for themselves from all whom they chose. And God said: 'My spirit will not forever strive on account of man, for that he also is flesh; and his days shall be a hundred and twenty years.' There were Nephilim in the land in those days and also after that, when the distinguished men came to the daughters of man, and they bore children to them; these were the mighty men of old; men of renown.

The first two verses of this unit describe two groups: the "distinguished men" and the "daughters of man." Whether the "distinguished men" here are regular mortals or not, it is clear that the "daughters of man" certainly are. In these verses the "distinguished men" are active, while "man" (Adam) and his daughters are the passive victims.

God's words in verse 3 are open to various interpretations: they may be meant as an expression of reconcilement, or the opposite – an expression of punishment or retribution. In any event, it is clear that God is talking here about "man," in the wake of some unworthy behavior on his part. This is puzzling, since in the preceding verses, as pointed out above, mankind is the passive, injured party. Even if, in the formal sense, the "distinguished men" are included within the category of "man," from a literary perspective the differing usages of the word make for very confusing reading, and serve to break the literary flow.

Apparently, this unit combines two separate levels of meaning, or "aspects." We adopt here the exegetical methodology known as the "*shitat habeḥinot*," developed by my Rav and teacher, Rav Mordechai Breuer. According to this approach, God writes the Torah in layers, with narratives or halakhic units that parallel one another – different "aspects" – each of which is able to stand alone and to be read in its own right, such that sometimes they appear to contradict one another. Often, these aspects are intertwined, creating a complex or multi-layered unit. This complex unit blurs the points of transition between one aspect and the other, but highlights the difficulties inherent in these transitions. Each story expresses its own independent content, which is important in its own right; however, there is some relationship between them, which justifies their integration into a single text. By delving into the difficulties that arise from the joining together of the two aspects – such as repetitions or contradictions – we are able to expose the two independent "aspects," and thereafter to explore their significance.

Aside from the local division of this unit into "aspects," we may divide the book of Genesis in general into two aspects. The one refers to God only as "*Elokim*," while the other (also) uses the Tetragrammaton. Obviously, there are also further stylistic and thematic characteristics that differentiate between the two aspects.

The story of the "distinguished men and the daughters of man" is usually categorized under the aspect that uses the Tetragrammaton to refer to God. However, in light of the difficulty that we have indicated above, it may make more sense to divide this unit. In verse 3 we find the Tetragrammaton, and therefore the categorization of this verse is clear. Verses 1–2, which represent a single unit which does not continue on to verse 3, would appear to belong to the aspect that is characterized by the name *Elokim*. Verses 4–5 mention explicitly the events referred to in verses 1–2, and therefore they too belong to the aspect of *Elokim*.

We shall not discuss here the meaning of the verses belonging to the aspect of *Elokim*, nor the significance of the merging of the two aspects into a single textual unit. For the purposes of our discussion, we shall focus only on the aspect characterized by the Tetragrammaton.

Verse 3 is the only portion of unit that falls into this category. Clearly, this verse cannot stand alone; it must be read as the continuation of some previous verse. Hence, we must seek the last preceding verses belonging to the same aspect.

Chapter five is devoted to the "generations," as evidenced by its introduction, style, and structure. For various reasons, such genealogical chapters are usually categorized under the name *Elokim*, even where they contain no divine name at all. In chapter five, however, there is one verse that deviates from the otherwise fixed structure and which uses the Tetragrammaton. We refer here to the verse cited above, describing how Noaḥ received his name: "And he called his name Noaḥ, saying: This one shall comfort us for our work and the toil of our hands caused by the ground, which **God** has cursed." Had the Tetragrammaton aspect stood alone here, the Torah would have presented Lemekh and the fact of Noaḥ's birth in accordance with the style of that aspect. However, since the text interweaves both aspects, the fact that a son is born to Lemekh belongs exclusively within the aspect of *Elokim*. The aspect of the Tetragrammaton covers only his name and its meaning.

Hence, within the Tetragrammaton aspect, verse 3 of chapter six should be read as a direct continuation of verse 29 of chapter five:

> And he called his name Noaḥ, saying: This one shall comfort us for our work and the toil of our hands caused by the ground, which God has cursed.

And God said: My spirit will not strive forever on account of man for that he is also flesh; and his days shall be a hundred and twenty years.

Thus, the verse must be understood as referring to the curse of Adam. Accordingly, the word *"yidon"* (strive) is meant in the sense of judging and punishing; i.e., "I shall not continue to argue with man and punish him by cursing the earth."

If this is the case, then the verse is indeed meant in a spirit of appeasement, and the rest of the verse should be understood as proposed by Ramban, in accordance with Psalms 78:38–39:

For He is compassionate, forgiving sin, and not destroying; often turning away His anger and not stirring up all of His wrath; He remembers that they are mere flesh; a wind that passes and does not return.

Here, in the wake of Lemekh's prayer, God declares that He will indeed turn away His wrath from man and no longer judge him according to the strict demands of the Attribute of Justice. Man is in need of the Attribute of Mercy, for he is mere flesh and blood – a mortal who departs from the world after a brief hundred-and-twenty years. According to the exegetical direction that we are now taking, Lemekh's wish does receive due attention. God accepts his prayer, in principle, and declares that through Noaḥ consolation will come to mankind for the curse of the earth.

We must now re-read the concluding verses of *Parashat Bereshit* (6:5–8) which, as noted above, are actually the introduction to the story of the Flood:

"And God saw that the wickedness of **man** [*ha-adam*] was great in the land, and all the inclination of the thoughts of his heart was only evil all the time. And God **repented** [*vayinaḥem*] for having **made man** [*ha-adam*] in the land, and He was **grieved** to His heart. And God said: I shall **wipe out** [*emḥeh*] **man** [*ha-adam*] whom I have created from the face of the **earth** [*ha-adama*] –

both **man** [*me-adam*] and beast and crawling things and birds of the sky, for I **repent** [*niḥamti*] that I **made them**. But **Noaḥ** found **favor** [*ḥen*] in God's eyes."

There are repeated expressions involving the Hebrew root *a-d-m*; as well as regret/comfort (*neḥama*), wiping out (*meḥiya*) and favor (*ḥen*), and expressions of action (*a-s-h*) and of melancholy (*itzavon*). These alliterations serve to link these verses to the words of Lemekh: "This one will comfort us [*yenaḥamenu*] for our work [*mima'asenu*] and the toil [*itzavon*, literally "melancholy"] of our hands, because of the land [*adama*] which God has cursed."

Man is a transitory creature; he passes on and does not return, but his wickedness has already become a matter of enormous scope and proportion. Man's evil inclination admittedly arises from the fact that he is mere flesh, but this inclination of his heart is only evil, all the time. For this reason, corresponding to *"zeh yenaḥamenu"* ("this one will comfort us") we find *"vayinaḥem HaShem"* (God repented), and corresponding to *"me'itzvon yadenu"* ("for the toil of our hands") we find *"vayitatzev el libo"* ("He grieved to His heart"). God would like to comfort man and relieve him of the melancholy of his heart, but the situation has reached a point where man's wickedness is grieving God and causing Him to regret having created man in the world. This being the case, God decides to wipe man off the face of the earth. Instead of *"neḥamat ha-adam min ha-adama"* (comforting man for the melancholy of the cursed ground), God brings about *"meḥiyat ha-adam min ha-adama"* (wiping man off the face of the earth).

God's direction of the world balances two considerations. On the one hand, man's weakness requires a measure of compassion, a "sweetening of the verdict." On the other hand, it is specifically his importance in God's eyes that causes God to be so grieved by his actions, and intensifies the severity of His retribution. At the time of Lemekh's prayer, the former consideration prevailed. In the wake of the behavior of the generation of the Flood, the latter consideration came to take precedence.

However, this change in approach does not nullify Lemekh's wish completely. Along with the divine decree comes a note of hope: "But

Noah found favor in the eyes of God." Noah may still bring about some sort of comfort and consolation.

Ultimately, Noah leaves the ark, builds an altar to God, and offers up his sacrifices. Then the text tells us (8:21):

> God smelled the sweet savor, and God said in His heart: I shall no longer **curse** the **ground** [*adama*] for **man's** sake [*ba'avur ha-adam*], for the inclination of man's heart is evil from his youth; nor shall I any more smite all of life, as **I have done**. For as long as the earth remains, sowing and harvest and cold and heat and summer and winter and day and night shall not cease.

Noah, through his sacrifices, "reminds" God that there is good in man, too. The consideration that "the inclination of man's heart is evil from his youth" is similar to God's statement at the time of Lemekh's prayer: "For that he also is flesh; and his days shall be a hundred and twenty years." Man's fundamental weakness arouses God's compassion, and He is reminded of His decision not to "strive" with man forever. On the other hand, man's increasing evil apparently makes it impossible to return to the situation prior to Adam's sin and to cancel his curse. Instead, God decides to fulfill Lemekh's prayer, but in a different way: through nullifying the possibility of absolute melancholy and the eradication of man from the face of the earth.

Thus, both Lemekh's prayer and God's promise – "My spirit shall not forever strive on account of man" – are realized literally, but not as intended. Noah brings a certain consolation in that there will not be another annihilation of man from the face of the earth. However, along with this promise comes the assertion that the punishment of "by the sweat of your brow shall you eat bread" will not be cancelled; rather, "sowing and reaping ... will not cease."

Above, we rejected the possibility that Lemekh's words are fulfilled in Noah's planting of the vineyard. However, the vineyard may yet be connected to this story. Seemingly, Noah, who grew up imbibing the prophecy of his father, was deeply disappointed by God's assertion that "sowing and reaping ... will not cease." Out of despair and disillusionment,

Noah tried to single-handedly bring about a nullification of the curse, by providing the consolation of wine. However, Noah's attempted evasion of God's decree was also a flight from reality. Its results were shame and humiliation, instead of the joy and comfort that he had intended.

Survival and Revival – On the Righteousness of Noaḥ

by Rav Chanoch Waxman

I.

Noaḥ's story ends tragically. We part from him not after the deliverance of a divine blessing (9:1–7) or the establishment of a divine covenant (9:8–17), but rather after the strange and disturbing events at the end of chapter nine.

> And Noaḥ began to be a husbandman, and he planted a vineyard: and he drank of the wine and was drunk; and he was uncovered within his tent. And Ham, the father of Canaan, saw the naked-ness of his father, and told his two brothers outside. And Shem and Yafet took the garment, and laid it upon both their shoulders, and went backward, and covered the nakedness of their father; and their faces were backward, and they saw not their father's nakedness. And Noaḥ awoke from his wine, and knew what his younger son had done to him ... (9:19–24)

The story abounds with difficulty. What happened? What did Ham, the father of Canaan, or Canaan and Ham on some interpretations,

51

do to Noaḥ? What does the text hint at in the opaque phrase "done to him"? The options suggested range from the relatively mild acts of observing and publicizing (Ibn Ezra, Ramban) on the one hand, to the far more sinister acts of castration or rape on the other hand (Rashi). Whether one interprets the action of Ḥam-Canaan as mere disrespect and mockery or as more serious crimes, the story depicts Noaḥ drunken, sexually vulnerable (and perhaps even abused) by his children. In short, he is completely disgraced – a surprising twist in the story of a righteous man.

II.

Complex parallels between the end of the Noaḥ narrative and the Lot story should help reinforce this sense of unease. Both the story of the destruction of the generation of the flood in *Parashat Noaḥ*, and the account of the destruction of Sodom in *Parashat Vayera*, present stories of God's destruction of a bad society/world. In line with this broad thematic parallel, we note numerous specific linguistic and narrative parallels. The Torah utilizes the word "*ra*," meaning bad or wicked, to describe both objects of God's wrath when they are first introduced (6:5 and 13:13). Similarly, the verb for destruction (*shaḥot*) is the same in both stories (6:13 and 19:13, 14, 29). In both cases, the term first appears in a speech by God or a divine emissary heralding the incipient destruction to the leader of the single family destined to escape the destruction – Noaḥ (6:13) and Lot (19:12–14). Furthermore, in both cases the Torah utilizes the same Hebrew root, *m-t-r* ("rain down"), to describe God's method of destruction. Just as the flood is wrought by "raining down" (7:4), so too the "brimstone and fire" storm that devastates Sodom comes "raining down" (19:24).

A closer look at these stories reveals that they parallel each other in more than just the theme of destruction and in language. In both cases a single family is saved, seemingly escaping just in the nick of time (see Rashi on 7:6–7 and 19:16–17, 21–24). Furthermore, in both narratives, God's mercy and rescue are connected to His "remembering" a single "perfect" man who "walks" with God. In the story of Sodom, God "remembers" Abraham (19:29), who had been commanded by God to "walk before Me and be perfect" (17:1). Consequently, due to Abraham's merit, God saves Lot. In the story of the flood, God "remembers" Noaḥ

(8:1), a man previously described as "perfect in his generations," a man who "walked with God" (6:9). Here, it is the virtuous Noaḥ himself who is saved. Unlike the undeserving Lot, saved only by virtue of his relation to a righteous man, Noaḥ is rescued on the basis of merit. He is the righteous man, both cause and object of God's rescue.

Finally, these destruction-rescue stories are parallel in one last and crucial fashion. We all remember the sad end of Lot. Alone with his children in a small enclosed space (19:30), he is drunk, sexually vulnerable, and exploited by his very own children – debauched and disgraced. But this, of course, is the end of Noaḥ: alone with his children, in a small enclosed space (9:21), drunk, sexually vulnerable, and exploited by his very own children – debauched and disgraced.

Mapping out the parallel, we note the following. In stage one, which we may term "the righteous man," Noaḥ is the cause of the rescue and stands in parallel to Abraham, the cause of the rescue from Sodom. Stage two, "destruction," apparently contains no human characters in either story, and need not concern us now. In stage three, "rescue," Noaḥ stands parallel to Lot, a wholly undeserving and morally crippled creature who had chosen to settle in Sodom despite the evil character of its citizens (13:9–13). But this is not necessarily disturbing. As pointed out previously, unlike Lot, Noaḥ is saved by his own virtue. The point of the parallel and contrast at this point is to denigrate Lot, not Noaḥ. However, in the fourth stage, "end," once again Noaḥ parallels Lot. Like Lot, he is withdrawn, drunk, abused and disgraced. Here the point of the parallel seems to be the opposite of stage three: not the denigration of Lot, but the denigration of Noaḥ. On the literary plane, Noaḥ moves from the Abraham role, the role of the righteous man, to the Lot role, the role of the undeserving man. At the end of the story of Sodom, we find Abraham standing and observing the destruction, literally and metaphorically "in front of God" (19:27–28). He stands outside the desperation and disgrace of Lot. But such is not the fate of Noaḥ. He stands only in the Lot role, inside the wretched drunkenness and disgrace, far from the face of God. Noaḥ has become Lot.

What strange circumstance has transformed Noaḥ into the equal of Lot? What has happened to our "perfect" and righteous man by whose virtue mankind was saved?

III.

Let us turn to the question of Noah's righteousness. In its preface to the story of the flood at the end of *Parashat Bereshit* (6:1–8) and also throughout the early parts of *Parashat Noah* (6:9–7:5), the Torah informs us repeatedly of Noah's unique status and righteousness. Noah is described variously as "finding favor in the eyes of God" (6:8), "righteous and perfect in his generation" (6:9), "the sole righteous one of this generation" (7:1) and as one who "walked with God" (6:9). Noah is different than those around him; he does not participate in the social, moral and sexual corruption of his era (see 6:1–12, Rashi on 6:11).

However, in addition to this method of description, the Torah also employs another, far subtler tool to emphasize Noah's uniqueness. After reporting the instructions given by God to Noah for building the ark and gathering the animals (6:13–22), the Torah informs us, "And Noah did according to all that God commanded him; so he did" (6:22). As if for emphasis, the phrase appears again in slight variation just a few verses later (7:5) after additional commands from God (7:1–4). At first glance, the conceptual pair of God's command and Noah's obedience might not strike us as significant; after all, when God talks, one should listen. But let us reconsider.

The term "command" has appeared in only one other context until this point. This is in fact the term utilized to describe God's forbidding the fruit of the Tree of Knowledge (2:16–17). Likewise, God Himself uses the command term in interrogating Adam. God inquires whether he has "…eaten from the tree that I commanded you not to eat from it?" (3:11).

Unlike Adam and Eve, who proved themselves incapable of obeying the simple command of not eating a particular fruit, Noah proves himself capable of obeying the most arduous commands. Noah does not evade, disobey or even reply. He simply carries out God's word, no matter how Herculean the task, no matter the size of the boat, the number of animals to be gathered or the amount of food to be collected. Noah's uniqueness lies not just in his uprightness and morality, but also in his obedience to the command of God.

IV.

Undoubtedly, as argued above, the command-response section of the flood narrative describing Noah's obedience and righteousness (6:13–7:5) provides crucial insight into our understanding of Noah, and consequently, the story of the flood. A deeper examination of the section should help us further sharpen our insight into Noah, the ark and the flood. Let us begin our examination at the end, taking a careful look at 7:1–5.

> And God said to Noah: Come, you and all your house into the ark; for only you have I seen righteous before Me in this generation. Of every clean [*tahor*] beast you shall take sevens, male and female: and of beasts that are not clean two, male and female. Of birds of the air, also sevens, the male and the female; to revive seed upon the face of earth. For in another seven days, I will cause it to rain upon the earth forty days and forty nights; and I will blot out every living substance that I have made from the face of the earth.
> And Noah did according to all that God commanded him.

Logically, the subsection contains the following points: 1. an instruction to Noah to enter the ark, 2. the information that Noah is a righteous man, 3. instructions to Noah regarding the animals, 4. God's intention to destroy the world, and 5. the statement that Noah did exactly as God commanded. But none of this is particularly new. In the command-response section until this point (6:13–22), Noah has already been told about entering the ark (6:18). With regard to the second point, we of course already know that God's rescue is due to the fact that Noah is righteous (6:9). Furthermore, Noah has already been instructed regarding the animals (6:19–20) and told that God intends to destroy the world (6:17). Finally, we already know that Noah did and does precisely as God commands (6:22). We may very well ask ourselves: What purpose does this second command-response section serve?

Perhaps the answer to this problem lies not in noting the similarities to what has come previously, but rather in focusing on the differences between the second command-response section and the narrative until this point. As pointed out by Ramban, the second section includes for the first time the command to gather seven male-female sets of *"tahor"* animals and birds. Previously, Noaḥ had been commanded to take into the ark "two," apparently one male-female set, of "all flesh," "the birds to their kind" and "the cattle to their kind" (6:18–19). According to Ramban, the purpose of the *tahor* animals is to serve as a resource for sacrifices after Noaḥ emerges from the ark. By implication, the entire second command-response section exists solely to implicitly command Noaḥ in the mitzva of sacrifices. But this explanation seems difficult to maintain. Could not this information and "command" have been folded into the first command-response section, as part of the command to gather animals?

Alternatively, we may focus on a second crucial difference between 7:1–5 and all that has come previously. In explaining the purpose of gathering the animals and entering the ark, the text utilizes the phrase, *"leḥayot zera al penei kol ha'aretz"* (7:3). However, previously, in the first command-response section, the term used as the rationale for gathering the animals and entering the ark is the subtly different: *"leḥaḥayot"* (6:18–20), bereft of the additional, *"zera al penei kol ha'aretz."* But what exactly is the difference?

In fact, the phrases possess very different connotations. The bare phrase, *"leḥaḥayot,"* is probably best translated as, "to keep alive," or colloquially, "to survive." In the first command-response section, the rationale of the ark is survival. God the Creator wishes that something of His labor be preserved. He chooses Noaḥ and two of each species as "survivors," or perhaps even "relics" – representatives of the world that once was. In contrast, the different and full phrase, *"leḥaḥayot zera al penei kol ha'aretz,"* is best translated as, "to make alive seed upon the entire face of the earth," or in more colloquial terms, "to revive life upon the earth." The rationale of the ark is far more than mere survival. Rather, it is about reviving the entire world. It is future-oriented rather than past-oriented, its inhabitants intended as prototypes for a new world rather than just survivors and relics of an old one. God wishes that the world be made anew and charges Noaḥ with the task.

On this account, the command to gather the *"tahor,"* clean, animals can be seen in a new light. Quite possibly, they are for the purpose of sacrifices. A world in which man expresses thanksgiving to God is far better than one in which he fails to acknowledge God. However, we might also claim that *"tahor"* here does not necessarily mean "clean" in the halakhic sense of permissible for sacrifice. Perhaps the term connotes "pure" in contrast to "corrupt," as in the "corruption of all flesh upon the earth," the all-encompassing distortion of nature which includes even the animal world (see Rashi on 6:12). Just as Noaḥ, the righteous man, is chosen as a prototype for a new humanity, so too the *tahor* animals, the uncorrupted flesh of the animal world, are chosen as a new majority in the animal world, to remake the world as a new and better place.

All of this should bring us to a good understanding of Noaḥ's character, the purpose of the ark, and the text of the first part of the flood narrative. Noaḥ is righteous, and has been unique in obeying God's command. The purpose of the ark is dual, and hence the text deals with a dual theme. It is about survival, but also about much more. It is also about revival, the process of remaking the world. Without doubt, Noaḥ fares well at the task of survival. He builds the ark, gathers the supplies and animals, and enters the ark exactly as commanded by God (6:22; 7:5, 9, 16). But what about the second task? What about reviving and remaking the world? How well does the righteous and obedient man bear this task?

V.

Let us take a look at the latter part of chapter eight, the emergence from the ark. God commands Noaḥ as follows:

> …Go out of the ark, you and your wife, and your sons and their wives with you. Bring out with you every living thing that is with you, of all flesh, both of birds and of cattle…and swarm on the earth, and be fruitful, and multiply upon the earth. (8:16–17)

Noaḥ is given three commands. The first is to leave the ark in male-female pairs. The second is to actively bring the animals out of the ark. Both of these commands anticipate and constitute preparation for the third command, the demand to swarm across the newly made earth and procreate. Noaḥ and his band stand at the cusp of a new world, both opportunity and responsibility, facing the demand to revive and remake the world. However, Noaḥ's response is quite different:

> Noaḥ and his sons went out, and his wife and his sons' wives... every beast, every creeping thing, and every bird and whatever creeps on the earth after their kind went out of the ark. (8:18–19)

Quite clearly, something has gone awry. In place of Noaḥ leaving the ark along with his wife, in male-female pairing, he leaves in the company of his sons. Likewise, Noaḥ is not depicted as bringing out the animals; they are left behind and seem to emerge by themselves without the help and assistance of Noaḥ. Rather than an image of a mixed group of male-female pairs emerging prepared to repopulate the world, we are presented with a linear image of three separate groups: men, women and animals. Furthermore, the apparent purpose of leaving the ark – the imperative to procreate, the third aspect of God's threefold command – is wholly neglected in the "response" stage. In fact, Noaḥ's segregated, linear emergence from the ark and neglect of the animals seems calculated to negate the procreation-repopulation imperative (see Abarbanel).

On the simplest level, we are confronted with an act of disobedience. For the first time, we find Noaḥ not being Noaḥ, not obeying the command of God. In fact, this is the first command of God to Noaḥ regarding which the text does not state, "And Noaḥ did as God commanded." On a deeper level, the refusal or perhaps inability of Noaḥ to procreate, swarm over the earth, assist the animals, etc., signals Noaḥ's inability to succeed at the "revival" aspect of his task. While confronted with the task of survival, Noaḥ excelled. He was the perfect divine servant. But now, confronted with reviving the world, he no longer obeys the word of God.

VI.

This key should help us unlock the mysteries of the remainder of the story of Noaḥ and the riddle of his "transformation." In line with the claims made above, Abarbanel points out that much of chapter nine can be viewed as a divine attempt to rescue Noaḥ, this time from himself. At the beginning of the chapter, God blesses mankind, expresses special

concern for mankind, and distinguishes man from the animals by allowing man to consume meat (9:1–7). The blessing begins and ends with
the imperative to "be fruitful, multiply and fill the world." God follows
with a covenant and a sign, a promise never to destroy the world again
(9:17). All of this is intended to bolster Noaḥ. God cares about mankind
and the world. He desires their revival. He has promised a covenantal
relation and permanent existence. Noaḥ should be revived and begin
to revive the world.

This brings us full circle to the end of chapter nine and the
drunken Noaḥ. Rather than finding a renewed Noaḥ, roaming and
remaking the world, we find Noaḥ in an enclosed space, withdrawn,
drunk, engaged only in the bliss of the bottle. Rather than engaging in
the imperative of procreation and filling the world, we find Noaḥ, naked
and sexually compromised by his son.

In sum, the story of the "end of Noaḥ" is not so much the story
of the transformation of a righteous man but the story of the limits of
Noaḥ's righteousness. His righteousness is capable of surmounting and
surviving great challenges, from upright existence in the midst of an
evil society, through the daunting multi-year task of building the ark
and living in it. It is even a righteousness that is capable of enduring the
destruction of the world and emerging to thank God for His mercy and
rescue. It is this very righteousness that fostered Noaḥ's spiritual survival
and thriving amidst the society of the flood generation. But at the end
of the day, it is a righteousness of survival. It is oriented solely along a
God-self axis that does not include the world. Consequently, it is not a
righteousness that is oriented to the world. It is not a righteousness that
cares about the world and is capable of its renewal, rebuilding and revival.

A final return to the Sodom-flood parallel and the Noaḥ-
Abraham-Lot triangle should help buttress this point. As pointed out
earlier, the person-parallels shift as the parallel progresses through its
various stages: "the righteous man," "destruction," "rescue" and "end."
In stage one, "the righteous man," Noaḥ is the cause of the rescue and
stands in parallel to Abraham, the cause of the rescue from Sodom.
As of stage three, "rescue," Noaḥ overlaps with Lot, but at least as the
cause of his own rescue. However, by the time we reach stage four, "end,"
Noaḥ stands in complete parallel to Lot, debauched and disgraced, his

righteousness in shambles. When making this point earlier, I claimed that stage two, "destruction," apparently contains no human characters and is not relevant to our person-parallel progression. In fact, the key word here is "apparently." The destruction of Sodom does indeed contain a human character. His name is Abraham.

The story of the destruction of Sodom begins textually with God sharing His plans of destruction with the "righteous man" (18:17–21). This section is framed on either side by verses describing the ongoing journey of the "men" towards Sodom and its imminent destruction (18:16, 22). Abraham's response is immediate and well-known: he prays (18:22–33). He prays for justice, for mercy, for the bad society of Sodom, for even ten good men. The silence of the "righteous man" in the flood story thunders by contrast. Noaḥ is silent. He builds, he gathers, he obeys, he enters the ark; the world is destroyed, he survives, and he even thanks God. But he never expresses a sentiment or prayer for the world around him. Once again, his righteousness is the righteousness of the self, an isolated and private righteousness. It is not a righteousness oriented to the world, capable of praying for the world before disaster, or rebuilding it afterwards.

Noaḥ is not Abraham in the second stage of our parallel. His righteousness may be thought of as a two-place relation, a pair consisting of self and God, rather than a triangular relation of God, self and world. From there on, it seems that the slow slide to complete overlap with Lot, the undeserving survivor, is just a slippery slope away. Perhaps we are to derive that righteousness of the self, isolated and private, is not only limited but also prone to decay. Perhaps the lesson is to be a little bit less like Noaḥ and a little bit more like Abraham, to construct a righteousness engaged with the world, a righteousness of revival and not just survival.

To Be a Man of the Earth

by Rav Yaakov Beasley

I. INTRODUCTION

After the widespread tragedy and wholesale destruction of the Flood, the eyes of the Torah turn to the person chosen to rebuild the human race and restore the order that existed on earth before mankind's descent into corruption and degeneracy. Indeed, the Torah, before the Flood, introduced Noah as follows:

> These are the generations of Noah. Noah was a righteous man [*ish tzaddik*] and whole-hearted in his generations; Noah walked with God. (Gen. 6:9)

Our hopes in Noah seem well-founded. He is the first person that the Torah labels as a righteous man. Even at birth, he was named with the prayer that "this one [Noah] will provide us relief from our work and the toil of our hands, out of the very soil which HaShem placed under a curse" (Gen. 5:29). Lemekh's words echo the hope that, at long last, the divine punishment meted out to Adam after the Garden of Eden – "Cursed be the ground because of you: by toil shall you eat of it … by the sweat of your brow shall you get bread to eat" (3:17–18) – has run its course and an antidote has been found.

After the destruction of the earth and its inhabitants through the Flood, we are given additional reason to hope that Noah is indeed capable of undoing Adam's original sin.[1] Upon leaving the ark, Noah offers sacrifices to HaShem, whose response is to declare, "Never again will I curse the earth because of man" (8:21). He blesses Noah with the original blessing to man, "Be fruitful and multiply, and fill the earth" (9:1). Commandments are given, the new relationship between man and animal is delineated, and finally, a covenant is established between God and humanity.

How does Noah respond to this new opportunity? The Torah continues:

> The sons of Noah who came out of the ark were Shem, Ham, and Yafet – Ham being the father of Canaan. These three were the sons of Noah, and of these was the whole earth branched out. And Noah the man of the earth [*ish ha-adama*] began, and planted a vineyard. And he drank of the wine, and was drunk; and he was uncovered within his tent. And Ham, the father of Canaan, saw the nakedness of his father, and told his two brethren outside. And Shem and Yafet took a garment, and laid it upon both their shoulders, and went backward, and covered the nakedness of their father; and their faces were backward, and they saw not their father's nakedness. And Noah awoke from his wine, and knew what his youngest son had done unto him. And he said: Cursed be Canaan; a servant of servants shall he be unto his brethren. And he said: Blessed be the Lord, the God of Shem; and let Canaan be their servant. God enlarge Yafet, and he shall dwell in the tents of Shem; and let Canaan be their servant. And Noah lived after the flood three hundred and fifty years. And all the days of Noah were nine hundred and fifty years; and he died. Now these are

---

1. Indeed, the description of the Flood and the earth's destruction contain many inverse literary parallels to the earlier account of the earth's creation. A fuller account of these parallels and how the story of the Flood serves as a thematic and literary undoing of the work of Creation can be found in R. Michael Hattin's article "Creation and Dissolution: A Study in Contrasts?" at the VBM Introduction to Parsha archives.

the generations of the sons of Noaḥ: Shem, Ḥam, and Yafet; and unto them were sons born after the flood. (9:18–10:1)

What an ignoble ending! From the lofty appellation of *"ish tzaddik"* – a righteous man, Noaḥ became an *"ish ha-adama"* – a man of the lowly earth.[2] Even here, he fails to rule over his creation, until he is left drunkenly sprawled out uncovered in his tent, where he becomes the unwilling victim of some despicable, reprehensible behavior from his own family. Only the respectful behavior of his other children offers him some modicum of respect. All that is left is for him to curse the perpetrator, and, like the generations that preceded the Flood, he lives and dies, adding nothing meaningful to the course of human history. Indeed, the words "And Noaḥ began [*vayaḥel*]" echo the story of Enosh who "began [the pasuk uses the word *huḥal*] to call in the name of HaShem," which rabbinic thought identified with the beginning of idolatry and the spiritual descent of man (see Rashi on 4:26; the beginning of *Mishneh Torah*, Hilkhot Avoda Zara). The Torah continues its account with his children, "And these are the generations of the sons of Noaḥ," while he becomes a footnote in history. What happened? How did this character, filled with the hopes of his generation, descend so rapidly to the state of shame and dishonor that marks his final appearance in the Torah?

II. ALLUSIONS TO OTHER STORIES

In order to answer these questions, we will rely on one of the basic approaches available to the reader, the discovery of literary allusions and connections to other stories, in the hope that we can use them to decipher the cryptic answers encoded within the text in front of us.

We turn first to the planting of the vineyard. Of all the plants available, what motivated Noaḥ to plant grapes? Glancing at other stories in Tanach, we find that the drinking of wine is often accompanied by sexual behavior, often immoral. For example, wine has sexual overtones in Song of Songs (1:2, 4; 4:10; 5:1; 7:2, 9; 8:2). Lamentations mocks the daughter of Edom:

---

2. *Midrash Tanḥuma, Bereshit* ch. 13. "Rabbi Yehuda the son of Rabbi Shalom said: In the beginning he was a 'righteous man,' and now he is a 'man of the earth.'"

> Rejoice and be glad, O daughter of Edom…you shall be drunken, and shall make thyself naked. (Lam. 4:21)

In chapter nineteen of Genesis, Lot's daughters use wine to repeatedly seduce their aged father, while David uses wine to get Uriah drunk in a vain attempt to induce Uriah to have intercourse with his wife Bat-Sheva, so David's adultery and her pregnancy could be concealed. What does this suggest about Noah's motivations?

We suggest, however, that the planting alludes to another event in Genesis – the planting by God of the Garden of Eden. Just as God engaged in planting, so too Noah engaged in planting. If so, then we can suggest that Noah's actions after the Flood mimic God's actions in Creation – an act of *Imitatio Dei*. Indeed, the entire section contains many parallels to the Creation story, which we will enumerate. This leads one to conclude, that just as the Flood served as the undoing of the original creation, our story of Noah and the vineyard serves to undo the attempt to start Creation again after the Flood.

Parallels:

1. Both stories begin with the blessing to "be fruitful and multiply."
2. God planted a garden; Noah planted a vineyard.
3. Both stories take a turn for the worse when the protagonist(s) consumes some fruit.[3]
4. After the eating/drinking of the forbidden fruit, the protagonist's naked state, and the efforts to cover it, become prominent details in the story.
5. Curses (and blessings) are distributed at the finale of the story (creating the parallel between Ham and the snake).

---

3. Rabbinic thought strengthens the parallel further. *Berakhot* 40a: "It was taught: Rabbi Meir said, 'The tree that the first man ate from was a vine, as there is no food that brings more curses upon man than the grape [wine].'" *Sanhedrin* 70a – "What is the meaning of 'a man of the earth'? Said the Holy One, Blessed be He, to Noah, 'You should have taken heed from what happened to the first man, whose downfall was through wine.'"

That Shem and Yafet are forced to walk backwards to cover their father becomes the symbolic theme of the story: any forward progress made by humanity after the Flood has been reversed. Indeed, their act is the pivot of the chiastic structure that frames this story.

A. And *Noaḥ drank of the wine* and became drunk…
   B. Ḥam *saw his father's nakedness*
      C. and told *his two brothers outside* [*the tent*]
         D. Then Shem and Yafet took a garment…
      C1. and [*the two brothers*] *walked backwards* [*into the tent*] and covered the nakedness of their father…
   B1. and *their father's nakedness they did not see*
A1. And *Noaḥ awoke from his wine*…

In this case, the chiasm reflects the text's contrast the differing reactions of Noaḥ's children to his predicament.

The precise nature of what Ḥam did while in the tent remains obscure. According to Radak, his offense was solely to see his father uncovered (and his willingness to share that information with his brothers). *Ḥazal* in the Talmud went much further then what is explicit in the text: they suggested that in fact either Ḥam castrated Noaḥ, or that he engaged in homosexual relations with Noaḥ (an alternative form of "uncreation"), and then castrated him. The parallels mentioned above to the incestuous Lot/daughters episode certainly point in this direction. The failure to interpret Ḥam's offense as simple voyeurism (itself a serious misdemeanor) and the interpretation that something more drastic occurred are supported by the verse "And Noaḥ awoke from his wine, and knew what his youngest son had done unto him." Clearly, something beyond simple peeking had to have occurred.

We suggest that Ḥam in fact committed an incestuous act with Noaḥ's wife (his mother). The rationales for this interpretation are several. First, the wording of "uncover nakedness" is only used in the book of Leviticus to describe heterosexual incest, not the homosexual act. More specifically, Leviticus 18:8 equates "the nakedness of your mother" with the "nakedness of your father." Furthermore, if Ḥam engaged in incestuous sex with his mother, the text's emphasis on his son Canaan becomes clear. Canaan is the product of this incestuous union, as Moab and Ammon are the product of Lot and his daughters. That explains why the text consistently identifies Ḥam as the "father of Canaan," and why Noaḥ chooses to curse Canaan upon awakening. The Torah also alludes to the possibility that this occurred in Ḥam's mother's tent. As Rashi notes, the written word (the *ketiv*) "the tent" in verse 21 has the feminine possessive suffix, "her tent," although we read (*keri*) the word as "his tent." Ḥam's act of sleeping with his mother would therefore be seen as an act of rebellion against Noaḥ's authority (as seen later with Reuben with Bilha, Absalom with David's concubines, and Adoniyahu's attempt to claim Avishag as his rightful bride from Solomon). We could suggest that this was *Ḥazal*'s intention in interpreting his act as castration – the ultimate removal of the father's creative power.

III. NOAḤ'S MOTIVATION

Whatever despicable act Ḥam committed, we return to the question of Noaḥ's motivations – was his drinking motivated by his desire to fulfill the directive to "be fruitful and multiply," to replant the world around him (just as God planted a Garden for man to live in); or was it the desperate act of a man who chose not to engage in the new reality around him? A careful reading of his exit off the ark may provide us with the answer. When God commanded Noaḥ and his family to enter the ark before the floodwaters would arrive, God stated:

> On that very day entered Noaḥ, and Shem, and Ḥam, and Yafet, the sons of Noaḥ, and Noaḥ's wife, and the three wives of his sons with them, into the ark. (7:13)

However, when God commanded them to exit the ark, he stated:

> Go forth from the ark, you, and your wife, and your sons, and your sons' wives with you. (8:16)

Rashi notes the change in the order of the command, and comments that while on the ark, relations between men and women were forbidden (hence the text's separation between Noaḥ and his sons/his wife and daughters-in-law). However, they were permitted to resume regular marital life upon exiting the ark (therefore, the text pairs Noah and his wife/his sons and their wives). However, if we examine the text closely, we see that Noah did not obey the divine directive. Instead, he left as follows:

> And Noah went forth, and his sons, and his wife, and his sons' wives with him. (8:18)

In direct opposition to God's wish to repopulate the desolate earth, Noah chooses to refrain from bringing new life forth. Perhaps this is a delayed reaction to the severity of the destruction around him; perhaps he did not feel equal to the task. Instead, he chose to avoid his destiny, to drown himself in his own handiwork. Whatever the interpretation of Ham's behavior, they all share Noah's new state of sterility – his inability to continue to produce. Sadly, the impression of the old, decrepit, infertile Noah is the last glimpse that the text allows us to view. What had begun with such high hopes and promises turned out to be another failed episode in God's attempts to find someone with whom He could create a lasting relationship and covenant. That would have to wait another ten generations.

Sefer Toledot, the Tower of Babel and the Purpose of the Book of Genesis

by Rav Menachem Leibtag

I. INTRODUCTION

The *Mabul* (the Flood) and *Migdal Bavel* (the Tower of Babel) are the two primary stories in this week's *parasha*. However, each of these two stories is preceded by a list of genealogies that appear to be rather irrelevant. Furthermore, at the conclusion of *Parashat Noaḥ* (Gen. 11:10–25) we find yet another set of genealogies (which introduces the story of *Avraham Avinu* [Abraham]). In this week's *shiur*, we explain how these "*sifrei toladot*" (lists of genealogies) create a "framework" for the book of Genesis and can help us better understand how these stories (i.e. the Flood and the Tower of Babel) contribute to its overall theme.

II. FROM A LIST TO AN OUTLINE

The book of Genesis moves quickly from one topic to another. The creation of the world is followed by the stories of the Garden of Eden and Cain and Abel. A description of the sorry state of mankind is followed quickly by the Flood. The attempts to rebuild the world lead to the building of the Tower of Babel. Finally, HaShem turns to Abram to assist His overall plan. We note that all of these stories relate in one form or other to God's *hashgaḥa* [providence], i.e. His intervention in the history of mankind as He punishes man (or mankind) for wayward behavior. For example, after Creation we find the following stories:

Adam & Eve sin and hence are expelled from the Garden of Eden.

Cain is punished for the murder of Abel.

The generation of the Flood is punished for its corruption.

The generation of the Tower of Babel is "punished" for building the Tower.

Afterward, the focus of the book of Genesis shifts from stories of "sin & punishment" to God's choice of *Avraham Avinu* – and the story of his offspring.

However, within this progression of topics, we find a very interesting phenomenon. The Torah introduces each of the general stories with a set of *toledot* (genealogies):

The *toledot* from Adam to Noaḥ (ch. 5) introduce the story of the Flood (ch. 6–9).

The *toledot* of Noaḥ's children (ch. 10) introduces the story of the Tower of Babel (11:1–9).

The *toledot* from Shem to Teraḥ (ch. 11) introduce the story of *Avraham Avinu* (ch. 12ff).

In fact, as surprising as it may sound, even the story of the Garden of Eden (ch. 2–3) is first introduced by *toledot*!

These are the *toledot* of the heavens and earth... (2:4).

Furthermore, later on in Genesis, we continue to find *toledot* – the *toledot* of Ishmael (25:12); *toledot* of Isaac (25:19); *toledot* of Esau (36:1); and *toledot* of Jacob (37:2).

The following table summarizes this pattern, and illustrates how *toledot* introduce each of the main topics in Genesis.

CHAPTERS	TOPIC
2	*Toledot shamayim va'aretz*
2–4	Man in (and out of) the Garden of Eden
5	*Toledot Adam* to **Noaḥ**
6–9	*HaMabul* – The story of the Flood
10	*Toledot Benei Noaḥ* – Shem, Ḥam & Yafet

11:1–9	*Migdal Bavel* – The Tower of Babel
11	*Toledot Shem* until **Teraḥ**
12–25	God's choice of *Avraham Avinu*
25–35	*Toledot* Yitzḥak – the story of Jacob & Esau
36	*Toledot Esav* – story of Esau's children
37–50	*Toledot Yaakov* – story of Joseph & his brothers

Although this pattern is rarely noticed, these *sifrei toladot* actually create a framework for the entire book of Genesis! In this manner, the *toladot* introduce each and every story in Genesis. To explain why, we must first take a minute to explain what the word *"toladot"* means:

The word *"toladot"* stems from the Hebrew word *"velad,"* a child or offspring. Therefore, *"Eleh toledot"* should be translated "These are the children of…" For example: *"Eleh toledot Adam"* (5:1) means "these are the **children** of Adam," – and thus introduces the story of Adam's children, i.e. Shet, Enosh, Kenan, etc. Similarly, *"Eleh toledot Noaḥ"* introduces the story of Noaḥ's **children** – Shem, Ḥam, and Yafet. (See Rashbam on Gen. 37:2 for a more complete explanation.)

Some of these *toladot* in Genesis are very short; as they simply state that the person lived, married, had children and died (e.g. the generations from Adam to Noaḥ). Other *toladot* are very detailed, e.g. those of Noaḥ, Teraḥ, Isaac, and Jacob. Nonetheless, **every** story in Genesis could be understood as a detail in the progression of these *toladot*.

This explanation raises a question concerning the first instance where we find *toladot* – i.e., *toledot shamayim va'aretz* (2:4). How do the heavens and earth have "children"?! The answer to this question may be quite meaningful. Recall that the first chapter of Genesis explains how God created *shamayim va'aretz* (heavens and earth) from "nothing" (*ex nihilo*). Then, immediately afterward in the next chapter, we encounter the first use of *toladot*:

Eleh toledot hashamayim veha'aretz behibaram… (2:4)

So what does Ḥumash refer to as the *toladot* of *shamayim va'aretz*, i.e., what are the **children** of heaven and earth? If we follow the progressive pattern of Genesis, then *"toledot shamayim va'aretz"* must refer to man himself (i.e. *Adam harishon*), for it is the story of his creation that immediately follows this introductory verse! This interpretation could help explain the significance of the verse that describes how God created man in chapter two:

> And *HaShem Elokim* formed man from the dust of the **earth** and blew into his nostrils *nishmat ḥayyim* [the breath of life]. (2:7)

This second ingredient may reflect the aspect of man which comes from (or at least returns to) heaven.

In contrast to the story of Creation in chapter one, which features a clear division between heaven and earth, God's creation of man in chapter two may reflect his unique ability to connect between heaven and earth.

Similarly, the next set of *toladot* – from Adam to Noaḥ (ch. 5) leads immediately into the story of the Flood. (Note how 9:28–29 follow the same "template" of the *toladot* in chapter five.)

This pattern of *toladot* that introduce stories continues all the way until the very end of Genesis. Therefore, we conclude that these *sifrei toladot* do more than "keep the book together"; they also help develop the theme of Genesis. We will now show how these *toladot* create not only a framework for Genesis; they can also help us identify its two distinct sections that create its primary theme. Let's explain:

III. THE TWO SECTIONS OF GENESIS

Despite this successive nature of the *toladot* in Genesis, they clearly divide into **two** distinct sections: God's creation of mankind (ch. 1–11) and the stories of our forefathers (ch. 12–50).

Though the majority of Genesis focuses on the family of *Avraham Avinu* (Section **Two**), in the first eleven chapters (Section **One**), the Torah's focus is on mankind as a whole. Even when the Torah includes special details about Noaḥ, it is **not** because he is designated to become a special nation – rather, it is because through Noaḥ that mankind will be preserved. After the flood, the Torah tells us how Noaḥ's offspring evolve into nations (ch. 10). Even though we find that Noaḥ blesses Shem and

Yafet (9:25–27), the concept of a **special** nation with a special covenant does not begin until the story of *Avraham Avinu*.

In contrast, chapters 11–50 focus on the story of *Am Yisrael* – God's special nation. In this section, Genesis is no longer universalistic; rather, it becomes particularistic. Therefore, this section begins with *toledot Shem* till Teraḥ (11:10–24) to introduce the story of *Avraham Avinu*, whom God chooses in chapter twelve to become the forefather of His special nation. The remainder of Genesis explains which of Abraham's offspring are **chosen** (= "*beḥira*," e.g. Isaac and Jacob), and which are **rejected** (= "*deḥiya*," e.g. Ishmael and Esau). This explains why Genesis concludes precisely when this complicated *beḥira* process reaches its completion – i.e., when **all** twelve sons of Jacob have been chosen, and none of his offspring will ever again be rejected.

Our final table summarizes how the *toledot* help define these two sections of Genesis:

I. UNIVERSALISTIC (chapters 1–11) – Creation of mankind		
Chapter	**Toladot**	**Story of ...**
1–4	*'shamayim va'aretz'*	Man in (and out of) the Garden of Eden
5–9	from Adam to Noaḥ	"*dor hamabul*" – the Flood
10–11	*Benei Noaḥ* to 70 nations	"*dor haplaga*" – the Tower of Babel
II. PARTICULARISTIC (11–50) – God's choice of *Am Yisrael*		
11	Shem to Teraḥ	leads up to *Avraham Avinu*
11–25	Teraḥ	God's choice of Abraham
25	Ishmael	his "rejection" (*deḥiya*)
25–35	Isaac	Jacob and Esau (their rivalry)
36	Esau	his "rejection" (*deḥiya*)
37–50	Jacob	Joseph and his brothers

However, if our original assumption that each sefer in *Ḥumash* carries a unique prophetic theme is correct, then there should be a thematic reason for the progression of events from Section One to Section Two.

Therefore, to identify the overall theme of Genesis, one must take into consideration how these two sections relate to one another. To help uncover that theme, we must take a closer look at the structure created by these *toladot*.

IV. SHEM & *SHEM HASHEM*

Note once again from the above table how each general topic in the first section of Genesis was first introduced by a set of *toladot*. In a similar manner, each of these units concludes with an event which in some way relates to the concept of *"Shem HaShem."* Our first unit, the story of Adam, concludes with a very intriguing verse:

> And also Shet gave birth to a son and called him Enosh, then he "began" to call out in the name of God [*az huḥal likro beshem HaShem*]. (4:26)

No matter how we explain the word *"huḥal"* in this verse, all of the commentators agree that God's intention was for man to "call out in His name." Note, however, how this verse concludes the section that began in 2:4 with the story of the Garden of Eden. Even though man was banished from the Garden of Eden and Cain was punished for murder, God still has expectations from mankind – man is expected to search for God, to "call out in His name."

Despite this high expectation, the next unit of *toladot*, which leads into the story of the flood, shows that man's behavior fell far short of God's hopes. God becomes so enraged that He decides to destroy His creation and start over again with Noaḥ. This unit which begins in 5:1 concludes in chapter nine with a special set of mitzvot for *Benei Noaḥ* (9:1–7), a covenant (9:8–17), the story of Noaḥ becoming drunk (9:18–29). However, even in this final story (of this unit) we find once again a reference to *"Shem HaShem."* After cursing Canaan for his actions, Noaḥ then blesses his son Shem:

> Blessed be God, the Lord of **Shem**... (9:26–27)

Now, it is not by chance that Noaḥ named his son "Shem." Most likely,

Noah's decision to name his son Shem was rooted in his hope that his son would fulfill God's expectation that man would learn to call out *"beshem HaShem,"* as explained in 4:26!

Noah blesses Shem in the hope that he and his descendants will indeed fulfill this goal. However, once again, we find that the next generation fails. In chapter ten, again we find a unit that begins with *toladot* – this time the development of the seventy nations from the children of Shem, Ham, and Yafet – and, again, just like the two units that preceded it, this unit also concludes with a story where the word *"shem"* emerges as thematically significant, i.e. the story of the Tower of Babel. As we will now explain, in this story, once again mankind is not looking for God; rather, they are interested solely in making a "name" (*"shem"*) for themselves!

V. THE TOWER OF BABEL

From a cursory reading of the first four verses of the story of the Tower of Babel, it is not clear exactly what was so terrible about this generation. After all, is not achieving *ahdut* (unity) a positive goal? Likewise, the use of human ingenuity to initiate an industrial revolution, developing man-made building materials – i.e. bricks from clay, etc. – seems to be a positive advancement of society. Finally, there appears to be nothing wrong with simply building a city and a tower. Why was God so angered that He decided to stop this construction and disperse mankind?

Hazal focus their criticism of this generation on its antagonistic attitude towards God (see Rashi on 11:1). One key phrase in the Torah's explanation of the purpose for the tower reflects the egocentric nature of this generation:

> *vena'aseh lanu shem* [**we** shall make a **name** for **ourselves**]. (11:4)
> (See *Sanhedrin* 109a)

Instead of devoting themselves to the **name of God**, this generation devotes all of their efforts for the sake of an unholy end. Their society and culture is focused solely on man's dominion and strength, while totally neglecting any divine purpose for their existence. (See Ramban on 11:4!)

Although this generation's moral behavior was probably much

better than that of the generation of the Flood, God remained disappointed, for they established an anthropocentric society (i.e. man in the center) instead of a theocentric one (i.e. God in the center). Their primary aim was to make a "**name** for themselves," but **not** for God. As God's hope for this new generation never materializes, He instigates their dispersion. God must take action to assure that this misdirected unity will not achieve its stated goal (11:5–7). Therefore, God causes the "mixing of languages" – so that each nation will follow its own direction, unable to unify – until they find a common goal worthy of that unity.

VI. ABRAHAM IS CHOSEN FOR A PURPOSE

Our analysis thus far can help us identify the thematic significance of this Tower of Babel incident within the progression of events in Genesis – for the very next story is God's choice of *Avraham Avinu* to become the father of His special nation! In a manner similar to the earlier stories in *Ḥumash*, the story of God choosing *Avraham Avinu* is first introduced (and not by chance) by tracing his genealogy back ten generations – so that it will begin with **Shem**, the son of Noaḥ! The thematic connection to *shem* becomes obvious.

From this perspective, the story of the Tower of Babel should not be viewed as just another event that took place – so that we know how and when the development of language began. Rather, this story "sets the stage" for God's choice of *Avraham Avinu*, for it will become the destiny of Abraham, the primary descendant of *toledot Shem*, to bring God's name back into the history of civilization; to "fix" the error of civilization at the Tower of Babel!

Therefore, it should come as no surprise to us that upon his arrival in the land of Canaan, the Torah informs us of how *Avraham Avinu* ascends to Beit El and builds an altar where he "calls out in God's name":

> And Abraham came to the Land, to Shekhem...and God spoke to him, saying: "To your offspring I have given this Land" ... and Abraham traveled from there towards the mountain range to the east of Beit El...and he built there an altar – and **called out in the Name of God.** (12:6–8)

Similarly, it should not surprise us that when the prophet Isaiah describes the "messianic age" (Is. 2:1–5), he speaks of unity of mankind, when all nations will gather together once again, but this time to climb the mountain of God (not a valley); when they arrive at the **city** of Jerusalem – to its special **tower** – i.e. the *Beit HaMikdash*, "the place that God has chosen for **His name** to dwell there" (Deut. 12:5–12), they will thus rectify the events that took place at the Tower of Babel. Finally, when the prophet Zephaniah describes ultimate redemption, we find once again an allusion to the Tower of Babel:

> *Ki az ehpokh el amim safa berura, likro kulam beshem HaShem le'avdo shekhem eḥad.* (3:9)

Parashat Lekh Lekha

The Land and the Land of Canaan

by Rav Yoel Bin-Nun

I. THE BORDER OF THE LAND OF CANAAN

The section of the "generations of the children of Noaḥ" describes how mankind split into nations and spread out across the earth in the aftermath of the Flood (Gen. 10:1, 5, 14, 18, 32). Important principles emerge from this account. All of mankind traces back to Noaḥ, thus obligating all of humanity to the mitzvot that were given to Noaḥ. Additionally, the account also emphasizes and expands upon points that are important to the Torah – e.g., the might of the kingdom of Nimrod (10:8–12), which is connected to the story of the Tower of Babel, and to Babel in general.

Of all the seventy nations included in the chapter (according to the count of Ḥazal), only with respect to the Canaanites is mention made of a border,[1] almost certainly due to the importance

---

1. Rashbam in his commentary to the Song of Ha'azinu, bases his commentary on the chapter in Genesis dealing with the generations of the children of Noaḥ. He understands the phrase "according to the number of the children of Israel" in Ha'azinu as referring to the twelve children of Jacob, corresponding to Canaan and his children. He adds: "And it is written there: 'And the border of the Canaanites was from Zidon' – because all of this was for Israel. But regarding all the other children of Noaḥ, there is no specification of any border..." This fits in with Rashbam's approach in other places – that the Torah expands upon a certain issue in one section

of the land of Canaan later in the Torah and its being promised to the patriarchs.[2]

Let us examine these borders:

> And the border of the Canaanites – was from Zidon – as you come to Gerar unto Gaza … as you come to Sodom and Gomorrah, and Adma, and Zeboim, unto Lesha. (Gen. 10:19)

Two things must be accepted to understand this verse properly:

1. "Zidon" mentioned in this verse is not only the city of that name,[3] but the entire region connected to Zidon and close to Lesha, i.e., the entire expanse extending from the city of Zidon to the Ayun

---

for some purpose that will be clarified later. See his commentary on "And Ham is the father of Canaan" (Gen. 9:18), a verse which Rashbam argues exemplifies this principle, and which he connects to the setting aside of cities of refuge on the east bank of the Jordan by Moses (Deut. 4:41).

2. Ramban writes: "… Know that the land of Canaan with its borders from the time that it was a nation was fit for Israel, it being the land of their inheritance, as it is stated: 'When the Most High divided to the nations their inheritance, when He separated the sons of Adam, He firmly established the boundaries of the nations, according to the number of the children of Israel.' But the Holy One, blessed be He, gave it at the time of the Dispersion to Canaan, he being a slave, to preserve it for Israel…" (Ramban on Gen. 10:9).

3. Oftentimes a city is mentioned in Scripture, but the reference is not only to the city, but to the surrounding area as well, in the narrow or even the wider sense. The verse, "when Joshua was in Jericho" (Josh. 5:13), certainly refers to the outskirts of the city, as *Ḥazal* understood (*Nedarim* 56b, and see Rashi ad loc.). Similarly, the verses mentioning "Givat Shaul," "Givat Binyamin" or "Giva" in the same breath with another city in the area (Migron or Rama – 1 Sam. 14:2; 22:6), and the division of Saul's army: "…two thousand were with Saul in Mikhmash and in Mount Beit-El, and a thousand were with Jonathan in Givat Binyamin" (1 Sam. 13:2). See at length R. Yoel Elitzur, "*HaTefisa haTeritorialit baKefar haAravi ubeGeografiya haMikra'it*," Teva VaAretz 22, 6 (September 1980).

It is possible that this is also the way to understand the bringing of Goliath's head to Jerusalem (1 Sam. 17:54) – the reference being to Bethlehem, in the region of Jerusalem, the land of Jerusalem. According to this, it is not necessary to say that David brought it only later, after he had already conquered Jerusalem.

and Litani rivers in the southern portion of the Bekaa valley in Lebanon (this being also the historical kingdom of Zidon).[4]

2. The word "Zidon" governs the two halves of the verse: "as you come to Gerar..." and "as you come to Sodom..." They both start in Zidon. The western border is from Zidon as you come to Gerar unto Gaza; and the eastern border is from Zidon, as you come to Sodom...until Lesha. Lesha is identified by the ancient translations with Callirrhoe, an ancient city of healing baths northeast of the Dead Sea.

In summary, the Canaanite borders described in this verse are the coastal valley from Zidon to Gaza and the Jordan Valley from Mount Hermon to the Dead Sea. In both cases, it may be assumed that Gaza and Lesha come to restrict the border; that is to say, Canaanite settlement did not actually reach Gerar or Sodom, but approached them.[5]

---

4. This verse in Genesis and verses in Joshua and Judges below present Zidon as an important city ruling over the southern coast of Phoenicia. This reflects the situation prior to the ascent of Tzor in the days of David and Solomon. Zidon was the most important city on the Lebanese coast during the second millennium B.C.E., while in the first millennium B.C.E. Tzor took its place, flourishing during most of the first Temple period and swallowing up its northern neighbor (see: II Sam. 5:11; 24:6–7; I Kings ch. 5, 9–10; II Chr. ch. 2). In the days of Ahab, Ethbaal the king of Tzor was even called "king of the Zidonites" (I Kings 16:31; 17:9–10), and at the end of the first Temple period, Zidon was an inseparable part of Tzor (Is. ch. 23; Amos ch. 1; Ezek. ch. 26–28). However, the conquests of the Assyrian and Babylonian kings weakened it, and once again Zidon and Tzor flourished as partly independent cities until the end of the Persian period.

   In any event it is clear from Joshua (11:8) that greater Zidon extended to the Bekaa valley in Lebanon, below Mount Hermon (compare there to verses 16–17). This is also explicit in the borders of the remaining land: "...and all the Lebanon toward the sunrise, from Baal Gad under Mount Hermon to the entrance of Ḥamat. All the inhabitants of the hill country from Lebanon as far as Misrephot Mayim, and all the Zidonites, them will I drive out from before the children of Israel..." (Josh. 13:5–6).

5. In general, the term *"ad"* (until – עַד) as used in Scripture marks the precise place or the precise time to which the verse is referring, and sometimes even the far limit of that place or time. When, however, the term *"ad"* is doubled in the verse, a different explanation is necessary. The most reasonable explanation is that the first *"ad"* marks the general area, whereas the second one comes to narrow it down to a

Clear proof that this verse describes the western and eastern borders, while leaving the southern border undefined (as opposed to what one might think – that it describes the western and southern borders, and not the eastern border) may be adduced from the description of the nations settled in the land by the Israelites who came to spy out the land:

> The Amalekites dwell in the land of the Negev, and the Hittites and the Jebusites and the Amorites dwell in the mountain: and the Canaanites dwell by the sea and by the side of the Jordan. (Num. 13:29)

The Canaanite border in chapter ten of Genesis corresponds to the border of Canaanite settlement as it appears in chapter thirteen of Numbers, and thus we can precisely understand the definition of "the land of Canaan" as a geographical unit: "The land of Canaan" is that area between the Jordan Valley and the coastal plain, i.e., the central mountainous massif – from Lebanon to the Negev – which is surrounded by these two valleys to the east and west. The inhabitants of the mountains, in their various tribes (especially the Hittites, the Hivites, the Perizites and the Jebusites), are referred to by the general term "Amorites," while the inhabitants of the valleys are referred to by the general term "Canaanites."[6] But when we relate to the entire area bounded by the two valleys inhabited by the Canaanites, it is called "the land of Canaan" as

---

precise place (and not to add to the first one). Thus, in the well-known verse, "And Abram passed through the land to the place of Shekhem to Elon Moreh" (Gen. 12:6), "Elon Moreh" is not in Shekhem itself, but in the surrounding area. See also "And he went on his journeys from the Negev even to Beit-El, to the place where his tent had been at the beginning, between Beit-El and Ai" (ibid. 13:3), where it is clear that the first "*ad*" marks the general area, whereas the second marks the precise spot, as the Torah explicitly states that we are not dealing with Beit-El itself. So too in our verse regarding Gerar and Lesha. This is also the understanding of S.D. Luzzatto in his commentary to our verse.

6. See Gen. 48:22; 14:13; Deut. 1:27 (compare to Gen. ch. 23); Josh. 7:7; and many others. Accordingly, the verse "For the iniquity of the Emori is not yet full" (Gen. 15:16) relates to all of the tribes of the mountains, as opposed, for example, to the Canaanites who dwelled in Sodom and Gomorrah, whose iniquity was already full – and for this reason these cities were destroyed in the days of Abraham.

an overall term, after the Canaanites who dwell in the valleys along its borders. Accordingly, the eastern border of "the land of Canaan" is the Jordan Valley, whereas the east bank of the Jordan is not "the land of Canaan." Transjordan is the plateau between the Jordan Valley and the wilderness, i.e., between the land of Canaan and the wilderness. The inhabitants of the mountains in Transjordan might be called "Amorites" ("Sihon king of the Amorites"), but since the Canaanites (who live in the valleys) do not have a settlement east of the Jordan River, the term "the land of Canaan" does not apply to it.

The borders of "the land of Canaan" in *Parashat Masei* clearly indicate that the east bank of the Jordan is not included within the realm of "the land of Canaan," and that the border between them runs through the Jordan Valley:

> This is the land that shall fall to you for an inheritance, the land of Canaan with its borders … and your south border shall be the outmost coast of the Dead Sea eastward … and the border shall descend, and shall reach the eastward projection of the Sea of Galilee. And the border shall go down to the Jordan, and it limits shall be at the Dead Sea: this shall be your land with borders round about. (Num. 34:2–12)

Another verse that distinguishes between "the land of Canaan" and "the [east] side of the Jordan" is found in the section dealing with the cities of refuge:

> You shall give three cities on this side of the Jordan, and three cities shall you give in the land of Canaan. (Num. 35:14)

Several other verses at the end of the book of Numbers explicitly state: "When you pass over the Jordan into the land of Canaan" (Num. 33:51; 34:2, 29; 35:10).

It is interesting to examine in this light the account of the borders of the "remaining territory" (Josh. ch. 13), which includes the entire coastal plain from the south to the north – an area that was not captured, because "all the Canaanites that dwell in the land of the valley have chariots of iron" (Josh. 17:16; Judges 1:19). When the book of Joshua was written, the southern portion of the coastal plain was in the hands of the Philistines-Caphtorites, and therefore the Torah states: "This is the land that still remains; all the regions of the Philistines, and all the Geshurites" (Josh. 13:2).[7] But this requires emphasis, for even when the Philistines were there in the meantime, the entire coastal plain was still regarded as included in the ancient Canaanite borders: "From Siḥor, which is before Egypt, as far as the borders of Ekron northward – which is counted to the Canaanite" (ibid. v. 3). This region includes the entire coastal plain, from the border of Egypt and the area under the control of Zidon to the feet of the mountains, as is stated in the following verse: "From the south, all the land of the Canaanite, and Mearah that is beside the Zidonites, as far as Aphek, to the border of the Amorites" (ibid. v. 4). The mountainous area itself is already the site of the settlement of the Amorites.[8]

II. "THE LAND" – THE LAND OF ISRAEL

The source of the term "the land of Israel" (*Eretz Yisrael*) as it is used today – as the land that was promised, consecrated, and designated for

---

7. The arrival of the Philistines-Caphtorites is dated, according to modern scholarship, to the beginning of the twelfth century before the Common Era. Thus, a distinction must be made between the early Philistines, the shepherds of Gerar and subjects of Abimelekh – who are mentioned in the book of Genesis, and who were later called by the name "Canaanites" – and the invading Philistines who came from Caphtor, i.e., the "peoples of the sea," the tribe of Peleset and other tribes. Y. Grintz makes this distinction, and his proofs are solid. To me, however, the verses in Deut. 2:23 and chapter 13 of Joshua relate already to the Philistines, the people of the sea. In light of this, the question of dating the settlement of the land of Canaan requires a separate discussion; see my article, "*HaMikra beMabat Histori vehaHitnahalut haYisraelit beEretz Canaan*," in: Y.L. Levin and E. Mazar (eds.), *HaPulmus al haEmet haHistorit baMikra*, Jerusalem 5761, pp. 3–16.

8. There are places where it would seem that the terms "Amorite and "Canaanite" are interchangeable or that they are general terms for the inhabitants of the land (compare, for example, Num. 14:43–45 to Deut. 1:41–44). But upon closer examination, it appears that we are dealing with places where there is a meeting between mountain and valley, so that they intermingle. Such was the situation in the Negev, where Canaanites lived in the valley of Arad-Be'er-Sheva, and Amorites lived in the Negev and Ḥevron Mountains.

the people of Israel – is in the words of *Ḥazal*. Nowhere is it used in this sense in the Torah. In those places where the term is found in the Torah, it means "the land of the people of Israel," the land in which Israel actually dwells, and sometimes also the land of the Kingdom of Israel, as opposed to the Kingdom of Judea. The first appearance of the term "the land of Israel" is only in the book of Samuel, in the description of the Philistines' suppression of Israel:

> Now there was no smith found through all the land of Israel [*Eretz Yisrael*]: for the Philistines said, Lest the Hebrews make them swords or spears: but all Israel went down to [the land of] the Philistines... (1 Sam. 13:19–20)

"The land of Israel" is contrasted here to "[the land of] the Philistines," and it refers to the territory in which Israel was actually settled; it does not include within its limits the land of the Philistines. As such, the term "the land of Israel" in Biblical Hebrew has no special religious, moral or conceptual weight – it is equivalent to "the land of Moab," "the land of Edom," "the land of the Philistines," and the like. In the Torah, this expression is not found at all, not even in the sense of the land in which the Israelites live, because the Israelites did not yet live there. In the meantime, it is the land of the Canaanites and the other nations who actually lived there.

On the other hand, we find in Biblical Hebrew, and especially in the Torah, another term, which indeed bears the special weight that would later be borne by the term "the land of Israel" in the wording of *Ḥazal* and in Modern Hebrew, in the sense of its special sanctity. I refer here to the term "the land" (*"ha'aretz"*) – with the definite article (the letter ה) – the land that is known, chosen, designated and promised to Israel.

What is more, the term "the land" – the Promised Land – represents in miniature "the land" in the sense of the entire earth. Originally "the land" referred to the entire earth (Gen. 1:1); man in general was created to inherit it, and to fulfill his mission in it (Gen. 1:28). Eventually, "this land" was chosen from the entire earth, and Abraham was chosen from among all of mankind. As soon as Abraham was chosen, he was sent to the Promised Land to fulfill the mission of "the way of the Lord, to do justice and judgment" (Gen. 18:19). Therefore, when Ḥazal used the term "the land of Israel," they referred to what the Torah called "the land" or "this land" – "To your seed I will give this land" (Gen. 12:7).

In contrast, "the land of Canaan" – with respect to the sense of connection and belonging under discussion – expresses an ordinary and natural sense of belonging, with no special meaning, as it is commonly found in people's consciousness. It is the very same relationship that we have in our consciousness to terms like "the land of Moab," "the land of the Philistines," or "the land of Egypt."

When the Torah reverses the formulation – "and the Canaanites were then in the land" (Gen. 12:6) – it means to say that at that time the Canaanites were living in the land, and at that time, it (so to speak) belonged to them. In truth, however, it does not belong to them, and they will not remain there forever, for it must be remembered that, as opposed to "the land of Canaan," there exists the broader concept of "the land" – the entire world (and its most select part, "the land" – the land of Israel), which belongs to God. He created the world, He parcels out land to particular nations, and He can also take it back from them if He so desires.[9]

---

9. See Rashi and Ramban on Gen. 1:1. Rashi's words are well-known, but Ramban adds to them and turns them into a universal principle, in accordance with the plain meaning of the words of Jeremiah, who said this about the conquests of Nebuchadnezzar: "Thus says the Lord of Hosts, the God of Israel... I have made the earth, the man and the beast that are upon the ground, by My great power and by My outstretched arm, and have given it to whom it seemed proper in My eyes. And now have I given all these lands to the hand of Nebuchadnezzar, the king of Babel, My servant... until the time of his own land come also" (Jer. 27:4–7). Rabbi Yitzhak's words cited by Rashi are clearly based on these words of Jeremiah, and Ramban expands upon them:

> ... For the Torah began with "In the beginning God created," and the story of the entire creation until the creation of man, and that He gave him dominion over His handiwork and set everything under his feet. And the Garden of Eden... was made for him to dwell in, until his sin caused him to be sent out from there. And the people of the generation of the Flood with their sins were sent out from the entire world, and only the righteous one among them escaped, he and his children. And their seed – their sin caused them to be dispersed in

From this follows the well-known understanding of these two verses:

> And Abram passed through the land to the place of Shekhem unto Elon Moreh. And the Canaanites were then in the land. And the Lord appeared to Abram, and said, "To your seed will I give this land," and there he built an altar to the Lord, who had appeared to him. (Gen. 12:6–7)

"The land of Canaan" which was mentioned in verse 5 is not the natural and absolute possession of the Canaanites living there; rather, like "the land"/the whole earth, it is in God's hands to give away, and the Canaanites' settlement in the land is only temporary, only as long as God wishes it to be theirs. But the King of the world can take it from them and promise to Abraham, who was righteous in His eyes, to give it to him in the future as an inheritance (and also to take it away again from Israel, if they practice the abominations of Canaan – see Lev. ch. 18).

When we reexamine the verse, we immediately see the importance of this distinction: Indeed, Abraham goes to the land "as the Lord had spoken to him" (12:4), and thus begins the special chapter of Abraham and his descendants, whose spiritual mission is connected to this land and its role in the world. But the journey to "the land of Canaan" in the natural-human sense began with Teraḥ (rather than with Abraham) – whether because of the importance of "the land of Canaan" for commercial routes as an international crossroad, or because of the natural qualities of the land of Canaan with respect to its soil or climate, or its proximity to the sea and to the wilderness, or because of a certain spiritual quality which Teraḥ discerned in the land of Canaan. The Torah itself does not explain what drew Teraḥ to the land of Canaan, and we can do nothing but conjecture – based on the plain sense of the verses

---

[many] places and scattered in the lands … If so, it is fitting that when a nation continues to sin, that it should lose its place and that another nation should inherit its land, for this is the judgment of God in the land from all time … But the servants of God, the seed of he who loves Him, will inherit it … And if they sin to Him, the land will vomit them up, like it vomited up the nations that were before them … (Ramban on Gen. 1:1)

and the plain sense of the world – that he was primarily drawn after the commerce.[10] The special spiritual quality of the land of Canaan is apparently also alluded to in the Torah, but it is clear that this attraction was not strong enough for Teraḥ, and that it did not bring him to make the effort to actually reach the land of Canaan. He therefore settled along the way, in Ḥaran.

The biggest surprise, however, lies in the fact that Abraham – besides journeying to the land at God's command – also continued the journey started by Teraḥ that had come to a halt. His journey as the head of his family therefore has two meanings: He goes both to the natural "land of Canaan," as the heir and executor of Teraḥ's plan, and to the chosen "land," which had been designated for him by the word of God.

Another possibility is that Teraḥ's journey was connected to his desire to find a cure for Sarai's barrenness, for this is the order of the verses: "But Sarai was barren; she had no child. And Teraḥ took ..." (11:30–31). According to this conjecture, it is easy to understand why Abraham continued this journey, whereas Teraḥ and Naḥor, who had children, gave up on it.

I would like to illustrate this duality of Abraham's journey to the land and in the land itself with the following parallels in the verses:

---

10. The occupation in trade at the crossroads in Syria and the land of Canaan is clear from the biblical narrative and from the nature of the "bridge" between Mesopotamia and Egypt. The Torah explicitly mentions this: "Dwell and trade in it" (Gen. 34:10); "And you shall trade in the land" (42:34); and it is also implied by the camel companies of Abraham (24:10) and Ishmael (25:18; and especially 37:22). Even in the places where the patriarchs are described as shepherds, it is clearly evident that this was only part of their occupation, and that the work was done by servants and members of the household (only Jacob was himself a shepherd during the period of his exile – 13:7; 26:12, 20, 25; 30:29 and onward; 31:38–40; 32:15–20).

When the sons of Jacob, who give all appearances of being shepherds (ch. 37–38), are required to stand before Pharaoh and describe what they do, they must plan in advance and coordinate positions to hide all of their other affairs and ascertain that everyone will say the same thing – that they are shepherds – so that Pharaoh will not scatter them in different places through public appointments (see ch. 47). Someone whose sole occupation is herding animals need not plan out how to present this simple truth.

And Teraḥ took Abram his son, and Lot the son of Ḥaran his son's son, and Sarai his daughter-in-law, his son Abram's wife; and they went out with them from Ur Kasdim, to go into **the land of Canaan** and they came to Ḥaran and dwelt there. (11:31)	
	Now the Lord said to Abram, Get you out of your country, and from your kindred, and from your father's house, **to the land** that I will show you. (12:1)
	So Abram departed, as the Lord had spoken to him; and Lot went with him: and Abram was seventy five years old when he departed out of Ḥaran. (12:4)
And Abram took Sarai his wife, and Lot his brother's son, and all their substance that they had gathered, and the souls that they had acquired in Ḥaran; and they went forth to go **to the land of Canaan, and into the land of Canaan** they came. (12:5)	
	And Abram passed through the land to the place of Shekhem to Elon Moreh. And the Canaanites were then **in the land**. And the Lord appeared to Abram, and said, To your seed will I give **this land**: and there he built an altar to the Lord, who had appeared to him. (12:6–7)

The clear and emphasized parallel between "And Teraḥ took" and "And Abram took," and especially between the key expression that repeats itself, "to go to the land of Canaan," serves as a decisive proof of the natural meaning of "the land of Canaan" – for it preceded God's words to Abraham, and therefore its significance can only stem from the nature of the world, and not from the revelation of the word of God. This also demonstrates the double meaning of Abraham's journey: as a continuation of Teraḥ's on the one hand, and as one that goes with the words of God on the other.

We established above that the expression "the land of Canaan" expresses ordinary natural belonging, with no unique dimension of sanctity, whereas the term "the land" expresses the special meaning borne by the expression "the land of Israel" as used by Ḥazal and by us, in the sense of special sanctity. This is true when we examine the matter from the perspective of the revelation of sanctity in history. From this perspective, the term "the land of Canaan" does not denote any sanctity, for on this historic plain, the definition of the essence and value of sanctity depends on historical events. From this perspective, the concept "the land of Israel" truly denotes the territory in which the Canaanites actually dwell. In contrast, "the land" expresses the territory in which Israel is commanded to act – to conquer, to inherit, and to settle – and, through this activity, the special sanctity and particularity find expression.

However, parallel to the sanctity that stems from revelation on the historic plain, there is likewise in the Torah a dimension of intrinsic and natural sanctity, special sanctity that is rooted in the thing by its very creation, independent of man's actions. "The land of Canaan," in the sense of the territory to the west of the Jordan River, indeed has natural sanctity, which lies within it from the time of its creation in the six days of Creation – unconnected to and independent of those dwelling within it. This is what causes its habitants to be regarded as particularly sinful. It is by virtue of this natural uniqueness that we can understand what the Torah says regarding the Canaanites even before Israel conquered the land:

> For all these abominations have the men of the land done, who were before you, and the land is defiled; that the land vomit not you out also, when you defile it, as it has vomited out the nations that were before you. (Lev. 18:27–28)

This natural uniqueness is found only on the west bank of the Jordan, between the Jordan and the sea, within the borders of "the land of Canaan" and in accordance with the borders mentioned in *Parashat Masei*.

III. THE TWO COVENANTS

Three promises were made to Abraham – the promise of *Lekh Lekha*, the promise of *Elon Moreh*, and the promise of "east of Beit El"; two covenants were made with him, and God took one oath to him (the oath of the *Akeda*). The oath of the *Akeda* itself is connected to the first promise through the shared term, "Get you out" (*Lekh Lekha*), which appears in the Torah only in these two places. In this way the journey to the land is connected to the journey to the site of the *Shekhina*, the site of the *Mikdash*. This is the structure of the promises, the covenants and the oath:

The promise: "Get you out of your county...to the land" (12:1–3)	
The promise of *Elon Moreh* (12:7)	The promise of east of Beit El (13:14–17)
The Covenant between the Pieces (*Berit bein HaBetarim*) (v. 15)	The covenant of circumcision (v. 17)
"Get you into the land of Moriah" – the oath of the *Akeda* (v. 22)	

Let us briefly examine the two covenants – the Covenant between the Pieces and the covenant of circumcision, and the differences between them: [11]

---

11. Biblical critics based much of their teachings regarding the (two) sources of the book of Genesis on this difference, along with the redundancies in the account of Creation and the story of the Flood. One who closely examines what we have said will see the fundamental difference between their position, which separates between the sources, and ours, which explains the two covenants as two aspects – two perspectives – within a single Torah. In this sense, our approach is fundamentally different than that of R. Mordechai Breuer. A precise analysis of these issues requires a much broader discussion, but this is not the proper forum for that.

The Covenant between the Pieces – *Berit bein HaBetarim*	The covenant of circumcision – *Brit Mila*
Mention is made of "the land."	Mention is made of "the land of Canaan."
Only the Tetragrammaton appears (and in the words of Abraham, the name of *Adnut*, which denotes the kingdom of God).	Only the names of *Kel Shakai* and *Elokim* appear (the Tetragrammaton appears in the beginning of the section, in the words of the Torah, but in the continuation we find only the name *Elokim*).[11]
Abraham prepares the parts, and God makes the covenant. Abraham is asleep, and the covenant is in a vision.	Abraham is awake and active and makes the covenant.
The land is the essence of the covenant.	The family of the patriarchs is the essence of the covenant.
The mission is historical-national.	The covenant is religious-natural – "To be a God to you, and to your seed after you."
A promise is made regarding the conquest of the full breadth of the land.	There is no mention of conquest. The land of Canaan is merely a place of residence (the patriarchs are strangers and sojourners).
Will be actualized in the distant future, in the fourth generation (the generation of Egypt).	Is established immediately. The land of Canaan is promised as an everlasting inheritance. Circumcision is a sign of the covenant for all generations.

The deep and essential difference between the two covenants cannot be blurred. We are presented with two approaches, two outlooks, two character patterns, two ways of thinking, two meanings of the people of Israel, the land of Israel, and all of Jewish history!

The first approach – that of circumcision – is a religious, natural and familial approach. Its foundation (as will be explained below) is in the creation of the world, in the nature of reality, in the uniqueness of the family and in the nature of the land – in both the manifest and covert senses. The covenant is already established in Abraham's lifetime, it is anchored in the family tradition of the house of Abraham; it finds expression in circumcision, as a sign for all generations.

This covenant does not depend on changing times and circumstances. It remains the same whether the "holy land," the everlasting inheritance of the seed of Abraham, is currently settled and ruled by Canaanites or Amorites, Egyptians or Philistines, Arameans or Ammonites, Assyrians or Babylonians, Persians or Greeks, Romans (pagans or Christians), Muslims or Christians, Turks or Arabs – "the holy land" does not change in any way! Just as the manifest nature of the land, with its mountains and its rivers, its deserts and its valleys, its minerals and its climate, does not undergo fundamental changes – so too its hidden nature, its unique sanctity, is not subject to fundamental changes.

Accordingly, anyone who undergoes circumcision as a family covenant belongs to the seed of Abraham, to the nature of the land, and in a certain sense, even to the sanctity of the land. Jews who lived in the "holy land" or came "to be gathered under the wings of the *Shekhina,*" to draw the abundance of holy spirit from the uniqueness of the "air of the land," never connected this to the nature and identity of the land's ruler, which in this framework seemed to them an inconsequential and superficial matter. The covenant that they made through their dwelling in the land and through their prayers, through the mitzvot that they observed, through the sanctity of the land that they contemplated – all have religious significance, but no historical significance whatsoever (and therefore no political significance either). "The holy land," even when it is under foreign rule, still remains an "eternal inheritance" for us – a family inheritance – and no stranger has a share in its unique sanctity and in the fulfillment of the covenant, save for one who belongs to the covenant of circumcision.

The deep expression of this sanctity also reveals itself in the possession of a burial place and in the burial of the dead in the land: the purchase of the Makhpela cave as a possession of a burial place of the patriarchal family, and Jacob's making Joseph take an oath not to bury him in Egypt, but "in my grave which I have dug for myself in the land of Canaan, there shall you bury me" (Gen. 50:5; 47:29–31; 49:29–32; 50:13). The sanctity of the land that reveals itself through the family burying place in which fathers and sons were buried, is the foundation upon which R. Ashtori HaParḥi, disciple of the Rosh (*Kaftor VaFeraḥ,* 10) based the idea of the inherent sanctity that lies at the root of living in the land, above and beyond the sanctity of the commandments dependent upon it.

Rabbi Yehuda HaLevi generally follows this approach in his *Kuzari*: nowhere does he mention sovereignty or rule over the land as a fundamental principle (see part II: 14, 44).[12] This, of course, was also the understanding of the kabbalists and the Hasidim: they set the nature of hidden sanctity as the true inner content of the lower world in general –

---

12. R. Yehuda HaLevi's (Rihal's) profound remarks about "the land of prophecy," which is "the land of God" (part I:109; part II:9–24; part III: end of 3, 11, 17; book's conclusion) emphasize prophecy as a natural-spiritual phenomenon found in the land of Israel, which is connected to the natural-spiritual essence found in the people of Israel (part II:12), but can only be realized in the land of Israel, and in particular when all of Israel is dwelling there, and the Temple is built – for then the *Shekhina* (the glory of God) rests there, and then the unique essence of the people of God in the land of God reveals itself in a most perfect manner. In all that he says, there is not a single mention of political sovereignty, neither directly nor indirectly, but perhaps only implicitly in the communal context (of all of Israel), that when they are dwelling in Israel, then the *Shekhina* can reveal itself through the Temple. The fact that Rihal's approach is not political sovereignty in the historical sense, but rather a natural-spiritual essence that is realized through the resting of the *Shekhina*, is all the more striking in the fact that he does not make a fundamental distinction between the days of the patriarchs and the days of the first Temple.

If we compare Rihal's approach to that of Rambam, we immediately see that it is precisely the Rambam who defines the idea of "the land of Israel" based on political sovereignty, in the concrete historical sense: "Whenever *Eretz Yisrael* is mentioned, the intent is the lands conquered by the King of Israel or a prophet with the consent of the entire Jewish people ..." (*Mishneh Torah*, Hilkhot Terumot 1:2). Fundamentally, of course, this is also the view of Ramban in his strictures on Sefer HaMitzvot (the well-known positive commandment 4). Rambam and Ramban are much closer in approach to each other than to that of the *Rihal*, which stands by itself!

Two common mistakes in understanding Rihal's position regarding the land of Israel must, therefore, be fixed. First of all, it should be noted that Rihal gives priority, essential and substantive, to the unique essence of the people, and only afterwards "the land also has a part in this" (*Kuzari*, part II:12). Second, Rihal does not at all stress Israel's conquest, rule or sovereignty, but only the sanctity of the *Shekhina* and the unique essence of prophecy. Rule over the land of Israel is at best a means of establishing the Jewish collective, which in the end will also merit the Temple and the resting of the *Shekhina* therein. Rambam, and not Rihal, is the great fighter for "the land of Israel" as a site of Jewish sovereignty, and after him follows Ramban, despite all the subtle differences between them. This is not the forum to expand upon the matter any further. My thanks to R. Zalman Korn, who enlightened me on this point.

and of the holy land in particular – as the land of prophecy, in a manner that all are amazingly fit for the true, sanctified nature of the upper worlds.

Accordingly, the giving of the Torah to Israel is but a revelation of the secret hidden in the universe, in the holy nation, and in the holy land, from the beginning of creation. Not only is it the case that even a distinguished scholar cannot say something new about the Torah – for every novel insight is but a revelation of some hidden secret – but even the exodus and the giving of the Torah did not involve anything new, because the Torah and Israel were already playing together in God's secret chambers many generations before Adam was created.

This approach does not allow room for upheavals or changes, nor for disappointments or crises. All is clear and existing, like the natural laws – all is known from the outset (and the permission granted is merely the permission to integrate into the order that is known from the outset).

The second approach reveals itself in the Covenant between the Pieces. From a conceptual-moral, historical and national perspective, it is based on an upheaval. Its essence lies in novelty. Its bearers are the heralds of social movements and spiritual streams, national and state leaders, legislators of law and social morality, creators of history and those borne on its waves. It is "novelty" that brought Abraham into the world. Prior to spiritual revolutionaries like Abraham and Moses, there was nothing in the world of value (this period is designated the "two thousand years of chaos"), because the cosmic-natural religiosity was immersed in its idolatry. "The way of the Lord, to do justice and judgment" was unknown, and, needless to say, nobody fought for its realization.

"The land of Israel" in the sense in which it appears in the Covenant between the Pieces is the center and focus of a moral-spiritual-historical revolution. From this perspective, Israel's rule in the land of Israel is not at all like non-Jewish rule, because Israel was assigned to build in the land a moral society, which keeps "the way of God, to do justice and judgment" (Gen. 18:19), in keeping with the objective of God's selection of Abraham and his descendants.

In this sense, the land of Israel does not have geographical borders, and all that it can have are historical borders in the expanse between the Nile and Euphrates rivers:

> Every place whereon the sole of your foot shall tread shall be yours, from the wilderness to the Lebanon, from the river, the Euphrates river, to the uttermost sea shall be your border. (Deut. 11:24)[13]

---

13. The "promised boundaries" are defined in the Torah as: "From the river of Egypt to the great river, the Euphrates river" (Gen. 15:18). Many commentators understand this verse as a geographical determination of fixed and solid borders, just as the borders mentioned in *Parashat Masei* (the borders of "the land of Canaan," Num. ch. 34) are essentially geographical borders. This is the understanding of Ramban in several places.

It seems, however, that there is a profound difference between the two borders that goes far beyond their geographical scope, and the various attempts to explain or remove the contradiction between the borders seem in the final analysis to be forced. It seems that we should go back to the plain sense of the text and to the precise formulation of Rambam, who fixes the borders of the land of Israel in accordance with the historical realization – i.e., the border of the returnees from Egypt (= the first sanctification), or the border of the returnees from Babylonia (= the second sanctification); only the land of Canaan, which is the sanctified core, must be conquered first (*Mishneh Torah*, Hilkhot Terumot 1:2–3). This is also explicitly stated in the book of Exodus: "I will not drive them out from before you in one year…Little by little I will drive them out from before you, until you are increased, and inherit the land. And I will set your bounds from the Sea of Reeds even to the Sea of the Philistines, and from the desert to the river" (Ex. 23:29–31), and three times in the book of Deuteronomy (7:22; 11:22–24; 19:8–9; and see *Mishneh Torah*, Hilkhot Melakhim 11:2). The disagreement between Ramban and Rambam is evident: Ramban understands (as does the *Sifrei*) that Deut. ch. 11, according to which "every place whereon the sole of your foot shall tread shall be yours" (Deut. 11:24) – which undoubtedly refers to an historical act of conquest – is essentially an added promise, beyond the geographical border of the land mentioned at the end of the verse. In contrast, Rambam, following the plain sense of the text, understands that this promise is stated in reference to what is found within the borders mentioned in the end of the verse (and perhaps here and there a little beyond that border, as is implied by a careful reading of the *Sifrei*). What this means is that the broad promised borders (mentioned at the end of the verse) constitute the expanse in which the people of Israel will realize their sovereignty in the manner of "communal conquest" (and according to the conditions attached to this term), and that the actual borders will be established through conquest, by way of "every place whereon the sole of your foot shall tread shall be yours" – that is to say, the places where the flag of Israel will fly with the consent of the majority of the people of Israel (see *Mishneh Torah*, Hilkhot Terumot 1:2–3).

Therefore, "the land of Canaan" (the holy, primeval core) has clear geographical borders, as stated above. But the borders of "the land" are not geographical, but rather

This understanding is connected to and stems from God's revelation in history in general, and in the history of Israel in particular, and, accordingly, it necessarily depends on the changing situations.

Therefore, Abraham cannot rule the land, because his seed did not yet ripen into "the nation of the God of Abraham" (until the exodus from Egypt), and because "the iniquity of the Amorites is not yet full" (Gen. 15:16). Hence, Abraham sees the vision of this covenant in a prophetic vision and in sleep. This covenant was only meant to be actualized at the end of four hundred years – and this, too, in accordance with the historical conditions, and in the framework of a historical process:

> I will not drive them out from before you in one year; lest the land become desolate, and the wild beasts multiply against you. Little by little I will drive them out from before you, until you are increased, and inherit the land. And I will set your bounds from the Sea of Reeds even to the Sea of the Philistines, and from the desert to the river. (Ex. 23:29–31)

The borders of the land according to this conception are the actual borders, the borders of conquest and settlement, the borders of historical actualization.

According to this understanding, the commandments depending on the land are consequences of the first sanctification (in the time of Joshua), the second sanctification (in the time of Ezra), and the third sanctification. The cosmic sanctity in the nature of the world and of the land from the time of creation is not what is essential regarding the commandments; rather, it is moral-social meaning ("the way of the Lord, to do justice and judgment") and the political-national-historical meaning which lies concealed in the exodus from Egypt and the giving

---

borders of historical actualization (through sovereignty or settlement, or perhaps both), within the expanse of the "promised borders," between the Euphrates and the Nile – each generation in accordance with what it merits to receive from God, the God of Israel!

of the Torah, until the final redemption, when the words of the prophet Jeremiah will be fulfilled:

> Therefore, behold, days are coming, says the Lord, when it shall no more be said, As the Lord lives, that brought up the children of Israel out of the land of Egypt; but, As the Lord lives, that brought up the children of Israel from the land of the north, and from all the lands into which He had driven them, and I will bring them back into their land that I gave to their fathers. (Jer. 16:14–15)

These two fundamental understandings underlie the two covenants, the covenant of circumcision and the Covenant between the Pieces, which are such opposites in all respects: regarding the names *"Elokim"* and *"Kel Shakai"* as opposed to the Tetragrammaton, regarding the definition of the land, regarding the nature of the covenant, and regarding the substance and meaning of the covenant.

IV. COMBINING THESE TWO COVENANTS IN THE EXODUS FROM EGYPT

From here we proceed to a small section of the Torah, upon which many important sections of the Torah depend, and over whose explanation rivers of ink have already been spilled, and still there is much to do – the beginning of *Parashat Va'era*. Based on an understanding of the covenants made with Abraham in the book of Genesis, so contradictory in their meaning, this section can be easily explained in a way that will prove the correctness of Rashi's interpretation of the section, though with an important difference. The entire section is brought below, with a clear differentiation being made between the expressions characteristic of the covenant of circumcision and those characteristic of the Covenant between the Pieces:

Expressions characteristic of the covenant of circumcision:	Expressions characteristic of the Covenant between the Pieces:
And God spoke to Moses,	
	and said to him, I am the Lord
and I appeared to Abraham, to Isaac, and to Jacob, by the God Almighty,	
	but by My name the Lord I was not known to them
And I have also established My covenant with them, to give them the land of Canaan, the land of their sojournings, in which they sojourned	
	And I have also heard the groaning of the children of Israel, kept in bondage by Egypt; and I have remembered My covenant. Therefore say to the children of Israel, I am the Lord, and I will bring you out of their bondage, and I will redeem you with an outstretched arm, and with great judgments
And I will take you to me for a people, and I will be to you a God	
	And you shall know that I am the Lord your God, who brings you out from under the burdens of Egypt.
And I will bring you into the land, which I swore to give to Abraham, to Isaac, and to Jacob; and I will give it to you for a heritage. (Ex. 6:2–8)	

Based on the expressions used in this section, it is absolutely clear that the Torah is relating here both to the covenant of circumcision on the one hand, and to the Covenant between the Pieces on the other. "My covenant" that "I have established" at the beginning of the section certainly refers to the covenant of circumcision, and "My covenant" that "I have remembered" (the next verse) undoubtedly refers to the Covenant between the Pieces, the essence of which is the exodus from Egypt and the inheritance of the land, and which must be remembered as we approach the exodus. The term "and I appeared" to the patriarchs "by the God Almighty" surely relates to the covenant of circumcision, and so too "the land of Canaan" and "the land of their sojournings." In contrast, "I am the Lord," "the land," "heritage," and "bringing out from bondage" are clear reflections of the Covenant between the Pieces.

In the same way, the expression, "and I will be to you a God," clearly relates to the covenant of circumcision ("to be a God to you, and to your seed after you," Gen. 17:7), whereas the expression "I am the Lord" clearly relates to the Covenant between the Pieces. In *Parashat Va'era*, the two expressions unite into a single one: "And you shall know that I am the Lord your God, who brings you out from under the burdens of Egypt." This combination is what provides us with a precise explanation of the exodus from Egypt as a single covenant that embraces two covenants: it continues the covenant of circumcision established already with the patriarchs, and it establishes the Covenant between the Pieces, whose time had arrived after four hundred years – so that Israel should see and believe and know, and Egypt should know, "that I am the Lord," the faithful keeper of the covenant.

The expression "I am the Lord your God," which appears here for the first time in the Torah, always expresses the exodus from Egypt as a unique phenomenon. Thus, for example, in the concluding verse of the Shema:

> I am the Lord your God, who brought you out of the land of Egypt to be your God: I am the Lord your God. (Num. 15:41)

The joining of the two covenants, with all of its meanings, explains this unique expression, and its context and significance wherever it appears in the Torah.[14]

---

14. For example, this is a necessary key for understanding the structure and meaning of the chapter of the commandments and sanctity in the nineteenth chapter of Leviticus, by way of the distinction between the concluding term "I am the Lord," which expresses God's providence as a constant presence, and the concluding term "I am the Lord your God," which is an expression that bases the obligation on the exodus from Egypt: "And if a stranger sojourn with you in your land, you shall

It is therefore Rashi who is closest to the plain sense of the text, when he explains the verses as referring to the fulfillment of the covenants, and not to the prophetic level of Moses (as they are explained by the Ibn Ezra, Ramban, and of course the Rambam, and many others). The patriarchs were familiar with and knew the name of God (the Tetragrammaton) in visions of sleep, but it was not known to them through the fulfillment of His covenant. Any explanation that is based on an understanding of this "knowledge" as information, or even as a level of prophetic perception, does not account for the section's context, and as such it can only be accepted as midrashic exposition, but not as the plain sense of the text.

Thus, the one covenant of the exodus from Egypt combines the two covenants that were made with Abraham with respect to his descendants, and these two covenants became the one covenant of Israel with the Lord their God, the God of their fathers, the God of Israel who were leaving Egypt to inherit the land – the land of Canaan.

The significance of this phenomenon from a conceptual perspective is that Israel's exodus from Egypt and the covenant of the exodus express at one and the same time both a continuation of the tradition of the patriarchs and a revolution. The continuity, at the center of which stands the covenant of circumcision, is natural, moral, family religiosity; whereas the revolution is the giving of the Torah to Israel as a free nation, on its way to the land to fulfill the national-historical destiny of the people of Israel in its land – by virtue of the Covenant between the Pieces. On the one hand, God speaks to Moses by virtue of the patriarchs: "I am the God of your father, the God of Abraham, the God of Isaac and the God of Jacob" (Ex. 3:6). On the other hand, there is the prophecy of Moses' mission. He alone takes Israel out of Egypt and receives the Torah, and only his prophecy obligates future generations in the mitzvot that are not a tradition from their fathers but rather God's

---

not wrong him. But the stranger that dwells with you shall be to you as one born among you, and you shall love him as yourself; for you were strangers in the land of Egypt: I am the Lord your God...Just balances, just weights, a just *efa*, and a just *hin*, shall you have: I am the Lord your God, who brought you out of the land of Egypt; therefore shall you observe all My statutes, and all My judgments, and do them: I am the Lord" (Lev. 19:33–37).

Torah. Only Moses, in addition to being a prophet, is he who receives the Torah and the commandments, the statutes and the judgments, and also king of the redeemed people of Israel, who leads and guides them to the land. All of these are just chapter headings of the great revolution that veers entirely from the tradition of their forefathers – "but by My name the Lord I was not known to them" (Ex 6:3). It can even be said that the Covenant between the Pieces is the visionary seed of the exodus from Egypt and the giving of the Torah that appears by Abraham – the future influencing the past – whereas the covenant of circumcision expresses the influence of the past on the future by way of the family tradition of circumcision.

Moses, whose entire upbringing was outside of his father's house, is perfectly suited for the revolution of the exodus from Egypt and the giving of the Torah, whereas Aaron ("his brother the Levite," Ex. 4:14, 27–31; and compare: ibid. 7:17) is the leader by virtue of ancestral tradition. Therefore, it is clear that the covenant of circumcision is a necessary precondition for the covenant of the exodus from Egypt that was made with the offering and eating of the Paschal sacrifice – the only two positive commandments that are punishable by excision.

Moses' stubborn refusal to bear the redemption and the people by himself strengthens our argument that it was only the joining of Moses and Aaron that made possible the full joining of the two covenants – tradition and revolution, the continuation of the religious-familial ancestral tradition together with the prophetic-Torah-national-historic leadership of Moses – into a single covenant of the exodus from Egypt, the giving of the Torah and the inheritance of the land, the seal of which is the expression "I am the Lord your God."

If we closely examine the Written Law, and also the Oral Law, we will easily find the commandments, the customs, the statutes, the laws and the traditions that stem from the tradition of our forefathers, in contrast to those that were given to the people of Israel "by the mouth of God through the hand of Moses." At times we find these two dimensions in the same commandments, laws and customs. The priesthood is the central axis of the continuation of the tradition, whereas prophesy and governance, judges and kings, are the central axes of the revolution. In this way we can explain the relationship between the two sections of the book of Exodus: the exodus from Egypt and the giving of the Torah on the one side, and the *Mishkan* on the other. In this way we can also explain the relationship between the book of Leviticus, which is primarily a priestly code, the book of Numbers, which deals mostly with governance, and the book of Deuteronomy, which is almost entirely comprised of the words of Moses as leader, king and prophet.

We find in the Torah periods and situations in which one of these two principles is most active, sometimes the one and sometimes the other. In the sin of the golden calf, for example, we find Aaron acting in the absence of Moses, whereas in the killing of the Egyptian and in the interference in the fight between the two Israelites, we find Moses acting alone. The fixed priesthood, the sacrifices, purities and plagues, are the realms of Aaron. Judgment and leadership are those of Moses. The book of Deuteronomy was said by Moses after the death of Aaron (exactly a half year later), and it is truly a precise continuation of the covenant of the exodus from Egypt, in the sense of the fulfillment of the Covenant between the Pieces.

However, the foundation of the covenant, upon which the exodus from Egypt, the giving of the Torah, and the inheritance of the land are based, is precisely the joining of the patriarchal tradition of the covenant of circumcision, and the revolution of the exodus from Egypt and the fulfillment of the Covenant between the Pieces, into one phenomenon – one double covenant – which cannot be encompassed by any narrow explanation. "The Torah of the Lord is perfect, restoring the soul" (Ps. 19:8) – when it is perfect, i.e., complete, it also restores the soul.

From Babel to Berit bein HaBetarim –
The Early Life of Abraham

by Rav Yaakov Medan

I. INTRODUCTION

The Torah's opening verses about Abraham give no reason for God's revelation to him. We are introduced to him at mid-life; he is already seventy-five years old. We are left with several questions: what is the beginning of the story? Why does God choose Abraham and send him to walk about in the land? In what way is Abraham different from the twenty preceding generations, all of which angered God? And even if we succeed in unearthing the story of Abraham prior to God's revelation to him, we must still ask: why does the Torah not explain why God chose him?

Since the Torah provides no reason as to the selection of Abraham, we must turn to Ḥazal. The Midrash recounts two stories (*Bereshit Raba* 38, 13) concerning Abraham's life during his first seventy-five years:

> "Ḥaran died before Teraḥ, his father" – Rabbi Ḥiyya bar Beriya said in the name of Rav Ada of Jaffa: Teraḥ was an idolater [idol merchant]. Once he went off to a certain place, and he left Abraham as shopkeeper in his stead. A person came who wished

to buy [an idol]. [Abraham] said to him: "How old are you?" The man replied, "Fifty," or "Sixty." Abraham said: "Woe to this man, who is sixty years old, and he must serve an idol created just yesterday!" [The man] was ashamed, and went away. Another time a woman came, bringing a bowl of meal. She said to him, "Take this; offer it to the idols." [Abraham] got up, took a hammer, smashed all the idols and placed the hammer in the hand of the biggest of them. When his father returned, he asked: "Who did this to them?" [Abraham] answered, "A woman came and brought them a bowl of meal; she told me to offer it before them. I offered it before them, and one said: 'I shall eat first,' then another said, 'I shall eat first.' The biggest among them got up, took a hammer, and smashed them." [His father] said, "What nonsense are you telling me – do they then have any understanding?" [Abraham] answered, "Do your ears not hear what your mouth is saying?!"

They took him and handed him over to Nimrod [the king]. He said to him, "Worship the fire!" Abraham answered, "Shall I then also worship water, which extinguishes fire?" Nimrod said to him: "Worship the water!" He answered: "Then should I also worship the cloud, which bears the water?" He said, "Worship the cloud!" [Abraham] answered, "Then should I also worship the wind, which disperses clouds?" [Nimrod] said, "Worship the wind!" He answered, "Shall I then worship man, who endures the wind?" He said, "You talk too much; I worship only fire. I am going to throw you into it; let the God whom you worship come and save you from it!" Ḥaran was standing there. He said, "Either way [I shall be safe] – if Abraham wins, I shall say, 'I am with Abraham.' If Nimrod wins, I shall say, 'I am with Nimrod.'" When Abraham entered the fiery furnace and was saved, they said to him: "On whose side are you?" He told them, "I am with Abraham!" They took him and cast him into the fire, and so he was burned with no chance of bearing children, and he came out and died before Teraḥ, his father. Therefore it is written, "Ḥaran died before Teraḥ, his father. "

Before explaining the midrashim, let us first say a few words about our basic attitude towards *Ḥazal*'s teachings. *Ḥazal* are not story-tellers, and obviously anyone who understands *Ḥazal*'s teachings literally is a simpleton. Neither is the purpose behind *Ḥazal*'s narratives to convey ancient legends, but rather, principally, to interpret the Torah. The source for any narrative by *Ḥazal* is usually to be found in some prior biblical incident. In many instances the Torah is cryptic and fails to recount details of events that represent the reason for things that we read about in the text. So it is in our case: there is no explanation for Teraḥ's sudden departure from Ur Kasdim, nor for God's selection of Abraham. *Ḥazal*, as biblical commentators, come to explain that which is opaque. For this reason they create legends which "fill the gaps" in the text.

In our case, as in many others, our question is: upon what do *Ḥazal* base their narrative? Why do they choose to recount specifically this story about Abraham?

It seems that *Ḥazal* followed the well-known principle, "The Torah text elaborates in certain cases and is brief in others." Wherever there are gaps in the biblical narrative, *Ḥazal* compare the character or the subject under discussion to a parallel biblical excerpt. This comparison provides the basis for a "filling-in" of the picture, to create a sort of "photomontage" that completes the missing pieces of the puzzle.

If we try to trace *Ḥazal*'s sources for the stories about Abraham, we arrive at two biblical narratives: the story of Gideon son of Yoash smashing idols is the inspiration for the first midrash quoted above, while the episode of Ḥanania, Mishael and Azaria in the fiery furnace represents the inspiration for the story of Abraham's own trial of fire. What causes *Ḥazal* to connect these stories to the life of Abraham? It is this question that we shall investigate in this *shiur*.

II. GIDEON AND THE SMASHING OF THE IDOLS

The story of Gideon is remarkably similar to the legend about Abraham: Gideon breaks his father's altar, used for idolatry – corresponding to Abraham's destruction of the idols belonging to Teraḥ, his father. The question is, why do *Ḥazal* "pair up" Gideon and Abraham, carrying over the story from one to the other? What is the basis for this comparison?

It seems that the parallel between Abraham and Gideon is based upon the story of the war of the four kings, since in many respects that war fought by Abraham is similar to Gideon's war against Midian:

1. *The number of fighters:*
   In *Parashat Lekh Lekha* we find an astounding military scenario: how could Abraham take only three hundred and eighteen men to fight against a mighty alliance of four kings, with a vast number of soldiers? A similar question arises concerning Gideon's fighters: they number a bare three hundred, against a massive army of a hundred and fifty thousand (see Judges 7:12; 8:10).

2. *Course of the war:*
   Abraham's battle tactic is, "He divided himself and his servants against them, by night" (Gen. 14:15). This was calculated to confuse the enemy forces and exploit the element of surprise to create panic in their camp. This tactic is especially effective when implemented against an alliance of different kings, where the allied armies are unfamiliar with one another. The classic example of such a battle is to be found in the story of Gideon, who comes upon the enemy forces with three groups of soldiers in the middle of the night, exploiting to the full the ensuing panic in the camp comprised of soldiers from Amalek, Midian and Benei Kedem. Based on this parallel, we may assume that Abraham, too, like Gideon, used the element of surprise in the middle of the night to startle the enemy. Since their camp, too, was comprised of forces representing different kings, this created chaos: in the dark the soldiers mistook identities and fought each other, eventually fleeing in all directions.

3. *Purpose of the war:*
   At the conclusion of Gideon's pursuit of the kings of Midian, we discover the reason for it: "He said to Zevaḥ and to Tzalmuna: Where are the men whom you killed at Tabor?" They said, "Like you – so were they, with the appearance of the sons of a king" (Judges 8:18). In other words, Gideon was trying to establish what had become of his brethren who were killed at Tabor – apparently on their way to call the men of Ephraim to war. Similarly, Abraham pursued the kings in order to find out what had happened to Lot, his nephew.

4. *Abraham and Eliezer vs. Gideon and Pura*

Rashi quotes the Talmud (*Nedarim* 32a), asserting that Abraham and Eliezer alone prevailed over the four kings:

> "Eighteen..." – Our sages taught: There was only Eliezer. The "three hundred and eighteen" refers to the numerical value of his name.

This midrash is most surprising: Is it not impressive enough that Abraham destroyed the camp of four kings with the help of only three hundred and eighteen men? For what reason do they reduce this number to Eliezer alone?

"The meaning of the text never contradicts the literal reading": we cannot deny the explicit verses teaching that Abraham wages war against the kings with the help of his servants. Therefore, what *Ḥazal* are trying to teach seems to be that although three hundred and eighteen men came with Abraham, Abraham and Eliezer alone would have sufficed to win. This type of message is certainly reminiscent of the story of Gideon and Pura, his attendant. The story of Gideon and Pura reminds us of the battle of Mikhmash, in which Jonathan, son of Saul, and his servant succeed in dispersing an entire camp. Since *Ḥazal* draw a parallel between Gideon's battle and that of Abraham, we may conclude that Abraham went down to the camp like Gideon, or Jonathan later on, and therefore they teach that Abraham descended with Eliezer alone.

These similar elements are the basis for *Ḥazal's* parallel between Gideon and Abraham, in light of which they raise another point of similarity: just as Gideon started his rebellion by smashing his father's altar, overcoming any fear of standing against the entire nation and placing God's altar as an alternative to that of Baal, so Abraham shattered his father's idols and introduced the alternative: worship of God.

III. THE FIERY FURNACE

As mentioned above, the story of Abraham's trial in the fiery furnace is inspired by the story of Ḥanania, Mishael and Azaria, recounted in chapter three of the book of Daniel. The story opens with a giant golden idol, sixty cubits – about twelve stories – high. This was no "tower reaching to the heavens," but rather a huge image of Nebuchadnezzar himself.

Such an idol would be an object of great admiration; the king's subjects would gaze at it with their heads bent backwards and their hearts raised towards their "father in heaven." Not to mention them in the same breath, the sight would be reminiscent of Moses lifting his staff at the top of the mountain, with *Benei Yisrael* gazing at the upraised staff and subjugating their hearts to God.

At the site of the idol a concert is performed: At a single moment all of the musicians begin to play, and at that same moment all of the nations, peoples and tongues bow and prostrate themselves. This image cannot but remind us of the story that we read in *Parashat Noaḥ*: "It was that the whole world was of one language and of the same speech" (11:1). However, there is a clear difference between the two stories: the episode of the Tower of Babel starts off with a single language that ultimately splits into many languages, many nations and many peoples, while Nebuchadnezzar's idol aims to unite the diverse nations, peoples and tongues into a single entity.

Nebuchadnezzar's status is something new to the world: no one before him had ever attained such a position – absolute power over the entire world. A world that is ruled by a king such as Nebuchadnezzar raises a most difficult question of faith: who is the king of the world? In the book of Daniel, Nebuchadnezzar's aim is explicit: he wants to nullify God's rule. In the preceding chapter, Nebuchadnezzar dreamt of a great idol, its head fashioned from gold, its neck and chest from silver, its abdomen from copper and the lower part of its body from brass. At the end of the dream, God's kingship comes and replaces the idol made from these perishable substances. In response, in the next chapter Nebuchadnezzar has an idol fashioned altogether from pure gold, so as to show that it is not God's kingship that will replace the idol described in his dream, but rather his own kingship that will last forever.

What we see is a sort of dialogue between the idol that Nebuchadnezzar sees in his dream, and the idol that he creates – a battle between God and Nebuchadnezzar. God appears in his dream as the king of all the world, but even then – in the dream – Nebuchadnezzar declares that God may be king in the dream, but he, Nebuchadnezzar, is king in reality. Instead of an idol that has only a head made of gold,

Nebuchadnezzar makes an idol that is fashioned altogether from gold, so that people will bow before it and rebel against God.

Indeed, were it not for Ḥanania, Mishael and Azaria, he would have succeeded. God's agents – representatives of the Jewish nation – stood firm and spoiled Nebuchadnezzar's vision, until ultimately the king himself is forced to acknowledge the truth. At this point, God's clear victory over the kingship of Nebuchadnezzar finds expression. Having reviewed the background to the midrash – the story of Nebuchadnezzar – let us now re-examine the story of the Tower of Babel and reconstruct Ḥazal's process of "photomontage" in the story of Abraham.

IV. WHAT'S WRONG WITH UNITY?

The sin of the generation that built the Tower of Babel is not stated explicitly in the text. The Torah only describes their initiative:

> They said: Let us build for ourselves a city, with a tower reaching up to the heavens, and let us make ourselves a name lest we be scattered over all the earth. (Gen. 11:4)

The verses convey the impression that the main problem concerned the city that they wanted to build (the city is mentioned in the story more often than the tower, and at the end we read, "So God scattered them... and they ceased to build the city,"), while Ḥazal indicate that the fundamental sin of the generation lay in the construction of the tower. Either way, when God sees the city and the tower,

> God said: Behold, they are a single nation and they all have the same language, and this is what they have begun to do. Now nothing will be withheld from them of all that they have planned to do." (11:6)

But what is it about the unity of the generation that is so bad? Isn't unity – under any circumstances – usually a good sign?

From the story of the Tower of Babel we learn something of the nature of the unity that existed in that generation: all had the same aim.

This was not **one nation** (*am eḥad*), but rather – as in Stalinist Russia – "**a nation of one**" (*am shel eḥad*). They were not "of **a single tongue**" (*safa aḥat*), but rather "of the tongue of one [person]" (*safa shel aḥat*). The builders were not "**of one aim**" (*etza aḥat*) but rather "of **the aim of one**" (*etza shel aḥat*) – of Nimrod, the mighty hunter who ruled over them. The collective conscience, the collective initiative and the collective thinking reflected not a unity and harmony of opinion, but rather the brutal and tyrannical coercion of a single individual, who thought and planned on behalf of everyone. This ruler – like other such rulers throughout history – was bloodthirsty; he brought about the unity of thought and belief in a single idea by means of a terrifying furnace into which anyone who dared to think differently would be mercilessly thrown.

If this is the type of unity that is proposed, then dispersion and division are preferable. Therefore, God's response is, "God dispersed them from there." It is better for all of humanity not to be subjected to the all-encompassing power of a single autocrat; rather, every person and every nation should choose its own ideals.

V. "THEY LEFT TO GO TO THE LAND OF CANAAN"

We are left with one final question: in the story from the book of Daniel we see how Ḥanania, Mishael and Azaria spoiled Nebuchadnezzar's plan. Having drawn a parallel between this narrative and that of the Tower of Babel, we are left looking for someone to spoil Nimrod's plan. And who is our candidate?

To answer this question, let us examine the end of the story:

> Teraḥ lived seventy years and he bore Abram and Naḥor and Ḥaran. And these are the generations of Teraḥ: Teraḥ bore Abram and Naḥor and Ḥaran, and Ḥaran bore Lot. Ḥaran died before Teraḥ, his father, in the land of his birthplace, in Ur Kasdim. Abram and Naḥor took wives; the name of Abram's wife was Sarai, and the name of Naḥor's wife was Milca, daughter of Ḥaran, the father of Milca and the father of Yisca. Sarai was barren; she had no child. Teraḥ took Abram, his son, and Lot the son of Ḥaran, the son of his son, and Sarai – his daughter-in-law, wife of Abram his son, and departed with them from Ur

Kasdim to go to the land of Canaan; they went as far as Ḥaran and sojourned there. Teraḥ lived two hundred a five years, and Teraḥ died in Ḥaran. (11:26–32)

It is clear to us from the end of *Parashat Noaḥ* that the birth of Abram represents a turning point in relation to the ten preceding generations. After the list of ten generations, the Torah suddenly begins to detail a new genealogy: "Teraḥ was seventy years old and he bore Abram and Naḥor and Ḥaran. And these are the generations of Teraḥ: Teraḥ bore Abram and Naḥor and Ḥaran, and Ḥaran bore Lot."

The Torah leaves many questions unanswered: why did Teraḥ behave as he did? Why would a person whose life was based in Ur Kasdim get up and leave his country and birthplace, and head for the land of Canaan?

Several hypotheses exist to explain this issue. Rav Yoel Bin-Nun writes in his article, "The Land and the Land of Canaan" (The Land and the Land of Canaan?), that Teraḥ's family was a family of merchants, therefore they wandered from place to place. He maintains that Abram's journey to the land of Canaan was actually a combination of two journeys: it was a continuation of the journey started by Teraḥ, his father, and at the same time a journey at God's request ("Go forth..."). Rav Mordechai Breuer, in his book *"Pirkei Bereshit,"* writes that the Torah gives no explanation for Teraḥ's journey to the land of Canaan because in truth it lacked any reason. It was an initiative in the direction of *Eretz Yisrael*, inspired by the divine ideal that extended to those generations.

We reject these explanations, and propose that the juxtaposition of the journey to Canaan with the episode of the Tower of Babel lends support to our claim:

> God **scattered** them from there over all the land, and they ceased to build the city. Therefore its name was called **Babel**, for there God mixed up [*balal*] the tongue of all the land, **and from there God scattered them over all the land.** (11:8–9)

The impression that arises from these verses is that some event took place in the land of Babel, as a result of which everyone was scattered and they wandered to many different places. Indeed, this is told to us explicitly in the story of Nimrod: "The beginning of his kingdom was Babel...**from that land Ashur emerged**"! For some reason, Ashur was forced to leave Babel. The reason, apparently, is the story of the Tower. Just as all the other nations emerged from Babel and wandered to other places, Terah also left Ur Kasdim and set off for Haran.

Let us now try to investigate further the matter of this "scattering." The Torah itself presents the scattering as a punishment for the having built the Tower, but in *Parashat Ha'azinu* we are given a different reason:

> When the Supreme God gave the nations their inheritance, when He separated the sons of man, He placed the boundaries of the nations according to the number of the children of Israel. (Deut. 32:8)

This verse reveals another explanation for the dispersion: it was all intended so that Abraham would reach the land of Canaan: "He placed the boundaries of the nations according to the number of the children of Israel"!

Combining these two contradictory reasons, we discover that the Torah is describing the two poles of the same idea. At one end we find Nimrod, who wants to rebel against God, and at the other end we find Abraham, who calls in God's Name. For Nimrod, the dispersion was a punishment: "God scattered them from there," while for Abraham this was an instance of divine guidance: "He placed the boundaries of the nations according to the number of the children of Israel."

Abraham, then, is the one who overturns Nimrod's plans. Abraham the Hebrew ("*HaIvri*") is on one side ("*ever ehad*"), while all the rest of the world – i.e., Nimrod – is on the other side, busy commanding everyone to bow and prostrate themselves to an idol! It is a short step, then, to complete the comparison between the story of Nimrod and that of Nebuchadnezzar, by placing Abraham in the role of Hanania, Mishael and Azaria.

VI. "YOUR DESCENDANTS WILL BE STRANGERS..."

The Covenant between the Pieces begins with bad tidings: Abraham is presented with the prospect of a four-hundred year exile, including slavery and suffering. *Ḥazal* debate the reason for this affliction, and – as is their way – couch their explanation in terms of divine retribution, reward and punishment:

> Rabbi Abahu said in the name of Rabbi Elazar: For what reason was Abraham punished, that his descendants would be enslaved in Egypt for two hundred and ten years? Because he pressed Torah sages into service, as it is written, "He led his trained servants, born to his house..."

> Shmuel said: Because he exaggerated in [his demands on] God's divine attributes, as it is written, "By what shall I know that I shall inherit it?"

> Rabbi Yoḥanan said: Because he kept people from joining the monotheistic faith, as it is written: "[The king of Sodom said to Abraham:] Give me the people, and take the property for yourself." (*Nedarim* 32a)

The three answers offered by the Talmud fall into two clear categories. One category includes those who follow the teachings of R. Yoḥanan of Tiberias – R. Yoḥanan himself, R. Elazar, his colleague and disciple, and R. Abahu, his disciple. In the second group, the Rosh Yeshiva of Nehardea in Babel – Shmuel – sits alone. The *Amoraim* of Tiberias connect the Covenant between the Pieces with the preceding *parasha* – Abraham's battle against Kedarla'omer and his company – and seek Abraham's sin within this context. Shmuel, in contrast, regards the episode of the Covenant as an independent unit, and seeks the sin within this unit itself, namely, in Abraham's words to God.

VII. "BY WHAT SHALL I KNOW THAT I SHALL INHERIT IT?"

Shmuel's understanding of Abraham's sin sits well with the literal reading of the text. Abraham asks of God some guarantee for the fulfillment of

His promise concerning the inheritance of the land. This demand would seem to express a deficiency in his supposedly perfect faith, justifying a harsh punishment. Indeed, in Shmuel's view, Abraham's punishment was "measure for measure": because Abraham asked, "How shall I know" (*Bameh eda*), he was informed of the future exile of his descendants with the words, "Know with certainty..." (*Yadoa teda*).

This interpretation raises two difficult questions. Abraham is the father of monotheistic faith and the greatest believer. How can we attribute to him the sin of deficient faith? The verses preceding the notification of future affliction represent a clear contradiction to the idea that Abraham's faith was anything less than perfect:

> He brought him outside and said: "Look, now, to the heavens and count the stars – if you are able to count them." And He said to him: "So shall be your descendants." And he believed in God, and He considered it righteous on his part. And He said to him: "I am God who brought you out of Ur Kasdim to give you this land for a possession." And he said: "Lord God, how shall I know that I shall inherit it?" (15:5–7)

The Torah speaks explicitly in praise of Abraham's faith. Why, then, would he not believe that the land would be given to him? It is possible that Shmuel's understanding is connected to that of the author of *Seder Olam*, as Rashi quotes in his name:

> "Four hundred and thirty years" – all inclusive. From the time of Isaac's birth until this point [the exodus], four hundred years had passed. From the time that Abraham [first] had offspring, the promise "Your descendants will be strangers..." was fulfilled, and thirty years passed from the time of [God's] decree at the Covenant until the birth of Isaac. (Rashi on Ex. 12:41)

This is most surprising: How could the Covenant have taken place when Abraham was seventy years old, when we are told explicitly at the beginning of our *parasha*: "Abraham was seventy-five years old when he left Ḥaran" (12:7)? Ramban (on Ex. 12:40) addresses this question, and mentions the opinion of the *Seder Olam* that Abraham actually ascended twice from Ḥaran to *Eretz Yisrael*: once at the age of seventy, and again at the age of seventy-five. This explanation is somewhat forced. In any event, his explanation implies that the narrative does not follow chronological order, and that the Covenant took place before the beginning of the *parasha*.

Perhaps we need not posit two journeys by Abraham to *Eretz Yisrael*; perhaps it is enough for us to move the Covenant to the end of *Parashat Noaḥ*, to the time when Abraham was living with his family in Ḥaran. Ḥaran is situated near the river Euphrates, which represents the border of the land promised to Abraham in the Covenant. In the Covenant between the Pieces, Abraham was promised not only the land of Canaan, as in the covenant of his circumcision, but all of "this land" – including the Keini, the Kenizi, the Kadmoni and the Rephaim.

Clarifying the picture that arises from this hypothesis, we have Abraham living with his father's household and his family in Ḥaran, when he receives a divine revelation at the age of seventy. In this revelation, God shows him from a distance "this land," which lies on the southwestern side of the Euphrates, and promises him: "I am God who brought you out of Ur Kasdim to give you this land as a possession." In the wake of this message, God commands him – five years later, when he is seventy-five years old – to leave his land, his birthplace and his father's home, and to go to that land which He will show him. At this stage, Abraham has not yet become the father and greatest of believers. He is the son of Teraḥ the idolater, and although he has discovered (through contemplation of the sun and moon) that it is God who created the world, and although he has already withstood the test of the furnace in Ur Kasdim, he still has questions and uncertainties as to his path and God's promises. Indeed, he is punished for these uncertainties in the affliction promised in the Covenant between the Pieces: "Your descendants will be strangers..."

When Abraham reaches the land five years later, by God's command, and God is revealed to him at his tent and guides him in all his endeavors – only then, in the land of God's inheritance, the land that God desires, does he ascend from one spiritual level to the next, until he becomes the greatest of all believers in God. Only then are we told, "He believed in God, and it was considered righteousness on his part."

According to our hypothesis, the encounter in chapter fifteen should be divided into two separate parts – verses 1–6 follow the war against the kings, and end with "And he believed in God, and it was considered righteousness on his part," while verses 7–12 with Abraham's questions occur in Ḥaran when Abraham is seventy years old.

VII. "BECAUSE HE PRESSED TORAH SAGES INTO SERVICE"

As mentioned above, the sages of *Eretz Yisrael* interpret the narrative in accordance with the order of the text. According to their understanding, the Covenant between the Pieces takes place immediately after the war against the kings, and the narrative as a whole is introduced with the words at the beginning of chapter fifteen: "After these things…"

Let us first discuss the approach of Rabbi Abahu in the name of Rabbi Elazar. In his view, Abraham was punished with servitude for his descendants "measure for measure" because "he pressed Torah sages into service." When I was a child, these words of R. Abahu used to be used as proof for the argument that Torah students should not be enlisted in the IDF. This claim proceeds from the exegetical assumption that Abraham is guilty of causing his "trained servants, born to his house" to neglect Torah, since the time spent in pursuit of the forces of Kedarla'omer and his company and in saving Lot was time wasted, in terms of Torah study. Abraham, then, should have conducted the pursuit alone or sent Eliezer. Clearly Torah study needed to be put aside for the purposes of the pursuit and to save Lot; after all, Abraham is not punished for wasting his own Torah-study time. He is punished only for pressing into service a greater number of fighters than was necessary for the battle against the four kings and their armies.

This interpretation is problematic in every respect. Can three hundred and eighteen fighters possibly be considered an excessively large army for the military challenge that Abraham faces? Is he supposed to rely on a miracle? Are all those "born to his house" really engaged day and night only in Torah, never leaving Torah for a moment in order to help take care of the needs of Abraham's household? Who, then, were his shepherds; who dug his wells, who was responsible for setting up his tent during his wanderings? Did Abraham never press those "born to his house" into service; did they never do anything for him?

Let us attempt to understand Rabbi Abahu's words differently. Possibly, *Hazal* had reservations as to the merit of the aim of the war that Abraham is about to embark upon: saving the kingdom of Sodom from the hands of Kedarla'omer. Perhaps they do not consider this sufficient justification for endangering the members of his household. If we question why *Hazal* are concerned for the safety of these gentiles and servants who took care of Abraham's herds, the answer is given: *Hazal* point out that these servants were Torah sages and fulfilled the commandments, with Eliezer instructing them in the teachings of Abraham, his master. Abraham should not have endangered these people without good reason.

Why do *Hazal* not present a similar claim concerning Abraham himself, for having endangered his own life in this battle? The answer is clear: A risk that a person takes upon himself is not the same as a risk that he places upon others – even if they are his servants. Abraham assumes the risk in order to save his relative, Lot, thereby fulfilling the commandment, "You shall not turn your back on your own flesh." He had a special obligation towards Lot, the son of his brother who was burned in God's name when he decided to accept the God of Abraham. But Lot was neither the relative nor even a friend of Abraham's shepherds and servants. On the contrary: he was their sworn adversary. Abraham, therefore, had no right to endanger them in order to save Lot.

VIII. "GIVE ME THE PEOPLE, AND TAKE THE PROPERTY FOR YOURSELF"

The final interpretation that we must address is that of Rabbi Yohanan, who also claims that Abraham's sin concerned the war against the kings. In his view, the problem was that Abraham prevented people from joining the monotheistic faith when the king of Sodom proposed, "Give me the people, and take the property for yourself."

Why should we expect Abraham to convert all the men of Sodom and bring them within the monotheistic fold? What good would come of a forced conversion of all these people? And since when are we commanded to make converts – especially when it comes to people like the evil sinners of Sodom?

From my teacher, Rav Yoel Bin-Nun, I learned that the approach of the teacher – Rabbi Yohanan – is the corollary of that of the disciple –

Rabbi Abahu. The assumption that there was some justification for saving the people of Sodom from their captivity and servitude is closely connected with the assumption that it would be possible to convert them and bring them to monotheistic faith. For this purpose it was proper even for Torah sages such as the members of Abraham's household to endanger themselves in order to save Lot and the men of Sodom together with him. But if Abraham decided to leave the men of Sodom and Lot alone, to allow them to return to their former evildoing, then there was no real reason for the war, and he was guilty of pressing Torah sages into service with no justification.

Let us explain Rabbi Yoḥanan's teaching in greater detail. After Abraham separates from Lot, who heads for Sodom, God appears to him and promises:

> Lift up your eyes and see, from the place where you are – northwards and southwards and eastwards and westwards. For all the land that you see – to you I shall give it, and to your descendants, forever. And I shall make your descendants like the dust of the earth, that if a person can count the dust of the earth – so shall he number your descendants. Arise and walk about in the land, its length and breadth, for I shall give it to you. (13:14–17)

This promise, as formulated here, applies not only to the land of Canaan, but to all of the great expanse from the river of Egypt up to the Euphrates. We are accustomed to understanding this as a vision for the distant future, but it is not so. God's intention in these words is for the present. Indeed, immediately after God's promise, the war of the kings erupts, with the kings from the other side of the Euphrates invading the eastern side of the Jordan river, attacking all of the kingdoms there, and perhaps even gaining indirect control of the western side of the Jordan.

Along comes Abraham and, in an instant, defeats these conquerors. In banishing them and the remains of their forces to the other side of the Euphrates, all the land up to the Euphrates falls into his hands. As he returns, crowned with victory, from his battle, it is no wonder that Ḥazal teach that all the kings vied to appoint Abraham king over them, for he had liberated them from the yoke of Kedarla'omer. Similarly, hundreds of years later, all the tribes of Israel came to Gideon, following his victory over Midian, and pleaded: "Rule over us, both you and your son and your grandson, for you have saved us from the hand of Midian" (Judges 8:23). Thus God fulfills His promise to Abraham to give the entire land into his hands.

But Abraham withdraws. He returns to his tent and chooses to relinquish his rulership over this vast area and over all that God has given into his hand. He obviously has his reasons: reigning over the land also involves assuming responsibility for its inhabitants – to educate them in the way of God, which is the way of righteousness and justice. Abraham sees before him the men of Sodom in all their wickedness, and concludes that he is not up to the task. He wants to establish God's nation from his own seed, to educate them from childhood, and thereby to prepare the people that will bear the banner of God's name in the world.

In this act, Abraham admits failure and foregoes the challenge that God has placed before him. His pangs of conscience over this decision are easily detected in his prayer to save the people of Sodom, some twenty-four years later.

Abraham had reason to fear that he had lost all his reward as well as God's promise, since he himself had decided to forego it. God once again promises him the land, and Abraham requests a covenant rather than just a promise, for the promise had been allowed to fall away:

And he said: Lord God, by what shall I know that I will inherit it?

IX. "THE EAGLE DESCENDED UPON THE CARCASSES"

According to the view of R. Yoḥanan, Abraham should have accepted rulership over the land; he should have forced upon its inhabitants the "way of God to perform righteousness and justice." His actions were deficient. Although it is difficult to regard his behavior as a sin, bringing in its wake divine retribution and punishment, clearly he did something wrong. Indeed, as we shall discuss below, the same conclusion arises from the unfolding of the Covenant between the Pieces.

For this covenant, Abraham is required to bring a three-year old heifer, a three-year old goat, a three-year old ram, a turtledove and a young pigeon, and to wait for God's appearance. Clearly, fire is supposed to descend from heaven onto Abraham's offerings, thereby sealing the covenant between him and God.

Let us depict the events here as described by my friend, R. Yisrael Sadiel of Kfar Etzion. Instead of the *Shekhina*, it was the "eagle" that descended upon the carcasses. The eagle (*ayit*) here is not a solitary bird. "*Ayit*" is a participle, like "*tzayid*" (hunting) or "*dayig*" (fishing). It appears, then, that a great flock of birds of prey – perhaps even of different types – descended upon the offerings that Abraham had prepared for the covenant. Abraham does not give up on fulfilling his part of the covenant: he lifts a thick stick and attacks this throng of menacing birds with all his strength. It is a battle that continues for many hours, a long, dangerous and exhausting fight described by the Torah in just a few words:

> The eagles descended upon the carcasses, and Abraham drove them away.

Throughout his desperate battle, Abraham must surely have his eyes raised heavenwards. He must be asking himself why God is holding back the descent of His fire upon the sacrifices that Abraham has painstakingly prepared in order to fulfill the covenant. But throughout the day, God is absent.

The sun is setting – it has reached the tops of the trees; Abraham has prevailed over the birds of prey, but has collapsed with exhaustion, or has fainted. It is specifically then that God comes, finds Abraham sleeping, and schedules the next meeting between them for four hundred years' time!

What is the symbolism of Abraham's Sisyphean battle against the eagles? This battle would seem to symbolize his spiritual and physical battle against the nations surrounding him, and against their wickedness – a battle that reaches its climax in the war of the kings. With his victory and the spiritual challenge that it brings – to introduce the way of God, the way of righteousness and justice, over the nations of the land, from the river of Egypt to the Euphrates – it is specifically at this point, at the climax of the battle, when Abraham shows signs of fatigue and doubt, and he withdraws.

As stated previously, in contrast to the two previous interpretations of his sin (as proposed by R. Abahu and by Shmuel), R. Yoḥanan proposes not a sin but a failure: the lack of courage to elevate himself to the level of repairing the entire world. Is this missed opportunity worthy of punishment? Indeed, my view is that R. Yoḥanan believes that the decree, "Your descendants will be strangers," is not a punishment, but rather a historical necessity in light of Abraham's withdrawal to his tent. R. Abahu emphasizes the slavery in Egypt – measure for measure for Abraham having pressed his servants into service. It is possible that Shmuel, who accuses Abraham of challenging God's promise, is emphasizing the "affliction" that is promised; namely, the literal suffering. In R. Yoḥanan's view, the emphasis should be placed upon the issue of being strangers. Had Abraham taken on rulership of the land and responsibility for the nations dwelling in it, to correct them and return them to God, they certainly would have joined themselves to the nation of the God of Abraham, and inherited the land forever. But since Abraham decided to withhold that potential sanctity from them and to bequeath the land only to his own descendants, a problem arose: to where would the nations, living in the inheritance that they had received from their forefathers in *Eretz Yisrael*, go? Could the native inhabitants of the land be banished for no justified reason, simply because God wanted to give the land to the descendants of Abraham?

God informs Abraham that, so long as the sin of the Amorites is not complete, God will not banish them from the land. The children of the Amorites were no saints in Abraham's generation; all were idolaters. But then – at the Covenant between the Pieces – the accounting of their sins began, and God's accounting for idolatry lasts up to four generations, as we read in the Ten Commandments, in the prohibition "You shall have no other gods before Me."

Until the sin of the Amorites is complete, and until God visits their sin upon them after four generations, there is no land for the descendants of Abraham. Therefore, the nation of Israel that is descended from Abraham is destined to be a stranger in a land that is not theirs. Even if Abraham's children will dwell, for part of this time, in *Eretz Yisrael*, they will still be considered strangers, for the Amorite inhabitants of the land will rule over them.

We may ask, then, why slavery and affliction are decreed upon Abraham's descendants. Why does God not suffice with, "Your descendants will be strangers," without adding that "they will enslave them and afflict them"? In truth, we must understand that the verse means only that the status of "strangers" will last four hundred years, while within those four hundred years there will be slavery and affliction for some undefined period. Indeed, this is what happened: the slavery and affliction did not extend throughout the four hundred years of "strangeness." Even the two hundred and ten years of exile in Egypt were not all years of slavery and affliction, for throughout Joseph's lifetime – and, according to Ḥazal, throughout the lifetime of his brothers – the slavery was postponed.

The slavery and affliction are a necessary historical result of being strangers for an extended period in the land of another nation. Naturally, there are host kings who are better and others who are worse, some more tolerant and others less so. Therefore, God set down a period for Abraham's descendants to be strangers, and declared that consequently there sometimes would also be periods of slavery and affliction. The status of being strangers arose, as stated above, from the fact that there was not yet an available land for *Am Yisrael*, so long as the sin of the Amorite was not complete.

Abraham's Aliyot

by Rav Mordechai Breuer *zt"l*

I. INTRODUCTION – THE TWO SEPARATIONS

The verses describing how Lot and Abraham separated from one another are problematic, raising several questions:

> Then Lot chose for himself all the plain of the Jordan; and Lot journeyed east; and they separated themselves one from the other. Abram dwelt in the land of Canaan, and Lot dwelt in the cities of the plain, and pitched his tent toward Sodom. (13:11–12)

> Then Abram removed his tent, and came and dwelt by Elonei Mamreh, which is in Ḥevron, and built there an altar to the Lord. (13:18)

1. The first half of verse 11 already states that Lot journeyed east, so there is no need to say in the second half of the verse that they separated themselves one from the other. Furthermore, the first half of the verse attributes the separation solely to Lot: "And Lot journeyed east"; while the second half of the verse attributes the separation to the two of them. It doesn't say: "And Lot separated himself from Abram," but "And they separated themselves one from the other."

2. Verse 12 states that Lot dwelt "in the cities of the plain." It is difficult to assume that Lot dwelt in all those cities at the same time. Instead, it stands to reason that he dwelt in one of them, close to Sodom, as the end states: "And he pitched his tent toward Sodom." It was, however, already stated in the previous verses (9–10) that Lot saw "the plain of the Jordan" and that he chose for himself "the plain of the Jordan"; it is, therefore, difficult to understand why it is does not say here as well the he dwelt in "the plain of the Jordan."

3. Verse 12 creates a clear parallel between Abram's dwelling in the land of Canaan and Lot's dwelling in the cities of the plain; similarly, there is a parallel between Lot's tent which reached Sodom (end of v. 12) and Abram's tent which was pitched in Ḥevron (beginning of v. 18). However, in the account of their respective dwelling places, the Torah puts Abram before Lot (v. 12); whereas concerning the respective places of their tents, it puts Lot (v. 12) before Abram (v. 18).

It seems, therefore, that the Torah describes Lot's separation from Abram in two parallel manners, depending on the two aspects of Abram's *aliya* to the land. The end of verse 11 (from the words "and they separated themselves") and most of verse 12 (until the words "the plain") describe the separation in the framework of the *aliya* that was undertaken in order to realize the plan of Teraḥ. In this framework, the separation is described as follows:

> And they separated themselves one from the other. (13:11)

> Abram dwelt in the land of Canaan, and Lot dwelt in the cities of the plain. (13:12)

This is a direct continuation of what was stated in verse 6. Since their substance was great, so that they could not dwell together, they separated themselves one from the other. Abram dwelt in the land of Canaan, and Lot in the cities of the plain. From this perspective, Abram and Lot separated because of their great substance, and the two of them were equally interested in the separation. Accordingly, there was no reason for Abram to give Lot priority, but rather they each separated "one from the other." Each person settled in the place that he chose to dwell. Since the Torah cannot simultaneously describe their respective settlements, it describes Abram's settlement before it describes that of Lot, as it is the Torah's way to describe the actions of great people prior to those of lesser individuals. According to this, it is also understandable that the Torah does not mention the names of the cities in which they settled, for in the framework of this *aliya* to Israel, Abram was only looking for the land of Canaan in general, and not a specific city that represents it. For this reason it only says that Abram dwelt "in the land of Canaan," whereas Lot settled in the cities of the plain, i.e., in one of the cities of the Jordan plain.

The rest of what is stated in verses 11–12, and 18 describe Lot's separation in the framework of Abram's *aliya* that was undertaken at the command of God. In this framework, the separation is described as follows:

> Then Lot chose for himself all the plain of the Jordan; and Lot journeyed east; and pitched his tent toward Sodom. (13:11–12)

> Then Abram removed his tent, and came and dwelt by Elonei Mamreh, which is in Ḥevron, and built there an altar to the Lord. (13:18)

This is a direct continuation of verses 7–10. After Lot saw all of the plain of the Jordan that "it was well watered everywhere," he chose for himself all the plain of the Jordan, and therefore he journeyed east, and pitched his tent toward Sodom; whereas Abram pitched his tent in Ḥevron, and built there an altar to the Lord. For it was the quarrel that led here to the separation, and since only Abram was interested in preventing the quarrel, he had to give priority to Lot. Accordingly, everything depended on Lot's desire: It was Lot who chose the plain of the Jordan; and only after he journeyed east, and pitched his tent toward Sodom, could Abram pitch his tent in Ḥevron. It is understandable that the Torah saw fit to mention here the names of the cities in which Abram and Lot pitched their tents; for in this *aliya* Abram sought not only the land in general, but also the city whose unique quality was most appropriate for him. From this perspective, there is a striking difference between Lot and Abram: Abram dwelt in Ḥevron, whereas Lot pitched his tent toward Sodom.

These are the two ways that the Torah describes the separation between Lot and Abram. This does not mean that they separated twice – once because of the great amount of property, and a second time in order to prevent strife. Rather, the Torah comes here to describe a single separation, which was caused by two factors, each of which on its own could have brought about the separation.

Verse 11 states that Lot chose for himself all the plain of the Jordan, and therefore he journeyed east. With this journey he acceded to the supplications of Abram, who wished to prevent quarreling. The Torah therefore adds that Lot's journey was caused by their great substance; and from this perspective the separation should not be attributed exclusively to Lot, but rather it should be described as a joint action: they separated themselves "one from the other."

We learn from this that the words, "and they separated themselves one from the other," should be read in two ways. Had Abram and Lot separated on account of the great size of their property, this expression would have been the direct continuation of verse 6, which describes their great substance. But since the separation came also in order to prevent a feud, the words "and they separated themselves one from the other" can also be understood as a direct continuation of "and Lot journeyed east." These two expressions come now to describe the two aspects of the separation: this is a separation that is understood both as Lot's journey east and as a separation "one from the other."

After describing the separation itself, the Torah mentions the places where Abram and Lot settled after they separated. It first mentions the lands and afterwards mentions the cities. However, the lands were chosen in the framework of the separation caused by Abram and Lot's great substance; and therefore Abram's settlement is described before that of Lot. However, the cities were chosen in the context of the separation brought about in order to prevent quarreling; and therefore Lot's tent is described before that of Abram. This allows the Torah to use the style of "opening with that with which it had closed." Lot's land closes the list of lands, while his city opens the list of cities.

According to this we can say that the clauses "and he pitched his tent toward Sodom" and "then Abram removed his tent, and came and dwelt by Elonei Mamreh, which is in Ḥevron" should also be read in two ways. Had the separation come only to prevent strife, these clauses would be a direct continuation of "and Lot journeyed east," which describes the separation itself. This would mean that only after Lot journeyed east (v. 10) and pitched his tent toward Sodom (v. 12) could Abram pitch his tent in Ḥevron (v. 18). But since the separation was also a consequence of their great substance, these two clauses can be understood as a direct continuation of "Abram dwelt in the land of Canaan, and Lot dwelt in the cities of the plain" (v. 12). It turns out that this is the way verses 12 and 18 should be explained against the background of the previous verses: After Lot journeyed east in order to prevent the quarrel – and at the same time Abraham and Lot separated themselves one from the other because of their sizable property – these are the places where they now dwell: in the framework of the separation because of the excessive property they settled in Canaan or in the cities of the plain; whereas in the framework of the separation in order to prevent strife they pitched their tents in Sodom or in Ḥevron.

II. SEPARATION FROM LOT – COMPLETING TWO *ALIYOT*

Abram's *aliya* – based on God's command – could not reach its conclusion as long as Lot "went with Abram." Accordingly, before Abram moved from Beit El to Ḥevron, a quarrel broke out between the shepherds; and in order to end the quarrel Lot agreed to journey east and pitch his tent toward Sodom, and in this way Lot ceased going with Abram. Only after Lot pitched his tent toward Sodom could Abram pitch his tent in Ḥevron – and thus complete his *aliya*. It is evident that the journey to Ḥevron – after Lot separated himself from him – is the crown of all of Abram's journeys in the land, for in Shekhem he built an altar, and in Beit El he built an altar and also pitched his tent. In Ḥevron, however, he built an altar and pitched his tent, and "came" and "dwelt" there in a permanent fashion:

Then Abram removed his tent, and came and dwelt by Elonei Mamreh, which is in Ḥevron, and built there an altar to the Lord. (v. 18)

Based on this we can now explain verses 13–17, which we skipped previously. Verse 13 describes the wickedness of the people of Sodom; whereas verses 14–17 record God's words to Abram after Lot had separated from him. Without a doubt, all of these verses are connected to Abram's *aliya* based on God's command. The Tetragrammaton is mentioned in these verses, for the *aliya* that was based on God's command was executed in the framework of the governance of the Attribute of the Tetragrammaton. Based on this, we must now explain these verses.

In verses 14–17 God repeats the promise that had already been given to Abram in Shekhem, only there the promise was worded in brief: "To your seed will I give this land," whereas here it is explained at length, and it includes both a promise about the land and about seed, and also the command to rise up and walk through the land. Furthermore, in Shekhem the promised land is referred to as "this land," whereas here Abram is commanded to lift up his eyes and look "northward, and southward, and eastward, and westward," and he is told that God will give him "all the land which you see." Only here does God fulfill the promised included in the words "the land that I will show you" (12:1), for only now does He show him the land, in the literal sense.

In Shekhem, Abram's *aliya* had only begun, for he had still not reached Ḥevron, and Lot was still "going with Abram." For this reason the promise regarding the land was still not given to him in full, and the promise of "that I will show you" was not yet entirely filled. Only when Abram was about to complete his *aliya*– and Lot had already ceased going with him – did the time arrive to complete God's promise and wholly fulfill "that I will show you." All this is explicitly stated in the introduction to God's words: "And the Lord said to Abram, after Lot was separated from him" (v. 14). Indeed, only after Lot separated from Abram – and Abram was able to go to Ḥevron – did the time arrive to say these things. Only then was Abram's *aliya* completed.

Of special significance is God's address to Abram: "Lift up now your eyes, and look from the place where you are" (v. 14); these words parallel what was said above regarding Lot: "And Lot lifted up his eyes, and beheld all the plain of the Jordan" (v. 10). The meaning seems to be as follows: Lot chose his land on his own; he "lifted up his eyes" and beheld all the plain of the Jordan, "that it was well watered everywhere, like the garden of the Lord, like the land of Egypt." But he did not understand that all this was only temporary – "before the Lord destroyed Sodom and Gomorrah" – because he did not pay attention to the fact that "the men of Sodom were wicked and sinners before the Lord exceedingly" (v. 13). Abram – his very *aliya* was "as the Lord had spoken to him." For this reason he did not choose his land on his own, but rather God said to him: "Lift up now your eyes, and look ... northward, and southward, and eastward, and westward," and it is God who promises to give him "all the land which you see." In this way Abram merited to dwell in Ḥevron that looked out upon Sodom; and from there he would later see the smoke rising from Sodom at the time of its destruction.

Just as Lot's separation allowed for the completion of Abram's *aliya* that was based on God's command, so too it allowed for the completion of the other *aliya*, which came to realize Teraḥ's plan. This is evident from an examination of all of the verses that describe this *aliya*.

> And Teraḥ took Abram his son, and Lot the son of Ḥaran his son's son, and Sarai his daughter-in-law, his son Abram's wife; and they went out with them from Ur Kasdim, to go into the land of Canaan, and they came to Ḥaran, and dwelt there. (11:31)

> And Abram took Sarai his wife, and Lot his brother's son, and all their substance that they had gathered, and the souls that they had acquired in Ḥaran; and they went forth to go to the land of Canaan; and into the land of Canaan they came. (12:5)

> And the land was not able to bear them, that they might dwell together: for their substance was great, so that they could not dwell together. (13:6)

> And they separated themselves one from the other. (13:11)

> Abram dwelt in the land of Canaan, and Lot dwelt in the cities of the plain. (13:12)

These verses describe Abram's *aliya* in three stages. First, Teraḥ took Abram, Lot and Sarai, and they "went out to go into the land of

Canaan," but they did not merit coming to the land of Canaan and dwell-ing there; rather, they only "came" to Ḥaran and "dwelt there" (11:31). Afterwards, Abram took Sarai and Lot and all their property, and they "went forth to go to the land of Canaan; and into the land of Canaan they came" (12:5); but they still did not "dwell" in the land of Canaan. Their substance was great, so that they could not "dwell" together (13:6). For this reason they separated themselves one from another. Only after they separated – so that Lot was no longer with Abram – did Abram's *aliya* reach its conclusion; for now Abram "dwelt" in the land of Canaan, whereas Lot "dwelt in the cities of the plain" (13:12).

The need for these three stages can be understood based upon what was explained above. For, according to this aspect of the *aliya*, they did not undertake the journey at the command of God; rather, they sought the land of Canaan based on some vague feeling that this land was destined for them. Regarding this, we must distinguish between three levels. Teraḥ, who was only "Abram's father," felt only the first buds of these feelings, for the land had not been designated for him, but for his son Abram. The feeling of connection to the land of Canaan was stronger in the heart of Lot, for to him was designated a land that lies on the border of the land of Canaan. However, it was only in Abram's heart that this feeling reached the level of perfection, for he could feel that the land of Canaan was designated for him. Hence:

Teraḥ, Abram and Lot – went out to go into the land of Canaan.

Abram and Lot – went out to go into the land of Canaan, and they came to the land of Canaan.

Abram alone – went out to go into the land of Canaan, came to the land of Canaan, and dwelt in the land of Canaan.

Regarding this matter, too, we can say that the actions of the forefathers are a sign for the children. Many wish to go to *Eretz Yisrael* based on some vague sense that it is their land. However, the intensity of this feel-ing is not the same; thinking about *aliya* does not always lead to action. Some rise up to go to *Eretz Yisrael*, but never come there, and certainly do not dwell there. Others set out for *Eretz Yisrael* and come there, but the land does not receive them well and so they do not end up dwelling there, but rather they leave soon after arriving. Only those whose sense of connection to the land is strong in their hearts merit fully realizing their *aliya*; they set out to go to Eretz Israel, they come, and they dwell there.

To conclude this discussion, we should note the common denominator between the two *aliyot* described in this *parasha*: each of these two *aliyot* developed in three stages. The *aliya* to *Eretz Yisrael* in general started with Teraḥ and continued with Lot, but only Abram merited completing it; the *aliya* to the land and its cities started with Shekhem, continued in Beit El, and reached its conclusion only in Ḥevron. It stands to reason that there is a connection between these three stages of *aliya* and the three stages in the selection of the nation; for the selection of Israel began with Abram, continued with Isaac, and only reached its conclusion with Jacob, who was called Israel.

III. LOT'S *ALIYA* – WHY WAS IT NECESSARY?

We are left with a question that arises from all that has been explained here. Abram's *aliya* could not be complete as long as Lot was found with him. Accordingly, it is difficult to understand what need there was for Lot's *aliya*, for the land had never been designated for him. It would have been fitting for Abram to go alone, "as the Lord had spoken to him," and to take only Sarai his wife with him. If it was God's will that Lot should dwell in the land that borders on Canaan, He could have brought him there directly. It was wholly unnecessary for Lot to first accompany Abram – as if the land had been designated for him as well – and only afterwards separate.

Apparently, Lot's *aliya* can be explained based on the general objective of the book of Genesis. Genesis comes to describe the selection of Israel, and it is well-known that this selection was done through a sifting process consisting of three stages. First, Abram was chosen from among the sons of Teraḥ, then Isaac was chosen from among the sons of Abraham, and finally, Jacob was chosen from among the sons of Isaac. This procedure for selecting Israel reflects how God governs the world in general. This world of ours is a world of duality, in which good and evil intermingle; no good enters into the world, without some evil alongside it. And since "God has made the one as well as the other"

(Eccl. 7:12), one can only take hold of the good by rejecting the evil. Accordingly, the light of Israel could also only have been revealed in this manner: at every stage of the foundation of the nation a selection was made, in the most literal sense – the good was chosen and the evil was rejected. Even after this selection, these two forces continue to stand against one another. The conflict symbolizes the world of duality, and it must take place, so long as the mystery of the world's unity has not been revealed. It will only be abolished in that ideal world, when there will be "one day... neither day, nor night"; when the Lord shall be one and His name shall be one (Zech. 14:7, 9).

That same divine selection, which chooses the good from among the evil, always takes place between two brothers who are similar with respect to their right to the land: both are sons of the same father; sometimes they are also the sons of the same mother, who emerged from their mother's womb at the same time. Thus the two of them stand alongside each other, ready and prepared to inherit the land, and the outside observer sees the two of them as enjoying equal rights. Only God, who sees through to the heart, knows how to distinguish between them; it is He who brings about that one of them will be rejected and lose his right to the land, while his brother is chosen and the land falls to him as his inheritance.

This selection never takes place through God's direct involvement; it always takes place on its own, according to the natural order of events: a feud breaks out between the two brothers, or the land is unable to bear them, and one of them arrives at the conclusion that his place is not in this land – and so he goes and "chooses" another land. In this way, he is rejected and his brother is selected.

Therefore, Abram did not go to the land of Canaan by himself, but accompanied by Lot. The idea that Abram expressed could not have entered the world only through its positive dimension; it had to be revealed through two matching elements, between which only God could decide. These two sides were represented by Abram and Lot, for they were two brothers who went on one journey and sought one land; the two of them "went out to go to the land of Canaan," and the two of them "came to the land of Canaan"; the two of them "went" and reached Shekhem and Beit El. And so it seemed as if the two of them were fit to inherit the land. It was only before the completion of the last stage of their *aliya* that the divine selection took place: Only Abram "dwelt in the land of Canaan" – whereas Lot "dwelt in the cities of the plain"; only Abram pitched his tent in Ḥevron, whereas Lot pitched his tent toward Sodom.

Here, in the selection made between Abram and Lot, the Torah alludes to the reason that Abram was chosen. For Lot chose on his own the plain of the Jordan; he thought that he was choosing "the garden of the Lord," but he did not know that the Garden of Eden cannot be found in Sodom – rather, its streams would be turned into pitch, and its dust into brimstone, and its land would become burning pitch (Is. 34:9). He chose the Garden of Eden, and he received perdition: "Its bonfire is of much fire and wood; the breath of the Lord, like a steam of brimstone, kindles it" (Is. 30:33). Just the opposite was said about the land that was given to Abram: even when it is desolate and in ruin, "this land that was blighted is become like the Garden of Eden" (Ezek. 36:35); God will eventually comfort its ruins, "and He will make her wilderness like Eden, and her desert like the garden of the Lord" (Is. 51:3).

"By What Shall I Know?" – Question and Covenant

by Rav Chanoch Waxman

I. INTRODUCTION

We tend to think of a divine covenant, a treaty with God, as something good – not just good, but wholly good. It is a gift from God, granted to the forefathers and passed on to future generations. We expect our covenants to include the promise of nationhood, possession of the land of Israel, the promise of divine caring and perhaps some form of religious responsibility. However, we do not expect them to include suffering.

The Covenant between the Pieces (*Berit bein HaBetarim*) shatters this expectation. In the very first formal covenant granted to Abraham by God, God promises suffering, and much of it.

> And when the sun was going down, a deep sleep fell upon Abram; and behold a horror of great darkness fell upon him. And He said to Abram, Know surely that your children shall be strangers in a land that is not theirs, and shall serve them; and they shall afflict them four hundred years… (Gen. 15:12–14)

The Covenant between the Pieces is primarily a formal guarantee of

God's promise of the land of Israel to Abraham's descendants (see 15:18–21), a clearly positive event. Yet as part of the process of contracting this covenant, Abraham is gripped by fear and horror, a premonition and foreshadowing of his children's suffering. As part of the covenant itself, Abraham is promised not just the land, but also exile and suffering. This seems strange and contradictory.

To rephrase this in more analytic terminology, why does the covenant include the promise of suffering? Why does God choose the moment of the formal treaty, the time of a great gift to Abraham, to inform him of the horrible future? In fact, why does Abraham need to know at all about the future exile in Egypt?

This series of questions leads us to the classic formulation of the problem. Above, I phrased the problem primarily in literary and dramatic terms: a problem of the inclusion of suffering, or the informing of Abraham. But if we shift for a moment to the theological and philosophical plane, we may phrase a crucially different question: what is the cause of the suffering? Why does God decree it?

II.

I have always been convinced that chapter fifteen itself provides some crucial clues for resolving these problems. Shortly before the instructions for the gathering of the animals, the splitting of the animals and the arrangement of the animals to be used in the covenant ceremony (15:9–11), God appears to Abraham and declares His intention to grant the land to Abraham as an inheritance (15:7). Abraham's response is immediate and pointed. "And he said, Lord God, by what shall I know [*bameh eda*] that I shall inherit it?" (15:8). A few verses later, after the "ceremony preparation" section mentioned above (15:9–11), we confront the section of "suffering" (15:12–14). Let us look carefully at part of the text again.

> And He said to Abram, Know surely [*yadoa teda*] that your children shall be strangers in a land that is not theirs, and shall serve them; and they shall afflict them four hundred years ... (15:12–14)

In delivering the decree of suffering, God utilizes the key word of

Abraham's question. God's statement "Know surely," a translation of a double usage of the word for "know," echoes Abraham's request for knowledge. Abraham asks for knowledge, and God grants it to him. Apparently, the inclusion of suffering in the covenant between the pieces is somehow related to Abraham's request.

III.

The overarching structure of chapter fifteen may well support this point. Let us take a look at the beginning of the chapter.

> After these things, the word of God came to Abram in a vision, saying, Fear not, Abram: I am your shield; your reward shall be very great. (15:1)

The preface of the sentence, "After these things," refers to the events of chapter fourteen, namely the war (see Rashi on 15:1), and clearly signals an organic connection between the war story of chapter fourteen and the covenant story of chapter fifteen. The linguistic and thematic connection between God as the shield (*magen*) of Abraham here (15:1) and God as the deliverer (*migen*) of Abraham's enemies into his hands (14:20) further strengthens this reading.

Finally, on the thematic plane, the last scene of the war story (14:17–24) depicts a meeting between Abraham, the victor in the war, and the King of Sodom, the representative of the coalition of five Canaanite kings defeated by the four Mesopotamian kings and subsequently saved by Abraham. The scene takes place in a location known as the "Valley of the King" (14:17) in the presence of Melchizedek, a priest of "the most high God." According to the standard way these things work, Abraham, the savior of the Canaanite principalities, should be accepted as ruler by the Canaanites, here in the "Valley of the King" in front of the representative of the high God. At the very least, some sort of tribute should be paid to Abraham and something akin to a noble-vassal relationship sealed by a formal treaty should be established. The King of Sodom plays his role perfectly. He offers Abraham all the booty of the war as the first part of a treaty initiative. However, Abraham refuses all reward. Only food for his allies is required. He turns down all reward, all formal relationship with Sodom and its coalition, and any hint of treaty and sovereignty (14:23–24).

In point of fact, Abraham turns down reward and treaty not just with Sodom, its allies and locality, but implicitly with a far vaster grouping and area. A careful reading of chapter fourteen yields the following conclusion: the four kings, who originate in Mesopotamia, travel across the eastern bank of the Jordan, carrying out numerous battles along the way. Near the southern end of the Dead Sea, they smite the five kings and then continue north towards Damascus through the west bank of the Jordan. They are on their way home. No more battles ensue. Their power and control is unchallenged; they are the rulers of the entire land of Canaan. In a certain sense, Abraham's defeat of the kings and his rescue of the Canaanites constitutes military hegemony over the entire region. It generates the possibility of reward, treaty and control over the entire area.

In the very next verse, "After these things" (15:1), God appears to Abraham and promises him great reward – not reward and treaty received from kings of flesh and blood, but reward and treaty received from the King of Kings, God Himself. In fact, the first verse of chapter fifteen constitutes a preface to the Covenant between the Pieces, a story of reward and treaty.

The interpretation of the covenant between the pieces as a reward for "treaty refusal" forces us to take a look at the structure of chapter fifteen. At first glance, the structure seems to dictate against this interpretation. The architecture breaks down as follows:

1. 15:1 – God's promise of reward;
2. 15:2–6 – Abraham's lament for children and the sign of the stars;
3. 15:7 – God's statement that He has brought Abraham from Ur Kasdim to give him this land as an inheritance;
4. 15:8 – Abraham's question, "How will I know?"
5. 15:9–11 – the ceremony preparations;
6. 15:12–16 – the promise of suffering;
7. 15:17–21 – the ceremony, treaty and conditions.

By some accounts (Ibn Ezra), the chapter should be divided into two halves, the first consisting of sections one and two above (the promise of reward, the lament for children and sign of the stars), and the second half consisting of the remainder of the chapter (the story of the Covenant between the Pieces). If this is correct, it seems hard to interpret the covenant between the pieces as a response to the treaty refusal of chapter fourteen.

In fact, I have implicitly argued for a different interpretation of the structure of chapter fifteen. The entire chapter constitutes a single unit focused on the Covenant between the Pieces from the very start (see Ramban). Section two, the lament for children and the sign of the stars, constitutes a digression, a textual and thematic interruption by Abraham. While God is concerned with granting the treaty, Abraham is concerned by his childlessness. God grants Abraham a sign and quickly returns to the topic at hand, the land and the treaty (section three).

On this account, the structure of the chapter consists of God's attempt to contract the Covenant between the Pieces and a series of digressions initiated by Abraham. Theoretically, if Abraham had not spoken in response, the action could have consisted of sections one, three, five, and seven – no sign of the stars, no question of "how will I know," and no promise of suffering. All of this (sections two, four and six) constitutes a series of questions and responses – digressions initiated by Abraham. They are secondary to God's central agenda in chapter fifteen.

Once again, this time from a structural-thematic perspective, we arrive at the same conclusion. The promise of suffering connects to Abraham's speech. The knowledge comes to Abraham as a result of his request for knowledge.

IV.

In commenting on Isaiah's accusation that "Your first father sinned" (Isaiah 43:27), Rashi pithily states: "By saying, 'By what shall I know?'" Apparently, in explicating Isaiah, Rashi expresses the opinion that Abraham's statement in chapter fifteen of Genesis – "God, by what shall I know that I shall inherit it?" (15:8) – constitutes a sin. This does not seem unreasonable. God has already repeatedly promised the land to Abraham and just stated that He brought Abraham from Ur Kasdim to give him the land to inherit. Abraham's response seems to be something along the lines of, "How do I really know that?" Abraham's reply appears brazen and skeptical.

If so, we may be inclined to interpret the "knowledge" of 15:12–14, the promise of suffering and exile, as almost a measure-for-measure punishment for Abraham's query. Abraham expresses skepticism, a lack of trust, and desires immediate knowledge, perhaps even immediate concrete fulfillment of the prior promises. The problem is precisely the long path, the delays and the difficulties. God greets Abraham's demand with a different type of knowledge – the knowledge that an even longer path, more difficulty and suffering lie ahead. This is in fact the opinion held by the *Amora* Shmuel (*Nedarim* 32a): the exile in Egypt constitutes a punishment for Abraham's demand.

Although this reading does explain the connection between Abraham's request (15:8) and the inclusion of the promise of suffering (15:12–14) argued for above, it seems a bit extreme. Does Abraham's crime justify a four-hundred-year punishment of his descendants? For that matter, Abraham's request may not even be a crime. Many biblical interpreters have read the question as an expression not of mistrust but rather of uncertainty. How does Abraham know that he will not sin in the future? How does he know that his descendants will not sin? How does he know that the current inhabitants will not repent? Abraham's question rises from the depths of his self-doubt, not his mistrust of God. Abraham asks for certainty, not out of impatience but out of confusion and concern. His desire for knowledge and guarantee is reasonable and legitimate (Ibn Ezra, Ramban, Seforno, Abarbanel).

If so, we have not yet arrived at an understanding of the connection. If we refrain from reading Abraham's request as a brazen expression of mistrust, we cannot interpret the inclusion of suffering as a measure-for-measure punishment. We still do not understand the inclusion of suffering in the covenant between the pieces.

V.

The imagery of affliction and suffering resurfaces in a striking fashion in chapter sixteen. The core scene of the chapter is, of course, familiar. Pregnant with Abraham's child, desperate to escape the suffering and affliction inflicted on her by Sarai, Hagar flees to the wilderness. There, alongside a spring, she is found, informed and instructed by an angel of God.

In describing Sarai's persecution of Hagar, the text (16:6) utilizes the same term for affliction utilized previously in the promise of suffering (15:13). Both *"vate'aneha"* (16:6) and *"ve'inu"* (15:13) are variants of the verb stem *a-n-h* .ע.נ.ה, the term for affliction and suffering. Similarly, the angel tells Hagar to return to her mistress to suffer (*vehit'ani*) under her rule (16:9), a second usage of the term for affliction. Finally, Hagar is instructed to name her son Ishmael, meaning "God hears," for God "has heard your affliction/suffering (*onyeikh*)" (16:11).

Interestingly, affliction is not the only linguistic and thematic echo of chapter fifteen found in chapter sixteen. In between being ordered to return to the clutches of her mistress (16:9) and being instructed to name her child Ishmael (6:10), Hagar is promised that her "seed" (*zar'ekh*) will be "much" multiplied (*harbeh arbeh*). Her descendants will be uncountable. But this, of course, is the promise and language of first half of chapter fifteen. Abraham is promised "much" (*harbeh*, 15:1), and told in the "sign of the stars" that his descendants will be uncountable (15:5).

Finally, the name Hagar, which appears seven times in the chapter (16:1, 3, 4, 8, 15–16), and the title, "Egyptian maidservant" or "maidservant," constitute a linguistic pun and thematic parallel to the status of *"ger"* (stranger) and *"eved"* (servant or slave) promised to Abraham's descendants (15:13). Hagar is a stranger in both name and fact. After all, she is from Egypt, a different land. She serves and slaves far from her place. This is exactly the promise made to Abraham. It almost need not be mentioned that she is Egyptian, a slave for residents of Canaan. The descendants of those Canaan residents will, of course, be strangers and slaves in Egypt.

In total, factoring in the promise of place and future nationhood made to Hagar's descendants at the end of the angel's instructions (16:12), the joint paradigm of both chapters fifteen and sixteen includes four elements: 1. the status of stranger-servant-slave, 2. affliction and suffering, 3. multiplication of seed bordering on the uncountable, and 4. future nationhood. What are we to make of this parallel?

The key to deciphering the meaning of the parallel may lie not in the overlap between the chapters, but in a central addition to the paradigm that occurs in the story of Hagar and the angel. As pointed out above, in between step three, multiplication of seed, and step four, future nationhood – and as a transition between the two stages – the angel informs Hagar that she is pregnant and will bear a son. He is to be named Ishmael, "for God has heard your affliction/suffering (*onyeikh*)" (16:11). God hears the suffering of the oppressed. In fact, on both the textual and logical levels, God's sensitivity and response to the suffering of the oppressed constitutes an intermediate stage between the negative and positive parts of the paradigm. God's "hearing" of the downtrodden leads Him to multiply them and give them nationhood and place. In fact, the paradigm contains a fifth and key element: God's "hearing."

Our paradigm is, in fact, the paradigm of "Oppression and Redemption," or, perhaps more accurately, exodus. This is confirmed not just by the parallel to the Covenant between the Pieces, which obviously anticipates the redemption from Egypt, but also by a quick glance at the book of Exodus. At the beginning of Exodus, we are repeatedly told that the Egyptians enslaved and "afflicted" the children of Israel (Ex. 1:11–14). Nevertheless, "the more they afflicted them (*ya'anu*), the more they multiplied" (1:12). The connection is obvious. Just as in the story of Hagar and the angel, and counter to the expected, the downtrodden grow and multiply.

Similarly, the beginnings of redemption from Egyptian affliction parallel the Hagar-angel story. As a preface to Moses' first meeting with God (at the burning bush, Ex. 3:1–4:17), the Torah tells us that the children of Israel groaned and cried from the burden of their work (2:23). God "hears" (2:24) and the redemption begins to unfold.

A careful tracking of the points above should bring us to a relatively counter-intuitive conclusion. The redemption from Egypt is not the first or only time that God has redeemed. It is not the sole example of this paradigm in history. God has also redeemed Hagar-Ishmael. They, too, have suffered, and have been granted by God, in His mercy and justice, multiplication, redemption and nationhood. In fact, this claim is confirmed by the prophet Amos. In comforting and, ironically, simultaneously chastising the Israelites, Amos states:

> Are you not as much to me as the children of the *Kushiyyim*, O children of Israel? says God. Have I not brought up Israel out of

the land of Egypt? And the Philistines from Caphtor, and Aram from Kir?" (Amos 9:7)

Apparently, Israel is not the only nation to have been redeemed and given place and nationhood. The same has happened to the Philistines, Arameans and the Ishmaelites.

The point seems to be that the "Oppression and Redemption" paradigm, involving suffering and God's response, does not necessarily involve any particular merit on the part of the sufferer and redeemed. Neither the Philistines, the Arameans, Hagar, Ishmael or the Ishmaelites are particularly virtuous characters according to the Bible. The very introduction of the paradigm, the story of Hagar and the angel, informs us that Ishmael, despite his inspired name and origins, will become no more than "a wild ass of a man" (16:12), one whose "hand will be against every man, and every man's hand against him" (ibid.). The paradigm is a manifestation of God's normal or natural mode of running the world, what we traditionally term "general providence," rather than the product of any special tampering with God's standard rules for history.

VI.

Let us briefly turn to the conclusion of chapter sixteen. At the end of the chapter, the Torah informs us that Abraham named his son Ishmael (16:15). I have always been bothered by this formulation. How does Abraham know to name the boy Ishmael? After all, Abraham is conspicuously absent from the core scene of the chapter, Hagar and the angel (16:7–14). The revelation and instructions are delivered to Hagar, not to Abraham. The simple answer is that Hagar reports the events to Abraham upon her return (Ramban). If so, Abraham's acceptance of her bizarre story and the consequent naming of Ishmael constitute a crucial turning point in Abraham's character and conscience.

On the simplest level, the naming reflects the recognition that it was wrong to abuse Hagar. God now grants His instructions to a wretched maidservant, not to Abraham, the normal address. On a deeper level, believing Hagar and naming the child Ishmael reflects learning and internalizing the lesson of the paradigm sketched above. God cares for the wretched and oppressed. He multiplies them and gives them nationhood. This is God's way, without condition, and without the requirement of special righteousness on the part of the oppressed.

To close the circle, the story of chapter sixteen, the conception and birth of Ishmael, is also a story about God and Abraham. It is about teaching Abraham the ways of God, the paradigm of "Oppression and Redemption." If so, the "promise of suffering," the inclusion of exile and affliction in the Covenant between the Pieces, and the events of chapter sixteen, the learning of God's ways, jointly provide an answer to Abraham's confusion and original question of "How do I know?"

Abraham is uncertain, after all; he or his descendants may be undeserving of nationhood. By what virtue will they inherit the land? God's response is two-tiered. First, He reveals to Abraham the fact – perhaps as punishment, perhaps for the eventual benefit of the Children of Israel, or perhaps as part of the normal ebb and flow of history and human free will – that his descendants will suffer and be afflicted in a foreign land. But this is only the first stage. Affliction triggers God's unconditional action. God hears the oppressed, brings them to their own place and grants them nationhood. Hence, God will similarly redeem Abraham's descendants. Even if Abraham sins, even if his descendants sin, God's rules of history, caring and redemption are immutable and unchangeable. God will grant Abraham's descendants nationhood and bring them to their land.

Hence, we have arrived at an alternate explanation of the connection between Abraham's request for knowledge and the inclusion of suffering in the Covenant between the Pieces. The connection is not necessarily one of sin and punishment. Rather, it is about the ever-evolving relationship between God and Abraham and the learning of God's ways. It is about learning the lesson of the "Oppression and Redemption" paradigm, the divine rules of history and divine caring for the oppressed. This lesson began in the Covenant between the Pieces and is continued, expanded and repeated in chapter sixteen.

VII.

In the above, I have attempted to explain the inclusion of "the promise of suffering" in the Covenant between the Pieces. Why does Abraham need to know? On the assumption that the knowledge he receives stems from his request for knowledge, I have explained the inclusion as either a product of a sin-punishment dynamic or, preferably, part and parcel of Abraham's ongoing education in the ways of God, a response to his uncertainty rather than his sin.

Along the way, I have argued for a particular reading of chapters 14–16, the core of *Parashat Lekh Lekha*. On the one hand, chapter fifteen, the covenant between the pieces, constitutes a response to Abraham's refusal of reward and treaty in chapter fourteen. On the other hand, through the ongoing dialogue between God and Abraham in the chapter, through the process of working through Abraham's desires and anxieties, it introduces a new paradigm, the model of "Oppression and Redemption," repeated and elaborated in the ensuing chapter, the story of Hagar and Ishmael.

Finally, I have also maintained that the redemption from Egypt, the story of the first part of Exodus, constitutes an occurrence of the "Oppression and Redemption" model. The children of Israel are strangers in a foreign land, enslaved and afflicted. They multiply, are heard by God, and eventually are brought to their land, to full nationhood. We might be inclined to draw the conclusion that this is all there is to the redemption from Egypt. It is a normal process, driven by God's response to suffering, part of the standard way that God runs the world. But this would be an error. The redemption of the Jewish people involves far more than just mercy and justice for the oppressed.

Let us take a look at the verse that prefaces the encounter at the burning bush, the first stirrings of redemption:

> And God heard their groaning, and God remembered His covenant, and Abraham and Isaac and Jacob... and God knew. (Ex. 2:23–4)

God not only hears, but also remembers the covenant and the forefathers. The redemption of the children of Israel is not just about the ironclad rule of Oppression and Redemption. It is not just about God caring for the pain and hearing the suffering of the afflicted. It is also about the covenantal relationship between God, the forefathers and their descendants. It is not just universal but also particular. It is not just normal but also supra-normal.

In the language of our discussion, it is not just about the link between chapters fifteen and sixteen of Genesis, the paradigm of Oppression and Redemption. Rather, it is also about the link between chapter fifteen and chapter fourteen of Genesis. It is a reward for the unique action of Abraham, who, forsaking all material and temporal compensation, received instead a unique relationship with God, a covenant with the divine.

Parashat Vayera

The Changed Abraham

by Rav Ezra Bick

T he story of Abraham and the angels is so full of incidental lessons – the mitzva of visiting the sick (God visiting Abraham, Rashi on 18:1), the mitzva of welcoming strangers (Abraham running about to feed the "men," cf. *Shabbat* 127a), the permissibility to tell a "white lie" (God changing the account of what Sara said about Abraham's age, Rashi on 18:13), the modesty of Sara (Rashi on 18:9) – that we are wont to ignore the perplexing nature of the story itself. For what purpose did the angels come to visit Abraham? The obvious answer is to inform him of the impending birth of Isaac. But this merely forces us to develop our question further.

1. Why is it important to inform Abraham that Sara will give birth in one year? God has promised him children since the beginning of *Lekh Lekha*. Neither Rebecca nor Rachel, who were both barren, received prior notice of their impending pregnancy. What is the importance to us, the readers, of the fact that there was a year's advance notice?

2. More specifically, God had already told Abraham the same thing just a day or two earlier. When commanding Abram to perform

mila, God changed his name to Abraham and Sarai's to Sara, adding, "I shall bless her and also give you from her a son" (17:16). A few verses later, God tells Abraham explicitly, "But Sara your wife will bear a son for you, and you shall call his name Isaac... and I will establish my covenant with Isaac, whom Sara will bear for you **at this time in the next year**" (17:19–21). This is nearly identical to the message of the angels.[1]

3. Why angels? As we pointed out, God Himself had told Abraham the same news. What's more, God has appeared to Abraham at the time the angels come to his tent. It surely appears very strange that God has sent angels to tell Abraham (or Sara) the good news when He Himself is in the midst of speaking to him. No sooner do the angels leave than God continues His conversation with Abraham. I think we are justified in not expecting someone like Abraham, to whom God spoke often, to have to rely on angels for the message of God. In the Torah, other than Abraham, we find angels speaking only to people who have not merited a more direct communication from God, such as Hagar, Lot, or Balaam. Generally, prophets are spoken to by God, while others have extraordinary experiences of meeting an angel. Abraham is spoken to twice by angels – here, and later at the climax of the *Akeda*. Why?

I think the answer to these questions, as well as the key to understanding *Parashat Vayera* in general, is rooted in the last section of *Lekh Lekha*. Brit Mila, the physical induction of Abraham into a covenant with God, introduced by the words, "Walk before Me and be perfect," constituted a transformation of the basic relationship of Abraham to

---

1. Ramban surmises that Abraham had not told Sara this piece of news, perhaps because he immediately performed mila, and then was ill. Hence the purpose of the angels' visit was to inform Sara of what Abraham already knew. Aside from the unlikelihood of Abraham "forgetting" to tell his wife that after thirty years she is about to bear a son, I think the Torah itself indicates that this is not so. God changed Sarai's name to Sara. From that point on, she is only called Sara, including by the angels when they ask about her. It seems clear that Abraham had already told her of her new name; how then could he not have told her of the birth of Isaac?

the natural world. In *Lekh Lekha*, Abraham reacts to the surrounding world according to the rules of nature and society, even as he is aided by God. He fights a battle with his private army. God helps him by granting him victory, but nevertheless he has to fight, using his own powers. Abraham lives on earth, even as, when he has a problem, God speaks to him from the heaven. But after Brit Mila, Abraham is no longer merely a saintly inhabitant of earth, a relatively better member of human society. Now, he walks with God. The Abarbanel perceptively deduces from the absence of Abraham's name in the opening verse – "God appeared to him in Elonei Mamreh," rather than "God appeared to Abraham in Elonei Mamreh" – that this appearance is an immediate continuation of the Brit Mila, despite the new *parasha*. But there seems to be no purpose for this appearance, no message from God to Abraham. The answer is that in this case, the appearance is its own purpose. After Brit Mila, God visits Abraham to spend time with him, in fellowship, for Abraham now belongs to the society of God and not that of men. Previously, God appeared to Abraham to tell him something specific. Here, it symbolizes their fellowship. Brit Mila has changed Abraham's status from that of a righteous individual to that of *"yedid HaShem,"* a part of the spiritual community. He is *"ba'al berit"* HaShem rather than *"ba'al berit"* Aner, Eshkol, and Mamreh.

Now we come to the visit of the angels. Ḥazal say that when they meet Abraham they are called "men," whereas when meeting Lot they are referred to as "angels," because Abraham was used to angels, so they appeared to him as men, whereas for Lot it was a novelty. I would like to suggest that this means that the presence of angels in Abraham's company, from this point on, is the presence of his fellows, his natural environment. "Walk before me and be perfect." Walking before God, as the retinue of the king, is what we imagine angels do. Abraham lives amidst the angels now, so angels appear to him as men.

What is the difference between the announcement by God of Isaac's birth in *Lekh Lekha* and that of the angel here? Notice the introduction – "I shall return to you in one year (*ka'et ḥaya*) and behold, a son, of Sara your wife." The angel doesn't merely predict the birth, he states that his presence will be with Abraham and it will be manifested in the presence of a son. In other words, the presence of angels, of God, of a heavenly environment in Abraham's house expresses itself naturally in creation and rejuvenation. Not "I will give you a son," but "behold, a son." Sara picks up on this immediately. "After I am worn, shall I experience rejuvenation?" In Abraham's case, it will be very unusual to have a child at such an advanced age, but for Sara, it requires transcendence of time, a return to her youth. Abraham has a child "in his old age" (21:2, 7), but Sara has actually become young again. Not having directly experienced Brit Mila, though included in its results (her name is changed too), Sara laughs in amazement at the thought. The usual flow of time has become meaningless in Abraham's house. The angels do not come merely to **inform**, they come to **produce** the effect itself (just as they destroy Sodom, and, according to Hazal, they cure Abraham). The presence of angels here symbolizes the spirit of God and its workings, not as a miracle from afar to correct a difficult situation, but rather as a total transformation of the conditions of Abraham's life in this world.

All of *Parashat Vayera* reflects this new transcendent state of Abraham. As the angels leave Abraham, God states, "Shall I conceal from Abraham that which I am going to do?" Abraham has become a partner of God's in running the world, a companion, one who shares in the responsibility. "Abraham will become a great and mighty nation and in him, **all the nations of the earth will be blessed.**" Can God act in Sodom without telling Abraham?

Abraham argues with God about God's role in the world – "The judge of all the earth, shall He not do justice?" Abraham is no longer merely an inhabitant of the lower world, but one who is engaged in defining how it should be run from above.

Why was Sodom destroyed? The Torah does not elaborate what was so unusually terrible about Sodom, other than a hint that they did not appreciate guests. Surely, there were other cities around the world that were not particularly hospitable that did not suffer this incredible plight. I think the answer is rooted in Abraham's new state – hence the same angels who visit Abraham destroy Sodom. Sodom is destroyed because *Eretz Yisrael* does not suffer evil. Compare:

> The last generation, your children who will come after you, and the stranger who will come from a far land, shall say, when they

see the plagues of that land (of Israel) and its sickness, which God has laid upon it. Brimstone, and salt, and burning all the land, not sown, nor growing, nor producing any grass, like the overthrow of Sodom and Gomorrah, Adma and Zeboim, which God overthrew in his rage and anger. And all the nations shall ask, why... And God rooted them out of their land. (Deut. 29:21–27)

The destruction of the people is not emphasized as much as the destruction of the land. Why is Sodom destroyed by angels who are coming from visiting Abraham after his Brit Mila? This, too, is a reflection of the elevation of Abraham above the natural order. *Eretz Yisrael*, the land given to Abraham, is no longer a normal land, obeying the natural laws of nature. It is the earthly home of the companions of God, a land which itself cannot suffer wickedness. The same angels (i.e. the presence of God) who, by their presence in Abraham's house, rejuvenate Sara and Abraham via Isaac, bring down brimstone and fire by their presence in Sodom.

In *Lekh Lekha*, Abraham saves Lot by attacking the kings who have taken him captive. In *Vayera*, he saves him once again simply because God, remembering his companion Abraham, separates Lot from his environment, a pale reflection of Abraham's separation from his environment.

Finally, Abimelekh takes Sara to his palace, as Pharaoh had done earlier. In the first case, a plague (which, of course, we know comes from God) afflicts Pharaoh, and he hurries to return Sara. This time, God Himself comes to tell Abimelekh to return Sara. The Midrash and the commentators can barely restrain their astonishment that Abimelekh merits the word of God. I think the focus should not be the merit of Abimelekh, but rather on the relationship of Abraham and God. Someone has caused Abraham a very serious and personal problem. God intervenes personally to set it right. God adds – "Now return the man's wife, for he is a prophet, and he will pray for you and you will live" (20:7). In relation to the inhabitants of the land, Abraham has almost magical powers to intercede with God and cure the sick. God is telling Abimelekh, "You have a problem, but Abraham has *"protektzia"* with Me; he is one of My own, so he can help you."

Vayera is a new *parasha* because it is a totally new stage in the life

of Abraham. It is rooted narratively, however, in the end of *Lekh Lekha*.
The Brit Mila of Abram concludes the story of a righteous man; the visit
of the angels to Abraham commences the story of heavenly man, what
Ḥazal call "*merkava liShekhina.*"

"At the Tent's Entrance" – Revelation to Abraham vs. Revelation to Moses

by Rav Tamir Granot

I n several instances in the biblical narrative, we find a phenomenon whereby one story "quotes" another – whether explicitly or by means of repeating linguistic expressions, a similar structure, or even a similar sketching of the narrative images. Reading the account of the revelation by God and the angels to Abraham, bringing tidings of the future birth of Isaac (Gen. ch. 18), we notes echoes of the description of the *Ohel Moed* ("Tent of Meeting") that Moses erected following the sin of the Golden Calf and in the subsequent story of the Second Covenant and God's revelation to Moses (Ex. ch. 33–34:10).

Let us first present the parallels between the two situations along the axis of the story of God's revelation to Abraham, following the order of the verses. Thereafter we shall elaborate slightly concerning each parallel in order:

GENESIS CH. 18:

He was sitting at the entrance to the tent (v. 1)

and behold, three men **were standing** before him [God reveals Himself] (v. 2)

And he ran towards them, and prostrated himself to the ground. And Abraham hurried (v. 2, 6)

And he said: My Lord, if I have found favor in Your eyes, do not pass over from before Your servant (v. 3)

And Abraham hurried **to the tent, to Sara**, and he said... **"and my husband [*adoni*] is old"** ... (v. 6, 12)

And afterwards you shall move on, since you have **passed to come to your servant** (v. 5)

Is anything too wondrous for God? (v. 14)

They shall **keep the way of God** (v. 19)

For I have known him (v. 19)

EXODUS CH. 33–34:

...Every man at the **entrance to his tent**...The pillar of cloud would descend and stand at the **entrance to the tent** and [God] spoke with Moses. [When Moses hides himself in the crevice of the rock, God also passes over the opening.] [2] (33:8–10)

And **he stood** with him there (34:5)

Moses hurried, and he bowed down to the ground and prostrated himself (34:8)

And he said: if I have found favor in Your eyes, God, let God then go amongst us, for they are a stiff-necked nation (34:9)

And his servant **Joshua Bin-Nun, a young man, did not move from inside the tent"** (33:11); **my master, Moses** – restrain them! (Num. 11:28)

I shall cause all My goodness to pass over before you. And it shall be, **when my glory passes** ... until **I have passed over**. And **God passed before him** ... (33:19)

So I and Your nation **shall be a source of wonder**; before all your nation **I shall perform wonders** (33:16, 34:10)

Let me know **Your ways** (33:13)

I shall know You by name (33:17)

Let us now examine these parallels in greater detail:

1. "God appeared to him in Elonei Mamreh, while he was sitting at the entrance to the tent, in the heat of the day" (Gen. 18:1) – God's revelation here is described using the verb "appeared" (*vayera*), which is quite common in such instances. Correspondingly, Moses asks "Show me [*hareni*] Your glory" (Ex. 33:19). But the place of revelation is interesting: **the entrance to the tent**. After describing what the Levites do after the Golden Calf, there is a description of the Tent of Meeting that Moses sets up. "... [and] the pillar of cloud would descend **and stand at the entrance to the tent**, and [God] spoke with Moses" (ibid. 33:7). In both stories the revelation takes place **at the entrance to the tent**. The parallel here is both thematic and linguistic. Further on, in the story of the Revelation at Sinai, we find a similar picture. God commands Moses, "You shall stand by the rock," and then, "It shall be, when My glory passes by, **I shall place you in a crevice of the rock**, and I shall cover you with My hand until I have passed ..." (ibid. 33:21–22). The rock is similar to the tent. God comes from outside the tent, and when He passes by, Abraham tries to detain Him, to speak to Him. God also comes from outside of the rock; when He passes by, Moses tries to take in whatever he can.

Still, the revelation at the rock is different from the revelation at the tent, for it takes place in a sphere that is super-human. Mount Sinai is also called "the mountain of God." Of course, we cannot say that the mountain is God's "house" (not even in the symbolic sense), for God descends to the mountain from the heavens. Apparently, the mountain is considered a place that mediates between the divine realm and the human one. Either way, its code of conduct is divine rather than human.

It is perhaps for this reason that Moses cannot eat while he is on the mountain – in keeping with the divine "code." This manifests symmetry with the story of Abraham's tent, where God – appearing as an angel – is described as eating, in keeping with the human code of courtesy. In both cases, the guest behaves in accordance with the code commonly practiced by the host.

To this we may add a further parallel: Moses leaves the camp and erects his tent in the desert, far from the camp. Only there can God reveal Himself to him, for the nation is not worthy of the presence of God's glory: "For I shall not go up among you…" Abraham, too, pitches his tent outside of any inhabited area, in the desert.

This is an important point that helps us understand his relations with the Canaanites: Abraham does not dwell among them; he does not become a citizen. This works to his disadvantage when he seeks a burial plot for Sara, but it does allow him to experience divine revelation – because he is outside of the pagan, morally blemished inhabited area. (Interestingly, Lot lives in Sodom, in a permanent dwelling. He is one of the locals. The difference between him and Abraham – with regard to their attitude towards the local population – is quite apparent.)

2. Similar language is used to describe the respective revelations: "And behold, three men **were standing** before him" (Gen. 18:2); "God descended in a cloud and **stood with him** there" (Ex. 34:5). The continuation of this latter verse is reminiscent of a verse that admittedly has nothing to do with the story of the angels, but is nevertheless common to Abraham and to Moses: "And he **called in God's name**" (Gen. 12:8; Ex. 34:5).

3. Both Abraham and Moses hurry to welcome the Divine Presence before it moves on: "He saw – **and he ran** towards them from the entrance to the tent." Immediately thereafter, we read, "And Abraham **hurried** to the tent and he said, 'Quickly prepare three measures of fine meal…'" (Gen. 18:2, 6). Concerning Moses, who sees the Divine Presence passing over, we read: "Moses **hurried** and bowed down to the ground and prostrated himself" (Ex. 34:8). In Abraham's case, too, the "hurrying" leads up to prostration: "He hurried towards them from the entrance to the tent, and prostrated himself to the ground" (Gen. 18:2).

4. We discover a surprising and most important point when comparing what Abraham and Moses say, at the time of the respective revelations:

> Abraham says: "My Lord, if I have found favor in Your eyes, please do not pass over from before Your servant." (Gen. 18:3)

> Moses says: "If I have found favor in Your eyes, my Lord, let my Lord go amongst us." (Ex. 34:9)

Attention should be paid to the fact that in both cases there is a request that God tarry and not move on. Both appeal to God with the appellation *"Adonai"* – "my Lord." In both instances, the request that God remain is uttered against the background of the presence of an angel, or angels. Abraham sees three men, but he addresses himself only to the most senior one, using a holy name. In Moses' case, the significance of the appeal is actually an attempt to change the divine decree that has come about in the wake of the Golden Calf. "I shall send an angel before you, and I shall drive out … for I shall not ascend among you, for you are a stiff-necked nation …" (Ex. 33:2–3). Moses asks that God remain and journey with the nation, not to remove Himself. Just as when God passes over, Moses tries to persuade Him to remain there with him by "reminding" God, as it were, that He Himself declared that Moses found favor in His eyes. So too, Abraham "reminds" God that he has found favor in His eyes, and therefore he entreats Him not to move on. And in both cases God agrees, remains, and does not move on.

5. There would seem to be a parallel between Sara's status and that of Joshua. Abraham runs to the tent, to Sara. Throughout the scene she remains inside, while the Revelation and the conversation between Abraham and God and the angels takes place at the entrance to the tent, under the tree. Similarly, we are told that Joshua – Moses' servant – does not move from inside the tent (Ex. 33:11), and the speech takes place at the entrance to the tent with Joshua inside. Both Sara and Joshua call Abraham and Moses, respectively, *"adoni"* – "my master": "My husband [*adoni*] is old …" (18:12); "My master [*adoni*], Moses – restrain them!" (Num. 11:28).

6. In both narratives, God's presence is described using the expression "passing over/on/by" (*la'avor al*). Abraham says, "...Feast yourselves, afterwards you will pass on, since you have passed by your servant" (18:5). In His words to Moses, God says, "I shall cause all My goodness to pass over before you," and thereafter, "And it shall be, when My glory passes over...until I have passed by" (Ex. 33:19; etc.), and finally, "And God passed over before him, and He called out..." (34:6).

7. In both cases the text makes use of the Hebrew root *p-l-a* (פלא). First, Moses asks, "How then shall it be known that I have found favor in Your eyes, I and Your nation? Is it not by Your going with us, that I and Your nation shall be **wondrous** [ונפלינו]" (Ex. 33:16); thereafter, God promises, "Before all your nation I shall perform **wonders** [נפלאות]" (ibid. 34:10). The "senior angel" chides Abraham, "Is anything too wondrous [היפלא] for God?" (Gen. 18:14). The significance of this expression in both narratives appears to be similar: something that is "wondrous" is unique, special, different, distinguishable from others. Moses asks that *Am Yisrael* be made wondrous – noticeably different – and God promises to perform wondrous acts that are unheard of in the world among other nations. Similarly, Abraham is asked, "Is anything too wondrous for God?" – meaning, is there anything that is foreign to God's power, anything that is different from what His abilities can accomplish?

8. In both cases the text speaks of "the way of God." The choice of Abraham is explained with the words, "For I know him...they will follow the way of God..." (Gen. 18:19), while Moses asks, "Show me Your way" (Ex. 33:13).

9. God's special relationship with each of these two personalities is described using the same expression: "**for I know him**" (Gen. 18:19); "For you have found favor in My eyes **and I know you** by name" (Ex. 33:17).

From the parallels discussed above, we conclude that the Torah is drawing our attention to a special connection between the two narratives. Let us now examine two possible ways of explaining the significance of this connection.

1. Revelation at the entrance to the tent: We have already mentioned that in both cases God's revelation takes place at the entrance to the tent. In the book of Exodus, this fact would appear to have added significance; the description of the "private" Tent of Meeting that Moses erects follows on God's announcement that He will not journey amongst *Benei Yisrael*. Moses draws the obvious conclusion – that he can no longer come into contact with the Divine Presence – and he therefore pitches "the Tent" outside of the Israelite encampment. It is from there that he conducts his quest for God: "And it was, that anyone who sought God would go out to the Tent of Meeting..." (Ex. 33:7). The commentators are divided as to the status of this tent. Rashi, along with many others who adopt his view, explains that this was a temporary arrangement that ceased with the establishment of the *Mishkan*. This would seem the most likely scenario, based on the narrative logic, and it would appear that whenever the Tent of Meeting is mentioned after this temporary period, it may be identified with the *Mishkan* that is familiar to us, which is also called the "Tent of Meeting." But the commentators who adopt this view fail to address the manner of the revelation. The difference between the Tent of Meeting – meaning the *Mishkan* – and the tent that Moses pitches is not only that the former sits in the very middle of the camp while the latter is outside of it. The more important difference is that in the case of the *Mishkan*, revelation takes place within it, at its heart: "from above the covering, between the two cherubim." Moses is always outside; he enters only when he is invited as God's guest, to His "house" – the *Mishkan*. In Moses' Tent of Meeting the situation is reversed: the tent is Moses' own, private domain. Joshua dwells constantly within this tent – something quite unimaginable in the case of the *Mishkan*. When God wants to speak with Moses, He descends and stands "at the entrance to the tent"; Moses goes out to Him and converses with Him. Here, Moses is the "host," as it were, and God the "guest." The visit is temporary and brief. It is only to show honor to the host that God reveals Himself in this place.

Moses' Tent of Meeting is erected precisely when the nation of Israel is not worthy of having the Divine Presence rest among them: "I shall not ascend among you" (ibid. 33:7). God comes to visit Moses by virtue of Moses' own personal stature. Even when the nation is undeserving – the prophet may be deserving. And it is precisely God's visit to Abraham that may serve as the prototype for such a revelation. God comes to Abraham because of his personal merit. He visits him – simply and literally. Abraham's tent – or, more accurately, the entrance to his tent – is the place of their meeting. Abraham, after all, supports his request, "Please do not pass on from before Your servant," with the preamble, "If I have found favor in Your eyes" (Gen. 18:3). The finding of favor is the justification for revelation to Abraham – as well as for the promise that follows. And Moses, likewise, exploits the fact that he, too, has found favor.

The episode in chapter twelve of Numbers – the story of Aaron and Miriam's complaint against Moses – can now be added to all that we have said above. Here, the main theme of the narrative is Moses' special elevated status in comparison with his brother and sister – his unique merit as a prophet. Obviously, in this instance, God chooses to reveal Himself in Moses' tent, not in the Tent serving the entire community, because He wants to emphasize that the revelation in this instance is by virtue and merit of Moses. Thereby, He demonstrates to Aaron and Miriam their mistake, for they said, "Has He not also spoken with us?" (Num. 12:2). God shows that His revelation to Moses is exclusive – and He does so through revelation at the entrance to Moses' Tent.

Attention should be paid to another connection between the revelations to Moses and Abraham respectively – a connection which requires close examination in its own right. The Torah testifies that Moses is the only person with whom God spoke "mouth to mouth" (Num. ch. 12), or "face to face" (Ex. ch. 33). The other prophets experienced prophecy in a dream or vision, or through the agency of an angel. Indeed, elsewhere in Tanach, wherever we find a full description of revelation (rather than just "So says God" or "God told him"), it takes place when the prophet is not awake (see, for example, the story of Balaam), or an angel is described as appearing to mediate. But here, in the story of Abraham (Gen. ch. 18), the situation is different: God reveals Himself to Abraham face to face, while Abraham is fully conscious and not dreaming. The proximity between God and the prophet (Abraham and Moses) is tangible. It is difficult to determine whether, in metaphysical terms, the revelation to Abraham is qualitatively different or whether it resembles the revelation through an angel that we find elsewhere. But, at least on the narrative level, it appears that the level of intimacy – the direct and close conversation between God and Abraham that takes place here – is very powerful, and is paralleled only in the case of Moses.

11. The status of Moses: We would like to suggest that the crux of the parallel concerns Moses' status. What the Torah means to tell us is that Moses here attains a status like that of Abraham. God Himself visits him, just as He visited Abraham, in his own personal tent. The visit is only to him, and it is by God Himself – not just an angel. Both Abraham and Moses find favor in God's eyes, and therefore He reveals Himself to them and answers their requests. If we continue this line of thought, we arrive at the possibility that the Torah is making an important statement about the forgiveness for the sin of the Golden Calf. At first, while Israel sinned and Moses was still atop the mountain, God suggested, "Now, leave Me alone that My anger may burn against them, and I shall consume them and make you into a great nation…" (Ex. 32:10). In other words, God tells Moses that he will be the father of a new nation. The expression "I shall make you into a great nation" echoes the promise to Abraham, the father of the Jewish nation: "God said to Abraham: Go forth… and I shall make of you a great nation" (Gen. 12:1–2). Again, following the visit by the angels, we read, "God said: Can I hide from Abraham… for Abraham shall surely become a great and mighty nation, and all the nations of the world will be blessed through him" (ibid. 18:17–18). God is suggesting that Moses take Abraham's place and become the new forefather of the nation.

Moses refuses the proposal, and supports his refusal by referring to the merit of the forefathers: "Remember for Abraham, for Isaac and for Israel… I shall multiply your seed" (Ex. 32:13). We usually think that the matter ended there, but perhaps this is not so. Maybe the text means to teach us that the Second Covenant, and the second set of Tablets – and especially God's acquiescence to the request that He go amongst the nation – are obtained solely by Moses' personal merit. Thus Moses becomes the forefather of the nation – not genealogically (i.e., not as father of the dynasty), as God proposes, but juridically – and perhaps also metaphysically, for the continued existence of the nation is all by his merit. Indeed, God explains His acquiescence with the words, "For you have found favor in My eyes, and I know you by name" (Ex. 33:17). Moses' stature and beloved status are the reason. And this understanding allows us to see that these two narratives, which at first glance appear so thematically different, actually deal with the same subject: the beginnings of the nation. The story of Abraham centers around the tidings of the son about to be born, representing the fulfillment of the promise, "I shall make your seed like the dust of the earth" (Gen. 13:16), and this is the beginning of the establishment of the nation. God makes the unprecedented gesture of coming right to the entrance of Abraham's tent in order to tell him about the beginning of the establishment of the nation. Similarly, God Himself comes and appears at the entrance to Moses' Tent to teach us that the second "start" of the nation is bound up with the merit of Moses himself. His merit and his prayer saved us, such that God agreed to go amongst us and to enter into a covenant with us.

The linguistic and thematic similarity that we have pointed out in the requests of the two personalities now assumes new significance: Moses asks that God go amongst the nation – i.e., that He "personally" fulfill the covenant, and not just send an angel. This request should be viewed as a re-establishment of the nation as God's nation. God's Tent of Meeting (*Mishkan*) is built in the midst of the camp only by virtue of the prayer offered by Moses from the Tent that is outside of the camp. Similarly, Abraham asks God not to pass by, and he thereby merits God telling him and Sara that the nation will be established through the descendant that will be born to them. We may therefore summarize by saying that the revelation to Moses is described as a mirror image of the revelation to Abraham, so as to link their respective status and to tell us that Moses is the forefather of the nation, like Abraham before him. Just as we are told concerning Abraham, "For I know him," we are told concerning Moses, "I know you by name." In both cases we see that the two personalities are uniquely chosen. In this regard, the concept of the "way of God" is also linked. Abraham is chosen in order that he will command his children and household after him to keep the way of God, to perform righteousness and justice. He immediately proves that he is worthy of this mission by arguing with God for justice on behalf of Sodom. Moses asks God to make His ways known to him, so that he will possess the wherewithal to plead before Him in the future. And God indeed reveals His ways, and Moses goes on to offer (after the sin of the spies) the prayers of the nation. Thus, the characteristic common to both personalities – nullifying personal interest for the sake of the community, for the nation of Israel, or even for Sodom – is the reason for the Torah attaching such importance to them. And this point may also serve to complete the picture: Abraham stands before God and demands justice: "Shall the Judge of all the earth not do justice?!" From him we learn that we may demand justice from the Master of the Universe. Moses demands a different principle: compassion and forgiveness, and God reveals these new ways to him. From Moses we learn that we may demand of God not only justice and righteousness, but also compassion and kindness.

All of the above gives rise to yet another central connection between the two narratives. Both revelations – that of God at the entrance to the tent, to Abraham, and that of God at the entrance of the Tent and in the crevice of the rock, to Moses – take place in the context of the prophet's request for mercy towards a sinful group of people about to be destroyed. Abraham prays for the wicked Sodom, while Moses begs for mercy on behalf of Israel, who have sinned concerning the Golden Calf. Perhaps the text is hinting to us, through all of the parallels, something about the reason for God's selection of Abraham and Moses as forefathers of the nation. They share a special ability to negotiate with God and to ask for mercy by invoking their personal merit on behalf of the collective – even a sinful collective.

"But My Covenant I Shall Establish with Isaac"

by Rav Chanoch Waxman

I.

Great joy, happiness and mirth: these are the central motifs of the first part of chapter twenty-one of Genesis, the story of the birth of Isaac. For example, shortly after reporting Isaac's birth and naming (Gen. 21:1–4), the Torah describes Sara's reaction:

> And God has made laughter [*tzeḥok*] for me, so that all who hear will laugh [Yitzḥak] with me. And she said, 'Who would have said to Abraham, that Sara should give children suck?' For I have borne Abraham a son in his old age." (21:6–7)

Sara celebrates God's miracle. It is an occasion for wondrous astonishment and joy, for herself, Abraham, and all who hear. In fact, Isaac's very name means "laughter" and symbolizes the joy and celebration. In line with this theme, the Hebrew root *tz-h-k* .צ.ח.ק, meaning laughter, appears repeatedly throughout the chapter (21:3, 4, 5, 6, 8, 9, 10, 12).

Nevertheless, all is not just merriment and mirth in this story. Sara's happiness is not yet complete. Without even a pause after the post-birth celebration, Torah describes the events of the day of Isaac's weaning. Upon seeing "the son of Hagar the Egyptian" engaged in "laughter," Sara demands that the "slave" and her "son" be sent away. In Sara's own words: "…for the son of this bondwoman shall not be heir with my son, with Isaac." There is yet a fly in the ointment, a reminder of Sara's long years of childlessness, degradation, and humiliation. Sara insists that the maidservant and her son be expelled and all be conferred upon Isaac, the only authentic heir. Despite Abraham's hesitation and worry regarding his son, God sides with Sara. Hagar and Ishmael are cast out.

The structure of the chapter and the sinister turn outlined above are, of course, understandable. The chapter is really about the "Triumph of Sara." The first section (21:1–5) describes God's "remembering" of Sara and the birth of Isaac, the first component in Sara's vindication. The third section (21:14–21) depicts the expulsion of Ishmael, the second component in Sara's victory. The middle section (21:5–13), analyzed above, provides the cause of Ishmael's expulsion, provides insight into the attitudes of the crucial characters, and acts as a transition between the two components of Sara's triumph.

But herein lies the nub of the matter. While we can easily parse Abraham's hesitation, and at least part of Sara's motivation, we cannot so easily fathom God's confirmation of Sara's demand. Why does He agree? What has Ishmael done besides laugh? Does God simply wish to grant Sara her wish? Are Hagar and Ishmael unsuitable in some way? Are we to chalk this up to the ever-mysterious divine wisdom? In sum, what in fact is the real cause of the expulsion of Ishmael?

II.

Let us turn to the third part of chapter twenty-one (21:14–21), the actual expulsion of Ishmael, treated above as no more than the second component of the vindication of Sara, part and parcel of the "Triumph of Sara."

The action unfolds as follows. Abraham gets up early in the morning, provides Hagar and Ishmael with provisions, and sends them away. They leave, wandering aimlessly in the desert (21:15). At this point, a crisis ensues – they run out of water. Hagar, convinced that Ishmael faces death, abandons him, and breaks down crying (21:15–16). But all is not lost. An angel of God calls to Hagar from heaven, reassures her, reunites her with Ishmael, provides water and promises great nationhood (21:17–20). Finally, we are told of Ishmael's marriage (21:21).

On some plane, it is difficult to maintain our previous interpretation of the section as no more than the second stage of Sara's vindication. For such a purpose, the Torah need only teach us the bare fact of the expulsion, the very first verse of the story. As a story of the triumph of Sara, no more need be said. If we imagine ourselves as typical pro-Sara readers eager to enjoy our foremother's triumph, we might ask: Why do we need to know the details? Who really cares about Hagar and Ishmael's crisis in the desert, the near death experience, the divine rescue, the promises and the marriage? Quite clearly, and counter to our first reading of the chapter, the story is in some real sense about Hagar and Ishmael. But once again, why do we need to know? In more analytic terminology, why does the Torah provide a detailed version of the "Ordeal of Hagar and Ishmael?"

Let us complicate the issue a little further. Upon close analysis, the ordeal of Hagar and Ishmael bears a striking resemblance to another story in *Parashat Vayera*. The narrative opens with the phrase, "And Abraham got up early in the morning," and depicts him as "taking" (21:14). No reader of the Bible can miss the echo. This is Abraham's first action in the *Akeda*, the story of the binding of Isaac. In the *Akeda*, the Torah utilizes the exact same phrase: "And Abraham got up early in the morning," and likewise depicts him as "taking" (22:3). This parallel is not just linguistic. In both cases Abraham rises early to accomplish a divine command. In both cases, the divine command involves a final parting from a son, the expulsion of Ishmael and the sacrifice of Isaac (21:11–12; 22:1–2).

All of this is just the tip of the iceberg. In both cases, a young lad, referred to by the term *"hana'ar"* (21:17–20; 22:5, 12), is endangered in the course of a journey. The respective journeys are described by a term comprising a variation on the Hebrew root *h-l-kh* ה.ל.כ., meaning "go" (21:14; 22:2–3). Furthermore, in both cases the danger threatens the lad as a result of the action of a parent. Hagar wanders aimlessly in the desert, and when dehydration consequently threatens, she casts her son away, leaving him to die under one of the shrubs (21:15–17). The danger to Isaac also stems from a parent. It is the hand and knife of Abraham that threaten Isaac's life (22:10).

More strikingly, in the respective climaxes of the stories, the endangered lad is saved by the call of an angel of God sounding from heaven (21:17; 22:11). In each case, the heavenly intervention is followed by "seeing," a vision that provides the solution to the problem of imminent death: water in the case of Ishmael (21:19), and the ram (as an alternate sacrifice) in the case of Isaac (22:13). Furthermore, in both cases the angel reiterates the promise of future nationhood before departing (21:18; 22:17–18).

Finally, after depicting the young man as having survived his life-threatening ordeal, both narratives turn towards marriage. Chapter twenty-one, the story of Ishmael, informs us of Ishmael's marriage (21:21). On a similar note, chapter twenty-two, the story of Isaac, closes with the genealogy of Naḥor, focusing on the birth of Rebecca, the future wife of our once endangered and now saved youth.

How are we to evaluate this parallel to the binding of Isaac? What does this mean for interpreting the latter part of chapter twenty-one and its inclusion in the Torah?

III.

Recently, some interpreters have begun to refer to the latter half of chapter twenty-one as *"Akedat Yishmael."* According to this line of thinking, the significance of the parallels sketched above lies in the revelation that there is in fact more than one story in the Torah detailing Abraham's submission to the divine will and subsequent "sacrifice" of a son: not just *"Akedat Yitzḥak,"* but also *"Akedat Yishmael,"* the "binding" (or rather expulsion) of Ishmael. Like many events in Abraham's life, the *Akeda* happens twice. Moreover, in a certain sense, the first *Akeda* is a necessary pre-condition for the second. After all, part of the test of *Akedat Yitzḥak* is the fact that all of Abraham's hopes now reside in Isaac. This psychology results not just from the divine decree that "... in Isaac shall your seed be called" (21:12), but also from the brute fact that Isaac is now effectively the only child.

While this is undoubtedly correct, it is only a partial understanding. Interpreting the latter half of chapter twenty-one as a precursor *Akeda* renders the story a narrative about Abraham, his challenge, his test and his success. But once again, we are no further along than before. The details of the "Expulsion of Ishmael" seem to be about Hagar and Ishmael, not about the triumph of Sara, nor about the trial of Abraham.

A review of the parallel between the two stories outlined above should help reinforce this point. Let us try to reduce the joint paradigm to its bare logical bones. In stage one, God orders Abraham to part from a son. In stage two, the lad and a parent (Ishmael-Hagar or Isaac-Abraham) go on a journey. Next, in stage three, during the course of the journey and through the action of the parent, the lad faces life-threatening danger. In stage four, the lad is saved by divine intervention and promised future nationhood. Finally, in stage five, we are given a glimpse of that promised future through a reference to marriage.

This is not just the paradigm of *Akeda*, the test of Abraham's faith. It is also a paradigm of "Journey, Danger and Rescue." The paradigm describes the "maturation journey," the "rite of passage" of the future progenitor of a nation who undergoes a near-death experience before being saved by God. As such, these stories are not just about Abraham and God, they are also about Isaac and Ishmael. As *Akeda*, the stories are about sacrifice and theological truths. As "Journey, Danger and Rescue," they are not just about theological truths. They are also about the parent-child pair and their journey into the crucible of crisis and impending death.

IV.

Defining the common denominator of the "Expulsion of Ishmael" and *Akedat* Yitzhak as an Isaac-Ishmael and parent-child focused paradigm should make us realize that perhaps the differences between the two stories are even more significant than the similarities. Let us turn our attention to some of the more obvious disparities.

In the *Akeda*, Abraham faces a frightening test. Despite all of God's previous promises, he is now required to give up his son – an apparently inexplicable and final reversal. Part of the dramatic tension of the narrative is how Abraham will react to the command, how he will hold up during the ordeal. The Torah relates to these questions in a clear fashion. Abraham is depicted as determined, purposeful and courageous. He gets up early in the morning, prepares the wood, takes Isaac and sets out (22:3). The strange nature of the journey, in which Abraham and Isaac set out for and arrive at "the place," the divinely chosen place, despite the lack of specific directions, further reinforces this point (22:2–4). Of course, it is Abraham's near performance of the act that most greatly emphasizes the themes of purpose, determination and courage.

To a great extent, these themes also characterize Isaac's actions in his own ordeal. Undoubtedly, as pointed out by Rashi (22:8), Isaac knows what is going on. Isaac's dramatic question, "Behold the fire and the wood: but where is the lamb for offering?" (22:7) already hints at Isaac's realization. Leaving behind the servants and failing to bring an animal can only mean one thing. Abraham's tantalizing reply, "God will show the lamb for sacrifice, my son," containing the clear conjunction of "sacrifice" and "son" (22:8), merely confirms Isaac's nascent knowledge. No further dialogue ensues. Isaac soldiers on carrying the wood for his own sacrifice (22:6, 8). He neither cries nor begs for mercy. He is purposeful, determined and courageous. He, too, in the famous phrase, is a "knight of faith."

The text not only emphasizes the parallel qualities of purpose and courage in Abraham and Isaac, but also their unity and togetherness. The Torah utilizes the phrase, "And the two of them went together [*yaḥdav*]," or a variation, three times throughout the narrative – not just before Isaac's full realization of the plan (22:6), but also after Abraham has all but told him outright (Rashi on 22:8); not just before Abraham put the knife to Isaac's throat, but also after, on the journey home (22:19). There is no breakdown, no collapse, and no division in the ordeal of Abraham and Isaac, in their story of "Journey, Danger and Rescue."

This picture mutates radically if we shift back to the first "Journey, Danger and Rescue" story. Unlike Abraham, Hagar possesses no reason to think that the previously granted divine promises have been revoked. After all, the previous promise of future nationhood for her children included "suffering under her mistress's hand" (16:9–12). If anything, her expulsion from Sara's house should appear as an opportunity to put the stage of suffering behind her and move on to a new and promising future. Yet Hagar's behavior in her journey is neither purposeful nor determined nor courageous. In despair, she wanders (21:14), turning her journey into a movement to anywhere or nowhere, the opposite of Abraham's mysterious arrival at "the place." In her purposeless wandering, she endangers her son. In her despair, she casts him away and breaks down crying.

The attitude of despair and breakdown that animates Hagar also spills over to Ishmael. During the preface to the divine rescue, the Torah states that "God heard the voice of the lad" (21:17), a clear echo of the crying "voice" of Hagar just four words previously. Just as Hagar breaks down and cries, so too does Ishmael. Furthermore, let us not forget Ishmael's age. He is at least sixteen years old. His passivity in the story is not the restraint of determination and sacrifice, but of disintegration and tears. Finally, let us not forget verse sixteen:

And she went, and sat down over and against him at the distance of a bowshot, for she said, Let me not see the death of the child. And she sat away from him and lifted up her voice and cried.

In pointed contrast to the *"yaḥdav,"* the togetherness of Abraham and Isaac, Hagar and Ishmael are divided, physically and existentially separate. This is their story of "Journey, Danger and Rescue," a story not of purpose, unity and togetherness in the face of justified cause for despair, but of despair, wandering, breakdown and division.

V.

We began our analysis of chapter twenty-one with a question. What is the reason for Ishmael's expulsion? Why did God agree to Sara's demand? As alluded to previously, numerous responses have been proposed, ranging from sinful behavior on the part of Ishmael (Rashi on 21:9), to the currently popular metaphysical doctrine that the chosen nation can be formed only through the process of "choosing," the pushing aside or purging of one of two possible heirs.

In analyzing the details of the third part of the chapter, the "Expulsion of Ishmael," treating it as a "Journey, Danger and Rescue" story and contrasting it with another such story of that type, *Akedat Yitzḥak*, I have implicitly argued for a new explanation of God's acquiescence. Unlike us, the readers of the Bible, or even Abraham and Sara, God knows the future. God knows the character and capabilities of Abraham and Hagar, of Isaac and Ishmael. God knows how Abraham and Isaac will react to the *Akeda*, to the ordeal of "Journey, Danger and Rescue." He already apprehends their capacities for faith, courage, purposefulness and togetherness. He knows they are cut from a certain cloth.

Likewise, he knows the essence of Hagar and her son Ishmael. He knows how they will respond to their comparatively mild trial of faith, their journey and danger. He knows that despair, division and breakdown are not the best materials from which to mold the nation of Abraham. Consequently, just as God first chose the long-suffering Sara and her child Isaac in the covenant of circumcision (17:15, 19, 21), so too God chooses Sara and her child Isaac here in chapter twenty-one.

To close the circle, the details of the "Expulsion of Ishmael" and the implied contrast to *Akedat Yitzḥak* are about letting us, the readers, in on these insights. By reading on, grasping what the character of faith is about and grasping what it is not about, we may also have begun to grasp the rationale for God's decision.

VI.

Before closing, I would like to explore another contrast between our two "Journey, Danger and Rescue" stories, specifically regarding the "Rescue" sections.

The rescue of Ishmael results from God's "hearing." This phrase appears as a preface to the angelic interference: "God heard the voice of the lad" (21:17), and in the angel's reassurance of Hagar: "Fear not, for God has heard the voice of the lad" (ibid.). This "explanation" of the rescue is not the least bit surprising. It is the very model enshrined and implicitly predicted in the naming of Ishmael (16:11). God hears the suffering of the downtrodden and oppressed, the expelled and the outcast.

In fact, we may identify at least four distinct ways in which the rescue of Ishmael is unsurprising. First, as mentioned earlier, God has never rescinded His earlier promise of nationhood for Ishmael. Second, as argued here, the mode of rescue involves "hearing" the pain and cries of the oppressed, a mode of rescue already identified explicitly with Ishmael. Third, it is part of an almost universal standard paradigm. Fourth, and finally, on a visceral and emotional level we identify and empathize with the rescue. It is only fair to save the suffering outcast.

In contrast, the rescue of Isaac is not easily explicable. In a shocking reversal, God has already seemingly reversed His statement: "But My covenant I will establish with Isaac" (17:21), and His declaration that "In Isaac shall your seed be called" (21:12). God has now demanded Isaac as a sacrifice. The rescue constitutes a second, and, in the context of the God-Abraham relationship, shocking and radical reversal. For Abraham, and for the reader who allows himself to forget his prior education regarding the notion of "*nisayon*," trial and test, the rescue is wholly unexpected. It comes as another surprise, a reversal of the reversal. Not for naught does the Midrash emphasize Abraham's inclination to somehow continue with the sacrifice (Rashi on 22:12, 13).

This theme of reversal is also hinted at in the time frame in which the reversal-rescue takes place. We are taught that "Abraham stretched out his hand, and he took the knife to slaughter his son" (22:10). In the very nick of time, the angel called. It is almost too late. Or is it perhaps already too late? In fact, we would expect that no one can react that fast, can be diverted when so focused. The reversal comes at the last minute, or in a certain sense, after the last minute, when it should have been too late.

Finally, the rescue is surprising in an emotional and visceral sense. Just as Abraham has submitted to the divine will and readied himself for sacrificing his son, so too we the readers of the *Akeda* have already succumbed to the terrifying logic of the events about to unfold. We have become numb and frightened by the power of God's will, bereft of any moral intuition about what should happen. Each time we are left relieved, gasping at the mysteries of the divine will.

In sum, the story of chapter twenty-one, the rescue of Ishmael, is marked by the expected, the normal, the comprehensible – the universal pattern of "Oppression and Redemption." But the story of chapter twenty-two, the rescue of Isaac, is marked by something altogether different: the concept of reversals, the unexpected, the inaccessible, and the forever-mysterious divine will. It constitutes a new pattern of redemption, defining a model of "Contradiction and Reversals," inexplicable reversal-difficulty followed by inexplicable reversal-redemption.

In fact, this distinction between the rescue of Ishmael and the rescue of Isaac, the redemption model of Ishmael's life and the redemption model of Isaac's life, is not a new difference between them. It is an old story.

Chapter sixteen opens with the story of the conception of Ishmael. Sara is barren. In accord with standard practice, Sara grants Abraham her maidservant and a child is conceived. Nothing strange. The story is familiar, understandable, natural, part of the regular way the world works. Not so the conception and birth of Isaac. Sara is barren, and in the natural scheme barren women cannot conceive. The very promise seems bizarre even to Abraham and Sara. Whether joyously, skeptically, or cynically, they laugh (17:17; 18:12). In Abraham's own words: "Shall a child be born to him that is a hundred years old? And shall Sara, that is ninety years old, give birth?" (17:17). It is absurd. But this is exactly the point. It is "absurd," unnatural, surprising and unexpected – a certain kind of miracle. It is the revivification of a barren woman at the age of ninety, the paradigm of "Contradiction and Reversal."

Let us turn our attention one last time to the expulsion of Ishmael, this time with a rich sense of the Isaac-Ishmael contrast. This expulsion in fact constitutes another "reversal," part of the Isaac-Ishmael contrast pattern. Ishmael is the firstborn. According to what might be termed the "ironclad law of primogeniture" prevalent in the ancient Near East, Ishmael cannot be expelled, exiled, replaced or contradicted as heir. But such is not God's will; God contradicts and reverses the natural, the normal way the world works, replacing Ishmael with Isaac. He reverses the natural and normal via one who, in his birth and near-death, as a child of a barren woman and as the rescued in the *Akeda*, embodies and represents by virtue of his sheer existence the concept of redemption through "Reversal and Contradiction."

If so, we have perhaps arrived at a further explanation of God's agreement with Sara's demand. It is not just about the character of Isaac. Rather, it is also about broadcasting a message, the message of "Contradiction and Reversal," the special and mysterious means by which God runs the history of His chosen people, Isaac and his descendants.

To conclude, the end of chapter twenty-one, the story of Hagar and Ishmael, is not just extraneous detail. Nor, for that matter, is God's affirmation of Ishmael's expulsion completely inexplicable. Rather, both the expulsion and the details of the subsequent ordeal in the desert are part of a sustained comparison of Isaac and Ishmael, part of an ongoing lesson in both the character of faith and the nature of God's providence.

The Birth of Isaac and the Banishment of Hagar and Ishmael

by Rav Elchanan Samet

Some seventeen years pass between Hagar's flight prior to Ishmael's birth (in *Lekh Lekha*) and their banishment from Abraham's household in this week's *parasha*. (Abraham was eighty-six years old at the time of Ishmael's birth [Gen. 16:16], and one hundred when Isaac was born [21:5]; about two or three years later Isaac was weaned [21:5].) There are several similarities between these two stories, forming a strong connection between them.

On the other hand, the circumstances have changed considerably since the narrative in last week's *parasha*: Ishmael, whose birth concluded that story, has become a youth in our *parasha*; Sara, who was then childless, now embraces her newborn son. In fact, the contrasts between these *parashot* are no less striking than the similarities, and both are quite clearly apparent.

Like the previous narrative, our *parasha* also arouses moral surprise and difficulty: Sara's demand of Abraham to "banish this maidservant and her son" seems quite harsh, and in fact brings Hagar and Ishmael to death's door when their water runs out in the desert. Indeed, in contrast with Abraham's agreement with Sara's complaints in the previous narrative – "Behold, your maidservant is in your hand" – here it appears that he does not agree with her: "And the thing was very bad in Abraham's eyes because of his son." However, those commentators who interpret the previous story as presenting Sara in a negative light (Radak, Ramban) see things differently in our *parasha*. The reason for this is clear: God explicitly tells Abraham, "Whatever Sara tells you, listen to her."

Nevertheless, God's support of Sara's demand does not mitigate our duty to explain the moral difficulty we sense in this story. On the contrary, we are faced here with not only the question of the morality of Sara, but also with the very justice of God, "a God of truth and without injustice; just and right is He" (Deut. 32:4).

The same four parameters that we used to explain the previous *parasha* may be useful again in clarifying this moral dilemma: i. socio-historical background, ii. literal interpretation, iii. literary analysis of the entire narrative, and iv. the context of this narrative within the life-story of Abraham and Sara.

I. SOCIO-HISTORICAL BACKGROUND

When Sara says, "For the son of this maidservant will not inherit with my son, with Isaac," it is clear that we must examine the laws of inheritance prevalent at the time. The Code of Hammurabi states:

> Par. 170: If a man's chief wife bears him children and his maid-servant [also] bears him children, and the father, while he still lives, tells the children whom the maidservant bore him, "[You are] my children," then he counts them among the children of his chief wife. After the father dies, the children of the chief wife and the children of the maidservant divide the property of the father's estate between them equally. The son of the chief wife is first to choose and take his portion of the inheritance.

> Par. 171: If the father, while still alive, does not say to the children whom the maidservant bore him, "[You are] my children," then after the father dies, the children of the maidservant do not receive a portion of the father's estate with the children of

the chief wife. The release of the maidservant and her children is assured; the children of the chief wife shall not demand servitude of the children of the maidservant."

Thus it appears that Sara seeks to protect Isaac's rights as sole heir. Why is she in such a hurry to demand that something be done in order to ensure this already? Experience has shown, from times of yore until today, that after a person's death, differences of opinion as to the wishes of the deceased can often arise between people who consider themselves heirs. Therefore, Sara wishes to make the legal situation clear while Abraham is alive. Abraham does something similar of his own initiative long after Sara's death, with regard to the children of his concubines:

> And Abraham gave all that was his to Isaac. And to the children of the concubines that Abraham had, Abraham gave gifts and he sent them away from Isaac his son, while he was still alive, eastwards to the eastern land. (25:5–6)

II. LITERAL INTERPRETATION: "BANISHING" AND "SENDING"

"Banishing" is a harsh action, all the more so when the subjects of this treatment are a woman and a boy, and where their destination is the desert. Hence, we are troubled: why does Sara demand this? Why is it necessary to banish Hagar and her son Ishmael in order to secure an uncontested inheritance for Isaac?

Indeed, Abraham does not "banish" them. After God tells him, "Everything that Sara tells you, listen to her," we are told that Abraham "sent her away" (21:14). It seems that the Torah is deliberately softening the harsh verb "banish" (from the Hebrew root g-r-sh, ג.ר.ש), using instead a softer verb (from the root sh-l-h, ש.ל.ה), reflecting Abraham's feelings and the character of his actions.

The root sh-l-h, in the *pi'el* (intensive) case, does sometimes have a meaning similar to that of the root g-r-sh (e.g. Deut. 22:7, 29). But in general, the word means "release," "letting someone go," "removing a restraint which prevents flight," etc. For example, release of slaves is generally termed "*shiluah*" in the Torah. Is it possible that this is the

Torah's intention in describing Abraham's action as *"vayeshalḥeha"* ("and he sent her")?

Par. 171 of the Code of Hammurabi stipulates that if the children of the maidservant are not included among the inheritors of the father, "The release of the maidservant and her children is assured." This is precisely the situation we have before us: with Abraham's decision that Ishmael is not to inherit him, Hagar and Ishmael are to be released. (Although Hammurabi's law stipulates that release follows the death of the master, in the case described there the master did not clarify anything concerning the inheritance until he died. It is possible that if he stated during his lifetime that the son of the maidservant was not going to inherit, then the son and his mother would earn their freedom even during the master's lifetime. Even if this was not so, it was perhaps in the interests of Abraham and Sara to advance their release while Abraham was still alive, for the reason mentioned above: in order to prevent arguments and misunderstandings following Abraham's death.)

Hence, perhaps this was what Sara had in mind, and this logically links the two parts of her statement: "Banish…for this maidservant's son will not inherit…" But where do we find the word *"gerush"* (banishing) used in the context of releasing slaves? "For with a strong hand he shall send them out [*yeshalḥem*] and with a strong hand shall he banish them [*yegarshem*]" (Ex. 6:1); and also, "When he lets you go [*keshalḥo*], he will surely banish you [*garesh yegaresh*] from here." We can explain this by keeping in mind that the slave did not always leave his master's house willingly.

It seems that Hagar did not wish to be released from her servitude in Abraham's house, inter alia because the circumstances of her release were a demonstrative declaration that her son had no part in Abraham's inheritance. This is why Sara uses the harsh verb *"g-r-sh"*; i.e., even if Hagar does not wish to be released from servitude, the law does not allow for her to continue to be a servant once it has been decided that her son will not be counted among Abraham's heirs. Therefore, she should be released, even if it is against her will. But in describing Abraham's actions, the text goes back to the original legal essence of the action: "sending away" or "freeing."

Sara's demand is thus an action with firm legal and moral underpinnings: she insists on a clarification of the exclusive rights to inheritance by her son Isaac, with the accompanying legal obligation – the release of Hagar and her son from servitude in Abraham's house. God's support of Sara's demand represents confirmation of the legality and morality of what Sara demands.

The stories of the forefathers in the book of Genesis are strewn throughout with threads of a double consciousness: one level of the actions of the biblical personalities is the earthly-mortal level, while the other is consciousness of the divine destiny. This consciousness brings its bearers to the realization that they are not simply private individuals, regular people, but rather God's chosen, set apart to establish His nation and to inherit His gift – the land of Canaan – in order to be a blessing to all the nations of the earth. This higher consciousness of the forefathers in Genesis turns their actions into events filled with historical import. Each significant event has fateful consequences for the future of the nation destined to descend from them.

We have explained how the conflict surrounding the identity of the mistress of Abraham's house was of deep significance: who would be Abraham's partner in realizing the divine destiny of establishing the nation of God's covenant? In our *parasha*, too, the identity of Abraham's heir goes much further than a regular question of inheritance. The more significant issue at stake here is which of the two sons will be the bearer of the covenant with God, upon whose foundation God will establish His nation in the distant future. For example, when God promises Abraham an heir in Genesis 15:3–4, this concerns the establishment of a nation as numerous as the stars, destined to inherit the land.)

This is hinted to in God's words in verse 12: "All that Sara says to you, listen to her voice, for in Isaac will your seed be called." This means that Isaac will be the father of the descendants promised to Abraham – destined to inherit the land and to be God's nation.

Furthermore, God tells Abraham: "Let it not be bad in your eyes for the boy and for your handmaid … And also the son of the maidservant will I make into a nation, for he is your seed" (21:12–13). In other words, fulfilling Sara's demand is also for the good of Ishmael himself, for he is also destined to be a great nation by virtue of being from Abraham's seed.

Faced with these numerous and multi-faceted justifications by

God, it seems that Abraham could have sent away the maidservant and her son for their own good, without this act seeming in any way wrong to him any longer. But the continued development of the story is not compatible with this optimistic view…

III. THE STORY'S STRUCTURE AND ITS
PLACE IN THE ABRAHAM NARRATIVE

There is open tension between God's calming words to Abraham concerning Ishmael's future and the unexpected development that takes place: "And she went and she wandered in the desert to Be'er Sheva. And the water was finished in the bottle… And she said: Let me not see the death of the child… And she lifted her voice and wept." Was Abraham made to send away Hagar and Ishmael under false pretenses? True, eventually God saves the child and tells his mother of his great future. But what, then, is the point of the desert scene that intervenes between the promise to Abraham and the beginning of its fulfillment at the end of the story?

In order to answer this question we need first to examine the structure of the story. Exposing the structure helps us to reveal hidden connections between the various parts and to clarify the place of each. In order to determine the story's structure, we need first to define its boundaries. I maintain that the story spans verses 1–21. What encompasses the entire story into a single literary unit is, first and foremost, the storyline: the birth of Isaac and his weaning, and the event which takes place at his weaning, cause Sara to be concerned for her son's future and to demand of Abraham that Ishmael be expelled. From that point onwards the story continues until its conclusion.

The twenty-one verses of the story can be divided into two halves of equal length, each of ten verses, with verse 11 – "And the thing was very bad in Abraham's eyes because of his son…" – serving as a sort of central axis for the story. The first half, verses 1–10, deals exclusively with Isaac. Even Sara's demand that the maidservant and her son be banished is substantiated with the good of Isaac in mind. This half opens with a tone of celebration and joy (verse 1 is structured in parallel clauses, a feature characterizing biblical songs of praise). This atmosphere prevails even in Sara's words in verses 6–7 (which also have the character of a song of praise), and it reaches its climax in the great celebration held when Isaac is weaned. But it is precisely at that point, on that joyous occasion that Sara sees Ishmael mocking, and she immediately demands of Abraham to banish him. This half of the story, which was so full of joy, ends in crisis.

Abraham's reaction, described in verse 11, is the climax of the conflict in the story, and it is the outcome of the first half: it is the birth of Isaac and his growth that have inevitably brought about this situation.

The second half, verses 12–21, deals exclusively with Ishmael and his fate (except for the words "for in Isaac shall your seed be called," the only mention made of Isaac in this half). This second half comes to resolve the conflict that culminated in verse 11, but the resolution is a winding, complicated one. Its path creates a "mirror image" of what took place in the first half: here we start with the expulsion of Hagar and Ishmael to the desert, we continue with their wandering and their great distress, and only towards the end does their fortune turn around with the appearance of the angel: Ishmael's life is saved, he grows up, and the story concludes with his marriage.

These two halves of the story, each one dealing with one of Abraham's sons, have a common theme, and this is perhaps the subject of the entire story: both describe the fulfillment of God's promises with regard to these two sons. Each son receives an independent promise – Ishmael in the form of an angel's words to Hagar (16:10–12), and Isaac in an angel's message to Abraham and Sara (18:10–15). In chapter seventeen (v. 19–20), the two sons receive a promise together:

> But Sara your wife will bear you a son … and I will establish My covenant with him for an eternal covenant, and to his seed after him. And as to Ishmael, I have heard you; behold I shall bless him and make him fruitful and make him very greatly numerous, he will bear twelve princes, and I will make him a great nation. And My covenant I will establish with Isaac whom Sara will bear you at this time next year.

Our *parasha* is therefore the story of the beginning of the fulfillment of the double promise. The realization of the promise as it pertains to

Isaac is his very birth at the appointed time, and this is highlighted at the opening of the story quite clearly ("as He had said ... as He had spoken ... at the time of which He spoke"). Even the name of the son who is born, Isaac, was already stated in 17:19, but here it is explained anew: not the doubtful laughter of a promise that has no apparent chance of becoming real, but rather the joyous laughter of its fulfillment. Furthermore, God's promise to establish His covenant with Isaac also begins to be realized in our *parasha*, when Sara demands that Ishmael be distanced from Abraham's house ("Whatever Sara tells you, listen to her voice, for in Isaac shall your seed be called").

On what does the fulfillment of the promise regarding Ishmael depend? It is precisely the sending away of Ishmael that is the precondition for the fulfillment of God's promise in his regard. Why? The juxtaposition of our story with that of Hagar's flight provides a solution. Ishmael will be able to develop in accordance with his inner personality traits – "And he shall be a wild man [*pere adam*]" – specifically in the desert of Paran (Rashbam on 21:21 comments that Paran hints at *"pere adam"*), far from Abraham's tent and his land of destiny. God hears Ishmael's voice "from where he was" – in the desert. There God hears him and will help him to find the secret of human existence in the desert – the well of water. It is there that God will accompany and watch over the boy's development (v. 20) into a hunter with bow and arrow. It is there that Ishmael will find his mate (v. 21) and will begin to multiply and establish the great nation that will have twelve princes. These tribes will excel in pursuing freedom and guarding it amongst all the nations, like the wild hind of the desert. (Abraham's seed descending from Isaac have a very different destiny, quite incompatible with the qualities of Ishmael's descendants: "Know that your seed will be strangers in a land that is not theirs and they will enslave them and oppress them for four hundred years.")

It appears therefore that the cutting off of Ishmael from Abraham's household and his wandering to the desert are a precondition for his becoming the father of a great and free nation, as promised by God. But this cutting off occurs only when he is already seventeen years old, with his formative years having been spent in the house of Abraham. His independent life, compatible with his qualities and historical destiny, is built on the foundations of the education he received from Abraham. (It should be noted here that Joseph, at the time that he was cut off from Jacob's house and went to Egypt for the fulfillment of his unique destiny, was also seventeen years old.)

Let us now return to the question with which we began: Why is Ishmael's departure to fulfill his destiny in the desert sown with such suffering, tears and mortal danger? Ishmael is not the only child who needs to be "reborn" after he comes close to death. Isaac, too, is "reborn" after he is bound on the altar and is nearly sacrificed. Moses, too, is "reborn" after he is placed as a baby in a basket in the river, as a last-ditch act of desperation by his mother. In all of these cases, the "rebirth" signifies the beginning of an existence on a different plane for the child concerned, a new destiny that attaches itself to his existence. In all instances, the purpose of this new existence is connected with the nature of the child's victory over death. In order to be reborn, the child has to reach death's door, and thereafter he is miraculously saved. This miracle brings about a change in his personality and shows him, his parents and all those around him that a new and different chapter of his life is now commencing, leading to the realization of his destiny.

Parashat Ḥayyei Sara

The Purchase of the "Burial Possession"

by Rav Yehuda Rock

T he story of Abraham's purchase of the "burial possession" (*ahuzat kever*) in Ḥevron is actually two stories with two different messages.

In this *shiur* we shall examine chapter twenty-three of Genesis using the exegetical methodology known as *"shitat habeḥinot,"* or "theory of aspects," an approach developed by my rabbi and teacher, Rav Mordechai Breuer. According to this approach, God wrote the Torah in "layers," with narratives (or halakhic sections) paralleling one another, each reflecting a different aspect or message, and each of which may be read independently, so that they contradict one another. Often, these narratives are interwoven so as to create a contiguous story. The contiguous story blurs the transition seams between one narrative and the other, but preserves the difficulties posed by those transitions. Each narrative expresses independent content with independent significance, and there is some relationship between them justifying their integration into a single story. By means of the difficulties arising from the combination of these narratives – such as repetitions or contradictions – we are able to expose the two independent "aspects," and then examine their respective significance. Here, as stated, we shall attempt to apply this methodology to the story of Abraham's purchase of the burial possession in chapter twenty-three of the book of Genesis.

We shall start by noting several textual difficulties. Thereafter, we shall see that separating this unit into two "aspects" causes these difficulties to disappear. Finally, we shall attempt to understand the significance of each aspect.

The chapter presents us with three main types of difficulties:

A. In verse 7 we read, "Abraham arose [*vayakom*]..." From where did he arise? He was in the middle of conversing with the children of Ḥet! Ibn Ezra suggests that the conversation took place with everyone sitting, and that at this point Abraham stood up in order to "bow" with his head. But doing this in the middle of a conversation where everyone is sitting seems odd.

   The expression, "Abraham arose," appears earlier in the unit, in verse 3, where the context is clear: after eulogizing and weeping over Sara, "Abraham arose from before his dead." Biblical parlance appears to perceive eulogy and weeping as being related to lying or sitting (as in the expression, "sitting *shiva*"), and leaving this state is a process of "arising" from mourning (once again echoed in the expression still accepted today – "getting up" from *shiva*). It seems that the expression may be meant in the same sense in verse 7, too. But if this is so, why does the text need to twice note the fact that Abraham arose from mourning? This repetition demands some explanation.

B. The expression "*kima*" is repeated elsewhere in these verses. In verses 17–18 we read: "The field of Ephron was established [*vayakom*]... as Abraham's," and then again in verse 20: "The field, and the cave that was in it, was established as Abraham's." Why does the text note twice the fulfillment of Abraham's purchase of the field and the cave?

   Admittedly, each of the verses contains something that is missing from the other, but they could easily have been combined into a single verse, along the lines of: "The field of Ephron that was in Makhpela, which was before Mamreh, was established –

the field and the cave that was in it and all the trees that were within all of its borders around – as Abraham's, as a purchase of a burial possession by the children of Het, in the presence of all those who entered the gate of his city." Thus it is not clear why the Torah notes twice, in two separate verses, the fulfillment of the purchase.

Aside from being repetitions, these verses are also contradictory. In verses 17–19 there is an emphasis on Abraham burying Sara only after the field is established as his. But in verse 20 it seems that the field was established as his after the burial.

Rashbam and Ibn Ezra explain that two different stages of "establishing" were involved. First, the purchase was fulfilled by means of the sale, as we read in verse 18: "as a purchase." At this stage, the field was considered Abraham's property, but it was not yet considered a burial possession. Only when Abraham actually buried Sara in the cave did the field and the cave become a possession of a burial place.

But this explanation is not satisfying. First, earlier in the *parasha*, in Abraham's two appeals to the Hittites, he asks: "Give me a burial possession" (v. 4) and "He shall give it to me in your midst for a burial possession." Thus, the "giving" itself was supposed to be the giving of a burial possession; there is no hint that Abraham would thereafter have to convert the field himself into a possession of a burial place. Second, if verse 20 is meant to describe the conversion of the field into a burial place by means of Abraham burying Sara there, then the verse should not mention "From the children of Het"! These words prove that verse 20 is talking about the fulfillment of the purchase of the field from the children of Het. Thus, we return to our question: why is the fulfillment of the purchase described twice, and was the purchase fulfilled before the burial or afterwards?

c. *Hazal (Bava Metzia* 87a) and the commentators note that there is an inexplicable transition in Ephron's position: he starts off willing to give the field to Abraham for free, but then demands payment. At first he declares, "No, my lord, hear me: The field I give you, and the cave that is in it, I have given to you. In the sight of the sons of my people I have given it to you; bury your dead" (v. 11). Not only does he not demand payment, but he appears to regard this gift as something obvious and already effected. Abraham insists on paying: "But if you [agree], please hear me: I will give the price of the field. Take it from me, that I may bury my dead there" (v. 13). In light of Ephron's initial generosity, we would expect that even if he accepts payment from Abraham, he would suffice with a nominal amount. Instead, he suggests the considerable sum of four hundred silver shekels: "My lord, hear me: a plot worth four hundred shekels of silver – what is it between you and me? And bury your dead" (v. 15). By comparison, four hundred shekels of silver is eight times the value of a virgin for marriage (see Deut. 22:29).

Lest we imagine that Ephron's latter words mention the value of the field as a mere aside, with no expectation of actually receiving this sum, the Torah testifies that Abraham understood Ephron's intention perfectly: "Abraham hearkened to Ephron, and Abraham weighed for Ephron the silver of which he had spoken in the presence of the children of Ḥet – four hundred shekels of silver in accepted currency" (v. 16). From Ḥazal's teachings, it seems that from the outset Ephron never really intended to give Abraham the field for free. But if this is the case, the Torah should have said so. Furthermore, if Ephron's seeming generosity is no more than a bargaining trick, why does the Torah not adopt its usual brief style, rather than take pains to describe each stage of the dialogue?

Let us now propose a separation of the unit into its constituent "aspects." The first two verses provide necessary background for the whole chapter, and include no repetitions or contradictions. Therefore, they should be regarded as an introduction that should not be divided between the "aspects," but rather remains common to both.

As mentioned, the "arising" (*kima*) in verse 7 should be interpreted as Abraham arising from before his dead. This "arising" must come as an immediate continuation of the end of verse 2, and it represents a repetition of verse 3. Therefore, everything that comes after verse 2 and before verse 7 should be categorized as belonging to one aspect (henceforth to be referred to as "aspect A"), and verse 7 itself as another aspect ("aspect B").

In B, verse 7 introduces Abraham's appeal to the people of the land. This appeal is described immediately thereafter, in verses 8–9. Therefore, verses 8–9 should be grouped together with verse 7, in aspect B. Already at this stage we can see a difference between the two aspects concerning Abraham's request.

In A, Abraham asks: "Give me a burial possession with you, that I may bury my dead from before me." He makes no attempt to purchase any specific field; he simply seeks a way of burying his dead. The children of Ḥet, understanding this as the crux of his request, answer: "Bury your dead in the choice of our tombs; none of us shall withhold his tomb from you for burying your dead." In other words, since your request is to bury your dead, you do not necessarily need a possession of a burial place which you will own; you can suffice with burying your dead in one of the tombs of the children of Ḥet. It is not clear whether this would indeed have satisfied Abraham, but it is clear in any event that the children of Ḥet understood that Abraham's main objective was to bury his dead.

In B, on the other hand, Abraham notes in his first appeal (as part of this aspect, disconnected from A) to the children of Ḥet that he is specifically interested in the Cave of Makhpela belonging to Ephron, son of Zohar, and that he wishes to pay "the full price" of it. Clearly, aside from burying Sara, Abraham also seeks to effect a purchase of the site.

Before we return to grouping the verses according to the two aspects, let us join the verses that are clearly connected to one another into units. First, attention should be paid to the fact that verse 10 contains two sentences (hereafter to be referred to as 10a and 10b): "And Ephron dwelled amongst the children of Ḥet," "And Ephron the Ḥittite answered Abraham in the hearing of the children of Ḥet and all who entered the gate of his city, saying." We shall address each of these sentences separately. It is clear that 10b is continued in verse 11, and therefore we shall treat 10b-11 as a single unit.

Verse 16 – "Abraham hearkened to Ephron, and Abraham weighed for Ephron the silver of which he had spoken in the hearing of the children of Ḥet – four hundred shekels of silver in accepted currency" – clearly relates to what Ephron says in verses 14–15: "Ephron answered Abraham, saying to him: My lord, hear me: a plot worth four hundred shekels of silver – what is it between me and you? So bury your dead." Therefore, verses 14–16 must be joined together as part of the same aspect.

Verses 12–13 – "And Abraham bowed before the people of the land. And he spoke to Ephron, in the presence of the people of the land, saying: But if you [agree], please hear me: I will give the price of the field; take it from me, that I may bury my dead there" – invite a response on Ephron's part. This response comes only in verses 14–15 (which we have already connected with verse 16). Therefore verses 12–16 are a single unit belonging to one aspect.

As we pointed out earlier, verses 11 and 15 contradict one another with regard to Ephron's intentions: in verse 11 he offers the field for free, while in verse 15 he asks an exorbitant sum. Moreover, verses 11 and 15 are the only verses in the chapter in which Ephron agrees to supply the field to Abraham, and each of the two aspects must therefore include one of these two verses. Therefore, verses 10b-11 should belong to one aspect, and verses 12–16 to the other.

It would seem logical to attribute verses 10b-11 to aspect A and verses 12–16 to aspect B (we shall return to the matter of 10a below). The reason for this attribution is that from Abraham's very first appeal we already discern a difference between the two aspects. The difference is that in A, Abraham requests – or at least seems prepared to accept – a free gift, while in B he insists on paying the full price for the field. Therefore, verses 12–16, in which Abraham insists on paying (v. 13), should be regarded as a continuation of his first request in B, while verses 10b-11, in which Ephron proposes a free gift to Abraham (and his proposal is accepted; Abraham expresses no opposition) should be categorized with aspect A.

As regards verse 10a, it is difficult to establish its place with certainty, but it appears to belong to aspect B. The reason for this is that if this verse were to belong to A, it would mean that the text first refers to Ephron simply by his name, "Ephron" (in this verse), and thereafter "introduces" him as "Ephron the Hittite." It is more logical that in A, the first time that Ephron is mentioned is in 10b, where he is introduced to the reader for the first time as "Ephron the Hittite." In B, Ephron has already been introduced in Abraham's words as "Ephron, son of Zohar," and thereafter he may be referred to simply as "Ephron."

It seems that the significance of 10b in aspect B is that it explains why Abraham appealed to the children of Het in the first place, rather than appealing directly to Ephron: it was because Ephron "dwelled amongst the children of Het"; he was a Hittite citizen, and according to ancient custom, burial required public approval (see A.Y. Beror, *Beit Mikra* XI:4 [5726]). Abraham spoke with the children of Het not merely in order to ascertain where Ephron could be found (the Torah would certainly not record such a trivial conversation), but rather because he needed their approval to bury Sara in their midst. For this reason, it seems, Abraham mentions only the cave in speaking to them, and not the field – since the purchase of regular land did not require public approval.

As stated, verses 17–18 – "Then the field of Ephron which was in Makhpela, which was before Mamreh – the field, and the cave that was in it…were made over to Abraham, for a purchase, in the presence of the children of Het, before all who entered the gate of his city" – are repeated in verse 20: "And the field and the cave that was in it were made over to Abraham, as a burial possession, by the sons of Het." Verses 17–18 should therefore be grouped with aspect B, it seems – first, because in these verses the location of the field is noted in detail, while in A thus far the text mentions a nondescript field with no indication of its exact location. Only in B does Abraham ask, in his first appeal to the children of Het (v. 9): "Plead on my behalf to Ephron, son of Zohar, that he may give me the Cave of Makhpela which is his, which is at the edge of his field." This matches the detailed summary in verses 17–18, and therefore verses 17–18 should be grouped under aspect B and verse 20 should be grouped under aspect A.

Verse 19, as we have mentioned, comes to emphasize that Abraham buried Sara after his purchase of the field had been fulfilled, in the wake of the description of the realization of the purchase in verses 17–18. Therefore verse 19 belongs to B. Verse 20, on the other hand, describes the fulfillment of the purchase in A, while A makes no mention of the burial of Sara.

We can now summarize the division of the chapter as follows:

COMMON TO ASPECTS A–B:

"Sara's life was a hundred years and twenty years and seven years, the years of Sara's life. And Sara died in Kiryat Arba, which is Ḥevron, in the land of Canaan, and Abraham came to eulogize Sara and to weep for her."

Aspect A:

(3) And Abraham arose from before his dead, and he spoke to the children of Ḥet, saying: (4) I am a stranger and a sojourner with you; give me a burial possession with you, that I may bury my dead from before me.

(5) And the children of Ḥet answered Abraham, saying to him: (6) Hear us, my lord; you are a mighty prince in our midst. Bury your dead in the choice of our tombs; none of us shall withhold his tomb from you for burying your dead.

(10a) And Ephron the Ḥittite spoke to Abraham in the hearing of the children of Ḥet, [and] of all who entered the gate of his city, saying:

(11) No, my lord, hear me: The field I give you, and the cave that is in it – I have given it to you. In the sight of the sons of my people I have given it to you; bury your dead.

(20) And the field and the cave that was in it were established as Abraham's, as a burial possession, from the sons of Ḥet.

Aspect B:

(7) So Abraham arose and bowed to the people of the land, to the children of Ḥet. (8) And he spoke to them saying: If you agree that I bury my dead from before me, hear me and speak on my behalf to Ephron, son of Zohar, (9) that he may give me

the Cave of Makhpela which is his, which is at the edge of his field. For the full price he shall give it to me in your midst for a burial possession.

(10) For Ephron dwelled among the children of Ḥet.

(12) And Abraham bowed before the people of the land.

(13) And he spoke to Ephron, in the presence of the people of the land, saying: But if you [agree], please hear me: I will give the price of the field; take it from me, that I may bury my dead there.

(14) And Ephron answered Abraham, saying to him:

(15) My lord, hear me: a plot worth four hundred shekels of silver – what is it between me and you? And bury your dead.

(16) Abraham hearkened to Ephron, and Abraham weighed for Ephron the silver of which he had spoken in the presence of the children of Ḥet – four hundred shekels of silver in accepted currency.

(17) Then the field of Ephron which was in Makhpela, which was before Mamreh – the field, and the cave that was in it, and all the trees that were in the field, that were within all the borders around it – were established (18) as Abraham's for a purchase, in the presence of the children of Ḥet, before all who entered the gate of his city.

(19) And afterwards Abraham buried Sara his wife, in the cave of the field of Makhpela which faces Mamreh, which is Ḥevron, in the land of Canaan."

Let us now examine each aspect, each narrative, and explain its significance in accordance with what it contains. In aspect A we find the following elements:

A. As noted, this aspect lacks the emphasis and detail concerning the location of the place – both in Abraham's request and in the description of the fulfillment of the purchase. Even the name of the place, "Makhpela," is omitted here. Abraham's request is simply, "Give me a possession of a burial place with you, that I may bury my dead from before me."

B. The progression of the narrative is as follows: Abraham appeals to the children of Ḥet, requesting a burial place. The children of Ḥet, understanding that the crux of the request is for a way to bury Sara, propose that she be buried in one of their tombs, and emphasize that any of them would readily agree to this possibility. One of the Hittites in the area is "Ephron the Hittite"; he volunteers to give Abraham his field and the cave that is in it. Ephron even emphasizes that the gift is definite and takes immediate effect: "Before the children of my people I have given it to you; bury your dead." By means of this public declaration the field and the cave are established as Abraham's, as a possession of a burial place by the children of Ḥet.

C. Abraham does not insist here on paying for the field; he accepts the free gift.

D. Abraham is treated with great respect by the Hittites ("You are a mighty prince in our midst"), unlike his treatment in B. Accordingly, he does not need to bow before them.

E. In this aspect, the actual burial ceremony is not mentioned; the reader is left to assume that it did take place.

Thus, the essence of the narrative in A is the story of how the Hittites, and Ephron, go out of their way to help Abraham with his request. The request itself is not the focus of the narrative, since the event of the burial itself is not even mentioned. Rather, the focus is on the fact that when Abraham needs something from the local people, he is given great respect, assistance, and a significant gift.

What this means is that God performed a kindness for Abraham in elevating his status in the eyes of the local people, thereby enabling him to purchase a burial place. This narrative, then, is about God's kindness towards Abraham, and perhaps also the beginning of the fulfillment of God's blessings to him – the blessings of making his name great and of the inheritance of the land (see Ibn Ezra and Ramban on v. 19).

In aspect B we find the following elements:

A. Emphasis on and details of the name of the field ("Makhpela"), and of its location, both in Abraham's request and, even more so, in the description of the fulfillment of the purchase.
B. Abraham's insistence on paying the full price for the field.
C. Abraham is subservient to the Hittites – he needs to ask their permission to purchase a possession of a burial place; he needs – twice – to bow before them.
D. Here the Hittites are also referred to as "the people of the land" (three times), a title that appears nowhere in aspect A.
E. The progression of the story is as follows: Abraham must apply to the children of Het, who own the place – "the people of the land" – with his request for license to purchase a possession of a burial place in their midst, in Ephron's cave. Thereafter, he asks Ephron to sell him the field. Ephron answers in an exploitative and scornful tone: You might as well not quibble about buying land for four hundred shekels of silver; the main thing is that you bury your dead. Abraham is forced to accept Ephron's dictates, and pays the sum that he demands. Abraham's purchase of the field is therefore fulfilled, and only afterwards is he able to bury Sara there.

Clearly, in B, the focus of the story is the purchase of the land. The narrative emphasizes and reinforces the ownership of Abraham and his descendants over the field of Makhpela, taking pains to note its description and its exact location, and that Abraham paid in full for this land, in the presence of those who were, at the time, "the people of the land." Aspect B also emphasizes the difficulties that Abraham had to overcome in order to be able to purchase the land: the subservience to the Hittites, the dictates of Ephron, and the exorbitant price that he had to pay. These difficulties, and Abraham's great efforts to overcome them, contribute towards strengthening his ownership: the plot is purchased through Abraham's suffering.

Aside from the independent significance of each aspect, we need to understand why the Torah chooses to present these two themes together in the same chapter. In other words, what is the meaning of the combination of these aspects?

The answer to this question is dependent on a broader understanding of the Abraham narratives. Abraham is commanded to leave his birthplace, where a secure and successful future awaits him, and he is promised a number of times that in the land of Canaan he will be blessed with descendants and with inheritance of the land. But throughout his life he is forced to deal with various difficulties and tests. The blessing is fulfilled only very slowly and partially, such that the bulk of it is fulfilled only later on, through his descendants (see Ibn Ezra and Ramban on v. 19).

The Torah makes no explicit mention of why the blessing is not fulfilled with Abraham himself. With regard to the inheritance of the land, there is some sort of explanation: "For the sin of the Amorites is not yet complete" (15:16). But no reason is given for why Abraham does not bear many children, like Jacob, so that the blessing could start to be fulfilled already during his lifetime. Likewise, concerning the land, it seems that he could have inherited more than he did in fact.

For this reason, the reader may be led to believe that the postponement of the fulfillment of the blessing had something to do with some deficiency in Abraham, who was not worthy of having the blessing fulfilled in his own person. It seems that it is precisely this sort of thinking that the Torah wants to prevent.

The Torah interweaves two narratives within its description of the same event. One emphasizes that God shines His countenance towards Abraham and seeks his success, while the other emphasizes that Abraham must deal with difficulties and delays, and purchase the land through the legitimate means of human society – "the full price" – so as to effect an absolute and clear purchase of the land – a purchase that is accepted in the eyes of the "people of the land" and which is eternally to be a possession of a burial place. This story also gives rise to an explanation as to the fulfillment of the blessing in general during Abraham's lifetime: Abraham is certainly worthy of having the blessing fulfilled during his lifetime, and God would gladly see him multiplying and inheriting the land personally. But if Abraham receives the land quickly and easily, it will be a temporary, transient ownership – "easy come, easy go." In order for the purchase of the land in general by Abraham's descendants – in each and every generation –to be a clear and absolute purchase, they must invest effort and experience suffering, and must also effect an acceptable, legitimate purchase (see *Mishneh Torah*, Hilkhot Beit HaBeḥira 6:16), in a process that is spread over generations. Only thus can they truly be worthy of a clear and eternal purchase of the land.

"The Field and the Cave Therein, Were Upheld unto Abraham for a Possession... "

by Rav Amnon Bazak

I.

One of the outstanding features in the Torah is the tremendous importance ascribed to the acquisition of land in *Eretz Yisrael*. Whenever such
a transaction is mentioned, it is described in great detail, all the minutiae
scrupulously recorded, and especially – the price. Our *parasha* tells of
the first field which was bought, and the beginning of the *parasha* – all
of chapter twenty-three – is devoted to the lengthy negotiations between
Abraham and Ephron the Hittite. In concluding the matter, the Torah
emphasizes and re-emphasizes:

> And Abraham weighed out the silver which he promised the sons
> of Het, four hundred shekels of silver in current coin. And the
> field of Ephron which was in Makhpela which is before Mamreh,
> the field and the cave therein, and all the trees in the field within
> all its surrounding borders, were established as the acquisition of
> Abraham before the eyes of the sons of Het amid all who came
> within the gates of the city... And the field and the cave within

were established as the possession of a burial ground of Abraham with the consent of the sons of Ḥet."

The Torah describes at length the refusal of Abraham to accept the field for free; he demands to pay Ephron its full value. The Torah emphasizes that the purchase is "before the eyes of the sons of Ḥet amid all who came within the gates of the city," and repeats – twice – that the field "was upheld" (*vayakom*) as Abraham's possession and burial ground.

Interestingly, whenever the Torah hereafter refers to the Cave of Makhpela, it proceeds to describe at uncharacteristic length the way in which the field was bought. Thus, for example, at the end of the *parasha*:

> And Isaac and Ishmael his sons buried him in the Cave of Makhpela, in the field of Ephron the son of Zohar the Hittite, which is upon Mamreh, the field **which Abraham bought from the sons of Ḥet,** that is where Abraham and his wife Sara were buried.

So too in the request of Jacob, before his demise (49:29–32):

> And he commanded them: "I am going to be gathered to my people. Bury me with my fathers in the Cave which is in the field of Ephron the Hittite, in the Cave in the field of Makhpela which is upon Mamreh in the land of Canaan, the field **which Abraham bought from Ephron the Hittite** for a burial ground, that is where they buried Abraham and his wife Sara...the field and the cave therein **were bought from the sons of Ḥet.**

Likewise at the fulfillment of the request (50:13):

> And his sons carried him to the land of Canaan, and buried him in the Cave of the field of Makhpela, the field **which Abraham bought for a burial ground from Ephron the Hittite, upon Mamreh."**

II.

The same phenomenon is evident in other cases as well. Jacob buys a field in Shekhem from Hamor, and again the Torah spells out the price:

> And he bought the field where he pitched his tent from Hamor, the father of Shekhem, **for a hundred *kesita*.**"

Later, when Joseph was buried there, the transaction is again described in detail (Josh. 24:32):

> And the bones of Joseph, which *Benei Yisrael* brought up from Egypt, they buried in Shekhem, in the field which Jacob bought from Hamor, the father of Shekhem, **for a hundred *kesita*,** and it became the inheritance of the sons of Joseph.

The book of Samuel concludes, as the backdrop for the book of Kings, with the purchase of the granary of Aravna the Jebusite. The story of the purchase is quite reminiscent of the acquisition of the field by Abraham: in both narratives, a highly esteemed figure (Abraham – "a prince of God in our midst"; David, the King of Israel) initiates contact with a Gentile (Ephron, Aravna) in order to buy a plot of land. In both cases we read of socially correct dialogue, replete with prostrations, in which the seller offers the land free of charge ("I have given you the field, and I have given you the cave therein"; "My lord the King may take and go up as he sees fit"). In both instances the buyer insists on paying the full price in silver. As Abraham, so David (II Sam. 24:24):

> And the King said to Aravna, "No, for I will surely buy it from you for a price, for I will not offer up sacrifices to the Lord my God for naught." And David bought the granary and the cattle for fifty silver shekels.[1]

---

1. It should be noted that the author of Chronicles I (21:24) appears to have been aware of this intended similarity, and in the parallel description of David's purchase he uses the expression "No, for I will surely buy **for the full price** [*kesef maleh*]," an idiom which was first used by Abraham when he bought the Cave of Makhpela.

III.

From the unusual length at which the Torah details these transactions, it appears the Torah aims to remove all possible doubt regarding the validity and legality of the sale. The statement of Ḥazal on the matter is well-known (*Bereshit Raba* 79:4):

> "And he bought the field where he pitched his tent" – Said Rav Yudan bar Simon, this is one of the three places regarding which the nations of the world cannot slander Israel and say "You stole them!" The places are: the Cave of Makhpela, the Temple, and the Tomb of Joseph. For of the Cave of Makhpela it is written – "And Abraham deferred to Ephron, and Abraham weighed out the silver..."; of the Temple it is written "And David gave to Arnan..."; and as for the Tomb of Yosef – "And he bought the field."

IV.

There is one more place whose acquisition is recorded (1 Kings 16:23–24):

> In the thirty-first year of Asa the King of Judea, reigned Omri over Israel... He bought the mountain of Samaria from Shemer for two talents of silver. And he built the mountain, and called the city which he built Samaria, after Shemer the master of the mountain.

Here, too, the verses spell out the exact price paid for the city. There are four places, then, where land in *Eretz Yisrael* was bought for a price: Ḥevron, Shekhem, Jerusalem and Samaria. The four have something else in common. These cities were the four which served as capitals during different periods: Ḥevron was made capital after the death of Saul, when David asks God where to have his capital (11 Sam. 1:11). Shekhem became the first capital of the kingdom of Israel: Reḥavam arrived in Shekhem for his coronation (1 Kings 12:1), but as a result of the "counsel of the children" to increase the people's burden, the kingdom split, and eventually Yerovam was crowned at Shekhem, which became his capital. Jerusalem was the capital of the united Kingdom of Israel: after the death of Avner and Ishboshet, the elders decide to accept upon themselves, as did their brethren in Judea, the kingship of David. His first step is the capture of Jerusalem, and its establishment as his capital (II Sam. 5:5). Samaria was the capital of the dynasty of Omri, which, despite its corruption, was the strongest and most central to rule over the tribes of Israel. Ḥazal noted this (*Sanhedrin* 102b): "Why did Omri deserve kingship? Because he added a major city to the Land of Israel, as it says: 'He bought the mountain of Samaria.'"

The common element to these four purchases was that they were bought not privately, but by the common entity representing the nation. In the case of the forefathers this is true by definition, once we accept that a forefather represents *Klal Yisrael*. In the latter two cases, the king bought the area for a national purpose – the place of the altar (and ultimately the Temple), and the capital of the kingdom of Israel. This is presumably the reason why they served as capital cities. The purchase gave them a status of national property rather than private or tribal property.

Could we claim that perhaps Abraham's and Jacob's purchases were merely private exchanges, acquiring it for them as individuals but not for the nation? Notice that in our *parasha*, the finality of the sale appears twice:

> The field of Ephron which was in Makhpela, which was before Mamreh, the field and the cave therein, and all the trees that were in the field within its surrounding borders, were established as an acquisition (*lemikna*) of Abraham..."

Two verses later, the Torah repeats this legal summary:

> "The field and the cave therein were established as a possession of a burial ground [*aḥuzat kever*] by the sons of Ḥet."

What is the difference between the two verses? The first enumerates the physical details of the sale, including the trees, and refers to it as a "*mikneh*" – a sale, an acquisition. The term means no more than "something bought." The second verse is less concerned with the details of the fields and refers to it as an "*aḥuza*" – a possession, an estate. What has taken place between the two descriptions? One verse: "After this, Abraham buried Sara his wife in the cave of the fields of Makhpela before Mamreh..." A commercial transaction by Abraham merely made the field the property of the individual Abraham. Burial of Sara, the matriarch, granted the field the status of *aḥuza* – the term used later in Leviticus (ch. 25) to describe *Eretz Yisrael* (*"eretz aḥuzatkhem"*) and the portion given to each Jew as his inheritance in the land (*aḥuzato*). Mere financial possession was not enough; the field had to be dedicated for a national purpose.[2]

A similar process appears to take place with Jacob's purchase of the field outside Shekhem. The verse in Joshua states that Joseph was buried in that field, and *"Vayihiyu livnei Yosef lenaḥala."* The plural verb *"vayihiyu"* leads the commentators to refer this statement to the bones – Joseph's bones were a *naḥala* of the sons of Joseph. Since bone cannot really be inherited, and *naḥala* is always associated with land, Radak explains that they viewed the burial of Joseph's bones as sealing the *naḥala*-status of the burial ground. The verse opens by reminding us that the Jews – the Jewish people – brought the bones of Joseph out of Egypt. Perhaps here too, Jacob's private purchase became *naḥala* only after it was dedicated to a national purpose: the burial of Joseph.

In the case of "Goren Arnan," the purchase was explicitly for the sake of an altar, which David immediately builds. David is king of Israel, so his purchase is public purchase by definition. (The verse in Samuel says the price was fifty pieces of silver. The corresponding verse in Chronicles says the price was six-hundred [1 Chr. 21:25]. The standard explanation is fifty from each tribe – fifty times twelve is six-hundred. In other words, it is crucial to ensure the national character of this purchase.)

These three places, then, are dedicated to the nation by virtue at their having been bought *"bekesef maleh"* – Joseph's burial place, the Cave of Makhpela, and the Temple mount.

---

2. In an extraordinary piece of arithmetic computation, the Arugat HaBosem proves that four hundred shekels – the price of the field of Makhpela – was enough to buy 2.4 million square cubits, based on the price of land given in Leviticus 27:16. In other words, there are four cubits [*"daled amot"*] each for 600,000 Jews.

"There Abraham Was Buried, and Sara His Wife"

by Rav Elchanan Samet

I. WHY SUCH A DETAILED ACCOUNT?

Biblical narrative is generally characterized by its extreme brevity: it focuses on the information that is necessary, while leaving out "filler." It generally contains no descriptions of nature, of social norms, psychological data or historical background. If any one of these elements appears in the narrative, it is either presented very briefly or only hinted at, and only if it is vital to the story itself.

There are some rare instances where biblical narrative appears to depart from this general rule, and elaborates on details that seem less than vital to the story. Commentators throughout the generations have noted such instances and have attempted to explain the reason for the departure from the regular biblical style.

The beginning of our *parasha* details at great length the description of the negotiations between Abraham and the children of Ḥet (and specifically with Ephron). These complicated and multi-stage negotiations occupy the majority of the opening story: sixteen verses (Gen. 23:3–18) out of twenty. In what way does this account further the aims of this specific biblical story? Could it not have been shortened, and its essence conveyed as follows: Abraham requested a burial plot from the children of Ḥet, and eventually purchased the Cave of Makhpela, where he buried his wife?

II. "FOR THIS THING ALONE IT WAS WORTHY OF BEING WRITTEN"

In order to understand the purpose of the story, let us examine its stylistic dimension: what are the key words here, those repeated more often than any others? Such words are usually called "leading words," since they lead or direct the reader to discover the principal significance of the story, or to discover hidden meanings within it. Usually the number of times that such words appear has its own significance, and most often the number is a multiple of seven. Our study requires that we pay attention to each appearance of the word: in what contexts is it mentioned? Does the word have a fixed meaning throughout the story or does it have a range of meanings? Does it appear in places that have special significance? How often does it appear in different parts of the story?

The word whose appearance stands out most clearly in our story is the Hebrew root *k-v-r* (to bury, burial place), which appears on several occasions here both as a verb and as a noun. We will return to its significance soon.

In many stories that center around a single character or a pair of characters, the name of the character/s may serve as a leading word. But sometimes the personal name is exchanged for a title as required by the story, and then we must count appearances of both the name and the title in order to reach the total number. In our story, Sara's name, and her title "Abraham's deceased," appear many times throughout. On what basis does the text choose to call Sara by her name or by this title?

The name "Sara" appears four times at the beginning of the story and once more at the end, while on eight occasions in the middle she is called "Abraham's deceased." The distinction is quite clear: Sara is called "Abraham's deceased" specifically during the course of the negotiations with the children of Ḥet – both in the narrative itself and by Abraham and the children of Ḥet. The reason for this seems to be that the children of Ḥet do not know Sara by name. To their view, she is "Abraham's deceased" – the deceased relative of someone who is very highly esteemed in their eyes. But in relation to Abraham himself, when he is not standing in front of the children of Ḥet, Sara is called by name – both during her life and afterwards, as well as when he eulogizes her and mourns her. Again, after the negotiations are over and Abraham buries her, she is called "Sara his wife."

The connection between the two leading words, *k-v-r* and Sara, is noticeable. It is no coincidence that the two terms occur an equal number of times in the course of the story: it is their combination that defines the subject and point of the story – finding a "burial place" in which "to bury" "Sara," "Abraham's deceased." You may ask: Does one need an analysis of the leading words to arrive at this conclusion? After all, the fact that this is the content of the story is quite obvious!

But if this is so, what is the explicit story coming to teach us – just that Abraham buried Sara? Why, then, all the elaboration? Benno Jacob, in his commentary on the book of Genesis, writes as follows:

> The purpose of the story is stated explicitly by Abraham himself. He requests a burial place for Sara his wife, who has died. In the purchase of the cave to bury Sara, Abraham expresses his love and honor for her. For this alone the *parasha* was worthy of being written."

We may offer the following two comments:

A. The main part of the story is the description of the effort invested by Abraham in order to show the proper respect for his wife, for the burial place was not easily acquired. The crux of his effort was in his intensive diplomatic negotiations with the children of Ḥet, with a rejection of their alternative proposals. The steep price that he was required to pay was also, ultimately, part of his effort.

B. The depiction of the household of Abraham and Sara is the first biblical description of a full human life, with the large and small human battles that it involves. The death of Sara is the first death in the family of the forefathers. Our *parasha*, then, is the first to describe someone's reaction to the death of the person who is closest to him, and his subsequent behavior. The *parasha*, therefore, has a primal character, instructing future generations as to how to deal with similar human situations (the mitzvot given to Israel at Sinai contain no explicit instructions pertaining to eulogy and respectful burial rites). All of this, then, may be categorized as "teachings of the fathers."

III. A SPLIT STORY

In our discussion of the leading words, we noted that the number of its appearances usually has typological significance. Thirteen is not one of the numbers generally associated with this phenomenon. This presents a difficulty with regard to the two leading words of our story, for two reasons: firstly – this is the number of times that each appears, and this is certainly not coincidental; secondly – this number is very close to another number that is much more typical for appearances of leading words in the biblical narrative: fourteen.

In order to understand the reason for this, we must first describe a literary phenomenon that is not sufficiently well known, which we call "the split story." There are stories in the Torah that are not narrated in one place in their entirety, but rather have one part – generally a few verses, but sometimes more – that is narrated somewhere other than in the body of that story. (For some examples of split stories, see the prose framework of Job [ch. 1–2; ch. 42]; the birth of Samuel [I Sam. 1:1–2:11; 2:18–21]; and the prophecy about Yoshiyahu [I Kings ch. 13] and its fulfillment [II Kings 23:15–20].) We propose that this story is split, and is concluded only close to the end of the *parasha*. Verses 7–10 of chapter twenty-five comprise the section that completes our story:

> And these are the days of the years of the life of Abraham, who lived a hundred and seventy five years. And Abraham expired and died in a good, elderly and full age, and was gathered to his people. And Isaac and Ishmael his sons buried him at the Cave of Makhpela, at the field of Ephron son of Zohar the Hittite, which was facing Mamreh. The field which Abraham had purchased from the children of Het – there Abraham was buried and Sara his wife. (Gen. 25:7–10)

For chronological reasons, it would obviously be impossible to include this earlier. The connection between this section and the story of Sara's burial is quite apparent, in terms of both content and style:

A. The story of Abraham's death is similar in style to that of Sara's death, and hence the conclusion of the story echoes its introduction:

> And the years of Sara were a hundred years and twenty years and seven years, **the years of the life of Sara**. And Sara died … (23:1–2)

> "And these are the days of **the years of Abraham**, who lived one hundred years and seventy years and five years. And Abraham expired and died … (25:7–8)

B. The Cave of Makhpela is mentioned as the burial place of both Abraham and Sara:

> And after that Abraham buried Sara his wife at the cave [*me'ara*] of the field of Makhpela, facing Mamreh … (23:19)

> And Isaac and Ishmael his sons buried him at the Cave of Makhpela … that is facing Mamreh. (25:9)

C. Both note the purchase of the field from the children of Ḥet (23:20 and 25:10).

D. The strongest and most important connection between the concluding section and the body of the story lies in the repetition of the final words:

> And thereafter Abraham buried Sara, his wife. (23:19)

> There **Abraham was buried, and Sara his wife**. (25:13)

Clearly, then, the concluding words of the concluding section of the story – "There Abraham was buried, and Sara his wife" – complete the number of appearances of both leading words of our story, the root "*k-v-r*" in relation to "Sara." Each leading word now appears in the complete story a total of fourteen times.

IV. STRUCTURE OF THE STORY AS A WHOLE

It is not only the stylistic and thematic analysis that confirms the connection between verses 7–10 of chapter twenty-five and the story of Sara's burial. The structure of the story as a whole now becomes clear, and it is typical of many biblical stories: it is divided into two equal halves, each comprising twelve verses. The second half opens with the third stage of Abraham's negotiations with the children of Ḥet (the negotiations with Ephron, 23:13–18). This stage represents a positive turning point, for it is successful and concludes with a weighing of the money and the purchase of the field from Ephron. The two previous stages of negotiations were unsuccessful, since they were met with a polite refusal on the part of the children of Ḥet and Ephron (and a submissive bowing down on the part of Abraham).

The two equal halves of the story correspond to each other with a developing chiastic parallel, as follows:

A. (23:1–2) Summary of the years of Sara's life, her death, eulogy by Abraham.

  B. (v. 3–7) Stage 1 of negotiations: Abraham requests a burial place from the children of Ḥet to bury Sara; they refuse.

   C. (v. 8–12) Stage 2 of negotiations: Abraham approaches Ephron with a request to purchase the Cave of Makhpela at the full price; he is refused.

   C1. (v. 13–18) Stage 3 of negotiations: Abraham insists on the payment, is answered in the affirmative, and purchases the field from Ephron.

  B1. (v. 19–20) Abraham buries Sara in the burial ground that he has purchased from the children of Ḥet.

A1. (25:7–10) Summary of the years of Abraham's life, his death and burial in Sara's burial place.

Let us examine this parallel more closely:

A and A1:

The stylistic correspondence between the opening and closing sections of the story was discussed in the previous section. The development here is clear: when Sara died there was no respectable place to bury her, but by the time Abraham died, the burial ground in which he had buried Sara was prepared.

B and B1:

B (verses 3–4)

> And he spoke to the children of Het, saying…
> Give me a burial place with you,
> that I may bury my dead from before me.

B1 (verses 19–20)

> And after that Abraham buried Sara his wife…
> for a burial place
> from the children of Het."

Here, too, the development is clear: Abraham made a request of the children of Het, which was met with polite refusal (B), but eventually, following stubborn negotiations, his request was fulfilled (B1). The order of events in the description of the realization of Abraham's request in B1 is in reverse order of their presentation in B.

C and C1:

Again, the parallel and the development are apparent. In C, Abraham encounters an indirect refusal of his request (in terms of person, property and sum), but after his repeated request in C1 (with a repeat only of the matter of payment, which is the controversial issue) he succeeds, and even beyond his request. He had requested the cave that is at the edge of Ephron's field, but ultimately acquired both the field and the cave.

Now we have a clearer picture of the structure not only of the story of Sara's burial, but also of the section of chapter twenty-five that is located later, at the end of the *parasha*. That section (excluding verses 7–10, which belong to the story of Sara's burial) also comprises two equal halves, with seven verses in each, and contains the two family branches that descended from Abraham other than that of Isaac.

The first half includes verses 1–6 and verse 11, with its list of the names of Abraham's children born of Ketura, whom he distanced from Isaac while he was still alive. Abraham gave them gifts and sent them far from Isaac, to the east, while giving everything that he had to Isaac. Verse 11 completes this selection by noting that after Abraham's death, God blessed Isaac, his son.

The second half of this literary unit, verses 12–18, lists the names of the children of Ishmael, Abraham's son born of the Egyptian Hagar. As we know from earlier on in the narrative, Ishmael too was distanced from Isaac by God's word during Abraham's lifetime, and indeed the place of Ishmael's descendants is "from Ḥavila until Shur, which is facing Egypt" – far from the borders of the land of Canaan, which was destined for the children of Isaac. It is only after the description of these two branches of Abraham's descendants that we begin with the *parasha* of "the generations of Isaac, son of Abraham."

V. THE FINAL SECTION OF THE SARA STORY

Does the addition of the final section concerning Sara's death in chapter twenty-five change the definition of our subject, such that it becomes "the story of the death and burial of Abraham and of Sara"? The answer seems to be in the negative. Twenty verses out of the twenty-four comprising the story are devoted to the death of Sara and to Abraham's efforts to bury her in an appropriately honorable burial place. The pair of leading words, which we found each to occur fourteen times throughout the story as a whole, likewise testifies that the subject is "the burial of Sara," and not the burial of Abraham.

What, then, is the contribution of the concluding section to the significance of the story in its entirety, as discussed above? This section is of vital importance to complete the description of the love and honor of Abraham towards Sara at the time of her death. Sara did indeed deserve to be buried in a private family burial plot purchased at the full price – and this is certainly a most respectable burial. But Abraham continues to be a "stranger and a resident" in the land; he continues as a nomad wandering after his flocks. What guarantee is there, then, that when the time comes he, too, will be buried in the burial place where Sara is buried? If perhaps he should die far away, and is buried in the place where he died, then the Cave of Makhpela will become, in relation to Sara, what the Tomb of Rachel is destined to become in relation to Jacob's beloved wife: the lonely grave of a person who was buried alone at the place where she died.

It is only at the time of Abraham's death, thirty-eight years after that of his beloved wife, when he too is buried in the Cave of Makhpela, that it becomes clear that Sara did indeed merit to be buried in a family burial plot (25:10) – "There Abraham was buried, and Sara his wife."

Chronology and Interpretation

by Rav Michael Hattin

I. INTRODUCTION

In the aftermath of the *Akeda* (Binding of Isaac), the Torah maintains a discreet silence concerning the lives of Abraham and Sara. Other than a brief genealogical list that traces the relationship of Rebecca to Isaac, the son of Abraham and Sara, there are no additional incidents recounted in the life of the aged matriarch or of her husband. Instead, this week's *parasha* of Ḥayyei Sara opens with the abrupt announcement of Sara's death. The rest of the section is devoted to the account of her burial, the marriage of Isaac to Rebecca, and Abraham's own demise. With Abraham's dismissal of his concubine Ketura and her offspring, and the proleptic but emphatic mention of Ishmael's death, Isaac's role as the successor and preserver of his parents' legacy is secured.

This week, we shall consider the chronology associated with Sara's death. In the process, it will become apparent that the issues raised by the discussion may have far-ranging implications for the entire enterprise of biblical exegesis. Along the way, a proverbial Pandora's box or two may be opened, but hopefully with less than harmful results.

II. THE AGES OF THE PROTAGONISTS

> The years of Sara's life were one hundred and twenty-seven, these
> were the years of Sara's life. Sara died in Kiryat Arba, that being
> Ḥevron, in the land of Canaan. Abraham arrived to eulogize his
> wife and to mourn her. (Gen. 23:1–2)

These terse verses introduce three salient points and no more: Sara's age
at the time of her demise, the location of her death, and the timely arrival
of Abraham at the scene. The text itself provides us with no clues at all
concerning the circumstances of her death or its cause.

The few details provided above may assist us in constructing
a more complete picture of the event, but the critical questions will
remain unanswered. Thus, knowledge of Sara's age allows us to calculate
the respective ages of Abraham and Isaac at that time. Recall that the
Torah had indicated on the eve of Isaac's birth that Abraham was one
hundred years old and Sara was ninety (Gen. 17:17; 21:5). Sara died at
the age of one hundred and twenty-seven, thirty-seven years after the
birth of her only son. Therefore, at the time of his wife's death, Abraham
was one hundred and thirty-seven and Isaac was thirty-seven. In themselves, these chronological details may seem inconsequential, but we
shall soon see that they are, in fact, critical.

The other additional temporal data that may be of significance
concerns the marriage of Isaac to Rebecca, his first cousin once removed.
According to a parenthetical reference in next week's *Parashat Toledot*,
Isaac was "forty years old when he took as his wife Rebecca, the daughter of Betuel the Aramean of Padan Aram, and the sister of Laban" (Gen.
25:20). Thus, if Isaac was thirty-seven years of age at the death of his
mother, then his marriage to Rebecca took place three years after Sara's
death. Again, although the calculation may seem trifling, it will potentially carry great exegetical weight.

III. THE CAUSE OF SARA'S DEATH

So far, although we have succeeded in generating a more comprehensive
chronology of Sara's loved ones, we still are left to ponder precisely what
precipitated her death. Is it possible for us to reconstruct not only the

potentially significant dates, but the pivotal events as well? According to many biblical commentators, the answer is a resounding "yes."

Sara's death is recounted in juxtaposition to the episode of the Binding of Isaac because she died on its account. When Sara heard that her son had been designated for slaughter and had almost lost his life, her soul left her body and she died! (Rashi on 23:2).

For Rashi and the many expositors that follow in his footsteps, Sara dies in the aftermath of the *Akeda*. Textually, this explanation is derived from the proximity of the *Akeda* account to Sara's death. In fact, no significant narrative intervenes between the two, as the penultimate episode of last week's *parasha* was the provocative Binding of Isaac (22:1–19). Recall that God had asked of the aged Abraham to surrender his beloved son Isaac on the altar of absolute trust. Abraham prepared the necessary provisions, journeyed to the land of Moriah, and steeled himself for the impossible deed. At the last moment, the sacrificial knife already raised, God's angel stayed his hand, and Abraham offered a ram in his son's stead. Abraham's absolute fidelity was rewarded with the promise of blessing and triumph for the nation that would one day emerge from Isaac his son. The account concluded with the observation that "Abraham returned to his attendants and they arose and journeyed together to Be'er Sheva, and Abraham dwelt in Be'er Sheva" (Gen. 22:19).

But for the brief interlude of Rebecca's almost unpronounceable genealogy, nothing else separates the event of the *Akeda* from the death of Sara:

> After these things it was told to Abraham that Milca also had borne children to Nahor his brother. Uz his firstborn, Buz his brother, and Kemuel the father of Aram. Kesed and Hazo, Pildash and Yidlaf, and Betuel. **Betuel was the parent of Rebecca.** These eight were borne by Milca to Nahor, Abraham's brother. His concubine Reuma bore Tevah, Gaham, Tahash and Maakha. (22:20–24)

IV. CALCULATING REBECCA'S AGE

Thus, Rashi and others maintain that it was the frightful news of Isaac's own brush with death that triggered his mother's demise. Additionally,

Rashi maintains that the report of Rebecca's pedigree is not only useful for the purposes of tracing her familial ties to her future husband Isaac, but is also significant for chronological reasons: "Upon their return from Mount Moriah...God informed them that Rebecca, Isaac's future mate, had been born" (Rashi on 22:20). For Rashi, the list of Rebecca's lineage that divides the *Akeda* from the announcement of Sara's death is therefore to be understood as the announcement of Rebecca's birth. She enters the world just as the aged patriarch and his much-loved son make their way back from their fateful encounter with God, the report of which fills Sara with fatal dread. Taking the matter to its logical conclusion, Rashi claims:

> At the time of the *Akeda*, Isaac was thirty-seven years old, for at that time Sara died...just then Rebecca was born. Isaac waited for three years until she was fit for marriage and then took her as his wife. (Rashi on 25:20)

Summing up the matter so far, we may say that Rashi succeeds in filling in the critical episodic gaps by bridging between the passages. We now know the cause of Sara's death, how old Isaac is at the *Akeda*, and the age of Rebecca at the time of her marriage. It must be stressed that Rashi's explanation and reconstructed chronology, well known to every ritually observant school child and accepted as authentic truth, is well established upon the bedrock of rabbinic tradition. The source for Rashi's comments is the venerable *Seder Olam Raba*, an early midrashic work of chronology that is often quoted in the Talmud. *Seder Olam Raba* records historical events from Anno Mundi ("Year of Creation of the World") until the failed Bar Kokhba Revolt of the second century CE – a period of roughly four thousand years. According to chapter one of this work, "Our father Isaac was thirty-seven years old when he was bound and placed upon the altar...at that time, Rebecca was born. Thus, our father Isaac married Rebecca when she was three years old."

V. THE ASSUMPTIONS AND THE PRELIMINARY PROBLEMS

Before addressing the thematic difficulties that are raised by Rashi's explanation, let us first take note of the assumptions upon which it is based. Firstly, Rashi assumes that no time whatsoever intervenes between the *Akeda* and Sara's death. The final verse of the *Akeda* episode recounts: "Abraham returned to his attendants and they arose and journeyed together to Be'er Sheva, and Abraham dwelt in Be'er Sheva" (22:19). The text itself gives no indication concerning the length of Abraham's stay in Be'er Sheva. Curiously, the location of Sara's death mentioned but a few verses later is recorded as Kiryat Arba or Ḥevron: "Sara died in Kiryat Arba, that being Ḥevron, in the land of Canaan. Abraham arrived to eulogize his wife and to mourn her" (Gen 23:2). How do we explain Abraham's return to Be'er Sheva while his wife Sara is apparently dwelling in Ḥevron? Could it be that Abraham was away from Sara for an extended period of time, and therefore she did not die, as Rashi claims, in the aftermath of the *Akeda*?

Rashi is careful to avoid the pitfall by explaining that "Abraham did not **dwell** in Be'er Sheva, because they were living in Ḥevron..." (Rashi on 22:19). Further, "Abraham **arrived** from Be'er Sheva to eulogize Sara and mourn her" (Rashi on 23:2). In other words, after the *Akeda*, Abraham and Isaac journeyed home from Moriah to Ḥevron. En route, they passed through Be'er Sheva, and Sara died while they were there. While plausible, Rashi's explanation does not address the use of the verb *"vayeshev"* to describe Abraham's stop in Be'er Sheva, a verb that is usually reserved for some sort of semi-permanent or permanent form of residence. Also, Rashi's geographical route is quite circuitous. Why would the aged father and his anxious son, eager to reunite with doting Sara, leave the well-trod route that links the crests of the Judean hills (southern Ḥevron and Moriah to its north among them) in order to detour through the arid foothills of Be'er Sheva that lie more than thirty kilometers south of Ḥevron?

Rashi's second assumption concerns the report of Rebecca's birth. Rashi supposes that the news of Rebecca's birth is synonymous with her birth, and that this news reaches him immediately after the *Akeda*. This is by no means certain. First of all, the text states that "After (*aharei*) these things it was told to Abraham that Milca also had borne children to Naḥor his brother...," and Rashi elsewhere acknowledges that "aharei" implies a lapse of time (see Rashi on Gen. 15:1, but see also super commentary of Ḥizkuni). More to the point, the text goes on to list the eight children that Milca bears to Naḥor, one of whom, Betuel, is the father of Rebecca:

> Uz his firstborn, Buz his brother, and Kemuel the father of Aram. Kesed and Ḥazo, Pildash and Yidlaf, and Betuel. Betuel was the parent of Rebecca. These eight were borne by Milca to Naḥor, Abraham's brother..." (22:20–23)

The thrust of the passage is to communicate the various offspring that Abraham's brother has sired since their parting many years before. It describes a series of children that were born over the course of quite some time. Of course, the significance of the list is that it introduces us to Rebecca, thus foreshadowing the pivotal events of this week's *parasha*. Nevertheless, there is no textual reason to assume that the news concerning long-lost Naḥor or his illustrious granddaughter implies Rebecca's concomitant birth at all.

VI. TEXT AND CONTEXT – MORE SERIOUS PROBLEMS

Rashi's explanation also introduces a series of overt exegetical difficulties. Recall that the *Akeda* is rightly regarded as Abraham's greatest trial of trust in God. In it he is called upon to sacrifice that which is most dear to him, the cherished realization of his lifelong yearning, the only hope for the continuity of his mission, his own flesh and blood, Isaac. The account unambiguously presents the unfolding story as Abraham's trial, and Abraham's alone. His son is portrayed as an unaware participant whose wide and trusting eyes fail to grasp the unfolding horror until almost the very end. The intuitive reading of the account indicates that Isaac is a young boy who believes in his loving father with absolute faith, as a child often must. Even the incomprehensible thought of death cannot dull his childlike acquiescence. However, if Isaac is a grown and mature man of thirty-seven years, then the trial of the *Akeda* is really his. He willingly surrenders his life to God, rather than Abraham taking it in His name. Is it really possible to reconcile the text of the *Akeda* account with Rashi's assertion that Isaac is thirty-seven years old?

Similarly, the notion that Rebecca was three years old at the time of her marriage to Isaac is untenable. Even allowing for the well-documented ancient Near Eastern practice of arranged childhood marriage, the text itself remonstrates against the possibility in this case. Recall that in the aftermath of Sara's death, aging Abraham sends his loyal servant Eliezer to Ḥaran, where Abraham's brother and extended family still dwell. Eliezer leads a caravan of ten camels laden with all manner of precious gifts, and embarks on his mission of securing a wife for Isaac from among his master's kin. Approaching Ḥaran as dusk falls, thirsty and weary from travel, Eliezer invokes an omen from God:

> Let the young woman to whom I shall say, "Please tilt your pitcher and allow me to drink," answer me by saying, "Drink, and I will also provide water for your camels." You, God, will thus have shown that she is designated for Your servant Isaac, and I shall know thereby that You have acted kindly with my master. (24:14)

Sure enough, the prayer having scarcely escaped his lips, a young woman passes him on the way down to the well. Approaching her as she ascends, her heavy pitcher upon her shoulder, Eliezer tentatively requests a drink. Quickly, she lowers the pitcher, provides him with water, and proceeds to enthusiastically water all ten of his camels. Now, the text has clearly indicated that approaching the well involves a descent (Gen. 24:16). Even assuming that Rebecca employs a small water jug that holds ten liters (two-and-a-half gallons), it still weighs ten kilograms (twenty-two pounds). Now, although we do not know how long it has been since Eliezer's last rest stop, we do know that thirsty camels are voracious drinkers. The Arabian camel can survive for many days without food or water by converting the fat in its telltale hump into energy, losing up to a third of its body weight between meals. When it does drink, however, it can consume as much as sixty-five liters (fifteen gallons) in less than ten minutes! It seems unlikely indeed that the labor necessary to provide water for ten camels, by repeatedly descending an incline to a well and then filling and refilling a heavy water jug, could be successfully performed by a three-year-old. Such an undertaking would be daunting even for a grown woman, let alone for a small child.

VII. OPPOSING INTERPRETATIONS

In light of all of the above, it is difficult indeed to adopt Rashi's chronology. Note carefully, however, that what makes Rashi's chronology problematic is not the reader's moral uneasiness with a marriage between a thirty-seven-year-old man and a three-year-old girl, but rather the textual awkwardness that such a chronology introduces. The subtle details that the Torah itself provides militate against adopting Rashi's interpretation. Counter-arguments that ask us to suspend our relativist ethical preconceptions in light of the Torah's absolute moral truths are therefore irrelevant here. How much easier our task would have been had the midrash that Rashi adopts calculated Isaac's age to have been three years at the time of the *Akeda*, and Rebecca's to be thirty-seven at the time of their marriage (when Isaac was forty – see 25:20)! Of course, we would have then concluded that Sara did not, in fact, die at the time of the *Akeda*, but many years later.

Not surprisingly, some of the classical commentaries do just that. Rejecting a chronological linkage between the *Akeda*, Rebecca's birth, and Sara's death, they are able to approach the text and interpret it without the insurmountable difficulties that Rashi's reading introduces.

> Our sages say that Isaac was thirty-seven years old at the time of the *Akeda*,

relates Rabbi Avraham ibn Ezra (twelfth century, Spain).

> If this is an authentic tradition, then we accept it. But from a logical standpoint, it cannot be correct, for then the text would have surely celebrated Isaac's righteousness in the episode, and his reward should have been double that of his father for having willingly surrendered himself to slaughter. The text, however, relates nothing at all concerning Isaac ... (Ibn Ezra on Gen. 22:4)

Ibn Ezra goes on to explain (not without introducing textual difficulties of his own) that Isaac was about thirteen years old at the time of the *Akeda*, thus placing the event some twenty years before Sara's death, and unconnected with the birth of Rebecca.

Similarly, in his lengthy comments, Ramban (thirteenth century, Spain) explains:

> God's command concerning the *Akeda* was communicated to Abraham in Be'er Sheva, for there he dwelt and to there he returned…That is why the journey [to Moriah] took three days…Ḥevron, in contrast is close to Jerusalem. After the *Akeda*, Abraham and Isaac returned to Be'er Sheva as the verse relates [22:19], and dwelt there for many years. If so, then Sara did not die at that time… After many years, they left the land of the Philistines [Be'er Sheva] and came to Ḥevron, and it was there that Sara died. (Ramban on 23:2)

Although Ramban goes on to offer a second interpretation, this time in defense of Rashi, he does not discard his initial reading of the passages.

Concerning the related matter of Rebecca's purported birth, Ibn Ezra and Ramban both are in agreement that there is no textual evidence to bolster Rashi's claim that the news of her birth is chronologically equivalent to her birth. The significance of the passage is only that it charts Rebecca's lineage and links her family to that of Abraham and Sara. It is therefore not possible to state with certainty Rebecca's age at the time of her marriage.

VIII. LOOSE BUT VITAL ENDS

Having come this far, two important tasks remain. The first is to attempt to delineate the parameters of midrashic authority. In other words, how can Ibn Ezra and Ramban reject a rabbinic source that is widely accepted? Can we confidently (but not complacently) follow in their footsteps without treading on the threshold of heterodoxy? Secondly, if indeed Rashi's reading is as implausible as it seems, how could he himself have adopted it? In other words, it goes without saying that Rashi and the rabbinic authors of the *Seder Olam* were as careful in their reading of the Torah's text as we could ever hope to be. How carefully they pored over its every nuance (as we should), how profoundly they considered the significance of its every letter (as we ought to), how lovingly they regarded it as the eternal word of God (as we must)! Surely, they were cognizant of the difficulties that their reading introduced. How are we to understand their willingness to surrender the clarity of the straightforward reading for exegetical gains that appear, on the surface, to be dubious at best?

IX. RAMBAN AND MIDRASH

Towards the end of his life, Ramban was forced to defend his faith and the faith of his people against the missionary attempts of the fanatical Dominican friars who enjoyed the support of King James of Aragon. In a famous disputation that took place in Barcelona in 1263 before the king and his ministers, Ramban was pitted against the apostate Jew Pablo Christiani and against the hostile and powerful Catholic establishment. Pablo considered himself expert in matters Jewish but was in fact exposed by Ramban as an ignoramus. During the course of the debate, Pablo attempted to bring evidence for Jesus' messianic pretensions from various midrashim that he carelessly quoted out of context. Ramban easily refuted his charges, but not without arousing the ire of the Church.

In celebrated remarks, which themselves have subsequently aroused lively debate in Jewish circles, Ramban drew a very sharp distinction between halakhic midrash and aggadic midrash. The former is concerned with explaining the mitzvot and how they are to be performed. The latter is homiletical in nature. Exposition of halakha is formal and rigorous, and its subject matter is anchored in the necessity of delineating correct performance of the commandments. *Aggada* is less exacting and more inspirational, and rarely deals with matters that are doctrinal. "Halakha" means "way" or "path," and demarcates the acts that form the backbone of Jewish ritual and ethical conduct. *"Aggada"* means "telling" or "story," and examines the narrative passages of the Bible with the objective of developing interest and fostering spiritual growth.

> We possess three genres of literature. The first is the Bible, or Tanach, and all of us believe in its words with a complete trust. The second is the Talmud, and it is an exposition of the mitzvot of the Torah, for the Torah contains six hundred and thirteen mitzvot. Not a single one of them is left unexplained by the Talmud.

We believe in the Talmud with respect to its exposition of the mitzvot. The third type of book that we possess is the Midrash, and it is like sermons…concerning this collection, for one who believes it, good. For one who does not believe it, there is no harm…" (Ramban, Book of Disputation, paragraph 39)

In other words, we must distinguish between traditions that explain and clarify the six hundred and thirteen mitzvot, and those that involve expositions of passages that are not concerned with halakhot, but rather with narratives. Concerning the latter, interpretation can be freer and acceptance less dogmatic. To put the matter in more concrete and extreme terms, the Torah says with respect to the commandment of executing justice that "…you shall take an eye for an eye, a tooth for a tooth, a hand for a hand, and a foot for a foot…" (Ex. 21:23–24). The Talmud discusses this passage at length and concludes that the Torah is in fact enjoining monetary compensation rather than bodily retaliation (see *Bava Kamma* 84a). Although seemingly at variance with the straightforward reading of the verse, we are nevertheless obliged to accept the tradition of the Talmud, because here we are dealing with the exposition of the mitzvot. In our passage, in contrast, Isaac's age at the *Akeda* has absolutely no bearing on mitzva performance. Therefore, Ibn Ezra and Ramban can question the tradition asserting that he was in fact thirty-seven years old.

At the same time, it may very well be the case that the claim of Rashi and the *Seder Olam* is in fact an authentic tradition that was orally transmitted at Sinai. Just because a passage is narrative in nature does not preclude the existence of authentic oral traditions concerning its correct meaning. Or, as Ibn Ezra himself put it: "Our sages say that Isaac was thirty-seven years old at the time of the *Akeda*. If this is an authentic tradition, then we accept it." But here, explains Ibn Ezra, the existence of such a tradition seems unlikely, since the texts themselves omit the critical details that would make it plausible. Perhaps we must uneasily conclude that it is no simple matter to reject a midrashic source. We do so not as a function of personal distaste, but rather in deference to scriptural evidence and with the support of other authoritative sources.

X. THE MIDRASHIC MATRIX

It is not enough to simply say that Rashi's interpretation is "wrong." Having concluded that it is untenable from a textual standpoint, the more important task now is to ascertain why Rashi may have proffered it. Too often, a midrashic source is dismissed as fanciful and improbable, and that is the end of the encounter. But such a superficial approach constitutes an unfortunate (but common) error. Instead, we must begin to ponder the deeper significance of the source, the implication of its reading that only on a surface level appears implausible. Perhaps Rashi's intent was to communicate far more important ideas, which only for the sake of brevity are couched in terms of the age of the protagonists.

Let us again consider the context of Rashi's chronology. By linking together the *Akeda*, Rebecca's birth and the death of Sara, Rashi is able to calculate Isaac's age as well as that of Rebecca. By doing so, Rashi encourages us to ponder the relationship between the episodes of the *Akeda* on the one hand, and the compassion of Rebecca on the other. It is the death of Sara that brings the two disparate events together. Sara dies as news of the *Akeda* reaches her, and Rebecca is born – the very same Rebecca who will graciously care for Eliezer and the camels in this week's central narrative. It is Sara's death at the stated age of one hundred and twenty-seven that allows for the construction of the chronology in the first place.

Recall the criticism of Ibn Ezra, who questioned the tradition that Isaac was thirty-seven years old at the time of the *Akeda*: "The text would have surely celebrated Isaac's righteousness in the episode, and his reward should have been double that of his father for having willingly surrendered himself to slaughter."

In other words, it is clearly understood that if Isaac is but a child, his role in the *Akeda* is minor, although he is its unfortunate sacrifice. Abraham surrenders his beloved son to God's fiat and Isaac is the trusting, innocent victim. But, in contrast, if Isaac is thirty-seven years old, then HE is the true hero of the *Akeda*. He knowingly, consciously, and willingly gives up his life in consonance with his profound trust.

XI. RASHI RECONSIDERED

Rashi is well aware of the straightforward reading of the text that considers Isaac a mere child and Abraham the object of God's test. Abraham is called upon to give up his most precious possession, his beloved and tender child. But there is another dimension to the *Akeda* – lived out by God's people throughout the course of their bitter history – in which we are called upon to give up not just the lives of our loved ones, but our own very lives themselves for the sake of our trust in God. We must do so not as blind, childish and senseless robots, but as sentient, thinking, mature adults with full cognizance of the awesomeness of the act. That is the *Akeda* of Isaac who is thirty-seven, and that is the additional insight into the text that Rashi's interpretation allows. Indeed, in Rashi's reading, Isaac is the real hero of the *Akeda*, and his remarkable acquiescence serves as the exemplar for all subsequent acts of self-sacrifice by his children – exalted deeds that are born out of deliberation, forethought, and complete trust in God. As Rambam (twelfth century, Egypt) remarks in his discussion of martyrdom:

> Whosoever has been called upon to die rather than abrogate the commands of the Torah and does so, has sanctified God's name. If his martyrdom transpired in the presence of ten other Jews, then he has sanctified God's name publicly, after the manner of Daniel, Ḥanania, Mishael, Azaria [Daniel ch. 3, 6] and Rabbi Akiva and his colleagues. These martyrs were put to death by oppressive regimes, and there is no higher degree than their example. (*Mishneh Torah*, Hilkhot Yesodei HaTorah 5:4)

Conversely, we may correspondingly consider Rebecca's act of compassion towards Eliezer and the camels in two lights. There is Rebecca the adult, the mature woman who altruistically provides for man and beast. That is the obvious reading of the text. But here, again, Rashi allows for an additional possible reading that is predicated upon Rebecca as a three-year-old child. What is the difference between the two? Sometimes, when we perform acts of kindness, we have many aims in mind. We seek to alleviate suffering and discomfort, and we also attempt to further our own personal interests, or at least protect them. That is the "selflessness" of adulthood, and often it incorporates an element of calculation and contrivance. After all, Eliezer the vulnerable foreigner brings with him ten camels laden with intriguing bounty. Perhaps there is gain to be made at his unsuspecting expense. As an example of this other type of "kindness" we need look no further than the example of Rebecca's own brother Laban, who so graciously greets the self-same Eliezer, all the while with an angle towards self-gain (24:29–32).

But there is another dimension to altruism, in which we suspend all thought of personal gain and instead concentrate fully on the act of compassion. In this version, the selfless act has an almost naive and childlike quality, particularly when it involves great effort and outlay on our part. By recasting Rebecca as a three-year-old child who superhumanly cares for Eliezer and the camels by repeatedly descending to and ascending from the well – heavy jug in hand – to provide water, Rashi alerts us to this more profound possibility.

In the thoughtful reading that Rashi advances, Isaac's real age has been transposed with that of Rebecca! The wide-eyed child victim has become the mature adult of absolute trust, while the astute and shrewd water-drawer who can easily identify a potential goldmine becomes the loving child who desires nothing but relief for the thirsty and weary travelers. Be kind and compassionate, without an eye to gain, with no desire for recompense, with only the needs of the recipient in mind. But be a servant of God with cognition and forethought, with maturity and understanding, with sentience and awareness, and not with immature and shallow devotion. Such is the thrust of Rashi's chronology.

AUTHOR'S NOTE:

See the chronology of the Flood, where Rashi also adopts the problematic interpretation of the *Seder Olam Raba*. Ramban refutes Rashi's reading on purely textual grounds and offers a different chronology. He introduces his interpretation with the following telling words:

> In some places Rashi himself takes issue with aggadic midrashim and exerts himself in order to explain the straightforward mean-

ing of the text. His example thus gives us license to do likewise, for there are seventy facets of Torah interpretation, and many midrashic sources preserve differences of interpretation between our sages. (Ramban on Gen. 8:4)

Parashat Toledot

The Birthright

by Rabbanit Sharon Rimon

The story of the sale of the birthright is one of the strangest stories in all of the Torah. Why does Jacob want to buy the birthright? Can a birthright really be "bought" or "sold"? Is Jacob exploiting Esau's weak state, forcing him to sell the birthright against his will? These and additional questions will be dealt with in this *shiur*.

Why does Jacob want to buy the birthright? What special status does the firstborn possess, that is worthy of a person exerting himself in order to acquire it? Clearly, the birthright accords the firstborn extra rights. The Torah recognizes the special status of the firstborn and commands a father to bequeath a double portion to him:

> If a man has two wives … and the firstborn son is [born] of the less loved, then it shall be, on the day he bequeaths to his sons that which he has, he cannot show preference to the son of the better loved [wife] over the son of the less loved [wife], who is the firstborn. Rather, he must acknowledge the firstborn son of the less loved wife, to give him a double portion of all that he has, for he is the beginning of his strength; the right of the firstborn is his. (Deut. 21:15–17)

The "right of the firstborn," entitling the firstborn to a double portion of the inheritance, was not unique to *Am Yisrael,* but was practiced throughout the ancient world. In light of this, Jacob may seek the birthright because of the extra rights that it confers, as Ibn Ezra suggests in his commentary on verse 31:

> The birthright means that he takes a double portion of his father's wealth. Some opinions maintain that the firstborn always retains a superior status in relation to the younger; [the latter] must stand up in his presence and serve him, as a son does to his father.

Despite the simplicity of this explanation, it leaves us with a great many questions. If it is money or honor that is at stake here, why does Esau spurn the birthright; why is he so easily induced to sell it?[1] Furthermore, why do we not see, later on, that Jacob indeed received greater honor or more property? And, more fundamentally – is this what Jacob was interested in? Is this an accurate portrayal of Jacob – a profit-seeker who exploits his brother's near-starvation to acquire status and property for himself? Surely not: just one verse earlier he is described as a "simple man dwelling in tents"! In addition, we must ask ourselves: why does the firstborn merit a greater portion of the inheritance, and a more highly respected status? Is this an arbitrary state of affairs with no particular significance, or is there some reason for it?

Ancient sources suggest that the firstborn received extra rights because he bore greater responsibility. The firstborn bore the yoke of providing for the household, together with the parents. Upon the death of his parents he would take upon himself the role of head of the family. It was for this reason that he received double – to compensate him for his extra investment of effort.

If this is so, then when Jacob purchases the birthright he not only acquires rights, but also – and more importantly – takes on obligations.

---

1. Ibn Ezra answers this question by asserting that at this time Isaac did not have much property, and therefore Esau was prepared to forego a double portion. See his commentary and that of Ramban, who disagrees.

Therefore, it would seem that the birthright means something more significant to him than extra rights with regard to the inheritance, or honor.

Let us examine the story of Jacob and Esau from the beginning. At the very dawn of the lifetimes of Jacob and Esau, Rebecca receives a prophecy that they are not two regular babies, but rather two nations. And these two nations will live in conflict with one another.

The *parasha* goes on to tell us about these two nations: "The boys grew up, and Esau was a proficient hunter, a man of the field, while Jacob was a simple man, dwelling in tents" (25:27). This is not a description of two individuals, but rather an essential depiction of qualities inherent in their respective personalities, destined to characterize the nations that will issue from them.

Esau is a "proficient hunter, a man of the field." His occupation is hunting: he shoots arrows, casting fear over man and animals. He kills. He is a man of the field; he is not a man of the home. He does not occupy himself with settling the world, establishing a home, sowing and planting.

In contrast, Jacob is a "simple man, dwelling in tents." The sages explain that Jacob sat and studied Torah, with Shem and Ever as his teachers. Ibn Ezra and Rashbam explain that the verse means "dwelling in a tent, with flocks" – i.e., a shepherd. Either way, Jacob is portrayed as a gentle person, civilized, wholeheartedly honest – the opposite of Esau.

The story of the birthright follows immediately after the description of the essence of Jacob and of Esau, and it seems to be a continuation of that fundamental characterization that differentiates between them. As we read the story, we can almost imagine the scene. Esau arrives home, back from the field. He is a burly, masculine type, filthy and tired after a day of chasing after prey. He finds Jacob at home, cooking stew. The situation, as described in the text, highlights the difference between these two brothers. We now understand the significance of the expression "a hunter"; we have a sense of how he looks at the end of the day, and how he behaves. At the same time, we behold Jacob, dwelling in the tent, preparing stew – dinner for the family. Esau, tired and famished, asks Jacob to give him food. His whole request expresses vulgarity: "Let me gulp, I pray you" – the expression connotes feeding an animal; it testifies to gluttony and haste. "From that red, red [stew]" – he does not even mention the dish by name, so eager is he to gulp it down. The repetition of the word "*adom*" (red) likewise speaks of his haste, as Rashbam explains:

> The way of a person who is in a hurry is to repeat himself when asking something of someone else. He is tired and hungry, and is saying, as it were, "Quickly, give me something to eat!"

Esau refers to the stew as "*adom*," because its red color catches his eye, and he repeats it twice. Rav Samson Raphael Hirsch comments: "The color tempts him no less than the food itself. It reminds him of the blood of a dying animal, the object of his desire, as he pursues it in the field."

At this moment there is a slight pause in the narrative, and the Torah inserts a comment: "Therefore his name was called 'Edom.'" The giving of a name is significant; it testifies to a person's essence. The essence of Esau is "*adom*" – the redness of killing, of hunting, and the burning haste – reflected in Esau's haste to consume the lentil stew. The color red symbolizes burning, and it is for this reason that it is so characteristic of Esau and of the nation that issues from him.

By commenting here, in mid-narrative, with regard to the name Edom, the Torah reminds us to pay attention to the fact that this is not a minor story of merely personal significance, but rather bears national significance; it is a story that characterizes Esau.

Following this important comment, the text once again takes up its narrative:

> Jacob said: Sell your birthright to me this day.

Jacob observes Esau's behavior – possibly for some time. At this moment, as Esau enters from the field and demands food – quickly, he suddenly experiences a flash of understanding: Esau's behavior is so vulgar, and unworthy of the firstborn of Isaac's household! It is clear to Jacob that it is impossible for Esau to be Isaac's successor. This is not the way of the tradition of Abraham and Isaac.

Jacob asks Esau to sell him the birthright. What is Esau's response?

> Esau said: Behold, I am about to die; of what use to me is the
> birthright?

Esau has nothing but scorn for the birthright. He attaches no value to it. Why does he hold the birthright in such low esteem? Some of the commentators explain that because he is a hunter, Esau's life is perpetually in danger; he could die at any time. Therefore he believes that he has nothing to gain from the birthright.

However, there seems to be something deeper to this: not only is Esau in perpetual danger, but his whole outlook is one of "Behold, I am about to die" – meaning something similar to, "Kill cattle and slaughter sheep, eat meat and drink wine; eat and drink for tomorrow we die" (Is. 22:13). The lust for the hunt and for meat to eat is a profound trait; it expresses spiritual emptiness. There is no spiritual or ethnical significance to this world; ultimately we all die, so we may as well eat – i.e., enjoy the pleasures of this world – as much as possible.

Jacob understands that such a person is not worthy of continuing the heritage of Abraham and Isaac, who devote their entire lives to imbuing this world with spiritual and ethical meaning, by means of cleaving to God.

However, it is not only Jacob who senses that the birthright is not suited to Esau. Esau himself feels the same way. He has no understanding of the value of the birthright, and therefore he asks with disdain, "Of what use to me is the birthright?" For this reason he is prepared to sell the birthright to Jacob, and he does it with great ease. The sale of the birthright for a lentil stew testifies to the insignificance of the birthright in Esau's eyes. He is prepared to sell the birthright for something of little value – a lentil stew. Moreover, for the sake of momentary bodily pleasure, he sells the birthright, which is a meaningful, spiritual matter. This testifies to Esau's essence: he lives with the motto, "Eat, drink and be merry, for tomorrow we die."

Hence, Jacob is not exploiting Esau's momentary weakness, nor does he deceive him. He proposes a deal that is profitable for both of them: Jacob wants the birthright; Esau does not want it. The sale is acceptable and desirable for both of them. It gives expression to the worldview of each of the brothers.

The story concludes as follows: "Jacob gave [*veYaakov natan*] Esau bread and the lentil stew." The usual format for a sentence in the Torah that describes actions in the past in accordance with the order of their occurrence is to employ the verb in the future tense, with the "conversive *vav*" (turning the future tense into past), followed by the subject of the sentence. For example, "Isaac loved [*vaye'ehav* Yitzhak]"; "Jacob cooked [*vayazed Yaakov*]"; "Esau came [*vayavo Esav*]"; "Esau said [*vayomer Esav*]," etc. Here, the order is reversed: "*veYaakov natan*." A sentence in this form means that the action in question took place previously. Thus, we conclude that Jacob fed Esau even before the sale of the birthright! Esau sold the birthright not in a moment of weakness, out of hunger, but with a full stomach and a mind at rest. The continuation of the verse emphasizes this: "He ate and drank, and got up and went, and Esau spurned the birthright." After eating and drinking, when he is no longer weary and faint, and when his mind is at rest, Esau gets up to go, despising the birthright. He does not regret the sale, but rather rejoices over it: of what use to him is the birthright? Esau does not sell the birthright on a momentary, hungry, weary whim. He sells it to Jacob because it is meaningless to him. To the extent that Jacob values and desires the birthright, so Esau scorns it and seeks to divest himself of it.

However, this interpretation is still deficient. We are not speaking here of two regular, individual brothers, but rather of Jacob and Esau, who are "two nations." Hence it seems that there is something deeper that lies behind this birthright. Indeed, Abarbanel does not suffice with the above explanation. He writes:

This was an attempt to inherit the blessing of Abraham, that God blessed him, namely the exclusivity of Providence for him and his descendants...This was the money and riches that Isaac inherited from his father Abraham, and this is the money, riches, and treasure that he will bequest to his children, not other possessions...Jacob believed that this divine inheritance could not be shared between him and Esau together, since not only did they have different natures, but also their natures and personalities were the polar opposites of one another. Jacob was a God-fearing man, loving God's commandments dearly, and he was therefore worthy of inheriting the divine destiny. But Esau was a man of evil ways, with no fear of God. He did not believe in God's Providence, nor did he seek His closeness. How, then, could he be the inheritor of the divine heritage?…Jacob knew that Esau would not suffer because of this [sale], since he did not believe in that destiny and did not desire that heritage, as it is written, "Of what use to me is the birthright?" … And Esau pondered and said to himself: If I put aside the way of my forefathers, of what profit is it to me that I be called their firstborn? For this birthright would not be to inherit assets…and even if it were concerned with spiritual goodness – I do not believe in it, or in the destiny of Abraham. Hence, of what use to me is the birthright?… Thus it becomes clear that Jacob sought the birthright solely because of the matter of the divine destiny, because he saw that Esau did not believe in it…

The birthright that Jacob wants to receive is the one that involves the right to receive the blessing of Abraham. This blessing is not material, but rather spiritual: special closeness to God and the inheritance of the land, which is God's land. Jacob was aware of the spiritual importance of the blessing, and therefore he sought to receive it. Esau, in contrast, was not worthy of this blessing, nor was he at all interested in it, because he did not follow the path of his forefathers.

The transfer of the birthright from Esau to Jacob was a process arising from the actions of both brothers. Jacob bought the birthright: not for lentil stew, but with his actions – by being a "simple man, dwelling in tents," continuing the path of his forefathers, Abraham and Isaac. Esau sold the birthright by choosing to be a hunter, a man of the field, a person unworthy of inheriting the blessing of Abraham. The sale described in our *parasha* is not a sudden, unexpected act, but rather the final development in a process, expressing all that has happened thus far.

It is possible that, in fact, Jacob had no need to buy the birthright at all. It would have come to him naturally, by virtue of his actions, and because of Esau's unsuitability. Even though Jacob is not the firstborn, his actions – and those of his elder brother – bring about a situation in which he will receive the blessing of Abraham. This conclusion, arising from our analysis here of the story of Jacob and Esau, also arises from a review of all the stories of the "firstborns" in the book of Genesis.

The first story reflecting this theme is that of Cain and Abel. Cain was the firstborn, but Abel – his younger brother – is the one whose sacrifice is accepted by God. Apparently, this sacrifice and its acceptance were significant in God's eyes – and therefore in the eyes of Cain and Abel, too: "God responded to Abel and to his offering, but to Cain and to his sacrifice He did not respond." The verse emphasizes that what was involved here was not only the acceptance of the sacrifice, but something much deeper: an indication of which path is acceptable to God. It is for this reason that it pains Cain so deeply that Abel's sacrifice is accepted while his own is not. Cain is certain that he, as the firstborn, is more worthy, but it turns out that God does not endorse his path. Even after Abel's death, the meaningful continuation of the world is not through Cain, but rather through a different son – Seth.

After the Flood, the world continues through Noah. Noah has three sons – Shem, Ham and Yafet. Clearly, Shem is the chosen son: he receives from Noah the blessing of closeness to God (see 9:18–29), and it is his dynasty that produces Abraham, who is chosen by God. But was Shem the firstborn? While all of the genealogical lists mention Shem first, and hence it would appear that he was in fact the eldest son, in Genesis 10:21 we read: "To Shem, too, were children born...he, the brother of Yafet, the elder." Rashi explains that Yafet was the eldest brother. Ramban, too (on verse 10:1) explains that the list of Noah's descendants begins with the descendants of Yafet, because Yafet was the eldest. Once again, the chosen son was not the eldest.

Abraham, likewise, was not the firstborn. While the Torah mentions him before the other sons of Terah – "These are the generations of Terah; Terah bore Abram and Nahor and Haran...," the Talmud (*Sanhedrin* 69b) explains that Abraham was the youngest son, and is mentioned first only because of his importance. How does the Talmud deduce this? From the sons of Noah. There, Shem is mentioned first, despite the fact that he is not the firstborn. From this the Talmud concludes that the genealogies of families listed in the Torah appear not in order of birth, but rather in order of importance.

The story of Abraham being chosen by God is not the last time that there is a choice. Genesis continues to address the issue of chosenness, and in a much clearer and more overt manner. Abraham's eldest son is Ishmael. While Ishmael is not born of Sara, he is still Abraham's firstborn. He is banished from Abraham's house (Gen. ch. 21) in the wake of Sara's demand. Sara understands that what is involved is a significant battle over the inheritance. The conflict is not an economic one, but rather a fundamental, essential one. Sara, observing Ishmael's base behavior, demands that the handmaid's son should not be one of Abraham's inheritors. He is unworthy of it. He is a "wild man, whose hand is against everyone, and everyone's hand is against him" (Gen. 16:12); he cannot succeed Abraham. God agrees with Sara, and tells Abraham, "Your seed shall be called through Isaac."

The next instance of chosenness involves Jacob and Esau. Both are sons of Isaac and Rebecca; they are twins, but even while still in the womb it is clear that there is a difference between them. It is clear that one of them will be chosen, and the one who is chosen will be the younger brother, as Rebecca is told through prophecy: "The elder shall serve the younger" (Gen. 25:23).[2] Indeed, further on, Jacob buys the birthright from Esau, and eventually also receives Isaac's blessing.

In Jacob's family, once again, the firstborn son – Reuben – is not the one who is chosen. Judah and Joseph receive the blessing and the leadership of *Benei Yisrael*. And in Joseph's own family, the younger son is once again chosen: Jacob deliberately crosses his arms so that his right hand rests upon the head of Ephraim, the younger brother, and he gives him the more important blessing (48:13–20).

One of the most important themes of Genesis is the matter of divine chosenness. Throughout the book we grapple with the question of who is chosen. Who is God choosing to represent God's way in the world? And throughout the book, the one who is chosen is not the firstborn. The entire book teaches that the physical fact of being the eldest does not automatically ensure the right to the firstborn blessing. God chooses the person who is worthy of receiving the blessing. God's blessing is given on the basis of merit, not chronology. While the Torah does recognize the status of the firstborn and his rights – as we saw above, in chapter twenty-one of Deuteronomy – this is so only on the personal,

---

2. Admittedly, the language of the verse is not unequivocal; the nature of Hebrew grammar allows for the opposite understanding: "*rav – ya'avod tza'ir*," i.e., "The elder shall be served by the younger." Still, it is clear that this is a secondary exegetical possibility; the plain meaning is that the elder will serve the younger. See Radak ad loc.

limited level. In Genesis, where the question concerns the essential representative of God's way in the world, there is no preference for the biological firstborn. Rather, God chooses the person who is most worthy, and it is only this choice that leads to the special blessing: the blessing of God's closeness and of inheriting the land.

Let us now return to our *parasha* and the story of the sale of the birthright. If the birthright has no relevance to the mater of chosenness and God's blessing, then what need is there for this entire narrative? Why must Jacob make the effort to buy the birthright if the firstborn in any case enjoys no preference with regard to divine chosenness and blessing?

It seems that the sale of the birthright expresses a different perspective: in order for Jacob to receive the blessing, he must acquire the birthright. He must become the firstborn.

Seemingly, an analysis of the story would lead us to conclude that it presents, in the clearest and sharpest possible manner, the fact that being the eldest does not entitle one to preference with regard to being chosen and blessed by God. Even if Esau would swear that he was selling the birthright, and even if Jacob were to pay a very dear price, Jacob cannot acquire from Esau the biological fact of being born first – this Jacob knows, and it is not this "birthright" that he is buying. Jacob seeks to buy the real "birthright" – the leadership of the family, representing the continuation of the path of Abraham and Isaac: guarding and observing "the path of God, to perform righteousness and justice." This birthright is not given automatically to the firstborn, but rather is acquired through actions. It is this birthright that Jacob "buys" – not with a pot of lentil stew, but rather by virtue of his actions; by virtue of his spiritual suitability for this special task.

The story of the sale of the birthright presents a picture of Esau, who is not worthy of being chosen, nor interested, and therefore despises that birthright. In contrast, we observe Jacob, who is interested in this true birthright – which is divine chosenness – and he makes an effort to "buy" it. The fact that the birthright can be acquired testifies to the fact that being born first does not automatically mean that a person is worthy of receiving God's blessing. To receive His blessing, one needs to be spiritually suited and worthy, to invest effort, and to seek to "acquire" the true birthright.

The Differences between Abraham and Isaac

by Rav Amnon Bazak

I. "ALL THAT HAPPENED TO ABRAHAM HAPPENED ALSO TO ISAAC"

Isaac is often portrayed as an exact parallel to Abraham, as reflected in the midrash:

> Note that all that happened to Abraham, happened [also] to Isaac. Abraham had to leave his place, and [likewise] Isaac had to leave. The identity of Abraham's wife was questioned, and likewise the identity of Isaac's wife. The Philistines were jealous of Abraham, and likewise of Isaac. Abraham eventually had a son, and Isaac also eventually had children. Abraham had a righteous son and a wicked son, and likewise Isaac. In Abraham's time there was a famine, and likewise in the time of Isaac, as it is written: "There was a famine in the land." (*Midrash HaGadol, Bereshit* 26:1)

On the basis of these similarities, many have concluded that Isaac had nothing new to offer the world. His greatness lay chiefly in his ability to preserve and secure the way of his father, Abraham.

In this *shiur*, I shall posit quite the opposite: points of comparison between Abraham and Isaac serve only to accentuate the differences between them. These differences demonstrate that Isaac repaired and completed the actions of his father, and as a result attained certain ends that Abraham himself had not achieved.

II. BARRENNESS

Both Abraham and Isaac were faced with the reality of a wife who was barren for many years. But their respective responses to this phenomenon are different. Concerning Abraham, we are told that Abraham does not pray directly for a son. On the contrary, he states – as a matter of fact – "Indeed, You have given me no seed" (15:2–4). Even if we understand this as a covert plea for a child, we note that he makes no mention of Sara in his words.

Radak questions whether Abraham did in fact pray for a son:

> Abraham did not pray for Sara as Isaac did for [Rebecca] – or perhaps he did pray but was not answered, for God wanted to display His wonders through her, for the love of Abraham; that she would bear a child at the age of ninety. (Radak on Gen. 16:2)

Rashi, on the other hand, explains Sara's anger at Abraham as arising from Abraham's disregard for her plight:

> "My anger is upon you" – for the wrong done to me, I place the retribution upon you, for when you prayed to the Holy One [saying], "What will You give me – for I go childless," you prayed only for yourself. You should have prayed for both of us, and then I, too, would have been blessed with a child, like you. (Rashi on 16:5)

By Isaac, however, both his prayer and his inclusion of his wife are clear: "Isaac pleaded (*vaye'etar*) to God for his wife, for she was barren…" (25:21). Naturally, we find that God answers him, measure for measure: "God accepted his plea (*vaye'ater*), and Rebecca, his wife, conceived."

III. FAMINE

Abraham and Isaac both face a situation of famine, and the Torah links their respective experiences:

> There was a famine in the land, and Abram went down to Egypt to sojourn there, for the famine was severe in the land. (12:10)

> There was a famine in the land, **besides the first famine, which had occurred in the days of Abraham,** and Isaac went to Abimelekh, king of the Philistines, in Gerar. (26:1)

Again, we find that while Abraham leaves *Eretz Yisrael*, Isaac remains within the boundaries of the land. The commentators are divided in their attitude towards Abraham's abandonment of Israel – Ramban regards it as a severe transgression, resulting in the decree of the Egyptian exile for his descendants, while Radak regards this course of action as evidence of Abraham passing a divine test. However, it seems that Isaac – who never considered leaving the land, but rather went off to the region ruled by Abimelekh "to sojourn in his land until the famine would be over" (Radak on 26:1) – behaved in a more praiseworthy manner. Indeed, in the wake of this act, Isaac receives a special blessing from God not transmitted to Abraham – he will remain in the land always. Though most of the blessings he received were admittedly already given to Abraham, one blessing is unique to Isaac: "And I will be with you." This blessing is given in the Torah only in connection with *Eretz Yisrael*, as we are told:

> God said to Jacob: Return to **the land of your fathers,** to your birthplace, **and I will be with you.** (Gen. 31:3)

> He commanded Joshua bin Nun, saying: Be strong and courageous, for you will bring *Benei Yisrael* to **the land that I promised them,** and **I will be with you.** (Deut. 31:23)

Because Isaac is so devoted to *Eretz Yisrael*, he merits an eternal connection with the land and the promise that God will be with him.

IV. "SHE IS MY SISTER"

On three different occasions we read of one of the patriarchs fearing for his life and deciding to pass off his wife as his sister – twice involving Abraham, in Egypt (ch. 12) and in Gerar (ch. 20), and once involving Isaac – in Gerar (ch. 26). A study of these three instances reveals a development: the first time the wife is taken altogether; the second time she is taken, but the king does not approach her; and the third time she is not taken at all. What is the meaning of these differences?

Concerning the first instance, again we find a dispute among the commentators as to how Abraham's act should be viewed. While Ramban (on 12:10) is unhappy with Abraham's behavior, Radak (on 12:12), once again, defends Abraham. However, even if we follow Radak's opinion, the *parasha* confronts us with a somewhat jarring expression:

> Please say that you are my sister, in order that it will be good for me on your account, and my life will be spared because of you. (12:12)

If there is really no alternative and it is a question of life and death, then the words "my life will be spared because of you" are quite in order. But what is the meaning of the previous phrase – "in order that it will be good for me on your account"? Rashi explains: "They will give me gifts," and it seems that his interpretation is correct, for we are told later on:

> He was good to Abraham on her account, and he had sheep and cattle and donkeys, servants and maidservants, and she-asses and camels. (12:16)

At a later stage in his life, Abraham expresses reservations about accepting money from evil people:

> Abraham said to the king of Sodom: I have raised my hand to the Most High God, Possessor of the heavens and the earth, that I will take nothing – from a thread to a shoelace – of all that is yours, that you shall not say, "I made Abram rich." (14:22–23)

Indeed, the second time Abraham encounters the same situation, he expresses no expectation of receiving any material profit:

> Abraham traveled from there to the land of the Negev, and he dwelled between Kadesh and Shur, and he sojourned in Gerar. And Abraham said of Sara, his wife: "She is my sister." (20:1–2)

While Abraham will receive gifts from the king who took his wife, this time the reward is not for the actual taking, but rather as compensation for the anguish caused to Abraham and Sara.

Isaac appears to achieve a complete repair of this scenario, for ultimately his wife is not taken at all. Instead, he remains in complete togetherness with Rebecca: "And … Abimelekh … saw, and behold – Isaac was intimate with Rebecca his wife" (26:8–10).

There seems to be one glaring difference between these three instances. In both of the stories about Abraham, the declaration that the woman is his sister is made immediately upon arrival in the new area:

> When he came near to come to Egypt, he said to Sarai, his wife: "Look, now – I know that you are a beautiful woman … Please say that you are my sister …" (12:11–12)

> And he sojourned in Gerar. And Abraham said of Sara, his wife: "She is my sister …" (20:1–2)

Isaac, on the other hand, waits until he is asked:

> The local people asked about his wife, and he said: "She is my sister," for he feared to say, "my wife" (26:7)

It seems, then, that Isaac and Rebecca lived there together as a regular husband and wife, and only when asked did he respond, "She is my sister." This dedication to the truth allowed Isaac to depart from it only at the last moment, under clear compulsion. Obviously, his response sounded suspicious, and it is reasonable to assume that this is what caused the king to look through the window specifically at this point, before taking the woman.

Abraham ascended from Egypt the first time with great wealth that he had received from Pharaoh in return for Sara: "Abram was very wealthy, in cattle, in silver and in gold" (13:2). In contrast, the Torah describes how Isaac, following the episode of Abimelekh, achieves his wealth by merit of his own labors: "Isaac sowed in that land and he received the same year a hundredfold, and God blessed him. The man grew great, and he continued to grow until he became very great" (26:12).

V. DISPUTE AMONG THE SHEPHERDS

Not much time passes, and again Isaac is beset with problems – this time from the direction of the Philistine shepherds:

> The servants of Isaac dug in the valley, and they found there a well flowing with fresh water. And the shepherds of Gerar strove with Isaac's shepherds, saying: "The water is ours," and he called the name of the well "*Esek*" ["striving"], for they strove with him. (26:19–20)

Again we are reminded of Abraham, who also had to deal with a dispute among shepherds (13:7). Here, again, there is a difference. Abraham's way of dealing with the dispute of the shepherds is to propose a compromise: "Is not all the land before you? Please separate yourself from me – if you take the left side then I will take the right; if the right – I will take the left" (13:9). Lot accepts his suggestion, and chooses the portion of land that pleases him.

At first glance, Abraham's suggestion seems to represent a worthy, peaceful solution. However, close inspection of God's reaction points to a certain reservation regarding Abraham's readiness to relinquish parts of the land, which were meant for him, to Lot:

> God said to Abram, after Lot had separated from him: lift up your eyes and see, from the place where you are – northwards and southwards, eastwards and westwards. For **all the land** that you see – I shall give it to you and to your seed forever. I shall make your seed like the dust of the earth, that if a person could count the dust of the earth, so could your seed be counted. Arise;

walk about in the land, its length and its breadth, for I shall give it to you... (13:14–16)

When God repeats Abraham's phrase "all the land," He is hinting that the land Abraham offers Lot is not meant for Lot at all; it is meant exclusively for Abraham and his descendants. It is not Lot who should "lift his eyes" and choose whichever portion he desires, but rather Abraham who should "lift his eyes" and know that the entire land has been given to him, for all eternity. The land is not supposed to be divided between "left" and "right," but should rather remain, in its entirety, the land of Abraham: from the north to the south, from the east to the west, its length and breadth. A completely different land is destined for the descendants of Lot:

> God said to me: Do not harass Moab nor challenge them to war, for it is not to you that I give of their land as an inheritance, but rather to the children of Lot that I have given Ar for an inheritance. (Deut. 2:9)

From this perspective, Isaac's determination to remain in the land and to fight for it is especially praiseworthy:

> They dug another well, and they strove also over that, and he called its name Sitna. He moved from there and dug another well, and they did not strive over it, and he called it Reḥovot ["broad places"], saying: Now God has made room for us, and we shall be fruitful in the land. (26:21–22)

Isaac does not offer the Philistines any portion of the land. His determination eventually prevails, and they cease to argue with him.

VI. PACT WITH ABIMELEKH

Although Abimelekh abducted Sara, and almost seized Rebecca as well, he ultimately approached both Abraham and Isaac, requesting that they enter into a peace pact with him. The stories share many similarities. In both instances, Abimelekh initiates the covenant after recognizing the divine assistance rendered to the patriarchs:

God is with you in all that you do. (21:22)

I have seen clearly that God was with you. (26:28)

In both cases, the patriarchs respond with a complaint concerning the injustice done to them by Abimelekh's servants:

Abraham rebuked Abimelekh on account of the well of water which the servants of Abimelekh had stolen. (21:25)

Why have you come to me, when you hate me and banished me from among you? (26:27)

Finally, each encounter concludes with a mutual promise between the patriarch and Abimelekh, which pertains also to the name of the city – Be'er Sheva:

Therefore he called the name of that place "Be'er Sheva," for there the two of them swore [*nishbe'u*]. (21:31)

They swore [*vayishavu*] each to the other…therefore the name of the city was Be'er Sheva. (26:31–33)

Once again, a closer look at the relevant chapters reveals fundamental differences between Abraham's way and that of Isaac. While Abraham immediately agrees to Abimelekh's request, and only afterwards mentions the injustice done to him (21:24–25), Isaac first presents his complaints to Abimelekh, and only after forcing the latter to admit that his approach is motivated by personal interests, does Isaac agree to negotiate with him (26:27).

Further on, it turns out that although Abimelekh asked Abraham only for a promise, Abraham is prepared to go even further – to forge a covenant (21:23–27). This point is of great significance. While a promise is merely an undertaking, a covenant expresses partnership and a qualitative connection between the two parties. Abraham's readiness to make a covenant with Abimelekh, after the latter had previously taken his wife

and after hearing Abimelekh's questionable apology for the episode of
the well is most surprising. The covenant is executed through an act of
expressing good faith, and an attempt to sort out the issue of the well
on the basis of mutual undertaking: "Take the seven sheep from me,
that you may be a witness for me that I dug this well" (21:30). However,
Ḥazal sharply criticize this act by Abraham.[1]

Isaac, interestingly, acts in exactly the opposite manner. When
Abimelekh asks of him what he never asked of Abraham: "Let me make
a covenant with you," Isaac agrees only to a mutual promise; he will not
enter into a covenant with a man such as Abimelekh. Although Isaac
offers the proper hospitality to Abimelekh and his men, he actually
gives them nothing.

This different approach is reflected in the different results. The
pact made with Abraham is violated after Abraham's death: "All the
wells that the servants of his father had dug in the days of Abraham
were blocked up by the Philistines and filled with dust" (26:15). The
agreement reached with Isaac, on the other hand, concludes with the
Torah reporting that "they departed from him in peace," and we hear
no more of any disturbances. It is specifically through highlighting the
moral distance separating Isaac from Abimelekh – leaving no possibility
of a covenant – that Isaac achieves a "cold peace" with him, which turns
out to be more effective than the covenant made by his father.

---

1. Abraham took sheep and cattle, and gave them to Abimelekh. Abimelekh said to
   Abraham: What are these here seven sheep? –

   The Holy One said to him: You gave seven sheep without My desiring it; by your
   life, I shall postpone the rejoicing of your children for seven generations.

   You gave him seven sheep without My desiring it; by your life, corresponding
   to this they will kill seven righteous men of your children, and these are they: Ḥofni,
   Pinḥas, Samson, and Saul and his three sons.

   You gave him seven sheep without My desiring it; correspondingly, his sons
   will destroy seven of your children's Sanctuaries, and these are they: the *Ohel Moed*
   and Gilgal, Nov, Givon, Shilo, and the two Temples.

   You gave him seven sheep without My desiring it; correspondingly, My holy
   Ark will remain in the field of the Philistines for seven months. (*Bereshit Raba* 54:4)

VII. ATTITUDE TOWARDS THE SINFUL SON

The final point that I shall address concerns a comparison noted by the Midrash: "Abraham had a righteous son and a wicked son, and likewise Isaac." What was the difference between Abraham's attitude towards Ishmael and Isaac's attitude towards Esau? Though Abraham protested against sending Ishmael away, the Torah does not record a single conversation between Abraham and Ishmael. The father's feelings for the son are discernable only at the end, after Ishmael's sin has brought about – with God's approval – the need to banish him from his home.

In contrast, Isaac reveals his feelings for his son Esau from the very outset: "Isaac loved Esau, for the hunt was in his mouth" (25:28). Though Isaac is well aware of Esau's character, he does not change course regarding his son, offering him a blessing before his death: "'Prepare me tasty dishes, such as I love, and bring it to me and I shall eat, in order that my soul may bless you before I die'" (27:1–4).

How beautifully the Midrash explains this relationship of Isaac towards Esau:

> "And Isaac loved Esau" – did Isaac then not know that Esau's actions were bad? Yet we are told, "Shall I not hate those who hate you, God?" [Ps. 139:21]. Why, then, did he love him?
>
> In truth, he showed love for him only to his face, in order to draw him closer. For if, when he loved him, Esau's actions were evil, how much more evil would they be if he hated him and distanced him! Our sages taught: The right hand should always draw near and the left hand push away. Therefore the Torah says that Isaac loved Esau. (*Midrash HaGadol, Bereshit* 25:28)

Isaac's plan – to bless Esau with blessings of material success while granting Jacob the blessing of Abraham – was not successful, because of Rebecca's intervention. This *shiur* does not discuss whether Rebecca was correct in intervening. But though Rebecca brings about a turnabout in the plan, the positive influence of Isaac's educational philosophy is still felt:

> Esau saw that the daughters of Canaan were bad in the eyes of

Isaac, his father. And Esau went to Ishmael, and took Maḥalat, daughter of Ishmael, son of Abraham, sister of Nevayot, in addition to his other wives, as a wife. (28:8–9)

Esau is not concerned by the fact that the daughters of Canaan are bad also in the eyes of Rebecca, his mother, who estranged herself to him. He is disturbed only by the fact that they are bad "in the eyes of Isaac his father," who openly showed his love for him. Moreover, even in his terrible rage at the deceitful act of Jacob, Esau manages – at least for the meantime – to hold back his desire to execute judgment for himself and to kill his brother:

> Esau said to himself: When the days of mourning for my father are at hand, then I will kill Jacob, my brother. (27:41)

Isaac teaches us a most important educational lesson. One's dealings with a son who has deviated from the path of his father must come from love. Only through love are we able to repair – even just a little – the way of the son.

VIII. SUMMARY

Abraham our forefather paved the way. His ceaseless moving – from the first "*Lekh lekha*" sending him to Israel, to the last sending him to Moriah – created a completely new path in the world. But – as in any new road – there is room for repair and completion of deficiencies, without which no new beginning could ever exist. This is the job of the continuer of the way – Isaac. With determination and conscientiousness, Isaac strengthens the connection with the promised land and deals with the corrupt inhabitants of the land. With great faith he addresses his wife's barrenness and also manages to influence even the evil ways of his son, Esau.

The Blindness of Isaac

by Rav Ezra Bick

Introductory Note:
This shiur will make liberal use of midrashim in order to understand the personality and spiritual qualities of Isaac. There is a widespread tendency to view peshat and midrash as mutually exclusive, seeing drush as appropriate for rabbis making a point in a sermon but not as genuinely addressing the text. I believe this is a fundamental misunderstanding of Midrash. The Midrash presents a sensitive second-level interpretation of the narrative, searching for the meaning and wider understanding of events. The language of the Midrash does indeed require decoding. Precisely because it deals so often with themes and understandings beyond the literal exposition of a story, it uses associations, metaphors, myths and other literary devices to convey its meaning. There are undoubtedly many midrashim that are homiletic in origin; nonetheless, the majority are interpretative. One of the goals of this shiur is to illustrate this point.

I.

Parashat Toledot recounts the entire career of Isaac. Abraham's life and deeds are described in *Lekh Lekha* and *Vayera* in a series of incidents involving heroism, devotion, sacrifice and moral excellence, and this is continued into *Ḥayyei Sara*. Jacob's life is detailed from *Vayetzeh* until the end of Genesis (viewing the struggle of Joseph and his brothers as belonging to the life of Jacob, i.e. how the mission is passed on – parallel to *Ḥayyei Sara* for Abraham and the second half of *Toledot* for Isaac). Isaac's life, his position in the trilogy of Avot, is completely encapsulated in one *parasha* – *Toledot*. And what did Isaac actually do in this *parasha*, other than having children and eventually sending them on their way? He dug wells! The only incident from Isaac's career described in the Torah is that he dug wells in Gerar. No drama, no great deeds of heroism, no struggle, no journeys. The last point is especially indicative. Travel and wandering are hallmarks of Abraham and Jacob. Abraham not only makes the long journey to *Eretz Yisrael*, he continually moves about within *Eretz Yisrael*, and makes a trip to Egypt as well. Jacob makes the round trip to Aram and is associated with several different places in *Eretz Yisrael*, completing his life in Egypt. Isaac's life is circumscribed by Gerar on the one side and the desert beyond Ḥevron on the other. The picture we receive is a sedentary one, uneventful, quiescent, passive. The Torah had nothing much to tell, it seems. Why, then, is Isaac an *av*, a father, an archetype? An archetype of what?

Let us begin by focusing on Isaac's blindness. "When Isaac grew old, his eyes weakened from seeing" (27:1). That Isaac had difficulty seeing is undoubted – the deception of Jacob in order to obtain the *berakhot* (blessings) depends on it. Nonetheless, it is tempting to interpret his blindness as not only physical but a perceptual, spiritual inability to distinguish: for instance, to distinguish between Jacob and Esau, and not only in the form of their faces. How is it that Isaac loved and favored Esau, when we assume he was unworthy of this preference? The answer is – he was blind, for some reason unperceptive, undiscriminating, and hence easily fooled.

There is one relatively strong indicator of this interpretation, despite its seeming "*drush*" character. Normally, the Torah introduces a necessary background piece of information not at the beginning of the story but precisely at the point where an explanation is demanded. For instance, although the fact that Sara is barren is clearly part of the background of the visit of the angels to Abraham, only when Sara is about to laugh at their announcement of the impending birth of Isaac does the Torah write, "And Abraham and Sara were old…" This is injected in the middle of the story, and, to modern ears, sounds like an interruption. This is, however, standard practice in the Torah. (See also, "And Rebecca had a brother…" [24:29].) In our case, the story begins with a statement that Isaac was blind and continues by stating that he called for Esau to come. If the significance of Isaac's blindness is to explain how Jacob could fool him, this statement need not appear before verse 5. On the contrary, its actual location indicates that his blindness is part of the explanation of why he sent for Esau. From that, it is one more step to conclude that we are dealing with lack of discernment rather than just physical blindness.

This principle, that explanatory material explains the nearest verse, is behind the midrashic principle of *"dorshin semukhin"* – proximity is a source of meaning. Naturally, the explanations need not be mutually exclusive. Not only is it possible that Isaac was blind in both ways, but a connection may be seen between the two. Isaac's physical blindness symbolizes and is reflected in his mental lack of discernment – the physical state of a biblical *Tzaddik* mirrors his spiritual state.

Why, then, was Isaac blind, unperceptive, not attuned to the world about him? The Midrash (*Bereshit Raba* 65:9) cites several explanations, some of which are quoted by Rashi. Let us examine two of them.

Based on the statement "His eyes were weakened from seeing," one midrash traces Isaac's blindness to something he saw during the binding (*akeda*). The latter phrase, "from seeing," is unnecessary, and the midrash chooses to understand it as causative ("seeing" caused his blindness) rather than modifying his blindness. One explanation is that Isaac, while bound on the altar, looked up and **saw** into the heavens, where the angels were weeping. The tears entered his eyes, seared them and, years later, caused his eventual blindness. An alternate version is that he saw the glory of the celestial throne and this sight alone resulted in blindness.

Both of these midrashim are clearly referring to spiritual blindness rather than physical blindness. After all, the verse explicitly states that Isaac became blind in his old age. Would the searing experience of angel tears have a delayed effect, if we are to understand that they in some way burn? Would the sight of the glory of heaven gradually attack the optic nerve, like a dormant virus, or would it, taking the story literally, burn away the tissues of the eye like a red-hot poker? The midrashim are describing an experience which reorients Isaac's perception, a tendency which increases with age and eventually, when it becomes totally dominant inwardly, is reflected in his physical blindness as well. But what exactly is the connection between the experience of the *akeda* and blindness?

I think the explanation of the first midrash is as follows: Angels are routinely used by the midrash to express an objective rational truth, even where God disagrees. For instance, the angels argue against the creation of man because "he is completely deceitful" – and Truth is the seal of God (*Bereshit Raba* 8:5). God's answer is to "cast Truth down" – not an answer which addresses their argument rationally. Similarly, the angels protest the *akeda* as being "foreign" to God (ibid. 56:5) – meaning, not in accordance with divine justice. In our midrash, the angels' tears express the objective tragedy of the *akeda* – the world, its spiritual foundations, weep at the sight of a father sacrificing his son. Isaac was witness and victim – willing victim, but victim nonetheless – of this act. He felt the tears of the angels, the tragedy and sadness of existence in a world where such an act is possible, while looking at his father's face, stern and determined, preparing to sacrifice him. Is it any wonder Isaac was unable to reject a son, even Esau?

The *akeda* was the formative experience of Isaac's life. While Abraham also was unwilling to reject his son, Ishmael, nonetheless he could be persuaded, by Sara and by God. Abraham appealed to God to accept Ishmael (17:18) – indicating that he recognized Ishmael's true nature. Jacob, of course, is famous for his willingness to discern and distinguish between his sons, beginning with Joseph and ending with individualized blessings (and not always blessings!) to his sons on his deathbed. Isaac, however, is unable to do so. This is due not to a simple lack of intelligence or insight, but to a heightened spiritual awareness of the value of fatherhood and sonship, an overwhelming sense of the tragic fragility of human continuity, of its cosmic significance (the angels are crying) and infinite value. This sensitivity will undoubtedly interfere with the practical side of fatherhood – you can't raise children if you refuse to distinguish between them. But is it not possible that it is nonetheless a crucial part of fatherhood, and Isaac is an *av*, a forefather of the Jews, precisely because he exemplified that ideal?

The second explanation of the midrash relates that Isaac peered into the heavens, and therefore was blind. *Ḥazal* are saying that Isaac's eye, following the *akeda*, was turned inward, or heavenward. Having seen so high, so holy a sight, having been in "that world," he was unable to also see and weigh and consider the problems of "this world." Isaac, in other words, was so overwhelmed by spirituality as to be relatively detached from mundane concerns. He was a dreamer, a visionary, contemplative, inward, detached – a *"Luftmentsch"* – and that is the sort of disability that blinded him to a clear distinction between Jacob and Esau.

The first midrash, while more tightly focused, is not actually presenting a different picture of Isaac. Whatever the nature of the cause, the result of the *akeda* is that Isaac's heightened spiritual sensitivity makes him unable to make hard-nosed distinctions in the mundane world. His mind is directed upward and inward; his field is depth of experience rather than practical living. From where in *peshat* did *Ḥazal* derive this picture? Consider the way Rebecca maneuvers Isaac. It isn't only that she succeeds, both in the case of the *berakhot* and in arranging for Jacob to be sent away, but she is apparently unable to approach Isaac directly. In his presence, Rebecca is unable to confront or persuade. The Netziv traces this back to the story in last week's *parasha* of Rebecca falling off the camel when first meeting Isaac. A touching story – but what is its significance? The Netziv explains that Rebecca's first impression of Isaac, returning from a "walk in the field," which the Netziv believes refers to a spiritual exercise of meditation, was so overwhelming in its spiritual force and intensity that Rebecca could never overcome the feeling of trepidation and awe in his presence, even when she knew intellectually that she was right concerning a particular matter.

This is indicated even more clearly by the lack of episodes in Isaac's biography. Isaac did not engage in remolding his external world; his experiences were inward, contemplative. He is a forefather – this sort of experience is a necessary and essential ingredient in the development of a full spiritual personality – but there cannot be much to tell. One episode in Isaac's life, repeated twice – digging wells – is the metaphor of this activity. Isaac doesn't conquer new heights, he deepens the achievements of the past. He not only digs wells in *Eretz Yisrael*, he **re-digs** the wells of Abraham. After Abraham, who climbed to the pinnacle of Mt. Moriah, spiritual development requires introspection – "*lasuaḥ basadeh*" (24:63), wandering through the field, digging within; and Isaac, in his all-encompassing fixation on the throne of glory, was the one to do that. The great achievements of Abraham will dissipate – the wells will become filled in – if Isaac will not return and deepen them, forgoing the advance into new areas in order to solidify what has been gained. His blindness, then, is part and parcel of his fatherhood.

Consider: God could have intervened and told Isaac to give the blessing to Jacob. When Abraham hesitated to banish Ishmael, God told him to do so, for Isaac was to be his successor. In Isaac's case, God neither cures nor instructs, and his blindness results in the *berakha* reaching Jacob by mistake – not despite the blindness, but through the blindness. Jacob receives a *berakha* in a manner where Isaac's blindness is part of the *berakha* itself. The blindness is not merely a disability; it is the obverse side of Isaac's depth, concentration, and single-minded dedication to the holy. Jacob, whose personality is so different, is a product of his grandfather and father – Isaac gives him the "*berakha* of Abraham" (28:4) – and he serves the God of Abraham and the "*paḥad*" of Isaac. *Paḥad*, fear and trembling, awe and retreat, is a necessary part of the integrated spiritual personality.

This understanding of Isaac's personality, in its one-sided extremeness, is based on Ḥazal's view of the forefathers as archetypes, all three of whom are necessary components of Jewish spiritual personality. Ḥazal understood this to be the deeper *peshat* of Genesis – a description of the roots of the people of God, rather than a collection of biographies. This requires that we search for the significance of each incident in the lives of the forefathers and relate it to the theme of their lives and of the book of Genesis, rather than merely determine its historical coherence. For that purpose, the midrash is unsurpassed.

Three Different Blessings

by Rav Tamir Granot

At the center of *Parashat Toledot* we find, of course, Isaac's blessing of Jacob. This is a well-known story, and the problems that it poses are equally familiar. As both early and later commentators have pointed out, the most difficult problem is the absence of any explicit judgment on the part of the Torah concerning Jacob's act of deception, carried out at Rebecca's instruction. The stealing of the blessing is undoubtedly a most important episode, and we want to learn the appropriate lessons from it – but the Torah provides no moral commentary; it simply recounts the events as they happened, with no evaluation.

We shall not address here the question of evaluating Jacob's act. What we shall focus on here is not the theft, but rather the blessings themselves. The question serving as our point of departure is a simple one. Jacob received, within a very short period of time (both chronologically and textually), three blessings, on three different occasions:

1. Isaac blesses him, believing him to be Esau (Gen. 27:27–29).
2. Isaac blesses him as he sends him off to Ḥaran to find a wife (28:1–4).
3. God blesses him in Beit El, in the dream of the ladder (28 :12–15).

Our question is: why does Jacob need three blessings; why will one not suffice? Obviously, from Jacob's perspective there is no problem. One blessing – the one that was meant to be given to Esau – he wanted, and indeed received, while the other two were bestowed upon him without any initiative on his part. But why does Isaac need to give him an additional blessing, over and above the one he has already received, and why does God add yet another blessing, in addition to Isaac's two?

One may offer an apparently simple solution. At the time of the first blessing, Isaac actually meant to bless Esau; hence, he apparently gave Jacob the blessing that he had prepared for Esau, rather than a blessing tailored to his own personality and destiny. When he sent Jacob off to Ḥaran, he blessed him as Jacob. And God had not blessed him up until this time, therefore He too added a blessing so as to confer a divine "confirmation," as it were, on that which a righteous man (Isaac) had decreed in the mortal realm.

However, to resolve the issues, we have to note that the three blessings are fundamentally different from one another. We expect Esau's blessing to be different from one meant for Jacob, yet why is Isaac's blessing different from God's? Furthermore, if the first blessing had indeed been appropriate for Esau, why did Jacob and his mother go to such efforts to attain it? And even if we want to posit that perhaps Rebecca and Jacob did not realize this in advance – why did Isaac agree to the blessing, and not give Esau the blessing meant for him?

To clarify the above questions, we shall first compare the blessings with each other in order to demonstrate the essence of the differences between them. Let us then examine the three blessings:

Isaac's blessing to Jacob disguised as Esau (Gen. 27:27–29)

(27) He approached and kissed him, and he smelled the scent of his garments, and he blessed him and said: "Behold, my son's scent is like the scent of a field that God has blessed.
(28) "May God (*Elokim*) give you of the dew of the heavens and the fatness of the earth, and much corn and wine.
(29) "May the nations serve you, and may peoples bow down to you; may you be a lord over your brethren, and may your mother's

sons bow down to you. May those who curse you be cursed, and may those who bless you be blessed."

Isaac's blessing to Jacob as he sends him off to Ḥaran (28:1–4)

(1) Isaac called Jacob and blessed him and instructed him, and said to him: "You shall not take a wife from the daughters of Canaan.

(2) "Arise, go to Padan Aram, to the home of Betuel, your mother's father, and take yourself a wife from there, from the daughters of Laban, your mother's brother.

(3) "May the Almighty God [*Kel Shakai*] bless you and make you fruitful and numerous, that you may be a multitude of peoples.

(4) "May He give you the blessing of Abraham, to you and to your descendants with you – that you may possess the land of your sojourning, which God gave to Abraham."

God's blessing to Jacob in the dream of the ladder (28:12–15)

(12) He dreamed, and behold – there was a ladder standing on the ground, with its head reaching the heaven, and behold – angels of God were ascending and descending it.

(13) And behold – God (YKVK, the Tetragrammaton) was standing over him, and He said: "I am the Lord God of Abraham your father, and the God of Isaac; the land upon which you lie – to you I shall give it, and to your descendants.

(14) "Your descendants will be like the dust of the earth, and you will spread westward and eastward, northward and southward; through you all the families of the earth shall be blessed, and through your descendants.

(15) "And behold – I am with you and shall watch over you wherever you go, and I shall return you to this land, for I shall not leave you until I have fulfilled that concerning which I have spoken to you."

Let us now focus on the differences between these blessings:

1. Preparation for and context of the blessing: Isaac utters the first blessing in the midst of eating his meal and drinking wine; this implies a mortal blessing. The second blessing relates to the purpose of sending Jacob away: marriage. The third blessing is unexpected; it offers Jacob support and encouragement.
2. God's name in the blessing: The first blessing includes the words, "May God (*Elokim*) give you…"; in the second, Isaac says, "May the Almighty God (*Kel Shakai*) bless you…"; in the third, we read "Behold, God (YKVK) stood over him…"
3. Content of the blessing: Isaac's first blessing to Jacob invokes material abundance of the land, dominion over nations and brethren, a curse to those who curse him, and a blessing to those who bless him. His second blessing to him speaks of being fruitful and multiplying, the blessing of Abraham, and the inheritance of the land of his sojourning – Canaan. God's blessing starts off with an identification: "I am the Lord God of your fathers…," there is the promise of the land – "to you I shall give it," there are descendants like the dust of the earth, expansion beyond the geographical limitations, and a blessing to all the families of the earth through him.

Examining the three blessings leads us to the following conclusions:

1. The second and third blessings are relatively similar to one another; at the center of both lies the promise of a multiplicity of descendants and of the land. The first blessing is an exception: it contains no promise as to dominion in the land or its inheritance; it speaks only of general abundance, with no mention of the classic element of descendants.
2. There are considerable differences in style between the second and third blessings, with additions and elaborations of one as opposed to the other and vice versa.
3. The first blessing is preceded by a process apparently aimed not only at arousing Isaac's affection for his son, but also at arousing a serene and joyful atmosphere conducive to divine inspiration. The meat and wine give Isaac vitality, causing him to want to

convey his blessing. The character of the blessing is entirely mortal and worldly. While it does contain a prominently religious element, ultimately it lacks any transcendental foundation.

4. Formulations of blessings are usually based on the pattern of previous blessings. The first blessing fits the general mold of a father's blessing to his son. In the third blessing it is easy to identify the elements of the various blessings to Abraham. Below we shall trace the exact sources.

5. The blessings invoke different names of God. In this context, a general principle should be pointed out: in the Torah we find frequent interchanges of God's names. The three most dominant names are the ones mentioned here: "*Elokim*," the Tetragrammaton, and "Kel Shakai" (less common than the other two). God's different names represent different aspects of His appearance and involvement in reality. *Hazal* set forth the following distinction: the name "*Elokim*" reflects divine justice, while the Tetragrammaton represents the trait of divine mercy. Since the etymology of both of these names is unclear, and since both cases represent unique grammatical forms, we have no way of understanding the names on their own; we can only arrive at their significance based on their respective contexts. In this regard, the first appearance of each, in the two chapters of Creation, is of particular importance. The name "*Elokim*" is used in the first chapter, which recounts the story of the creation of nature in general, in a process of orderly development and fixed laws. The name is connected to the fact that God is the source of nature, the source of natural law and regularity in the world, and this is also a context for what *Hazal* refer to as the "trait of strict justice" or the "trait of law."

The second section of the Creation story (ch. 2–3) is recounted using the name YKVK. The greater part of this section describes the creation of man and woman. It contains much of what is absent from the first section – particularly concerning the personal connection between God and man and the closeness between them, as manifest in God's concern for him, His placement of him in the Garden of Eden, the commandment He gives him, etc. Hence, we deduce that the use of the name YKVK should be regarded as a private, personal name – or, as arises from God's words to Moses at the burning bush, where Moses asks: "They shall say to me, what is His name?" and God's answer is *"Eh'yeh"* and YKVK (we shall not elaborate here on the difference between these two names). Thus it appears that the name *"Elokim"* expresses God's relationship with the world in terms of function and rule, while YKVK is His "private" name.[1]

In light of the above analysis, we can better understand the different blessings:

In the first blessing, the divine name that is used is *"Elokim"* – a general name, referring to the Creator of nature; this name relates to all humans on the same level. It is therefore natural that Isaac uses it in a blessing whose source is human and whose character and content are universal.

In his second blessing, Isaac uses the name *"Kel Shakai."* The source of this name is to be found in the story of Abraham's circumcision, where God identifies Himself to Abraham using this name. Hence, we must seek the reason for this name in that context – as we shall do below.

In the third blessing, God appears with the text referring to Him as "YKVK." From the context of this blessing and its purpose, the reason is clear: this is a private revelation, a substantial part of which reflects the divine will to encourage Jacob and promise him support. God reveals

---

1. This idea is expressed in a straightforward way by R. Yehuda HaLevi in his book, The Kuzari:

    The Rabbi said: *Elokim* is a term signifying a ruler or governor...

    For He is called HaShem [YKVK] after His uniqueness. This is as if one asked, "Which *Elokim* is to be worshipped: the sun, the moon, the heaven, the zodiac, any star, fire, wind, angels, spirits, or any other – each of these has its own activity and domain, and each of them is a factor responsible for existence or annihilation?" The answer to this question is, "HaShem [YKVK]!" As if you said, "So-and-so!" and called him by his proper name, "Reuben" or "Simeon" for instance, supposing that the names "Reuben" and "Simeon" convey their true personalities. (Part IV:1)

Himself to Jacob for the first time, and, understandably, presents Himself using the name by which He was known to the forefathers: "I am YKVK, the God of your father Abraham…" But as we noted concerning the second blessing, here, too, it should be noted that the use of this name takes us back to a previous blessing – one or more of the blessings to Abraham. Let us examine the relationship between (some of) Abraham's blessings and Jacob's blessing, which share the characteristic of being given in the name YKVK:

Dream of the ladder:

> And behold, YKVK stood over him and said, "I am YKVK, the God of your father Abraham, and the God of Isaac. **The land upon which you lie – to you I shall give it, and to your descendants. Your descendants will be like the dust of the earth, and you shall spread westward and eastward, northward and southward, and through you shall all the families of the earth be blessed.**" (Gen. 28:13–14)

The blessing of "*Lekh Lekha*" (Gen. ch. 12):

> YKVK said to Abram, "Go forth … and I shall make of you a great nation, and I shall bless you and make your name great, and you shall be a blessing. "I shall bless those who bless you, and those who curse you – I will curse; **and through you shall all the families of the earth be blessed.**" (12:1–3)

The blessing following the separation from Lot, to the east side of Beit El:

> YKVK said to Abram, after Lot had separated from him. "Lift up your eyes and see, from the place where you are – **northward and southward and eastward and westward. For all the land which you see – to you I shall give it, and to your descendants, forever. And I shall make your descendants like the dust of the earth**, that if a person may count the dust of the earth – so

shall he count your descendants. **Arise and walk about in the
land, throughout its length and breadth, for to you I shall
give it.**" So Abraham packed his tent and moved and settled in
Elonei Mamreh which is in Ḥevron, and he built an altar there
to God. (13:14–18)

It is easy to see that all of the elements of God's blessing here to Jacob
are taken from the first two blessings that were given to Abraham (which
was a single blessing in two parts, since it was only after Lot separated
from him that Abraham merited the blessing in its entirety). In other
words, God's blessing to Jacob is in fact a conferral of His first blessings
to Abraham. The blessing that Jacob receives in the dream, when God is
revealed to him, is the continuation of God's blessings to Abraham – the
two that are given to him at the outset of his move to Canaan, and the
third at the Covenant between the Pieces. As we might have predicted,
God's appearance to Abraham at the Covenant between the Pieces is
with the name "YKVK" – and only this.

Attention should also be paid to the fact that what immediately
follows God's two revelations to Abraham, as well as His revelation to
Jacob, is the establishment of an altar (Abraham) or monument, which
Jacob swears is destined to be the "house of God." Using the name
YKVK – and only this name – God appears to Adam personally and
shows concern for him, accompanies him and commands him. And it
is only to God – by His "private" name – that one may offer sacrifices or
build altars. Thus Noaḥ, who builds an altar, does so to "YKVK," who is
revealed to him: "YKVK smelled the sweet savor…" It is impossible to
offer sacrifices to the First Cause, to the Infinite, to the Source of Laws,
etc. Sacrifices are always brought to YKVK, who is revealed through
private revelation.

Let us now compare the second set of blessings:

Isaac's blessing as he sends Jacob off:

Isaac called to Jacob and blessed him and commanded him, and
he said to him, "You shall not take a wife from the daughters of
Canaan. Arise, go to Padan Aram, to the home of Betuel, your

mother's father, and take yourself a wife from there, from the daughters of Laban, your mother's brother.

"May *Kel Shakai* bless you **and multiply you and make you numerous, that you may be a multitude of peoples. And may he give you** the blessing of Abraham – to you and to your descendants with you, to possess the land of your sojournings, which God gave to Abraham. (28:1–4)

At Abraham's circumcision:

Abram was ninety-nine years old, and YKVK appeared to Abram and said to him, "I am *Kel Shakai*; walk before Me and be wholehearted. I shall give My covenant between Me and you, **and I shall multiply you exceedingly much.**"

And Abram fell upon his face, and God spoke to him, saying: "Behold, this is My covenant with you: **you shall be the father of many nations.** And your name shall no longer be called 'Abram'; your name shall be 'Abraham,' for I have made you the father of many nations. And **I shall make you most exceedingly fruitful**, and I will make nations of you, and kings shall emerge from you. And I shall establish My covenant between Me and you, and your descendants after you, in their generations, as an eternal covenant, to be God for you, and for your descendants after you. **And I shall give you** – and your descendants after you – the **land of your sojournings**; all of the land of Canaan, as an eternal inheritance, and I shall be their God." (17:1–8)

The similarity between the blessings is clear, as is a further point: the spirit of chapter 1 of Genesis hovers over the blessing to Jacob, since the source of the promise to make him numerous lies in the command to Adam, "Be fruitful and multiply, and fill the land and conquer it…"

The name *"Kel Shakai"* has its source in the story of Abraham's circumcision. The message of the circumcision is clear. It promises continuity of descendants – and hence also the birth of Isaac. In fact, the promise of the land is secondary, for only if Isaac is born will it be possible for the promise to be fulfilled in its original sense – that the child born to Abraham and Sara will inherit the land. Circumcision, as an act of covenant, performed upon the organ of procreation, connects the act of circumcision itself to the promise of progeny. The name *Kel Shakai,* which appears specifically here, at the circumcision, is therefore related to this concept of divine abundance and fertility. Rashi explains the name as follows: "I am the One whose deity (*elohut*) is sufficient (*dai*) for every creation." Obviously, this name is an abbreviation – *she-dai,* "Who is (or contains) sufficient" – but it also expresses the idea of unlimited abundance that emanates from God.

Isaac's use of this name is therefore understandable – to pass on to Jacob the blessing of fertility that was given to Abraham. It is precisely for this purpose that he is sending Jacob away – to find a wife! The invocation of the name *"Kel Shakai"* is meant to refer to the promise that Abraham received at the time of his circumcision, and particularly to the connection between these two blessings. Isaac is telling Jacob, "I am blessing you with the blessing of progeny and hope, even though you now are being forced to leave the land, which you will merit to receive as Abraham's blessing – to inherit the land of your sojourning."

We conclude that the three blessings to Jacob are completely different in their essence and in their purpose:

The first blessing is a worldly one – the blessing bestowed by a mortal spirit. It has only generalized significance. Isaac makes no mention in this blessing of Abraham's successor, the inheritor of the land – i.e., it contains no historical or religious perspective. It concerns only property and material abundance. It seems that this is where Rebecca's mistake lies: she believes that Isaac is going to make a decision as to passing on the blessing of Abraham, with all that it entails. Believing that Esau is unworthy of being chosen, she initiates the act of deception. Isaac, it appears, did not believe that it was his job to appoint the successor of Abraham. It is possible that he did not believe that either of his sons would necessarily be chosen. There are no grounds to be certain that what we know after the fact was also clear to Isaac at the time. The historical fact that one of his sons was rejected and the other chosen to continue is not a necessity. Hence, Isaac simply wanted to bless his elder son, who would take over and assume responsibility for his property after his death. Indeed, in terms of character, Esau was certainly suited for this role. Thus, as we have seen, what Isaac bestowed upon Jacob-disguised-as-Esau was no more than a general, universal blessing.

The other two blessings have a dual nature, like the blessing to Abraham. God forged two covenants with Abraham: circumcision, and the Covenant between the Pieces. Each of these creates a different mode of commitment and relationship. As we have noted, the first blessings to Abraham are essentially bound up with the Covenant between the Pieces. We shall not elaborate here on the fundamental difference between the two covenants; for our purposes, suffice it to note that one covenant was not enough, and that each covenant required its own blessing and its own covenantal act.

When Isaac sends Jacob to Ḥaran, he bestows upon Jacob the blessing that continues the covenant of circumcision – for two reasons:

1. The purpose – to marry and establish a family. Circumcision likewise concerns fertility.
2. Isaac cannot bless in place of God. The name YKVK can only come from revelation, and from it God's blessing emanates. Isaac can pray for Jacob concerning the continuity of the covenant of circumcision – the crux of which, in contrast to the Covenant between the Pieces, is not divine revelation or a divine act, but rather a human act. Therefore, he prays: "May *Kel Shakai* bless you and make you fruitful and numerous…and grant you the blessing of Abraham…"
3. Finally – God's blessing in the dream of the ladder is the continuation of the first blessings to Abraham and of the Covenant between the Pieces, with which it concludes. Like the episode of the Covenant between the Pieces, the blessing here is accompanied by a divine commitment. From this perspective, God's revelation in the dream of the ladder is the continuation of His revelation to Abraham in the vision, in the Covenant between the Pieces, and the events themselves are indeed quite similar. It is worth re-emphasizing the opening words: "I am YKVK," uttered in both instances. God reveals Himself using His name, and promises, committing himself to his word.

In summary: at the beginning we questioned the need for three separate blessings to Jacob, and the differences between them. We arrived at the conclusion that there is a distinction between the first blessing, representing a private initiative on Isaac's part, with no parallel (except for Jacob's blessings to his sons, which are of similar character), and the two latter blessings, which are a sort of complementary pair that continue the blessings to Abraham, and particularly the two covenants: the Covenant between the Pieces and the covenant of circumcision. The blessing and selection of Abraham are passed on in their entirety, with all of their components, to Jacob. Each blessing relates to a different one of God's names, since each divine name reflects a different aspect of divine manifestation in the world.

Parashat Vayetzeh

Perceiving Providence

by Rav Reuven Taragin

I. *VAYETZEH* – AN INDEPENDENT, COHESIVE UNIT

Although *Parashat Vayetzeh* presents stories covering more than twenty years, it contains no breaks. This presentation highlights the *parasha's* status as an independent unit, and reflects the relationship between its various stories. The relationship between the stories is reinforced by the parallels between the beginning and end of the *parasha*. The *parasha* opens with Jacob's voyage from Canaan on the heels of an angelic dream, within which God promises to be with and protect him in exile and eventually return him to Canaan, and concludes with the ultimate fulfillment of these promises – Jacob's return. The journey back ends as the first one began, with Jacob's encounter with *malakhim*.

Additional textual similarities link the conclusion of the *parasha* to its beginning:

CHAPTER 28	CHAPTERS 31–32
Vayelekh Ḥarana...	*VeYaakov halakh ledarko*
Vayalen sham	*Vayalinu bahar*
Vayifga bamakom	*Vayifge'u bo malakhei Elokim*
Ein zeh ki im beit Elokim	*Maḥane Elokim zeh*
Vayashkem Yaakov baboker	*Vayashkem Laban baboker*
Vayikaḥ et ha'even...	*Vayikaḥ Yaakov even*
Vayasem ota matzeva	*vayerimeha matzeva*
Vayikra shem hamakom hahu Beit El	*Vayikra shem hamakom hahu Maḥanaim*

Within this framework of Jacob's departure from and return to Canaan, the Torah presents five stories pertaining to the interim exile years. Like the opening and concluding portions of the *parasha*, these stories also exhibit a distinct relationship:

> A 28:10–24 – Jacob's departure / angels
> > B 29:1–14 – Jacob's escape to Laban
> > > C 29:15–30 – Jacob's labor for his wives
> > > > D 29:31–30:24 – The birth of the children
> > > C1 30:25–42 – Jacob's labor for money
> > B1 30:43–31:55 – Jacob's escape from Laban
> A1 32:1–2 – Jacob's return / angels

The births at the center of the *parasha*'s structure seem, at first glance, to be out of place. How does the birth narrative, which seems to convey mere technical data, function as the *parasha*'s turning point? We will see that, in addition to expressing Jacob's ability to flourish in exile, the births also redefine the preceding stories and introduce the following ones. This point becomes more evident after a careful study of the birth narrative.

Like the *parasha*, the birth narrative subdivides into two chiastically related sections:

> A 29: 31–5 – Birth of four children to Leah
> > B 30: 1–2 – Story (not of birth)

C 30: 3–8 – Birth of two children to Rachel's maid
C1 30: 9–13 – Birth of two children to Leah's maid
B1 30:14–16 – Story (not of birth)
A1 30:17–24 – Birth of four children to Leah/Rachel

Both sections describe God's favoring of one sister and the reaction of the other. The difference between the two sections lies in the sister chosen as benefactor. In the first section God "opens the womb" of Leah while closing that of Rachel. Leah chooses names for her children that reflect her recognition of and thanks to God for his merciful intervention. After listing Leah's four births, the Torah depicts Rachel's reaction. Instead of turning to God, the sole granter of child, she assails Jacob. The latter stresses her error by angrily retorting – "Am I in place of God, who has denied you fruit of the womb?" (30:2). Only after her misplaced complaint does Rachel grudgingly offer her maid in her place.

The second section opens with Leah's realization of the termination of God's providence on her behalf – "Leah saw that she had ceased to give birth" (30:9). Although we now expect Rachel to be the next to give birth, God "hears" her (v. 22) only after "hearing" Leah (v. 17). One wonders why Rachel is heard so late in the story and in far lesser proportion than Leah?

The answer lies in the structure of the narrative, which focuses on the divergent reactions of the two sisters to the same circumstances. As opposed to Rachel, who offers her maid only after having incorrectly complained to Jacob, Leah immediately presents her maid in her place. Like the first matriarch, Sara, as soon as Leah realizes that she can no longer contribute personally, she selflessly steps aside and hopes to continue to do so vicariously.

The difference between the two is expressed through the second story – that of the mandrakes – as well. Notwithstanding the symbolism of the mandrakes, Rachel's sale of a night with Jacob reflects a denigrating lack of appreciation of the sanctity of the conception experience. Ramban's appraisal of the mandrakes as fertility flowers attributes new significance to the transaction. Rachel has not yet realized the need to rely on God. There is no reason not to utilize the available medicine, but doing so at the expense of a night with her husband once again reflects Rachel's improper value system.

Leah, on the other hand, recognizes God's exclusive role as bearer of the "birth key," and happily exchanges the flowers for an additional night with Jacob and another window for God's providence. God rewards Leah's faith with three more children – two boys and Dina. Based on the parallel to the first section and a fair basis of distribution, all four boys should have been born to Rachel; two were given to Leah in recognition of her exemplary faith.

On an ironic note, the midrash concludes:

> One lost and the other lost; one gained and the other gained. Leah lost the mandrakes and gained two tribes and the firstborn; Rachel gained the mandrakes and lost tribes and the firstborn. (*Bereshit Raba* 72:2)

Eventually, even Rachel concedes that God – not Jacob or mandrakes – grants child, and beseeches Him with the birth of her first child for a second. Her request, rooted in her painfully learned lesson, is eventually granted, but at the cost of her life.

The message of the birth narrative facilitates the transition from the first to the second section of the *parasha*. Despite God's promises to Jacob at the *parasha*'s beginning, Jacob only meets frustration. Although he reaches his destination safely, his stay with Laban soon turns into backbreaking work on behalf of a wife he doesn't actually receive. The reader cannot help but wonder: how did God allow such a thing? What happened to the promised protective aid?

While the first part of the *parasha* reinforces the hidden nature of God's providence within it by not mentioning His name, the birth narrative compensates by mentioning His name fourteen times. Within the narrative, we are presented with Leah's recognition of God's exclusive control of nature. Appropriately, Jacob's unintended wife directs Jacob and us to recognize God's hand, even in its obscurity.

Only after Leah's clarification does God reveal His providence – first in the form of the angel who assists Jacob in outsmarting Laban, and finally by personally intervening to secure Jacob's escape.

In the second section of the *parasha*, there is no doubt as to providence's presence through the depiction of its recognition by all characters. First, Jacob realizes (after sensing Laban's unwarranted jealousy) that it has been "only the God of his fathers" (31:5) who has cared for him. The angel's aid in outsmarting Laban proved to Jacob that the angels he had seen at his journey's inception had indeed remained with him all along.

Jacob makes this point to his wives – Laban's daughters – and challenges them to fulfill God's command to abandon their home and family. Leah and Rachel, the first to have recognized God's providence, of course immediately concede (31:17). In doing so, they reaffirm their place with Abraham and Rebecca, who likewise abandoned their families in compliance with God's will.

The ultimate recognition of God's providence comes from Laban, in the context of his pursuit of Jacob. Despite God's demand that Laban refrain from telling Jacob "good or bad" (31:24), Laban proceeds with his verbal attack. Although Laban realizes that he will not succeed in repossessing his family and possessions, he feels that he bears a just claim. Was he not the catalyst of Jacob's growth? Did he not offer Jacob refuge, work, and a wife when the latter had nowhere to turn? Did he not deserve at least to be informed of Jacob's migration? Additionally, Laban is intent on finding his gods, whom he views as responsible for his, as well as Jacob's, success.

When Laban first arrives, Jacob allows him to vent his frustration, but his aggressive, suspicious search of Jacob's possessions as if they were his own forces Jacob to respond. Jacob reminds Laban that despite Jacob's faithful service, Laban took every opportunity to deceive him – "Had not the God of Abraham and the Fear of Isaac been with me, you would have sent me now away empty-handed. God saw my plight and the toil of my hands and He showed it last night" (31:42).

Jacob explains the true significance of the heavenly revelation. God's protection of Jacob reflected His exclusive role in his success. By protecting Jacob, God was merely asserting his deserved right to Jacob; Laban deserved not even the right to give his blessing. God used the phrase *"tov ad ra"* (good or bad) to remind Laban of the conclusion he himself had reached as a youngster after having heard the providential story of Abraham's servant – "And Laban and Betuel said: It has come from God; we cannot tell you anything bad or good [*ra o tov*]" (24:50).

In addition to God's revelation to Laban, his inability to find his own gods was meant to signify their and his own irrelevance to Jacob's success.

The meeting ends with Laban's request to formalize a treaty. Jacob responds by constructing two stone structures – a *"matzeva"* (v. 45) and a *"gal"* (v. 46). Significantly, the creation of the *matzeva* precedes that of the *gal*, and is carried out by Jacob alone. Before assenting to Laban's request and joining him in the construction of the *gal*, which symbolized their mutual treaty, Jacob expressed his thanks to the One truly responsible for his success – God. The *matzeva* created here parallels the one Jacob constructed in response to God's promises at the beginning of the *parasha*. By constructing this second *matzeva*, Jacob expressed his appreciation of God's fulfillment of the promises He made during the angelic vision, which Jacob had commemorated by creating the first.

Jacob's recognition of the consistent providence shown to him during his years in exile with Laban readied him for his return to Canaan and his encounter with Esau, and serves as the precedent for his descendants – a nation whose ideology centers on the belief in providence's universal consistency.

The Matzevot

by Rav Joshua Berman

J acob, over the course of his life, erects four "*matzevot*," four pillars (monuments), twice in *Vayetzeh* and twice in *Vayishlaḥ*.

A. On the morning after the dream in Beit El: "Jacob arose in the morning and took the stone which he had placed at his head and erected it as a *matzeva*, and he poured oil over it" (Gen. 28:18).

B. When Laban pursues Jacob, he says to him, "Let us now make a covenant, I and you, and it shall be a witness between me and you." In response, the Torah states, "Jacob took a stone and set it up as a *matzeva*" (31:45).

C. When Jacob returns to Beit El, God appears to him, changes his name to Israel and grants him the blessing of land and seed. The conclusion is, "…Jacob erected a *matzeva* on the place that He had spoken to him, a stone *matzeva*, and offered a libation on it and poured oil over it" (35:14).

D. When Rachel dies, Jacob erects a fourth *matzeva*: "Jacob erected a *matzeva* on her grave, which is the *matzeva* of Rachel's grave unto this day" (35:20).

There are a number of questions which arise in this context: Why are these places chosen by Jacob? Why does Jacob pour oil over the two in Beit El, but not over the others? And finally, what is the specific significance of a *matzeva* for Jacob, who – unlike Abraham and Isaac, who built altars – is the only patriarch to erect *matzevot*?

The common basis for all four *matzevot* can be found in the dream which appears at the beginning of the *parasha* (ch. 28). The description of the dream includes two references to the Hebrew root *n-tz-v* (the root of "*matzeva*"). "A ladder is set ["*mutzav*"] up on the ground, its head reaches the heaven, and the angels of God go up and down on it. And God was erect ["*nitzav*"] over him" (28:12–13).

The use of the same root in the dream and in Jacob's response is an indication that the *matzeva* which Jacob erects on the following morning does not only commemorate the event of the dream itself, but also its contents. There is another literary parallel between the ladder and the *matzeva*. In the dream, we are told that:

1. The ladder exists;
2. it is erected on the ground;
3. and its head is in the heavens.

When Jacob erects the *matzeva*, the same format is followed:

1. We are told that there is a *matzeva* – "He took the stone which he had placed at his head";
2. Then the foot of the stone – "he erected it as a *matzeva*";
3. Then the head of the stone – "he poured oil over its head."

Notice: the Torah doesn't write that he poured oil over it ("*aleha*") but "over its **head**" ("*al rosha*"), emphasizing the parallel to the ladder.

In order to understand why a *matzeva* is the appropriate commemoration for the dream, we must first understand the meaning of the dream.

There are numerous interpretations of Jacob's dream. A common thread to many of them is that the dream represents the protection of God over Jacob (and the Jewish people, by extension). Rashi, for instance, explains that the angels are escorting Jacob on his trip. Accordingly, Jacob's *matzeva* is a monument, physically and linguistically resembling the dream and its contents. Physically, the *matzeva* is rooted in the ground and its "head" is anointed, sanctified, like the ladder whose head was in the heavens (Ramban: "and God was erect on **it**" – on the ladder). In terms of content, it symbolizes Jacob's faith that God will watch and protect him, both in *Eretz Yisrael* and in exile (Rashi: "and God was erect over **him**" – over Jacob).

In the same manner as the dream explains the significance of the first *matzeva*, we can understand the others. The key is to follow the continuation of the dream. At the conclusion of the vision, God promises three things to Jacob:

> "I am the Lord, the God of your father Abraham and the God of Isaac. The land in which you are lying, I will give it to you and your seed. And your seed shall be like the dust of the earth, and you shall burst forth to the west, the east, north and south; and all the families of the earth shall be blessed in you and your seed. And I shall be with you and protect you wherever you go; and I shall return you to this ground, for I shall not abandon you until I have fulfilled that which I have spoken to you."

Jacob will, in the course of his life, erect a *matzeva* when each of these promises – land, children, and protection – is fulfilled, for each one is a fulfillment of the vision of the ladder and of the promise of "*HaShem nitzav alav*," God watching over him.

The first *matzeva* that Jacob erects afterwards is when making a pact with Laban, when he is about to return to *Eretz Yisrael*. This *matzeva* follows twenty years of tension and conflict between Jacob and Laban concerning his employment, his salary, his wives, and his children. Specifically, it follows ten days of flight and pursuit, after Laban declares that he is capable of doing harm to Jacob and that the only reason he does not do so is because "the God of your father said to me last night: beware of speaking anything to Jacob, either good or bad" (31:29). This *matzeva* is a commemoration of Jacob's salvation – it commemorates the promise of protection.

The previous chapter contains numerous references to the need for God's protection of Jacob, and places the entire episode in the light of the promise of protection. Immediately after Jacob realizes that his relationship with Laban is souring (31:1–2), God says to Jacob, "Return to the land of your fathers where you were born and **I will be with you**" (31:3). The opening of the promise of protection was "and I shall be with you" (28:15). Jacob, too, in his oath at the time, had said, "If God shall be with me and protect me on the way that I am going" (28:20).

When Jacob tells his wives about this message of God, he begins by stating, "I see that your father's manner to me is not as it was in the past, and the God of my father has been with me" (31:5). The angel (31:13) urges Jacob to leave Laban, saying, "I am the God of Beit El, where you anointed a *matzeva*..." i.e., your flight is under the protection of the dream and the *matzeva*.

Jacob, when caught by Laban, reminds him: "Were it not that the God of my father, the God of Abraham and the Fear of Isaac **were with me**..." (31:42).

Hence, when Jacob erects the *matzeva* to commemorate Laban's peace with him, it is clear that it symbolizes that God was **with him**; i.e., that the promise of protection made in the dream of the ladder has been fulfilled.

Jacob returns to Beit El, erects a *matzeva* and anoints it with oil (35:14). If we trace this *matzeva* to the promises of the dream, it would appear that it corresponds to the promise of the land. The *matzeva* commemorates Jacob's return to *Eretz Yisrael*. The question, of course, is why he waited until he arrived in Beit El rather than erecting it at his first stop, in Shekhem. A second question relates to the *matzeva* itself: why did Jacob first erect an altar and only afterward a *matzeva*?

If we examine the command given by the angels to Jacob in our *parasha* to return to *Eretz Yisrael*, we see that he reminded Jacob not only of the protection of God, but also of Jacob's oath after the dream. "I am the God of Beit El where you anointed a *matzeva*, where you swore an oath to me – now, get up and leave this land and return to the land of your birth" (31:13). In other words – return to *Eretz Yisrael* and fulfill your oath. Jacob has sworn, "This stone which I have set up as a *matzeva* shall be a house of God" (28:21), which most commentators (Rasag,

Ramban, Ibn Ezra, Radak) understand to mean that the place, Beit El, will be sanctified to the service of God. His mission, the reason for his return to *Eretz Yisrael*, is to fulfill that vow.

Like Abraham, Jacob's first destination in *Eretz Yisrael* is Shekhem, and, like Abraham, he builds ("erects") an altar there. The verb used to describe the building of this altar is from the root *n-tz-v* – the only occurrence of this verb with an altar in Tanach! Jacob's purpose is to erect a *matzeva*, but the place has to be Beit El. He already begins the process of "erecting" in Shekhem, since he has indeed come back to the land, but it is incomplete. Jacob has to fulfill his vow first – to make Beit El a place of worship of God. In fact, God commands Jacob to build an altar in Beit El (35:1). Apparently, an altar is the fulfillment of "... shall be a house of God." After Jacob builds the altar, God appears to him, directly rather than in a dream, and repeats the promises of the dream. Only afterwards does Jacob, assured that he has fulfilled his vow, erect the *matzeva* of return. At this moment, he knows he has returned to the land, acquired it by the renewed promise of God, and can now begin to settle it. He not only pours oil over this *matzeva* to sanctify it as a house of God, he performs a double sanctification: "He offered a libation on it and poured oil over it."

The last *matzeva* follows Rachel's death, and is over her grave. Rachel's death is entwined with the birth of Benjamin. The birth of Benjamin is special in many respects: it was in *Eretz Yisrael*, it was after Jacob had become Israel – but most of all, it was the last of Jacob's progeny, the completion of "*Beit Yaakov*." Immediately afterwards the Torah states, "The sons of Jacob were twelve" (35:22). Tragically, Rachel's tomb also signifies the fulfillment of the promise of seed "and you shall burst forth to the west, the east, the north and the south." Jacob erects this *matzeva*, but does so over the grave of his wife, as its fulfillment rests on her death.

All four *matzevot*, then, are connected by the dream of the ladder and its promises to Jacob: The first commemorates the dream itself; the second, the protection of God; the third, the promise of the land; and the fourth, tragically, the blessing of children. The presence of God in Jacob's life ("*nitzav alav*") and the ensuing sanctification ("*verosho magia hashamayma*") are symbolized by Jacob's *matzevot* and the anointing in Beit El, the "gate of heaven."

Fleeing and Marrying, Reality and Vision

by Rabbanit Sharon Rimon

> *Jacob departed from Be'er Sheva and he went to Ḥaran. (28:10)*

Why does Jacob leave Be'er Sheva and head for Ḥaran? There are two reasons, both set out at the end of last week's *parasha*. The first reason is that Rebecca was told the words of Esau, her eldest son, and she sent and called for Jacob, her younger son, and said to him: Behold, Esau your brother is comforting himself over you, (planning) to kill you.

> And now, my son, obey me and arise, flee to Laban, my brother, in Ḥaran. Dwell with him for a few days until your brother's fury is turned away. (Gen. 27:42–43)

Immediately thereafter, the Torah goes on to provide the second reason for Jacob's flight:

> So Isaac called Jacob and blessed him and commanded him and said to him, Do not take a wife of the daughters of Canaan. Arise, go to Padan Aram, to the home of Betuel, your mother's father,

and take for yourself from there a wife from the daughters of Laban, your mother's brother. And may the Almighty God bless you and make you fruitful and cause you to multiply, that you may become a multitude of peoples ... And Isaac sent Jacob, and he went to Padan Aram, to Laban son of Betuel the Aramean, the brother of Rebecca, the mother of Jacob and Esau. (28:1–5)

I. FLIGHT

Are both reasons equal in weight? From the way in which they are presented, the first reason seems to take precedence. Rebecca wants, first and foremost, for Jacob to get away from Esau. However, when Rebecca approaches Isaac, she makes no mention of the fact that Esau is planning to kill Jacob. Rather, she presents a different pretext for sending Jacob to Ḥaran. The pretext she chooses is that Jacob must find a wife who is not one of the "daughters of Canaan."

The narrative then accompanies Jacob on his way to Ḥaran. Along the way, God is revealed to Jacob, and He conveys to him both the promise of the land and the promise of descendants. He also promises to protect him and to bring him back to Canaan. Following this revelation, Jacob makes an oath:

> If God will be with me, and **guard me on this way** that I go, and **give me bread to eat and a garment to wear, and I return in peace** to my father's house, then the Lord will be my God. (28:20–21)

Jacob makes no mention of the great promises of the land and of descendants, nor does he ask for divine assistance in finding a wife. He asks only that God look after him and bring him back to the land. It seems, therefore, that Jacob's mind is on fleeing. Therefore, he asks God for protection, and to return home safely.

When Jacob reaches Ḥaran, he sits by the well, and it is there that he encounters Rachel for the first time. He is enthusiastic about this meeting, but we are not told here that he is struck by her beauty, nor even by her personality. It should also be noted that their dialogue contains no mention of marriage. The verses emphasize a different point altogether:

And it was, when Jacob saw Rachel, the daughter of **Laban, his mother's brother**, and the flocks of **Laban, his mother's brother**, then Jacob approached and rolled the stone from the mouth of the well, and he watered the flocks of **Laban, his mother's brother**. And Jacob kissed Rachel, and he lifted his voice and wept. And Jacob told Rachel that he was **her father's nephew** [literally – brother], and that he was **the son of Rebecca**. And she ran and **told her father.** (29:10–12)

The encounter between Jacob and Rachel is tightly wound around their family connection. Jacob is excited to meet someone from his mother's family. Not a word is said about marriage. Even in his conversation with Laban, there is no mention of a request to marry Rachel. Only a month later, Laban starts a conversation with Jacob about something that has nothing to do with marriage: "Just because you are my brother, should you then serve me for nothing? Tell me what your wages shall be." Only in the wake of this proposal does Jacob ask to marry Rachel.

Thus, while Jacob does set off for Ḥaran for two reasons – to escape from Esau and to find a wife – it seems that for him, getting away from Esau is the main reason. He does not appear to be thinking about marriage. Only when Laban mentions the subject of wages for his work is Jacob "reminded" of his father's instruction to find a wife, and then he raises the idea of marrying Rachel. The Torah does not depict Jacob's choice of Rachel as being based on her actions, nor does it describe any divine assistance in bringing about the match. The text relates a regular, human story of "falling in love" with a woman who is "of beautiful stature and of beautiful appearance." Even now, when Jacob finally asks to marry Rachel, he still makes no mention of the fact that Isaac had sent him to Laban's house in order to find himself a wife.

II. ISAAC'S MARRIAGE VS. JACOB'S MARRIAGE

There are some obvious parallels between the story of Eliezer's quest for a wife for Isaac and Jacob's path to Rachel. In both cases, the father commands that no Canaanite woman be considered; the woman chosen for marriage should be from Ḥaran. In both stories, the journey to Ḥaran ends at the well, where the first encounter with the woman takes place, and in both cases, the woman turns out to be from the family of Naḥor. Following the meeting with the woman, there is a meeting with the family.

Based on the above outline, the two stories appear to be quite similar. Nevertheless, it is specifically the similarities between them that serve to highlight the significant differences between them.

A. Isaac does not go out to seek a wife for himself. The quest for his wife is initiated by Abraham, and it is Eliezer who is dispatched to bring the woman. Isaac is involved in neither the choice of the woman nor the decision. Jacob, in contrast, is sent himself to Ḥaran to find a wife, and he decides on his own whom to choose.

B. Isaac is forbidden from leaving the land and going to Ḥaran; Jacob goes to Ḥaran.

C. For Isaac, the journey to Ḥaran has only one purpose: to find a wife for him. For Jacob, the journey is also a flight from Esau.

D. Jacob experiences a divine revelation on the way.

E. In the case of Isaac, throughout the narrative there is an emphasis on divine signs that Rebecca is the right woman to choose. In Abraham's directive to his servant, he says: "The Lord God of the heavens…He will send His angel before you, that you may take a wife from there for my son" (24:7). Eliezer in turn does not rely on his own discretion, but asks for God's help in finding the right woman. When he finds Rebecca and understands that she is the one, he once again emphasizes that it is God who had made his mission successful.

F. How is the woman chosen? For Isaac there is a "character test," accompanied by divine assistance. For Jacob, there is no test. He sees Rachel and decides on his own that he wants to marry her.

G. As noted, Eliezer announces the purpose of his visit immediately upon arrival at Betuel's home; he will not eat with the family until he has made it clear why he has come, at Abraham's command. Jacob, in his first meeting with Laban, makes no mention of marriage at all. A month later, when he does talk about marriage, he says nothing about his father's command, but rather asks simply to marry Rachel.

H. In Isaac's case, there is a return journey to Canaan immediately upon finding the woman. For Jacob, the return takes much longer; he remains in Ḥaran for many years.

What is the essential difference between the story of the match for Isaac and the story of the match for Jacob? In Isaac's case, there are two great ideals that guide the search. The practical difficulties are set aside; it is clear that God will help to overcome them. Additionally, Isaac has no personal involvement in the match. The marriage is directed from Above; the choice is explicitly left in the hands of God.

For Jacob, the entire episode reflects an altogether human plot. A man is fleeing from his brother; he reaches some relatives and stays with them. In the natural course of events he falls in love with one of the daughters, and asks to marry her in return for his labor. There is no appeal by Jacob for divine aid in finding a wife, nor does there seem to be any divine intervention in the course of events.

III. MARRIAGE

Clearly, the picture that emerges from the above description is not an accurate one. When Jacob leaves Be'er Sheva for Ḥaran, he is indeed fleeing from Esau, but he also receives a command from his father to find a wife. Together with this command, he receives the all-important blessing, the blessing of Abraham: the promise of the land, and the promise of descendants. The blessing that is bestowed upon Jacob does not come to him by chance. He wants it, and he plans Esau's sale of the birthright to him – symbolizing a transfer of the rights to this blessing. Jacob wants this blessing, with all of the commitment that it involves: bearing descendants who will be worthy of continuing the path of Abraham and Isaac in the world.

Thus, it is not possible that Jacob would "ignore" his commitment to marry a worthy wife. Even if he were not forced to flee from Esau, he would have to find a wife from Ḥaran, rather than marry a Canaanite woman. Jacob reaches Ḥaran with the knowledge that he must choose one of Laban's daughters to marry. When Rachel comes to the well and he discovers that she is Laban's daughter, he has no need for any further tests. Jacob does not simply fall in love with a woman whom he meets by chance. He headed for Laban's home with a view to marrying one of his daughters, and that is exactly what happens.

IV. CHOICE AND DECEPTION

The only room for choice that is left to Jacob is the question of whether to marry Leah or Rachel, since both are daughters of Laban. Here there is room for personal preference, and Jacob prefers Rachel. Why does he choose her? We might expect his choice to be based on some test of character, as in the case of Rebecca, but the Torah describes his motives as being quite different:

> ...But Rachel was **beautiful of stature and of beautiful appearance**.
>
> And Jacob **loved** Rachel, so he said: I will serve you for seven years for Rachel, your younger daughter...
>
> And Jacob served for seven years for Rachel, and they seemed to him like just a few days, for **his love** for her. (27:17–20)

The choice of Rachel is based on "regular," human love. This simple human preference once again emphasizes the natural, human behavior which we noted previously. Once again, we feel that Jacob's marriage is a routine, natural, human affair that starts with his flight from Esau and ends up with him "falling in love" with Rachel.

Jacob proposes that he will serve Laban for seven years and receive Rachel in return. Laban agrees. Jacob then goes on to fulfill his commitment. After he has paid the full price in labor, he asks to marry her, as agreed. Up to this point, Jacob has been in control of his marriage plans. But now Laban interferes, disturbing the proper course of events:

Laban gathered all the people of the place and made a feast. And it was, in the evening, that he took Leah – his elder daughter – and brought her to him, and he came to her.

Laban deceives Jacob and marries him to Leah instead of Rachel. His behavior is not all that surprising; what does surprise us is the success of his ruse. How is it that both Leah and Rachel are silent, revealing nothing of the exchange? How is it that Jacob fails to discover the deceit? And once he finds out how he has been deceived, why does he remain married to Leah? Why does he not divorce her? If Laban has disturbed the proper course of Jacob's marriage, how is it that his deceit is ultimately accepted and Leah remains married to Jacob – later on even becoming the mother of most of his children, including the progenitors of both the priesthood (Levi) and royalty (Judah)?

V. REALITY AND VISION

Further reflection on the story as presented above leads us to a different understanding of its significance. We see a natural, human process in which Jacob flees from Esau, reaches Laban's house, and falls in love with Rachel; Laban deceives him and causes him to marry Leah, and then Jacob finally manages to marry his beloved Rachel, too.

At the same time, there is another process going on: a divine plan, in which Jacob sets out to find a wife from among Laban's daughters, meets Rachel at the well, and believes that she is the right woman for him – the wife that Isaac had in mind, the woman for whose sake he was sent to Ḥaran. He asks to marry her, out of natural, human preference, but God brings about a situation in which he marries both Leah and Rachel. In other words, it is not Laban's deceit that leads to Jacob's marriage to Leah, but rather God's will. Laban's deceit is merely a vessel through which the proper marriage in God's eyes is brought about.

The image of Jacob that arises from the narrative is that of a man who lives within his human, existential reality and deals with all of its complexities and difficulties in an independent, human way. At the same time, he is not devoid of vision. Jacob has received Isaac's blessing – the blessing of Abraham – and God Himself was revealed to him as he set out on his journey, reiterating this most significant blessing. It is with this vision that Jacob heads into exile, to deal with his difficult, complex, human reality.

Indeed, the story of Jacob's life is not an easy one. He has to find a way to deal with Esau in such a way as to obtain his father's blessing; he is forced into exile and into dealing with Laban's trickery; he finally flees Laban's house in fear; he deals with a complicated family life involving four wives, two of whom are sisters with complicated relations between them; his daughter Dina is raped, and in the wake of his sons' response he fears that the people of the land will wage war against him; the relations between him and his sons are complex and strained, to the point where they sell Joseph.

Jacob's life descends to the depths of human experience; he struggles at every stage. However, this is not the only dimension to his life. At every important stage of his life, God appears to him and inspires him with vision. The complexity of Jacob's life is apparent at every stage. Many things that happen to him reflect dual causality: a human, natural process and a divine one. The departure from Ḥaran is not only an escape from Esau, but also a move inspired with the mission of finding a wife, and accompanied by God's blessing. The return to Canaan is not motivated solely by fear of Laban, but also accompanied, once again, by a divine revelation. The arrival in Beit El is not only prompted by the fear that the men of Shekhem are going to kill him, but also in response to God's command to return to there. The descent to Egypt is likewise not prompted solely by the desire to see Joseph. God's word accompanies Jacob's journey, imbuing the descent with a meaningful spiritual dimension:

> God said to Israel in the visions of the night, and He said: Jacob, Jacob. And he said, Here I am. And He said: I am God, the God of your father. Do not be afraid to go down to Egypt, for I shall make a great nation of you there. I shall descend with you to Egypt, and I shall surely also bring you up again. (46:2–4)

Jacob himself, when describing his life to Pharaoh, testifies to the great difficulties that he has encountered. He compares his life with that of his fathers, and the comparison appears to be intended not only on the quantitative level, but also in terms of his quality of life. Jacob, unlike Abraham and Isaac, has been through some very difficult experiences. He has battled with the reality of this world, with its basest, ugliest phenomena. Ramban comments:

It seems that Jacob was white-haired, and appeared very old, and Pharaoh was surprised at his old age since most people at that time did not live so long; their years were shorter. It was for this reason that he asked him, "How many days are the years of your life" – for I have not seen anyone as old as you in all of my kingdom. And Jacob answered him that he was one hundred and thirty years old, and that this should not surprise [Pharaoh], for this was little when compared with the lives of his fathers, who had lived longer. But since his life had been bitter with labor and sighing, he was white-haired and appeared much older.

The difference between Isaac's marriage and Jacob's marriage is a reflection of the difference between them throughout their lives. Jacob, unlike Isaac, does not live his whole life in Canaan, and he does not live exclusively in the "upper worlds." He goes into exile and is sucked down into the ugliest, most complex realms of reality. He deals with them himself, in a human, independent manner. This aspect of his life is reflected in his name, "Jacob" (recalling his grip on Esau's heel (*ekev*) during their birth).

However, deep in his heart, in the innermost part of himself, he is accompanied all along by a great vision. It is this vision that bestows his other name – "Israel." Jacob continues to bear both names, because both realities continue to exist within him to the end. And it seems that it is specifically this complex challenge that is the source and root of *Am Yisrael*. Jacob's family is the founding family of the nation. The nation is called "*Am Yisrael*," but sometimes they are also referred to as "Jacob." The grappling with all aspects of reality, including its most difficult challenges, while all the time bearing the great vision accompanying the entire journey – that is the foundation of *Am Yisrael*, the children of Jacob.

"And He Found Mandrakes in the Field"

by Rav Yonatan Grossman

Reviewing the continuum of the birth of Jacob's sons, we note that it is interrupted twice. First, after the birth of Leah's first four sons, a difficult and emotional dialogue is recorded between Rachel and Jacob. In the wake of this dialogue, Rachel gives her maidservant Bilha to Jacob, and the Torah then continues its listing of the birth of the sons. The second interruption in the narrative occurs after the two maidservants have each borne two sons. At that point, we find the story of the mandrakes (Gen. 30:14–16).

The need to record the conversation between Jacob and Rachel (the first interruption) is clear: it has a tangible effect on the building of Jacob's household, for as a result Jacob takes Bilha, and later also Zilpa, both of whom merit to take part in the establishment of the House of Israel. In contrast, the story of the mandrakes (the second interruption) is rather surprising. We may assume that during the seven years over the course of which Jacob's children were born, several other incidents took place, but the Torah makes no mention of them because the text is focusing here on the birth of the sons. What is the relevance of the story of the mandrakes in this context? In what way did it influence the establishment of Jacob's family?

In order to solve this question, let us first analyze this section itself, and then try to identify its significance in the overall context of the story of Jacob's family.

The story of the mandrakes opens with a description of Reuben's act: "And Reuben went, during the wheat harvest, and he found mandrakes in the field" (v. 14). Attention should also be paid to the seemingly superfluous noting of the time when this story occurs: "during the wheat harvest." What does it matter to us whether it took place during the wheat harvest or in the middle of winter? What is its true purpose?

In the Talmud, the sages address this question and use the verse to learn something of Reuben's character: "Rava bar Yitzhak said in the name of Rav: From here we learn that righteous people do not take stolen goods." In other words, there is a surprising contrast between the description of the time, "the wheat harvest," and what Reuben brings home – "mandrakes." Mandrakes grow in the wild. Considering the season when "Reuben went," we might have expected that he would return home with a sack full of grain, like Ruth upon her return from Boaz's field.

Immediately after describing how Reuben finds the mandrakes, the text records him handing them to Leah: "And he brought them to Leah his mother" (v. 14). Note that the verb used here is not "he gave," but rather "he brought." Reuben does not regard himself as the possessor of the mandrakes, as being in a position where an act of acquisition is necessary in order to effect a change of ownership. He "brings" them to Leah; in other words, they are his in the same way that they are hers. (Needless to say, as the story develops, both sisters relate to the mandrakes quite differently.)

The mention of the family relationship ("his mother") in conjunction with Leah's name is greatly significant. It is echoed again in the subsequent verses: "Please give me some of **your son's** mandrakes … Will you then also take **my son's** mandrakes … In exchange for **your son's** mandrakes … I have indeed hired you with **my son's** mandrakes." The text seems to be emphasizing to us the exceptional closeness between Reuben and Leah. He acts by virtue of her being "his mother," and she sees him as "her son." This emphasis provides an opening for us to understand Reuben's motives in the story.

At times it seems that Reuben is merely the background to the central encounter of the story between Rachel and Leah. But specifically because the fact that Reuben finds the mandrakes appears to add nothing to our understanding of the story, the Torah seems to be trying to teach something concerning Reuben as well.

The fact that, immediately after finding the mandrakes, he brings them to his mother reveals his emotions. Reuben is Leah's first-born son; night after night he sleeps close to her in the tent from which Jacob is conspicuously absent. Night after night Reuben wipes his mother's tears, and it is quite likely that it is to her first-born son that Leah opens her heart, bemoaning her painful relationship with her sister, and her husband's unfair treatment of her. Reuben's act of bringing mandrakes to his mother reflects a strong desire on the part of the son to comfort his mother, to bring her some happiness, to remind her that he is worth more to her than ten husbands.

From this perspective, we should view the connection between the two stories that open with the expression "and Reuben went." The expression "Reuben went" serves to introduce another episode in the book of Genesis: "And Reuben went and lay with Bilha, his father's concubine" (35:22). The connection between these two images is clear: in both instances Reuben is actively affecting the dynamics of the family relationships. In the story of the mandrakes, Reuben admittedly serves only as the background to the agreement that is reached between Rachel and Leah. However, the very fact that the Torah tells us how the mandrakes reached Leah's hands connects Reuben to the development of the events. In any event, it would seem that these two acts by Reuben are connected on a deeper level. In both instances, Reuben is seeking to restore his mother's honor.

We cannot know what Reuben thought, on the morning after the "mandrakes agreement," when he found that the mandrakes he had given Leah as a gift were in her sister Rachel's tent. Perhaps Leah explained to him that in handing them over, she had gained Jacob himself, but a five-year-old child would have trouble understanding why his mother would agree to relinquish a gift that he had labored to acquire for her.[1]

---

1. It is reasonable to assume that Reuben was about five years old. It should be remembered that after this story, Leah bore another three children (Issachar, Zebulun

VAYETZEH: *"And He Found Mandrakes in the Field"*

Either way, the close relationship between Reuben and his mother becomes apparent in this brief narrative. In light of this, Rachel's request of Leah – "Please give me some of your son's mandrakes" – could sound quite insolent, coming from the favored wife, but we must keep in mind Rachel's own profound distress. In this request she maintains her position from the previous dialogue that interrupted the narrative of the births of the children – her plea to Jacob. There she asked that Jacob give her children, and now she asks that her sister give her the talisman for childbearing – the mandrakes.

From this perspective, Reuben's title as "your son" assumes a different significance as Rachel utters it. We noted previously that the emphasis on Reuben's filial relationship with Leah is meant to impress on our consciousness their close connection, as well as the significance of the mandrakes for Leah. Now, it seems, the same title serves to emphasize Rachel's frustration at her own situation. "You, Leah, have a son," says Rachel. "Please give me some of the mandrakes that your son brought." We can almost see the mandrakes slipping unnoticed out of the conversation: "Please give me some of your son."

Rachel's suffering is unbearable. It is not enough that God has withheld children from her; there is a sense that her whole family is turning their back on her. First there is Jacob's aggressive response to her desperate plea, hinting that she herself is guilty for her barrenness: "Am I then in the place of God, who has withheld children from you?" (30:2). Now Leah, her sister, is similarly displeased with her request, and hints that Rachel is unworthy: "Is it a small matter that you have taken my husband; will you take my son's mandrakes too?" (30:15).

Leah defines Jacob as "my husband" (*ishi*), not "our husband" (*ishenu*). This definition reflects the reality, in which Leah married Jacob first, and only afterwards did Rachel join the household as Jacob's beloved wife. Still, these words cast an ironic light on the events, for Leah

---

and Dina), and that all her children were born within the space of seven years. It is possible that *Ri Bekhor Shor* is correct in asserting that Dina was Zebulun's twin sister (and therefore there is no mention of the pregnancy, in contrast to the usual formulation), but even then Reuben could not be older than five. I cannot understand the Radak's calculation that "Reuben was then about seven years old" (in his commentary on 30:14).

and Rachel know that Jacob wanted Rachel – and only Rachel – from the start; hence, in a certain sense, it is Leah who joined the household unfairly and "took the husband" of Rachel from her.

This sentence, then, which should have been formulated in precisely the opposite way, testifies most clearly as to the psychological complications that exist in this family. Leah, by her words, reveals her point of view of their reality: Rachel is stealing her husband from her. Obviously, Rachel views things differently, and communication between the two sisters is all but impossible.

Following the agreement between them, the text moves on to describe its fulfillment. Surprisingly, the Torah introduces the realization of the agreement with Jacob's return from work: "And Jacob came from the field in the evening, and Leah went out towards him and she said..." (30:16). It seems that the Torah could have sufficed with noting, immediately after the sisters' agreement: "And he lay with her that night." But, as we see so often, it is specifically the "incidental" details that contribute so much to our understanding of the emotional world of the characters described, and of the message that the text seeks to convey.

Here, again, the description seems to relate to two levels: both that of Jacob, who is returning from the field, and that of Leah, who is going out to meet him. The expression, "And Jacob came from the field," seeks to remind the reader of the previous occasion when this expression appeared (and it is, in fact, the only other appearance in the Torah): the story of the sale of Esau's birthright to Jacob. There, it was Esau who came from the field: "And Esau came from the field and he was tired" (Gen. 25:29).

What is the Torah trying to teach us by creating this connection? In both cases, the Torah describes two siblings who agree to a certain exchange. Esau is interested in consuming a pot of lentils, and Rachel is interested in acquiring mandrakes. In both instances, the price paid for the desired acquisition is not a tangible one, but rather a right: the birthright on one hand, and a night with Jacob on the other.

In light of the connection between the stories, we can understand Hazal's criticism of Rachel for "selling" the privilege of intimacy with Jacob. Rashi, basing himself on *Bereshit Raba*, explains: "Because she treated lightly her intimacy with that righteous man, she did not merit to be buried with him." Keeping in mind the comparison to Esau, the criticism does indeed come to the surface, for the story of the sale of the birthright concludes with a covert judgment of Esau: "And Esau despised the birthright." Thus Ḥazal project the same conclusion onto Rachel – that she did not appreciate her privilege as she should have.

But the comparison between the two stories is also related to the character who has not yet been mentioned by name: Jacob. Surprisingly, Jacob is the object that is being passed from hand to hand. The sisters decide between themselves whom Jacob will sleep with that night, and it is clear that they have no thought of consulting with him or receiving his approval. In fact, Jacob's passivity in the narrative of the birth of the children has already been emphasized earlier on, in the conversation with Rachel, concluding with her suggestion that Jacob take her handmaiden – "Here is my handmaiden, Bilha – come to her" (30:3). Lo and behold, there is no reaction whatsoever on Jacob's part! The text describes him as doing as his wife has suggested, offering no words of his own. Moreover, when Leah then adopts the idea and gives her handmaiden, Zilpa, to Jacob, there is no mention of even a request that Jacob agree to this. Certainty, a dialogue must have taken place; it is reasonable to assume that Jacob also answered Rachel, expressing his agreement. But in the Torah's omission of these words, there is undoubtedly a lesson to be learned about Jacob's character in these scenes.

Jacob's passivity also stands out in his reaction to Leah in the exchange agreement – or, more accurately, his lack of reaction. Here, again, the Torah makes no mention of Jacob's feelings in the face of this bizarre sale. Did he try to change Rachel's mind? Was he angry at his wives? Or perhaps he actually understood Leah's distress and went to her tent willingly? We may offer many different hypotheses, but the silence of the text speaks louder than any of them.

As noted, part of the significance of the connection between this "sale" of Jacob and the sale of the birthright is that it highlights a change in Jacob's status. Once before, it was Jacob who initiated an exchange agreement with his brother, and now it is Jacob who becomes the object that is exchanged.

In contrast to Jacob, Leah is depicted as quite active. This is apparently the intention of the text in emphasizing her "going out" to meet

Jacob: "And Leah went out to meet him, and she said: You will come to me, for I have indeed hired you for my son's mandrakes" (30:16). Leah cannot wait any longer in her tent. We can almost imagine her sitting in the tent, looking out of the window from time to time and perhaps sending her children outside so that they can inform her of his arrival. The moment he reaches the area of their encampment, she "goes out to him," immediately uttering the final result, so important to her: "You will come to me" (v. 4). The reason for this result comes only afterwards: "For I have indeed hired you …" The special double formulation (*sakhor sekhartikha*) also contributes to the ceremonial atmosphere of Leah's declaration.

Now we shall complete the circle. The story began with Reuben finding mandrakes "in the field" and bringing them to Leah: "and he brought [*vayaveh*] them to Leah, his mother." Now Jacob returns from "the field," and Leah tells him: "You will come to me [*elai tavo*]." The exchange is hinted at also in the words themselves: in exchange for Reuben's mandrakes from the field, Leah will receive Jacob "from the field."

We must now address the question with which we began: what is the significance of this narrative for the story listing the birth of Jacob's sons? To answer this, we must note another point. After the birth of Leah's four sons, we are told: "And she ceased to bear." This statement is most surprising, if we take into account the fact that over the course of seven years Leah bore a total of seven children (six sons and a daughter!). What is the meaning of the expression "ceased to bear," if she then went on to bear another three children?

It would seem that the birth of Leah's last three children should be seen as a divine response to the story of the mandrakes. The very fact that in the wake of that story God heard Leah's cry, and blessed her with another two sons and a daughter, indicates that the text is inclined towards Leah in its judgment. The Torah hints, in its declaration that Leah "ceased to bear," that we should not expect to read of any further children issuing from her. But behold – after the story of the mandrakes, Leah does indeed bear more children. This can only be a reward for Leah, for being prepared to forego the mandrakes in favor of Jacob. In the words of R. Levi:

Observe how beautiful the sale of the mandrakes was in the eyes of the Creator: for through the mandrakes two great tribes of Israel came into being – Issachar and Zebulun. Issachar sits and is occupied with Torah study, while Zebulun goes out by day and comes to support Issachar [with his material profits], such that the Torah prevails in Israel." (*Bereshit Raba* 72:5)

The text hints at this idea in the introduction to Leah's next childbirth following the story of the mandrakes: "And God heard Leah, and she conceived and bore..." (30:17). This introduction also appears at the birth of Leah's first child, and again at Joseph's birth to Rachel. On these two occasions, God gave the matriarchs their respective firstborns, and so the expression is appropriate in these cases. Why does it appear again in connection with Leah? Its repetition at the birth of Leah's last children seems to indicate that there was a need for special divine providence. In other words, Leah had truly already "ceased to bear," and it was only in the wake of the mandrakes episode that God opened her womb again.

It appears that Rachel, in her desire for the talisman of fertility and her foregoing of Jacob, actually delayed her pregnancy even further, while Leah – who agreed to relinquish magical omens for Jacob – merited bearing another two sons who would help build Jacob's household. This idea is echoed in *Ḥazal*:

Rabbi Eliezer taught: This one lost and the other one lost; this one gained and the other one gained. Leah lost the mandrakes but gained two tribes and the birthright; Rachel gained mandrakes but lost both tribes and the birthright. (*Bereshit Raba* 72:3)

Rabbi Shmuel bar Naḥman taught: Leah lost the mandrakes but gained tribes and the right of burial with Jacob; Rachel gained the mandrakes but lost tribes and burial with him.

In summary, the story of the mandrakes reveals the tensions hidden beneath the surface of Jacob's household. There is Reuben, attempting to comfort his mother; the plight of the barren Rachel, who cannot even find a sympathetic ear; the plight of lonely Leah, who feels that her husband has been snatched from her; the inability of the sisters to communicate properly; and Jacob – who is unsuccessful in bringing peace between his wives.

Ultimately, the problems are solved only with divine intervention: "And God heard Leah," "And God remembered Rachel and God heard her." It is not some miracle fertility drug that solves the family's problems, but rather the prayer that is heard by the Creator. In this context, we may make mention of the literary connection with which we began: the connection between this story and Reuben's sexual impropriety concerning Bilha ("and Reuben went"). Both stories seem to describe an "exaggerated" human attempt at intervention in the events. Rachel seeks to seize the keys of reproduction – keys that belong only to God, while Reuben seeks to determine the order of leadership in the family – an order for which Jacob is solely responsible.

Parashat Vayishlaḥ

"And Jacob Was Left Alone"

by Rav Chanoch Waxman

I.

The night before meeting his brother Esau, while alone in the dark, Jacob grapples with a strange and mysterious visitor.

> And Jacob was left alone; and a man wrestled with him until daybreak. And when he saw that he was not able, he touched the hollow of his thigh; and the hollow of Jacob's thigh was put out of joint… (Gen. 32:25–26)

Injured but not defeated, Jacob refuses to release his adversary until the latter blesses him (32:27). In response, his assailant names him Israel, "for you have contended [*sarita*] with God and man and have prevailed" (32:28–29). Based upon his antagonist's statement that he had contended with "God," and his unsuccessful attempt to learn the identity of the man (32:30), Jacob concludes that this was no mere man. He names the place Peniel, meaning "face of God," "for I have seen God face to face and my life has been spared" (32:31).

This short story abounds with difficulty. Who was the mysterious assailant? On the assumption that the man is in fact a divine emissary, why did God send him? What is the meaning of the injury, the blessing and the re-naming of Jacob as Israel? In sum, reading the story places us metaphorically in the position of Jacob. We, too, wrestle with a mysterious yet clearly significant unknown.

II.

In grappling with the story, I have become convinced that a key to interpreting the story can be found in Rashbam's comments. Rashbam notes a parallel between the textual context of Jacob's wrestling match and the story of David's river-crossing (II Sam. 17:21–24). Immediately preceding the story of the struggle, the Torah informs us that Jacob got up in the middle of the night, took his wives, children and possessions and crossed at Jabbok. This closely parallels the later story of David. Just as Jacob "got up," so too David "got up" (II Sam. 17:22). Just as the Hebrew root for crossing (*a-v-r*, ע-ב-ר) appears three times in the Jacob story to describe a middle-of-the-night event, so too the root appears three times in the David story, and likewise describes a middle-of-the-night water traversal (II Sam. 17:21–22). Finally, as Rashbam notes, the two crossings happen in geographic proximity one to the other. Immediately after the river crossing, David arrives at Maḥanaim (II Sam. 17:24). This, of course, is the place Jacob has last been located (Gen. 32:3), the approximate geographic locale of his crossing.

Rashbam concludes that just as David crosses to flee Absalom, so too Jacob crosses to flee. The two are both stories of avoidance and flight. Jacob's nocturnal crossing constitutes an attempt to run away, to avoid meeting his brother the next morning.

A careful reading of the larger context of the struggle story provides further support for Rashbam's revolutionary claim. The beginning of *Parashat Vayishlaḥ* describes Jacob's preparations for meeting Esau. After receiving word from his emissaries that Esau, accompanied by four hundred men, already marches to greet him, Jacob is gripped by fear and anxiety (32:7–8). He divides his camp into two and prays for divine help (32:9–13). Nevertheless, despite his fear, he apparently remains steadfast in his intention to meet with Esau. At this point, Jacob has but one more preparation to make. As night begins, either just before or just after going to sleep [how just after??] (32:14), Jacob engages in a final activity. He gathers together an offering for his brother sends it off in the hands of his servants (32:14–22). His threefold preparation complete, Jacob goes to sleep, as ready as he can be (32:22).

Surprisingly, immediately after being informed of Jacob's lying down for the night, and right before the story of the struggle, we find Jacob up and about, crossing the Jabbok.

> And he got up that night, and took his two wives and two maid-servants, and his eleven sons, and crossed over the ford of Jabbok. And he took them, and sent them over the brook, and sent over that which he had. (32:23–24)

Is this some new preparation for meeting Esau? I think not. Jacob has already arranged his camp in preparation for the upcoming confrontation (31:8–9). In pointed contrast to the previous splitting of his camp, he gathers together all of his people and possessions. He is breaking camp and initiating a journey. The sense of reversal of Jacob's previous preparations is further emphasized by the image of "getting up that night" (32:23), the precise opposite of the "sleeping there that night" (32:22) that closes out Jacob's preparations. Jacob seems to have undergone a last-minute change of plans.

To put all of this together, something has changed during the night. Whether out of fear, despair, habit, shame or a sense of not deserving divine protection, Jacob has decided to slip away into the dark.

From this reading of the context of the struggle, Rashbam reaches the obvious conclusion – and so should we – that God sends the angel to prevent Jacob from fleeing. The angel grasps Jacob at the last minute, after all have crossed over, and Jacob alone remains. They wrestle and thrash about in the dirt (Rashi and Ibn Ezra on 32:25), thus physically preventing Jacob from running away. When the angel realizes that he cannot prevail and Jacob seems on the verge of breaking away, he "touches" Jacob on his thigh, apparently dislocating his leg and thereby preventing Jacob from slipping away.

If so, we may conclude that the story of the struggle really constitutes a story of frustrated flight. At the last minute, Jacob wavers. God sends the angel, seizes Jacob and forces him to meet Esau. Jacob is injured, preventing his flight. Nevertheless, numerous issues remain

unresolved. What about the blessing and the name change? For that matter, why does God insist on Jacob's meeting Esau? Why not let Jacob
slip away into the night?

III.

In trying to puzzle out God's insistence on Jacob's meeting Esau, it seems
reasonable to posit that God does no more than help Jacob accomplish
his own original intentions. After all, it was Jacob himself who initiated
the original contact with Esau, without explicit divine prodding. He
sent the messengers (32:4–7). While, as Rashbam maintains, God may
in fact desire the meeting, God's role in the story seems primarily supportive, a dovetailing of divine will with Jacob's initiative. This returns us
to the central problem of the story: What motivates Jacob to meet Esau?

Jacob's third preparation, his sending of an offering (*minḥa*) to
Esau (32:14–22), may provide the key. In instructing his emissaries as to
what they should tell Esau, explaining the stream of gifts, Jacob tells them:

> And say, "Behold, your servant Jacob is behind us, for he said: I
> will cleanse his anger\face [*akhapera panav*] with the offering
> [*minḥa*] that goes before me, and afterwards I will see his face
> [*panav*]; perhaps he will accept me [*yisa panai*]." (32:21)

The combination of a *minḥa* (offering) and the Hebrew root *k-p-r*
(כ-פ-ר), meaning "cleanse" (Rashi on 32:21), possesses overtones of
atonement. It would appear that Jacob seeks forgiveness. How else
would Esau's anger be purged?

The remainder of Jacob's statement further strengthens this point.
Jacob states his desire that perhaps "*yisa panai*" – literally, that Esau will
lift his face. The verb for lifting or raising, from the root *n-s-a* (נ-שׂ-א)
is often associated with forgiveness and relationship. For example, after
Cain's *minḥa* is rejected and his "face falls," God informs him that if he
is good, he will be "lifted up" – an apparent reference to his "fallen face"
(4:6) – with the possibility of divine forgiveness, acceptance and relationship (4:5–7). In sending his *minḥa*, Jacob wishes for exactly what
Cain failed to achieve; namely, an elevation of his face by his master, a
renewed relationship and reconciliation.

Finally, let us turn to one last image utilized by Jacob. Jacob's refers to "seeing his face" (*er'eh panav*), the face of Esau. This, of course, is the classic image used for pilgrimage to the sanctuary of God. Throughout Exodus, numerous references are made to "not seeing the face of God empty-handed" (Ex. 23:17; 34:20). Just as the children of Israel must journey to God bearing gifts in order to express loyalty, achieve reconciliation and maintain their relationship, so too Jacob sends gifts for the purposes of service, loyalty and relationship.

In sending his *minḥa*, Jacob wishes to telegraph to Esau his position as a supplicant, a servant who desires to express fealty to his master. He desires to appease Esau's anger and to establish a relationship with him. He seeks atonement and reconciliation.

If so, we may infer that this complex of desires constitutes Jacob's motivation not only for sending the *minḥa*, but also for originally contacting Esau. The text can easily be interpreted along these lines. From the very start, in his original sending of emissaries to his brother Esau, Jacob places himself in the "servant" position and his brother Esau in the "master" position. He refers to "my master Esau," and "your servant Jacob" (32:5). He wishes to "find favor in his master's eyes" and implies that whatever he owns exists for the sole purpose of serving his master (Abarbanel on 32:6). By no accident, the terms "brother," "master" and "servant" appear repeatedly throughout the entire narrative (32:4–33:17), each one appearing at least eight times. These terms capture what the story is all about.

To complete the picture, let us take a look at a final proof. The morning after the struggle with the angel, Jacob finally confronts Esau (33:1–11). Needless to say, he defines himself as the servant (33:5), Esau as the master (33:8), and talks about finding favor in his master's eyes (33:8, 10). More importantly, he bows down – not just once, but seven times (33:3). Even after Esau has embraced Jacob, kissed him and cried, the bowing continues. Group by group, Jacob's wives and children approach and bow to Esau (33:6–7).

This scene should sound familiar. Recall one of the blessings Jacob had stolen from Esau: "Let peoples serve you and nations bow down to you: be a master [*gevir*] over your brother and let your mother's sons bow down to you" (27:29).

The meeting of Jacob and Esau constitutes the antithesis of the theft of the blessings. In place of Esau serving and bowing, it is Jacob who serves and bows. In place of Jacob acting the master, and receiving the tribute and obeisance of the descendants of Esau, it is Esau who plays the master, symbolically receiving the fealty of the future tribes of Israel. Everything plays out exactly as Isaac had intended. But this is also precisely what Jacob intends. Jacob contacts Esau in order to arrange this scene. He seeks his brother, in order to symbolically return to him the blessings he has stolen, a crucial step for achieving atonement and reconciliation.

IV.

Much of the argument above is not new. Particular segments have already been noted by Rashi, Ramban and Abarbanel. Nevertheless, most commentaries have hesitated to draw the necessary conclusions. For example, Ramban, in commenting upon the "servant-master" language discussed above, implies that Jacob acts "as if" the sale of the birthright were irrelevant, "as if" he seeks to make up for the theft of the blessings. Jacob deliberately presents a false front to Esau. He acts out of fear alone and seeks no more than to save his neck. On this account, Jacob's behavior in parashat *Vayishlaḥ* constitutes the third time Jacob has pulled the wool over Esau's eyes.

In general, it is almost impossible to disprove this kind of claim, a claim that posits a true interior motivation disguised by an external false front. In the technical language of philosophy of explanation: it is not falsifiable. Almost any evidence can be countered by the claim that we face just more of the false front. Nevertheless, I believe that the text tilts strongly against the "false front" interpretation and in favor of the "sincere apology and reconciliation" approach.

As pointed out above, the bowing of Jacob's family to Esau occurs after Esau and Jacob have embraced, kissed and cried (33:4). Offhand, there seems no reason to doubt the apparent mutual sincerity. At the very least, Jacob must already realize that Esau has no intention of killing him. If Esau intended to kill him, he already would have done the deed. If it is a false front, a mask worn over the fear, why keep it up?

Moreover, at this point, after the threat has evaporated, a crucial conversation occurs between Jacob and Esau (33:8–11). Jacob continues to employ the "servant-master" language and insists that Esau accept his offering. Esau declines and replies, "I have much [*rav*], my brother" (33:9). While Esau only means to tell his brother Jacob that he has enough possessions, he manages to conjoin the word "*rav*," also meaning "older," with the word "brother." This linkage creates an unmistakable echo of "*verav ya'avod tza'ir*," "and the older shall serve the younger," the phrase appearing in the oracle of Rebecca and the genesis of the entire Jacob-Esau conflict (25:23). While Jacob, the younger, now proclaims himself Esau's servant, Esau defines himself as "*rav*" (possessing much \ older) versus Jacob. On the level of subtext, Esau's refusal of Jacob's offering subversively contains the acknowledgement that it is the younger brother who serves the older, and not the reverse. Once again, we see another reversal of the supposed superiority and lordship of Jacob over Esau. But once again, if it is all a false front and Esau no longer threatens Jacob, why are they talking about something that happened before they were born?

Let us go on. Jacob refuses to accept no for an answer. Twice using the word for "please," he practically begs Esau to accept the offering (33:10). Moreover, he compares the experience of having his face seen and accepted by Esau with that of being seen and accepted by God (33:10). As if this were not enough, Jacob describes Esau's actions until this point as "*vatirtzeni*," a term normally referring to divine acceptance of sacrifices (Lev. 1:3). Is this a bluff? Rather, Jacob insists upon concrete acceptance of his offering because it is about far more than augmenting Esau's wealth. For Jacob, it is about a very real and concrete act of atonement, a way to physically correct his previous treatment of Esau.

If any doubts remain, let us take a look at the very next verse. Jacob beseeches Esau:

> Please take [*kaḥ*] my blessing that has been brought to you, for God has been merciful to me... (33:11)

If we choose merely to scratch the surface of Jacob's statement, the term "blessing" here means only the offering being proffered to Esau. But this would be naive. The language of "taking" and "blessing" is the exact language found in the aftermath of the theft in *Parashat Toledot*. Isaac informs Esau that Jacob has "come in trickery and taken [*velakaḥ*] your blessing" (27:35). Esau responds that he now finally understands the true meaning of the name Jacob: "He has supplanted me (*vaya'akveni*) twice; he took (*lakaḥ*) my birthright and now he has taken (*lakaḥ*) my blessing!" (27:36). Flash ahead twenty years to the meeting of *Parashat Vayishlaḥ*, the first conversation between Esau and Jacob since that fateful day. On the level of subtext, at the very least, Jacob symbolically offers to give back the blessing he has taken.

V.

Let us return to the story of the struggle with the angel and try to close the circle. As argued above, the first part of *Vayishlaḥ* constitutes the story of the reconciliation of Jacob and Esau, the story of Jacob's efforts to achieve atonement and make it right. Jacob leaves the house of Laban determined to reconcile with his brother and correct his earlier actions. But things turn out not to be simple. Jacob receives word that Esau is already on the march with four hundred men. Jacob assumes that Esau approaches with murderous intent.

Jacob must now contend not only with the flesh-and-blood Esau, but also with the mythic Esau of his imagination. He must not only wrest atonement from the real Esau, but must also grapple with his fear. Jacob gives ground to neither his fear nor the mythic Esau of his imagination. He remains determined and focused. He prepares his camp, prays, and devises a strategy to achieve reconciliation (32:7–22). But then he goes to sleep. In the dark of the night, Jacob wavers. The struggle proves overwhelming. Out of fear, habit, guilt, a sense of a lack of deserving divine protection, or a mix of them all, Jacob rises and attempts to run away.

This brings us back to the story of the struggle with the angel. God sends the angel to prevent Jacob from fleeing and to compel the confrontation between Jacob and Esau. Why is this important to God? For the very same reason it has been important to Jacob. God also knows that Jacob needs to make up for his behavior of twenty years past, that he requires atonement and reconciliation. Jacob is now injured; he cannot run. He has no choice but to face Esau. But there is more to God's action than mere support of Jacob's original intentions. When God forces Jacob to struggle with an angel, he thereby proves to him that he can meet almost any challenge. He teaches Jacob that he can complete the struggle and face his brother (Ibn Ezra, Abarbanel). Even when causing Jacob's temporary physical collapse, God in fact helps and bolsters Jacob. He challenges him to find new existential resources, to complete the task and atone for his past.

This leaves us with the blessing and the name change, the final and most difficult piece of the puzzle. Jacob's angelic adversary blesses him by renaming him Israel. More precisely, he tells him, "They will no longer say your name is Jacob, but Israel, for you have contended (*sarita*) with God (*Elokim*) and with men and proven able" (32:29). On the simplest level, the name stems from the conflict with the angel that night. The "God" that Jacob has struggled with is the divine emissary he has spent the night entangled with. He has not succumbed and has proven able.

But there is much more to it than this. Let us consider for a moment who the "men" are that Jacob has struggled with. Is this a reference to Laban, Jacob's previous adversary? But this places the renaming slightly out of context. Is this a reference to Esau? But Jacob has not yet met up with Esau. Perhaps the verb "contended" (*sarita*) should not be read as referring solely to the past. Perhaps the angel's statement is more prophecy and prediction than history. Jacob will successfully contend with Esau that very morning.

Alternatively, the angel's statement does indeed refer to the past and to the men that Jacob has just been struggling with. But who are these "men"? I think we already know the answer. They are the mythic and murderous Esau of Jacob's imagination, and Jacob himself – his fears, his prior character and his past actions. These are the struggles in which Jacob has been engaged. As argued previously, Jacob already contends with Esau even before meeting with him. He already struggles with the problem of how to achieve reconciliation and atonement. He already contends with his fear, sometimes successfully and sometimes unsuccessfully. Furthermore, the entire story of the meeting of Jacob and Esau consists of Jacob's struggle with his past self. It is about his struggle with the Jacob of misdirection, tricks and wiles, the Jacob who could never confront his self, the brother he has tricked or the moral-divine imperative of repentance.

To pull all of this together, God sends the angel to struggle with Jacob and thereby force Jacob to confront and make up with Esau. That very struggle with the angel constitutes a physical manifestation and metaphor of the numerous external and internal struggles that animate the character of Jacob both before and after the nighttime wrestle. In the course of his attempt to be more than the Jacob of tricks and wiles, he contends with the angel, with his clan-brother Laban, with his flesh-and-blood brother Esau, with his fear, with the divine imperative of seeking atonement, and with his very own self and character. His renaming by the angel captures this past, present and future theme precisely. He will no longer be Jacob, bent like the heel he once grasped, the one who garnered blessings by latching on to others, by the means of deals and tricks. He will no longer be known as the one Esau justly accused. Rather, he will be Israel, he who has struggled in so many ways and proven able. He will be known as Israel, a man whose blessedness stems from his struggles.

Simeon and Levi in Shekhem

by Rav Amnon Bazak

I. THE PROBLEM

Chapter thirty-four in our *parasha* is devoted in its entirety to the episode of Simeon and Levi in Shekhem. The story presents a serious challenge to its readers, for the brothers' act has far-reaching moral implications, and in this case it is very difficult to identify the Torah's attitude toward their actions. In general, the Tanach conveys a negative judgment in one of two ways: either by means of an explicit statement, indicating that the act was bad (for example, in the story of David and Bat-Sheva: "The thing that David did was bad in God's eyes" [II Sam. 11:27]); or indirectly, through mention of the punishment meted out to the perpetrator (for example, the death of Judah's sons after the sale of Joseph). Here we find no direct punishment of Simeon and Levi, and although their actions are not looked upon positively by their father, Jacob, the reason for his displeasure is essentially tactical:

> You have brought trouble upon me to make me odious to the inhabitants of the land – the Canaanites and the Perizites, and since I am few in number they will gather against me and strike me, and I will be destroyed – both I and my household." (Gen. 34:30)

Furthermore, even after Jacob's statement of this reason for his censure, it is Simeon and Levi who have the final word on the matter: "They said: Shall he treat our sister as a harlot?" (34:31).

However, when Jacob takes leave of his sons before his death, he expresses much harsher criticism of Simeon and Levi, extending beyond the danger that their act may have brought upon him:

> Simeon and Levi are brothers; vessels of cruelty are their swords. Let my soul not enter their council; let my honor not be united with their assembly. For in their anger they killed a man, and in their self-will they lamed an ox. Cursed is their anger for it is severe, and their wrath, for it is harsh; I shall divide them in Jacob and scatter them in Israel. (49:5–7)

But here, again, the intention is not clear, and the commentaries propose different ways of understanding Jacob's words. Indeed, the Rishonim are divided in their approach towards the act of Simeon and Levi. On one hand, Rambam writes:

> How are they [the nations of the world] commanded concerning justice? They are obligated to establish judges in every region to judge concerning these [other] six commandments, and to exhort the people. A non-Jew who transgresses one of these seven commandments is to be put to death by the sword. For this reason all the men of Shekhem were deserving of death, for Shekhem kidnapped [Dina] and they saw and they knew of it, but they did not judge him. A non-Jew may be put to death by [the word of] a single witness and by [the verdict of] a single judge, without [the need for] forewarning, and by relatives. (*Mishneh Torah,* Hilkhot Melakhim 9:14)

The Ramban, however, disagrees:

> This is not correct, for if it were so, then Jacob should have been the first to go in and put them to death. And if [the reason for

his failure to do so was because] he feared them [the men of Shekhem], why did he express anger at his sons and curse their wrath later on, and punish them by dividing and scattering them?! (Ramban on 34:13)

Accordingly, he concludes that this act by Jacob's sons was a sin:

> Regarding the matter of Shekhem: Since the men of Shekhem were wicked and [Jacob's sons] considered their blood like water [i.e. Simeon and Levi felt it was permissible to spill their blood], therefore Jacob's sons wanted to exact revenge on them with a vengeful sword. So they killed the king and all the men of his city for they were his servants, heeding his commands. And the circumcision that they had performed was worthless... for [the townspeople] had performed it merely to please their master. Jacob now informed them that they had endangered him, as it is written, "You have brought trouble upon me to make me odious..." and also, "Cursed is their anger..." for they had acted cruelly towards the people of the city in saying to them – in his presence – "'We shall dwell with you and we shall be a single nation,'" and the townspeople accepted this, but [Simeon and Levi] broke their word. Perhaps they [the inhabitants of Shekhem] would have returned to God, and they [Simeon and Levi] killed them needlessly, for they had done them no harm at all.

In Ramban's view, then, the sin of Jacob's sons lay in violating their commitment to the men of Shekhem, who had done them no harm, and who may have repented later on. The source of this critical perception of the brothers' act is in Jacob's speech to his sons in parashat *Vayḥi*.

II. NOTHING AT ALL OF THE "ḤEREM" SHALL REMAIN IN YOUR HAND

Another *parasha* in the Torah seems to hint at the episode of Shekhem: the *parasha* of the "condemned city" (Deut. 13:13–19). Let us list the parallels between the two *parashot*:

A. Both concern people who set out to convince the people of their city:

Ḥamor and Shekhem, his son, came to the gate of their city and they spoke to the men of their city, saying… (Gen. 34:20)

Good-for-nothing people will go out from among you and brainwash the inhabitants of their city, saying… (Deut. 13:14)

These are the only two instances in the Torah where the expression "the inhabitants of their city" is used.

B. Both instances describe a serious act that takes place in the city:

For he had committed a disgrace in Israel by lying with Jacob's daughter; such an act should not be done. (Gen. 34:7)

This abomination was committed among you. (Deut. 13:15)

C. In both cases, the people of the city are punished by the sword for their grievous act:

They came upon the city unhindered, and they slew every male. And they put Ḥamor and Shekhem, his son, to death by the sword. (Gen. 34:25–26)

You shall surely smite the inhabitants of that city by the sword. (Deut. 13:15)

However, this comparison actually serves to highlight two central differences between the two *parashot*. Firstly, as Ramban noted, the *parasha* of the "condemned city" deals with a case in which all of the people of the city have indeed been led astray to idolatry by idlers – as opposed to Shekhem, where the people of the city "had done them no harm at all." Secondly, there is an obvious difference concerning the spoils. The Torah emphasizes the conclusion of the mission to save Dina as follows:

It was on the third day when they were in pain that Jacob's two sons, Simeon and Levi, Dina's brothers, took each man his sword and they came upon the city unhindered, and they killed every male. And they put Ḥamor and his son, Shekhem, to death by the sword, and they took Dina from Shekhem's house, **and they departed**. (Gen. 34:25–27)

It was specifically then, when no "military need" remained, that Jacob's sons helped themselves to the spoils:

> Jacob's sons came upon the slain men and they plundered the city whose inhabitants had defiled their sister. They took their sheep and their cattle and their donkeys, whatever was in the city and whatever was in the fields. And all their wealth and all their children and their wives they took captive and plundered, and all that was in the house. (ibid. 27–29)

This is in complete contrast to the *parasha* of the condemned city, which concludes with a clear warning:

> You shall destroy it [the city] and all that is in it, and its livestock, by the sword. You shall gather all of its spoils into its open place and you shall burn with fire the city and its spoils, in their entirety, to the Lord your God. It shall be a heap forever; it shall not be rebuilt. Nothing at all of the "*ḥerem*" shall remain in your hand, in order that God may turn back from His fierce anger and grant you mercy, and be merciful towards you, and multiply you as He promised to your fathers. (Deut. 13:16–18)

Why does the Torah emphasize so insistently the importance of not taking from the spoils of the condemned city? The *Or HaḤayyim* writes (Deut. 13:18):

> "In order that God may…grant you mercy and be merciful towards you" – the intention behind these words is that, since God commanded that all of the inhabitants of the condemned city be put to death by the sword – even its livestock – this act will give rise to a cruel nature in people's hearts. This is as the

murderous Ishmaelites have told us in "The King's Saying," that they experience great passion when they kill a person, and the root of mercy is cut out from them and they become cruel. So too will this quality become rooted in the murderers of the idolatrous city. Therefore God gives them a promise that He will give them "mercy" – although natural circumstances would grant them the characteristic of cruelty, the Source of mercy will renew upon them the attribute of mercy, to nullify the attribute of cruelty that is born in them as a result of their act. The Torah says, "He will be merciful towards you," demonstrating thereby that so long as a person is in the category of one with a cruel nature, God will treat him accordingly, for God is merciful only towards a merciful person. (*Shabbat* 151b)

Putting to death all of the inhabitants of a city is a very difficult mission, and by nature such an act is likely to bring about the dulling of a person's moral sensibility. The Torah therefore promises that if a person acts for the sake of heaven, the Holy One will miraculously replant the attribute of mercy in the hearts of the murderers (this is the meaning of the promise, "That He may grant you mercy and be merciful towards you and multiply you"), and cancel the moral damage caused by the act.

However, for this purpose there is an obvious precondition: that the entire act be undertaken solely for the sake of heaven, and not to further any personal aim. The Netziv, in his commentary *Ha'amek Davar*, explains:

"...That He may grant you mercy": [Mercy is required] because the killing of the condemned city causes three evils in Israel:

1. One who kills another person becomes cruel by nature. If an individual is put to death by the court, an agent of the court has already been appointed for that task. But if an entire city must be put to death, then, whether we like it or not, we shall have to accustom a number of people to killing and being cruel.

2. There is no inhabitant of that city who does not have relatives in

another city; thus hatred increases in Israel [because the relatives will hate those who carry out the sentence].

3. The act brings about a lack and diminishing of Israel.

Therefore the text promises that by virtue of the fact that one engages in this act without deriving an y benefit from plundering, therefore God will turn back from His fierce anger, and give you mercy – the attribute of mercy.

In light of the above, the sin of Jacob's sons is revealed in all of its severity. Even if the killing of Shekhem and Ḥamor was justified, and even if the case could be made for killing all of the men of Shekhem, the plundering of the city was not only unjustified, but actually nullified any possible moral justification for killing the city's inhabitants. The taking of the spoils casts a dark moral stain on the act itself, presenting it as an endeavor undertaken out of personal interests.

Now it is easier for us to understand Jacob's rebuke that "Simeon and Levi are brothers; vessels of cruelty are their swords ... For in their anger they killed a man, and in their self-will they lamed an ox. Cursed is their anger for it is severe, and their wrath, for it is harsh...."

Jacob introduces his rebuke of Simeon and Levi specifically with the issue of the "vessels of cruelty." It is the taking of the vessels that proved that their "anger" was indeed severe and their wrath harsh, and hence that there was no justification for killing the men – which itself was also undertaken out of "anger."

III. "REMOVE THE FOREIGN GODS"

How much more grievous, then, is the plundering when it becomes clear what the spoils taken by Jacob's sons included "foreign gods." Jacob, who himself has just expressed the concern, "You have brought trouble upon me to make me odious to the inhabitants of the land," now receives a divine command to return to the Land, but he understands on his own that there is a precondition: the removal of the foreign gods. From where could Jacob's household have obtained foreign gods? The Midrash (*Sekhel Tov, Bereshit* 35:2) explains:

> "The foreign gods that are among you" – which they took from
> Shekhem, as it is written, "And all that was in the house" (34:29) –
> this refers to the idolatry."

Before returning to the holy land, Jacob's children must therefore cleanse
themselves of all that they took. They must divest themselves of the
spoils: the act of taking them was negative in itself, and all the more
so because it included artifacts of idolatry. It must all be buried in the
place from which it was taken. Only now is "the fear of God" upon the
inhabitants of the land assured. In other words, had Jacob's children not
rid themselves of the spoils which they should not have taken in the first
place, Jacob would have been correct in his prediction that "I shall be
destroyed, I and my household."

IV. "SIMEON AND LEVI ARE BROTHERS"

In any act that may be tainted by a suspicion of personal benefit, the test
of whether it is undertaken for the stated purpose or out of personal
interest is what the person will do in a situation that is not to his benefit.
If, in this situation, the person still acts in accordance with the stated aim,
this serves to prove his honesty. But if he acts in the opposite manner,
his behavior casts doubt even on his original act.

Simeon and Levi supposedly acted out of a desire to protect their
sister. As stated, a heavy cloud of suspicion hung over their act after the
plunder of the city. Would Simeon and Levi have been so quick to protect Dina if it had involved going against their personal interest? The
answer to this question is soon revealed:

> They saw him from afar, and before he could approach them,
> they conspired against him to kill him. They said to each other:
> Behold, here comes the dreamer! (37:18–19)

Who exactly are the speakers here? Rashi elsewhere (on the verse
"Simeon and Levi are brothers" – 49:5) quotes Ḥazal as follows:

> "They said to each other, Let us kill him" – who are the speakers?
> We cannot propose either Reuben or Judah, since they did not

agree to killing him. It could not be the children of the handmaids, for they did not hate him so utterly, as it is written [37:2], "The lad was with the sons of Bilha and the sons of Zilpa." Issachar and Zebulun would not speak before their elder brothers. Thus we are forced to conclude that the speakers are Simeon and Levi, whom their father calls "brothers."

This midrashic teaching reveals the depth of the plain meaning of the text. Simeon and Levi, who not long ago cried indignantly, "Shall he treat our sister as a harlot," do not stop here to ask themselves, "Shall we treat our brother as a murderer?" In their haste to pass the death sentence on their brother, another stain is cast on their behavior in the episode of Shekhem.

It seems that this is also what connects the episode of Shekhem and the sale of Joseph in Jacob's rebuke of his sons, as Rashi perceives it:

"For in their anger they killed a man" – this refers to Ḥamor and the men of Shekhem…

"And in their self-will they lamed [*akru*] an ox" – they wished to uproot [*la'akor*] Joseph, who is called "an ox," as it is written [Deut. 33:17], "The firstborn of his ox; grandeur is his."

It is specifically the fact that in their anger they killed the men of Shekhem, and in their self-will they wished to uproot Joseph, that proves that Jacob viewed these two acts in an equally grave light, and that their motives were illegitimate.

This, it seems, may also be the reason why Jacob's moral rebuke is delayed until this late date. Immediately after the act, Jacob's claim against his sons was only a tactical one, for from a moral perspective his sons could still claim that they had acted with proper motives. Their treatment of Joseph, their brother, proved retroactively that it was not moral considerations that had driven their actions.

"Power of Judgment" – Simeon and Levi in Shekhem

by Rav Tamir Granot

I. INTRODUCTION

This week's *shiur* focuses on chapter thirty-four of Genesis, which describes the episode of Shekhem, or – as it is more commonly known – the episode of Dina. As in many other stories in the book of Genesis, and in Tanach in general, we are faced here with a problem of judgment. What is this dilemma?

The Torah describes a series of actions and behaviors. They may be considered negative or morally reprehensible, or alternatively positive and praiseworthy, depending on the reader's point of view, his set of values, his way of analyzing the story, etc. If we believe, for example, that Simeon and Levi were correct in slaughtering the men of Shekhem and in deceiving them in their proposal of circumcision and the related agreement, then their behavior becomes a paradigm for emulation and imitation. If, alternatively, we believe that they were mistaken, or – even worse – they sinned, then the lesson that we learn from them is, obviously, how **not** to behave.

How are we to approach this problem?

At the outset, let us set forth our working assumption, that the problem must be addressed as an exegetical question, rather than as a problem in the sphere of ethics. We assume this for two reasons:

A. Often – even when addressing Tanach, but also in our treatment of life's dilemmas – we make judgments before we have a full picture with all of the facts. In the story in question, the moral issues are weighty ones. They have the power to exert a powerful influence on our judgment. Therefore, we must first address the facts. When considering a written account, "addressing the facts" means exegetical analysis that creates a clear picture of what happened.

B. When we learn Torah, what we need to clarify is not our moral position concerning the events, or how we judge the characters in question, but rather the Torah's position, or the prophetic position. In other words, what is the internal-biblical judgment? The answer to this question may be attained only by means of an exegetical analysis of what the text says. Only rarely does the Torah express a direct and unequivocal judgment of its characters. We have no doubt, for example, as to the guilt of Cain, since God testifies to it explicitly and Cain is punished. In many other instances, however, the text leaves us without any clear, unequivocal answers: Did Sara sin in her treatment and expulsion of Hagar? Did Abraham sin in presenting Sara as his sister? Did Jacob sin in acquiring the blessing through deceit?

It is possible that, in some cases, the absence of any explicit judgment is itself meant as a judgment: the silence of the text may imply criticism. But many times the Torah does judge its characters, without saying so explicitly. The judgment is implied by asides strewn throughout the story, by literary hints, by the structure of the plot and the internal dialogues, or by the development of events connected to the character at the center of the dilemma. An example of these techniques of judgment is to be found in the story of Dina.

II. THE CENTRAL DILEMMA

It seems that our central problem in assessing the Torah's position with regard to the deed of Simeon and Levi is the tension that arises between the story here and Jacob's words to them at the end of his life.

Here, the impression we get is that, from a purely moral point of view, Jacob is not opposed to their actions. We read: "Jacob said to Simeon and Levi: You have brought trouble upon me, to make me odious among the inhabitants of the land."

Jacob speaks here as what we would call, in today's terms, a pragmatic leader. He thinks about what may now transpire as a result of Simeon and Levi's actions. Using plainer language, Jacob tells his sons: we are going to be regarded as a violent clan, as hot-heads. We just arrived from outside the country, and we're already rioting among the locals. None of the country's inhabitants, upon hearing what has happened, will be prepared to accept this.

But Simeon and Levi are not taken aback by his response; they reply with stinging words of their own: "They said: Shall our sister be treated as a harlot?!"

The Torah concludes the narrative with this rhetorical question that serves to clarify their moral motivations to Jacob. In light of their proud stance and their severe answer, Jacob's complaint seems like an expression of meekness, of weak leadership.

Who is given the final word? There can be no doubt that we conclude the chapter with the proud declaration by Simeon and Levi ringing in our ears, with Jacob trailing far behind.

But this is not the only proof that the Torah supports Simeon and Levi. Later, we read on about Jacob's journeys, and come across further evidence of vindication:

> They journeyed, and the fear of God was upon the cities that were around them, and they did not pursue after the children of Jacob.

This verse is not coincidental. This is another form of judgment. The verse tells us that, contrary to Jacob's fears that the nations of the land would gather against him and that his sons' action would represent a stumbling block for the family, the reality turns out quite the opposite. The fear of

God (both literally and in the superlative sense) falls upon the nations of the land, and they do not pursue "the sons of Jacob" – not "Jacob" or "Jacob's household," but "Jacob's sons" – i.e., Simeon and Levi, and, by extension, the other brothers. In other words, if we had any doubts until this point as to which claim – the pragmatic one proposed by Jacob or the moral one propagated by Simeon and Levi – held greater weight, it now turns out that even on the pragmatic level, Jacob was mistaken. A proud stance and revenge not only did not worsen their situation, but apparently served to strengthen their position in the eyes of the nations of the land.

We may summarize by saying that the story of Dina itself seems to point to a fault and weakness in Jacob's leadership, and to a justification – both moral and pragmatic – of the actions of Simeon and Levi in slaughtering the men of Shekhem.

When we get to Jacob's blessing to his sons, the picture is reversed. Jacob now voices a scathing condemnation of their act: "Simeon and Levi are brothers; instruments of cruelty are their swords. Let my soul not be part of their counsel, nor my honor be joined to their assembly. For in their anger they killed a man, and willfully lamed an ox. Cursed is their anger, for it is fierce, and their fury – for it is cruel. I shall divide them among Jacob and scatter them among Israel."

Various commentators have attempted to interpret this fierce criticism – practically a curse – in the most generous possible way. In this regard, we note especially those who suggest that Jacob's condemnation refers to the sale of Joseph, rather than the deed in Shekhem, and explain that the "curse" is really meant for their benefit. Rashi, commenting on the words "cursed is their anger," notes that it is their anger that is cursed, not them themselves. But on the literal level of the text, it is very difficult to avoid the clear intention of what Jacob is saying. Jacob's accusation concerns the episode of Shekhem – since this is the only place where Simeon and Levi act and are mentioned by name. Jacob's words also leave little room for doubt. The expressions "instruments of cruelty," "killed a man," etc., can be understood – at least as far as we know from the Torah – only as a reference to Shekhem.

But the seriousness and profound significance of Jacob's words is borne out not only by their severe content, but also by their historical realization. His curse/prophecy, "I shall divide them among Jacob and scatter them among Israel," was fulfilled both in the case of the tribe of Levi, whose cities are scattered throughout the tribes of Israel and who receives no portion among his brothers, and in the case of the tribe of Simeon, who settles mainly within the portion assigned to Judah, but fails to obtain an independent portion. In the blessing given by Moses at the end of his life, in *Parashat Vezot HaBerakha*, the tribe of Simeon is omitted altogether. The realization of Jacob's blessing also testifies to the fact that this is not merely the outburst of an elderly patriarch seeking to avenge his dignity, but rather the words of a prophet, emanating from a strong sense of morality and expressing the will of God. It is specifically for this reason that the contradiction between Jacob's blessing – with its harsh condemnation of the episode of Shekhem, and the narrative itself – which seems to support the actions of Simeon and Levi, appears so irreconcilable.

In fact, the question must be asked on two levels:

From Jacob's point of view: if his criticism is indeed so fearsome and based on morality, why did he not voice this at the time of the incident, or immediately thereafter?

From the Torah's point of view: how does the Torah judge the actions of Simeon and Levi, and how are we to view them?

III. ANALYSIS OF THE STORY AND CLUES TO JUDGMENT

Let us examine the story of Dina using some exegetical tools:

Whenever we read a narrative – and this applies even to secular literature – a distinction must always be made between the plot itself (which is described from the internal perspective and includes the actions of the characters, background, descriptions of scenery, people, etc., and – obviously – dialogues and monologues), and comments emanating from the narrator (which are external to the action and secondary, from the point of view of the plot). At present, we are interested in the judgmental dimension. Our story contains several such comments:

> Jacob's sons came from the field when they heard of it, and the men were grieved and they were very angry, for he had done a disgraceful act in Israel by lying with Jacob's daughter; such a thing should not be done. (34:7)

Jacob's sons answered Shekhem and Ḥamor, his father, with guile when they spoke, for he had defiled Dina, their sister. (v. 13)

The sons of Jacob came upon the fallen, and they plundered the city, for it had defiled their sister. (v. 27)

These verses all contain asides that are not part of the story. The comment in verse 7 is particularly blatant. What is its role? On the simplest level, it explains the ethical-emotional motivation for the anger and fury of Jacob's sons. But the choice to describe the motive from an external perspective awards it objective significance. This is not a mere feeling or a window into someone's heart; it is a reason with universal validity. If we pay attention to the statement expressed in the verse, we notice that its formulation is altogether anachronistic: "For he had done a disgraceful thing in Israel" – what is "Israel?" The concept of "Israel" does not exist at the point in time in which the story takes place; Jacob and his sons are not yet a nation, and certainly not "Israel." Only at the beginning of the book of Exodus does the title *"Benei Yisrael"* ("the children of Israel") first appear, and even there, "the children of Israel" is meant in the literal sense, not as the name of a nation. Clearly, the Torah's intention here, then, is to express the absolute nature of the disgrace embodied in this act from the perspective of the values of the eternal nation of Israel, not just the emotions of the characters involved. The final phrase emphasizes this: "Such a thing should not be done!" This seemingly superfluous addition can only be understood in light of what we have said above. The Torah is judging the act of rape and thereby providing external justification for the future decision by Jacob's sons, led by Simeon and Levi.

The comments in verses 13 and 27 also explain the motivations of the deceit and the acts of killing and plundering, thereby providing external justification. From an informative point of view, they are entirely redundant. We are familiar with the background, and the motive is clear. Hence, this is not additional information, but judgment. The purpose of the text in inserting this external comment is to provide a moral basis for their actions.

Another point that we would like to address is the various titles by which Dina is referred. This is an important literary technique, as a change of name or title indicates a change of attitude or relationship. Dina could have been referred to simply as "Dina" throughout the story, and this would undoubtedly be the simplest option. The text chooses to use different titles, and we must examine this technique throughout the chapter:

> (1) **Dina, daughter of Leah, whom she bore to Jacob,** went out to see the daughters of the land. (2) Shekhem, son of Ḥamor the Hivite, prince of the land, saw **her** and he took **her** and lay with **her** and raped **her.** (3) And his soul was drawn to **Dina, daughter of Jacob,** and he loved **the girl,** and spoke kindly to **the girl.** (4) And Shekhem said to Ḥamor, his father, saying: Take **this child** for me, to be my wife. (5) Jacob heard that he had defiled **Dina, his daughter,** but his sons were with the cattle in the field, and Jacob held his peace until they returned… (7) And the sons of Jacob came from the field when they heard of it, and the men were grieved and were very angry, for he had done a disgraceful thing in Israel, to lie with **a daughter of Jacob;** such a thing should not be done. (8) Ḥamor spoke with them, saying: "The soul of my son, Shekhem, desires **your daughter;** please give **her** to him as a wife" … (13) The sons of Jacob answered Shekhem and Ḥamor, his father, with guile, as they spoke – for he had defiled **Dina, their sister**… (17) "But if you do not listen to us – to circumcise yourselves – then we will take **our daughter** and go." (18) Their words pleased Ḥamor and they pleased Shekhem, Ḥamor's son. (19) The young man did not delay to perform this, for he desired **Jacob's daughter,** and he was the most honored of all of his father's household… (25) And it was on the third day, when they were in pain, that Jacob's two sons Simeon and Levi, **Dina's brothers,** each took up his sword, and they attacked the city with no resistance, and they killed every male… (27) The sons of Jacob came upon the fallen, and the plundered the city for having defiled **their sister**… (30) And Jacob said to Simeon and to Levi: "You have brought trouble upon me, to make me odious among the inhabitants of the land – the Canaanites and

the Perizites; since I am few in number, they shall gather against me and smite me, and I and my household shall be destroyed." (31) But they said, "Shall **our sister** be treated as a harlot?!"

The following is a list of all the different titles for Dina that appear in the chapter: **Dina, daughter of Leah, her, girl, child, daughter of Jacob, his daughter, their sister, our sister, our daughter, Dina's brothers.**

We shall now propose a hypothesis for the role of each title:

Dina – simply – her name.

Daughter of Leah – emphasizing specifically the connection to Leah, not to Rachel or the handmaids.

Her – colorless title highlighting the attitude towards her as an object.

Girl – her actual status.

Child – a title of disdain.

Jacob's daughter – emphasizing the emotional and moral obligation that rests upon him as her father.

His daughter – as above.

Their daughter, our daughter – emphasizing their connection to her. With regard to Simeon and Levi, this hints particularly to the fraternity via their mother, Leah.

Our daughter – a Freudian slip. She is not their daughter, but they act as though she is.

Dina's brothers – only they. They are concerned for her and act as true brothers.

If we take another look at the order of appearances of the different titles in the chapter, the situation that arises is a dismal one indeed. At the outset, we read: "Dina, daughter of Leah, whom she bore to Jacob, went out…" The text supplies her lineage in full, although it does not say, "The daughter of Jacob, whom Leah had borne to him"; rather, it links Dina specifically to Leah. Rashi detects this, and – following Ḥazal's lead – he explains: "'daughter of Leah' – rather than 'daughter of Jacob.' Because of her 'going out' she is called the 'daughter of Leah,' for she, too, was a woman who went out [*Bereshit Raba*], as it is written: 'Leah went out to greet him' – and it is concerning her that the idiom came about: like mother, like daughter."

But perhaps the text is hinting in a different direction. The Torah wants to remind us that Dina is specifically Leah's daughter. This idea is made even clearer when we move to the end of the story, where Simeon and Levi declare to Jacob, "Shall our sister be treated as a harlot?!" (The word order in Hebrew reads, "Like a harlot shall he make of our sister?") The story concludes with "our sister" (*aḥotenu*), and it stands out against the background of the introduction, where the text mentions that she is Leah's daughter. Indeed, she is their sister, born of the same mother, and Simeon and Levi feel that this is definitely relevant. Why does Jacob himself not take any action? Why is he paralyzed with fear? Why does he not think that this is an abomination and disgrace? The answer emerges from the mouths of Simeon and Levi: we acted as brothers, with brotherly love burning in our hearts. You, our father, have not acted as required of a father. The statement here is a harsh one, difficult to hear, but the silence that follows testifies that Jacob admits to more than just a grain of truth in their accusation.

If we examine the appearance of the various titles during the course of the story, it seems that they confirm our hypothesis. Shekhem treats Dina as an object for exploitation. In his eyes, she starts off as "her," no more. Later, there follows a process during which he perhaps falls in love, perhaps suffers slight regret, maybe discovers that she is the daughter of an important man, and his attitude changes. Therefore he now refers to her as a "girl" or "child."

When Jacob hears that Shekhem has defiled Dina, "**his daughter**; that a disgrace has been committed in Israel, to lie with a **daughter** of Jacob," we expect Jacob to act like a father whose daughter has been assaulted. But upon reading the description of his reaction, our impression is that his response is somewhat anemic: Jacob hears…and holds his peace. This absence of emotion is particularly striking against the background of the reaction of the brothers: "they were grieved," "they were angry."

The expectation that Jacob will treat Dina as his daughter is not realized, and it is apparently for this reason that his sons assume the helm. When Shekhem and Ḥamor make their proposal, instead of Jacob answering – as appropriate for the head of the household – it is the brothers who reply: "The sons of Jacob answered Shekhem and Ḥamor, his father, with guile as they spoke…" Henceforth, Dina is referred to not as "the daughter of Jacob," but rather as "their sister" or "our sister," since it is only her brothers who act in accordance with the appropriate sense of fraternity. The Freudian slip, "We shall take our daughter," is simply an extreme expression of the fact that they have assumed Jacob's place, to the extent that Dina is considered as though she is their daughter.

Finally, when the action takes place, we read: "Jacob's two sons, Simeon and Levi, Dina's brothers, took up each man his sword…." The insertion, "Dina's brothers," is, of course, superfluous, and its role here is not to fill in information, but rather to provide an explanation. It is they, Dina's brothers, sons of Leah, who behave properly and as expected of brothers, acting to deliver her and to protect her honor. Jacob, meanwhile, sits at home.

In light of this analysis, it arises that the story of Dina should be understood against a broader backdrop that represents the source of most of the problems that arise in Jacob's household, and which arises from Jacob's preference for Rachel over Leah. At first, his ardent love for Rachel leads to Leah's jealousy. Ultimately, his great love for Joseph, son of Rachel, leads to the jealousy of Leah's children. In between these two endpoints, his relative apathy concerning the fate of Leah's daughter galvanizes her brothers, Simeon and Levi, born of the same mother, into action that gets out of control and ends in mass slaughter.

The third problem is the deceit practiced by Jacob's sons. The text itself attests to this trickery: they "answered with guile, when they spoke." But this is not necessarily a criticism. Deceit is a means – and morally justifiable, under certain circumstances. It is undoubtedly permissible, for instance, to use deception in order to capture a terrorist. Thus, the question of judgment does not necessarily turn on the word "deceit." But we propose a more balanced view of deceit, arrived at through an analysis of the literary repetition of the proposed agreement between Jacob's sons and the men of Shekhem. The repetition in our story concerns the agreement, which is first presented by Shekhem and Ḥamor to Jacob and his sons.

Shekhem and Ḥamor say:

> Make marriages with us; **give us your daughters, and take our daughters for yourselves. And dwell with us, and the land shall be before you: dwell and trade in it, and** acquire property in it. (34:9–10)

The brothers respond to Shekhem and Ḥamor:

> **But thus we may consent to you: if you will be like us – that every male among you shall be circumcised. Then we will give our daughters to you, and we will take your daughters for ourselves, and we will dwell with you and be a single nation.** (v. 15–16)

Shekhem and Ḥamor then tell the inhabitants of their city:

> Those men are peaceful towards us; **let them dwell in the land and trade in it, for behold – the land is large enough for them; let us take their daughters as wives for us, and let us give our daughters to them.**
>
> **Only by this will the men agree to dwell with us, to be a single nation: if all the males among us are circumcised, as they themselves are circumcised.**
>
> **Their cattle and their property and all their animals – are they not ours? Let us only consent to them, that they may** dwell with us. (21–23)

Comparing the different versions, we see that there is a prominent addition that appears in the latter two versions but is absent in the first: the demand of circumcision. This, after all, is the crux of the brothers' intention. But this point is not enough. Attention should be paid to the other details. The original proposal is fairly generous. It includes several promises: free intermarriage, free trade, and equal civil status: "acquire property in it."

In their repetition, the brothers agree, in principle, to receiving equal status: "We shall be a single nation." But they add the requirement of circumcision, and also repeat exactly the proposal of intermarriage. The interesting changes are to be found in the repetition by Shekhem and Ḥamor, detailing the agreement before the inhabitants of their city:

They repeat the principle of civil equality (to be a single nation), as well as the requirement of circumcision, but make changes and additions in order to make the proposal more palatable to their subjects and to present the agreement as though it benefits them.

They invert the proposal of intermarriage, declaring: "We shall take their daughters for ourselves," instead of the original "you shall give us your daughters" – i.e., it will be by our will, not by their will. And conversely: "And we shall give our daughters to them," instead of the original "you shall take our daughters for yourselves" (and also not "we shall give to you") proposed by Jacob and his sons. In other words: we shall give – at our discretion.

They add: "Their cattle and their property... are they not ours?" In other words, their property belongs – or will ultimately belong – to us. This intention, of course, is hidden from Jacob and his sons.

Likewise, the addition: "Behold, the land is large enough for them" comes to soften the threat that the inhabitants of Shekhem may feel concerning their sources of subsistence – their pasture grounds and fields. Ḥamor and Shekhem imply that Jacob's household need not necessarily dwell right next to them.

The picture that arises from the above should change the prevalent view of Shekhem and Ḥamor as innocent men who agreed to be circumcised and were tricked. They are hard-boiled politicians who make a cold calculation of profitability and even cook up a plot of their own. This picture may certainly serve to change our view of the deceit practiced by Simeon and Levi.

IV. SUMMARY AND SOLUTION OF THE DILEMMA

There is no doubt that, in various ways and using different techniques, the text of chapter thirty-four supports the actions of Simeon and Levi. A number of elements converge to produce this conclusion: the judgmental comments and aside, the analysis of the different titles used in reference to Dina, the development of the agreement between Jacob's sons and Shekhem and Hamor, as well as the recriminations traded by Jacob and Simeon and Levi at the end of the story. The opening and closing of the narrative serve to reinforce this general impression, while the Torah's comment in chapter thirty-five – "The fear of God was upon the cities…and they did not pursue after the children of Jacob" – provides irrefutable vindication of Jacob's sons' claim.

Since this conclusion is unequivocal, we are forced to re-examine the principal dilemma that we presented at the outset: i.e., the contradiction that arises between the narrative itself, with all of its aspects, and Jacob's blessing – or, more accurately, his curse – to Simeon and Levi. We propose that the solution be sought by paying attention to the respective locations of the two different evaluations of the act and its significance.

The supportive judgment is the internal evaluation within the story; it arises from the development of the plot, while the negative judgment is pronounced from afar; it is uttered in a general, rather than personal context – related to the future of the tribes. This distinction is the key to understanding the matter. Jacob is depicted in the story as manifesting weakness, and the text is unforgiving in its indirect criticism of him. His timidity may be a symptom of a general fear of conflict (Esau, Laban, etc.), or derive from an element of alienation from Dina as Leah's daughter. In any event, it is unthinkable that Jacob should stand aside and do nothing, failing to react to the rape of his daughter and not lifting a finger to save her (it must be remembered that the Torah tells us, "They took Dina from Shekhem's house, and left": i.e., during the negotiations, Dina was still there). When the brothers take over the reins that Jacob should properly have grasped, he loses the right to attack them for losing control of the horses. When the wagon driver is asleep, the horses do as they please. And the horses are not driven by moral considerations or a perspective of absolute justice; they are motivated by their heated emotions – their anger and zealousness on behalf of their sister's honor. Therefore, the Torah silences Jacob and presents his opposition as a weak leader's fear for his household – a fear which turns out to be unjustified.

But this understanding cannot justify all actions. Even if the brothers are justified and correct in their anger and zealousness, there are still proportions and limitations of punishment, revenge and justice. Jacob's curse concerns proportion. And proportion is the crux of the moral question. The justification for harming a person who is guilty – in order to exact revenge and in order to save others – is entirely clear. But why must every male in the city be killed? And why do they plunder the city? We note, in contrast, how *Megillat Ester* takes pains to note that "they did not lay their hands on the plunder." Ultimately, their inability to channel their most justified emotions into a morally justified course of action brought about the situation of a mitzva that turned into a sin, and caused the brothers to be cursed. But it was only at the very end of his life that Jacob was permitted to express this. At the time, the Torah held him responsible, too – because had he acted, events would not have transpired the way that they did.

In conclusion, it must be noted that even Jacob's curse is not the final word on the matter. A decree may be altered. The tribe of Levi merited to turn its zealousness in a positive direction – so much so that this tribe became God's servants in the Temple; instead of the inheritance taken from them by Jacob's curse, they receive "the portion of God." Anger directed by a leader, in accordance with law and judgment – as manifested by Moses after the sin of the Golden Calf, where the tribe of Levi joined his campaign – is a holy instrument in times of crisis.

Beit El

by Rav Ezra Bick

P arashat Vayishlaḥ is dominated by two dramatic confrontations of Jacob, once with Esau (the person and the angel) and once with Shekhem (the person and the city). I would, however, like to discuss a short incident, which follows the two major ones: the return of Jacob to Beit El. This takes place "on the road," as Jacob travels from Shekhem, and continues onward towards Efrata (Bethlehem) (Gen. 35:16) and Migdal Eder (35:21), finally arriving "home" at Ḥevron (35:27). While it is true that Jacob builds both a *matzeva* and an altar there, and receives a divine vision and promise, we have gotten so used to God reiterating the promise of the Land to our forefathers that we are likely to skip over this section without proper attention. I propose that we stop and spend some more time at this "roadstop."

After the conclusion of the Dina episode in Shekhem, God tells Jacob to go up to Beit El and build there an altar "to the God who appeared to you when you were fleeing before Esau your brother" (35:1). Jacob, after first instructing his household to get rid of all idolatrous articles, travels to Beit El and builds the altar (v. 5–7). Subsequently, God appears to Jacob (v. 9–13) and then he raises a *matzeva* (v. 14), and, apparently, immediately departs, continuing his journey south in the direction of Ḥevron (v. 16).

A few questions and points to consider on the first half of this story (v. 1–8):

1. Why does Jacob decide to clean out his house from idolatry now?
2. God tells Jacob to "rise and go up to Beit El" (v. 1). Jacob calls on his family to "rise and go up to Beit El" (v. 3). What is the meaning of the striking phrase "rise and go up"?
3. Both God and Jacob call his destination "Beit El." Nonetheless, when he gets there, the Torah states, "Jacob came to Luz, which is in the land of Canaan, which is Beit El" (v. 6). Why are we told now that the city is named Luz?
4. And, in the same verse, what is the significance of the phrase "which is in the land of Canaan"? If this were Jacob's first stop in Canaan, this would make sense, but since Jacob has already been in Canaan since he arrived at Shekhem, it is very strange to be identifying sites within Canaan as "in the land of Canaan." In fact, this appellation appears only when Jacob arrived at Shekhem, his first stop (33:18), and here, but not at any of Jacob's other stops on his way south.
5. Jacob, in Shekhem, speaks to "his house and all who are with him" and suggests travelling to Beit El. At Beit El, we find "Jacob arrived…he and all the people ['*am*'] who are with him." Somewhere along the way, his "household" has become his people ("*am*" – in the sense of "a people, a nation" and not as the plural of person).
6. Deborah, the nursemaid of Rebecca, dies and is buried at Beit El. What was she doing there, and what does this have to do with the story?
7. Jacob had sworn, when he awoke from the dream in Beit El when he was fleeing Esau, that the *matzeva* that he had erected then would become "a house of God." In fact, he will soon erect a *matzeva* in Beit El and offer a libation on it. If the purpose of

his journey now is to fulfill the vow, why does God tell him to build an altar? Why is that the first thing he does, and only after the subsequent vision of God does he re-erect the *matzeva*?

Jacob arrives in *Eretz Yisrael* twice: once when he comes to Shekhem (33:18), and once when he comes to Beit El (35:6). The expression "which is in the land of Canaan" is a clear indication that this is Jacob's point of arrival in a new land. This is confirmed by the expression (in the first case) "when he came from Padan Aram." Jacob entered Shekhem **when he came from Aram.** Now, when Jacob arrives in Beit El, we do not have this additional phrase. But just a few verses later, we find, "God appeared to Jacob again, **when he came from Padan Aram**, and blessed him" (v. 9). Since we know that this took place in Beit El – "Jacob called the name of the place where God spoke to him Beit El" (v. 15) – it turns out that Beit El is also designated as an arrival point.

This point is, I think, greatly emphasized by the name-switch of Beit El in the story. God tells Jacob to go to Beit El. Jacob tells his family that they are going to Beit El. Yet, when they finally get there, we are told that Jacob has arrived in Luz – which is Beit El. In other words, the goal is clearly Beit El, a location saturated with *kedusha*, with the name that Jacob gave it to commemorate his meeting with God and his vision of the gate of heaven. However, until Jacob gets there, the place is actually the Canaanite city of Luz. The Torah has to tell us that this place is the same place called Beit El beforehand; hence the phrase "Luz, which is in the land of Canaan, which is Beit El." The conclusion is an editorial comment, for those who forgot that Luz is the same place as Beit El and therefore are likely to be confused. But the uncommented narrative reads, "Jacob came to Luz in the land of Canaan." In other words, before this point, Jacob is not in the environment we associate with *Eretz Yisrael*, a land of holiness, a land where there is a place which is "the house of God and the gate of heaven." Despite the geographical border of Canaan, which Jacob has crossed some time earlier on his way to Shekhem, Jacob has not actually returned yet to the land of his fathers. Only after Jacob builds the altar does the narrative refer to the place as Beit El.

The reason is that, at this point in the biblical narrative, at least as concerns Jacob, the land of Israel is a reflection of the life of Jacob. Israel is the land where the forefathers carry out the divine design of building the Jewish nation. Jacob has been "out on vacation" from that project for all of the years that he has been in Laban's house. He has to re-inaugurate his career and his status as a forefather, and only from that point on will he be back on the course, and, as a corollary result, back in *Eretz Yisrael*.

The place for this inauguration is Beit El. The reason is spelled out in the command of God: "Make an altar there to the God who appeared to you when you fled before Esau your brother." Beit El was the place from which Jacob left *Eretz Yisrael*. (The midrash which states that from Beit El Jacob proceeded directly to Aram with "*kefitzat haderekh*," a miraculous warp of space, makes this true literally). The vision in the beginning of *Vayetzeh* is Jacob's farewell to Israel, to the land of holiness and the presence of God. The content of God's message there is that he will protect Jacob and be with him in exile, and return him home. In other words, Jacob "dropped out" there, and that is the place where he returns to his destiny.

Jacob understands this, and therefore cleanses his family from the dust of idolatry that might have come with them from Aram. Habits that were appropriate in Aram, leniencies that were acceptable, must be done away with before commencing the great push onward in Jewish history. It is not a question here of avoiding sin. The emphasis is, as Jacob states, "and purify yourselves and change your clothes." Jacob is declaring a new beginning. Both God and Jacob therefore call this journey "rising and going up." The reference, of course, is not merely to the altitude of Beit El. "Rise up" means to raise oneself, to stir and gather one's powers, to ascend spiritually. God is telling Jacob to make *aliya*. The altar that He commands Jacob to build there is not the fulfillment of Jacob's vow but an altar of consecration, reminiscent of the altar that Abraham built when he entered the land of Israel (12:7 – in Abraham's case, it was in Shekhem! – and later in Beit El: 12:8).

There is one further difference between Jacob before Beit El and after. By accepting his destiny, by re-inaugurating his career as a forefather – and remember, Jacob is the final forefather, the one who is followed by a nation and not individuals – Jacob transforms his family from a "house" (*bayit*) into a "people" (*am*). In Aram he was the father of a family, albeit a large one. Once we see him as a forefather in *Eretz Yisrael*, he is the leader of a people. By the time he gets to Beit El, he has become "Jacob and the people who are with him" (v. 6).

I have answered all of the questions I raised, except that about Deborah, Rebecca's nursemaid. I am not sure, but I suspect that she represents the world of Aram. At Galeid, Jacob divorces himself completely from Aram. Deborah is the last remnant of that world. As a nursemaid, she signifies the nurturing that Rebecca received in her father's house. That connection is now cut completely, that chapter in Jacob's life closed. Jacob is completely a man of Israel and *Eretz Yisrael*.

The second part of our story begins when God appears to Jacob and blesses him, changing his name. God then says:

> I am *Kel Shakai*, be fruitful and multiply; a nation and a community of nations will come from you, and kings will come out of your loins. And the land which I gave to Abraham and to Isaac shall I give to you, and to your seed after you shall I give the land. (35:11–12)

Does this blessing sound familiar? It is practically word-for-word the blessing which Isaac gave Jacob when he left to flee to Aram, even to the name of God:

> And *Kel Shakai* shall bless you, and make you fruitful and multiply you, and you shall be a community of nations. And He shall give you the blessing of Abraham, to you and your seed with you, to inherit the land you inhabit, which God gave to Abraham. (28:3–4)

It is as though the twenty years that Jacob spent in Aram (and fourteen more, according to *Hazal*, that he spent in the yeshiva of Shem and Ever) are merely a dream. God picks up exactly where the story left off when Jacob left. The *birkat Avraham*, Jacob's career as a forefather, has been in suspended animation, frozen in time. Jacob is now returning to the point where he left, both geographically (Beit El) and spiritually. Jacob's years in Aram should be placed in parentheses.

In fact, that is what Jacob does. He places those years within parentheses, a *matzeva* on each end. When he left for Aram, he raised a *matzeva* and prayed for protection on his journey out of *Eretz Yisrael* – in other words, on his exit from national history. When he returned, when he realized that he had completely returned "from Padan Aram," had reached "the land of Canaan," and had resumed his role as forefather, where not children but "nations and community of nations will come from him," he then erected another *matzeva*, in the same place, at the same point, thereby bracketing the years of personal development and drawing the straight line from his blessing at the hands of his father so many years before and the continuation of the role implicit in those blessings now. The two *matzevot* are brackets around the years that Jacob's career was suspended, the years that he was out of *Eretz Yisrael*.

God is giving Jacob a new name, and granting him the exact same blessing that Isaac had given him years earlier. The blessing is the continuation of the blessing of Abraham (and indeed is quite similar to God's blessing to Abraham when He changed Abram's name – "I shall multiply you exceedingly and make nations of you; and kings will come out of you" [17:5–6]). The entire episode is based on the idea that this point, Beit El, the place where Jacob took his leave of *Eretz Yisrael*, is the place where he can return to his role as a forefather. This is, on the one hand, the place which serves as the entry-point to *Eretz Yisrael* for Jacob, when we consider him in his historical role (rather than as an individual) – that is what we saw in the first half of the story. On the other hand, it is the place where God confirms his new identity as Israel, father of a nation. That this revelation of God is not connected to Jacob's circumstances after the incident in Shekhem, but to his return from Aram to *Eretz Yisrael*, is quite explicit in the description the Torah gives. "God appeared to Jacob **again** when he came from Padan Aram, and blessed him" (35:9). This revelation is dated "when Jacob came from Padan Aram," although we know he has been in Shekhem for some time. But even more explicitly – God is appearing to Jacob **again** – a clear reference to the dream of the ladder. This revelation continues that one.

This explains a curious phrase that repeats itself three times at the end of our story.

> God ascended from him, at the **place He spoke with him**. And Jacob erected a monument, **at the place He spoke with him**... Jacob called the place **where God spoke to him there** Beit El. (35:13–15)

Rashi (in printed Ḥumashim the comment appears on v. 14, but it should be on v. 13) comments, "I do not know what this is teaching us." I would like to suggest that the emphasized phrase does not refer to the place where God spoke to him now, but to where He spoke to him thirty-five years before, on the night of the dream of the ladder. The first verse states that God ascended from the spot where He had spoken before; in other words, this now is the conclusion of that prior revelation. Everything that took place in the meanwhile can be skipped, or blocked out. Similarly, Jacob erects the new monument not in the spot where God spoke now, to commemorate a special occasion, but in the spot that God spoke **then**, as a parallel to the previous monument. The name Beit El, we already know, refers to the first revelation, which has been continued now as though there were no interruption, and that is why Jacob reconfirms the name of the place. The whole purpose of the story is to bring us, literally, to the point where we left off at the beginning of *Parashat Toledot*. We are back at "the place He spoke to him."

Parashat Vayeshev

Who Sold Joseph?

by Rav Menachem Leibtag

I. INTRODUCTION

Could it be that the brothers did not sell Joseph?! As shocking as this statement may sound to anyone familiar with the story of Joseph & his brothers; a careful reading of that narrative in Ḥumash may actually support this possibility! In the following *shiur*, we explore this fascinating possibility (and its consequences) while taking into account some important geographic considerations.

After throwing Joseph into a pit to die, the brothers were able to eat. However, the Torah does not tell us if they sat near the pit, listening to Joseph's screaming and pleading, or if they sat far away – to enjoy some 'peace and quiet'?

What difference does it make? This tiny detail affects our understanding of almost every aspect of the story that ensues. Our *shiur* will entertain each possibility – showing how this 'missing detail' may be what leads several commentators to conclude that the brothers may never have sold Joseph after all!

II. THE BROTHERS' PLAN A

As Joseph arrives at Dotan, the brothers conspire to kill him (37:18–20). However, their plan concerning how to kill him is revised several times. The original plan was to kill Joseph as soon as they saw him [**Plan A**]:

> They [the brothers] saw him from afar, and ... they conspired to kill him. And they said to one another, behold the "dreamer" is coming. Now, let's kill him and throw his body into one of the pits ... (37:18–20)

Note how the brothers originally plan to kill Joseph immediately (on the spot) and then "bury him" in a pit – most likely to "hide the evidence" (should their father later accuse them).

Although Reuben opposes Joseph's murder, he realizes that the brothers would not accept his opinion. Therefore, instead of arguing with his brothers, he devises a shrewd plan that will first postpone Joseph's execution, and enable him at a later time to secretly bring Joseph back home.

III. REUBEN'S PLAN B / SECOND DEGREE MURDER

As you read Reuben's plan, be sure to differentiate between what Reuben **says** (to his brothers) and what Reuben **thinks** (to himself):

> ... And Reuben said ..."Do not shed blood, cast him into a pit [in order that he die] out in the wilderness, but do not touch him yourselves – "

[Then, the narrative continues by informing the reader of Reuben's true intentions ...]

> ... in order to save him [Joseph] from them and return him to his father. (37:22)

Reuben's "official" plan (that the brothers accept) is to let Joseph die in a less violent manner, i.e., to throw him alive into a deep pit to die, instead of murdering him in cold blood. However, Reuben secretly plans to later return to that pit and free him.

Note how Reuben even suggests the specific "pit" into which to throw Joseph – *"habor hazeh asher bamidbar"* – most probably so that he can later sneak away to that pit and save him, as opposed to the brothers' original plan to throw him into "one of the pits" (37:20) – possibly a pit closer by.

Unaware of Reuben's true intentions, the brothers agree. Joseph arrives, and – in accordance with **Plan B** – the brothers immediately strip Joseph of his special cloak and throw him alive into the pit (37:23–24). Afterward, the Torah informs us, they sit down to eat (v. 37:25).

IV. WHERE ARE THEY EATING?

Until this point, the plot is clear. Now, two important details are missing which affect our understanding of the rest of the story.

1. Where did they sit down to eat, i.e., close by or far away?
2. Where is Reuben – eating with them, or off on his own?

Even though the Torah does not tell us, we can attempt to answer these two questions by employing some "deductive reasoning."

1. Where are the brothers eating?

Recall that the brothers are grazing their sheep in the Dotan area (37:17) (today the area of Jenin, between Shekhem and Afula), which is on the northern slopes of central mountain range of Israel. The *"midbar"* (wilderness) that Reuben is talking about is found some five to ten kilometers to the east of Dotan (that *"midbar"* is found along the eastern slopes of the entire central mountain range).

Considering that the brothers throw Joseph into a pit "out in the midbar," it would definitely make sense for them to return afterward to their campsite in the Dotan area to eat (37:16–17). (Besides, it would not be very appetizing to eat lunch while listening to your little brother screaming for his life from a pit nearby [42:21].)

And even should one conclude that it would have been just as logical for them to have sat down to eat near the pit, when we consider the whereabouts of Reuben, it becomes quite clear that they must have sat down to eat farther away.

2. Where is Reuben?

Considering that Reuben's real plan is to later save Joseph from the pit, it would only be logical from him to either stay near the pit, or at least remain with his brothers. Certainly it would not make sense, according to his real plan, for him to go far away, and to leave his brothers by the pit!

However, from the continuation of the story we know for sure that Reuben did not stay near the pit, because he returns to the pit only **after** Joseph is sold! Therefore, if Reuben left the pit area, then certainly the brothers also must have left that area. Hence, it would only be logical to conclude that the brothers are indeed eating away from the pit, and Reuben must be eating with them! After all, not joining them for lunch could raise their suspicion. Furthermore, the Torah never tells us that he left his brothers. In summary, we conclude that Reuben remains with his brothers, as they all sit down to eat away from the pit.

V. JUDAH'S PLAN C / A "QUICK BUCK"

Now that we have established that Reuben and the brothers are sitting down to eat at a distance far away from the pit, we can continue our study of the narrative, to see if this conclusion fits with its continuation:

> And the brothers sat down to eat, and they **lifted up their eyes** and saw a caravan of Ishmaelites coming **from the Gilad** carrying [spices] ... to Egypt. Then Judah said to his brothers, "What do we gain by killing our brother ... let us sell him [instead] to the Ishmaelites; after all, he is our brother, our own flesh," and his brothers agreed. (37:25–27)

From Judah's suggestion, it becomes clear that the brothers truly planned to allow Joseph to die in the pit and were unaware of Reuben's intention to save him. If indeed Reuben is still sitting with his brothers, then this new plan (to **sell** Joseph) puts him in quite a predicament, for if the brothers would sell Joseph, his own plan to rescue him would be ruined. Reuben has only one alternative – he must "volunteer" to fetch Joseph from the pit, in order to free him – before his brothers may sell him.

Before we continue, we must provide a little background on Israel's geography, which is essential towards understanding the verses that follow.

VI. THE ANCIENT TRADE ROUTE

Recall that Joseph met his brothers while they were grazing their sheep in the hilly area of Dotan (37:17), north of Shekhem. During their meal, the brothers "lifted up their eyes" and noticed a caravan of **Ishmaelites** traveling down from the **Gilad** (the northern mountain range in Jordan), on its way to Egypt (37:25). Most assume that this convoy will soon pass nearby the spot where the brothers are eating. However, when we consider the geography involved, it is more probable to arrive at a very different conclusion!

This caravan of Ishmaelites (camels et al.) most likely should be traveling along the ancient trade route (better known as the Via Maris), which crosses through *Emek Yizrael* (the Jezreel Valley) on its way toward the Mediterranean coast. Therefore, this convoy, now sighted by the brothers as it descends from the Gilad Mountains in Transjordan, must first pass through the Beit She'an valley, continuing on towards Afula and Megiddo in *Emek Yizrael*, on its way towards the coast. Certainly, it would not pass the hilly area of Dotan, for it would make no sense for the caravan to climb the Gilboa mountain range to cross through the Dotan area to reach the coast.

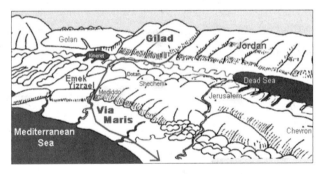

Dotan, today the area of Jenin (about twenty kilometers north of Shekhem) lies about ten kilometers south of this main highway (the Via Maris) as it crosses *Emek Yizrael*. In altitude, Dotan sits about three- to four-hundred meters above *Emek Yizrael*. Hence, from the hills of the Dotan/Gilboa area (where the brothers are eating lunch), one has a nice view of both the Gilad and parts of the Jezreel Valley. However, the trade route itself follows through a valley that cuts between the mountains.

This explains why the brothers are able to see an Ishmaelite caravan (convoy) as it was descending from the Gilad towards Beit She'an on its way to *Emek Yizrael*. Even though it was in sight, it was still far enough away to allow the brothers at least several hours to meet it, when it would pass some ten kilometers to the north. Therefore, in order to sell Joseph to that caravan, the brothers would have to first fetch Joseph from the pit, and carry him on a short trip till they meet the caravan in *Emek Yizrael*. They have ample time to first "finish their meal," go fetch Joseph from the pit in the *"midbar"* (on their way to the valley), and then meet the convoy to sell Joseph.

VII. SOMEBODY GOT THERE FIRST

With this background, we now return to the story of *"mekhirat Yosef"* in *Humash*. Let's take a careful look at the next verse, noting its grammar:

> And a group of Midianite **traders** passed by, and **they** pulled, and they lifted Joseph out of the pit, and **they** sold Joseph to the Ishmaelites for twenty pieces of silver, and brought Joseph to Egypt. (37:28)

Based on the wording of this verse, it's quite clear that the Midianites and the Ishmaelites are two different groups of people! To support this, note how the Torah describes the Midianites as local **"traders"** (*"soharim"*), while the Ishmaelites are described as international **"movers"** (*"orhat Yishmaelim"* – a transport caravan). A simple reading of this verse implies that a group of Midianite traders happened to pass by the pit (they most probably heard Joseph screaming), and pulled him out. As these Midianites are "traders," they were probably on their way to sell their wares (now including Joseph) to the Ishmaelite caravan.

If this explanation is correct, then the Midianites themselves pulled Joseph out of the pit and sold him. Where were the brothers during all of this? Most probably, still eating! Recall our explanation above: the brothers had thrown Joseph into a pit out in the *"midbar"* and returned to their grazing area to eat. They are far enough away that they do not see or hear what transpired between Joseph and the Midianites!

And where was Reuben? Again, as we explained above, he must

have been eating with his brothers. However, as soon as he heard Judah's new plan (and the brothers' agreement) to sell Joseph, he would have to get back to the pit (before his brothers) to save Joseph – and that's exactly what he does! But it's too late. Note how this explanation fits perfectly into the next verse: "And Reuben returned ["**vayashov**"] to the pit, and behold, Joseph was no longer in the pit!; Then, he tore his clothes" (37:29).

Reuben is not the last brother to find out that Joseph was sold (as commonly assumed). Rather, he is the first brother to recognize that Joseph is missing!

What can Reuben do? Shocked, he immediately returns to his brothers [probably eating dessert by now] with the terrible news:

> And he returned ["**vayashov**"] to his brothers and said, "The boy is gone! And for myself, what am I going to do?" (37:30)

Note the word *"vayashov"* ("and Reuven **returned**") in both verse 29 and verse 30. This proves that the brothers could not have been eating near the pit, for if so, Reuben would not need to "return" to them. Since Reuben and his brothers are eating away from the pit, Reuben must first **return** to the pit, then he must **return** back to his brothers to tell them the news – hence twice the verb *"vayashov"*!

VIII. WHAT DO THE BROTHERS THINK?

At this point in the story the brothers must be totally baffled, for they have no idea what happened to Joseph. Assuming themselves that he was most probably eaten by an animal, they don't want their father to think that he may be missing, nor would they want their father to accuse them of killing him – so they plot once again. They will trick their father into thinking that Joseph had been killed by a wild animal on his way to visit them. They dip Joseph's coat in blood and have it sent to their father (37:31–32). This plan works, as when Jacob sees the coat:

> And he recognized it and said, "My son's 'ktonet,' ḥaya ra'a akhal-atu; tarof, taraf Yosef – [Joseph was surely devoured by a wild beast]." (37:33)

Ironically, the end result of this final plan echoes the brothers' original plan (see "*ve'amarnu – ḥaya ra'a akhalatu*" [37:20] – compare 37:33). Jacob reaches the same conclusion that the brothers themselves may have reached, but for a very different reason!

Even more ironic is how the brothers final plan "to sell Joseph" came true, even though they never sold him; and how (they thought that) their original plan – for Joseph to die – came true, even though they never killed him.

In retrospect, one could even suggest that the brothers may have never been able to "gather the courage" to either kill or sell Joseph. Despite their various plans and intense hatred of Joseph, just as they had quickly retracted from their first two plans to kill Joseph (37:22, 26), they most probably would have retracted from their plan to sell him as well.

Nevertheless: they talked; they planned; they plotted; and – in God's eyes – they are considered guilty, even though they never actually killed or sold Joseph.

IX. WHAT DOES JOSEPH THINK?

So far, our explanation has followed Rashbam and the Ḥizkuni. Even though this interpretation seems to explain the verses quite well, there is a verse in *Parashat Vayigash* that seems to "ruin" this entire approach. When Joseph finally reveals himself to his brothers, he states explicitly:

I am Joseph your brother, whom you **sold** to Egypt. (45:4)

Based on this statement, it's quite clear that Joseph himself thinks that his brothers sold him! But if our above interpretation is correct, Joseph should have thought that the Midianites had sold him, and not his brothers! In fact, this verse is most probably the primary basis for the more popular interpretation that the brothers indeed did sell Joseph.

The Ḥizkuni, bothered by this verse, explains that Joseph knows that the Midianites sold him, but since the brothers threw him in the pit, it was the brothers "who caused me to be sold to Egypt." Alternately, one could explain, based on the above *shiur*, that Joseph truly did think that his brothers had sold him, even though the brothers themselves had no idea concerning what really happened. Joseph was not aware of any of the brothers' conversations. All that he knew was that, as soon as he arrived, his brothers took off his coat and threw him into the pit. A short time later, some Midianites passed by, took him out of the pit, and sold him to the Ishmaelites, who later sold him to the Egyptians. Joseph, trying to piece together what had happened, probably assumed that his brothers had set it all up beforehand. In other words, he thought that the brothers told the Midianites that they had thrown Joseph in a certain pit, and that they should take him from there to sell to the Ishmaelites.

X. HASHEM'S PLAN

Even though the brothers had three different plans for "getting rid" of Joseph, God had a different plan. The Hand of Providence led the brothers to believe that **their** "dream" (to rid themselves of Joseph) had come true. In reality, it was their plotting that eventually led to the fulfillment of Joseph's dreams to come true. Finally, as will be seen in the story that follows, this was all part of God's long-term plan for the people of Israel to become a nation in the land of Egypt, as the forecasts of the *Berit bein HaBetarim* now begin to unfold.

Judah and Tamar

by Rav Mosheh Lichtenstein

Τ he location of the episode of Judah and Tamar, inserted by the Torah in the very midst of the Joseph story, requires explanation. Why relate the story of the older brother, Judah, before concluding that of his younger brother Joseph? The action is suspended with Joseph in mid-journey (he has not yet reached Egypt) when the Torah embarks upon the story of Judah and his sons.

One approach would be to deny our premise that one story interrupts the other, claiming simply that the story of Judah and Tamar is the more appropriate episode for the development of the *parasha's* theme. Two possible alternatives suggest themselves to support this line of thought. One option is to regard the Torah as treating the story of the family, with its sibling rivalry, leadership struggles, and cliques (the first half of the *parasha*) as distinct from the individual histories of the various brothers/tribes. Though we are accustomed to thinking about "Joseph and his brothers," making it essentially the story of Joseph (and therefore the Judah and Tamar story is an obvious interruption in the flow of the narrative), this is not necessarily the only perspective. Should we view the previous chapter as relating to *Beit Yaakov* – Jacob's family as a family – and not to Joseph, the story of Joseph in Egypt would no longer be a direct continuation of the sale episode but rather an entirely new chapter devoted to Joseph and what befell him as an individual. Therefore, it need not immediately follow the sale episode. Hence, in the ensuing transition from family to individual history, Judah takes precedence over Joseph, either because of his seniority, or because of the brevity of his narrative, or due to the insular nature of his personal history. Be it as it may, the sequence of our *parasha* is preserved.

Alternately, the *parasha* could be understood to focus upon the fortunes of Jacob and his household in *Eretz Yisrael*. The opening verses of the *parasha* make it clear that the history of Jacob in *Eretz Yisrael* is a unique chapter, distinct from the story of his life in exile up to that point, and therefore, only the local episodes are an integral part of this story. Thus, the Egyptian element, which is a story of exile, is postponed until after the conclusion of the *Eretz Yisrael* narrative. Actually, there is not only a geographic distinction between the two, but also a basic difference in personal status; Judah is a patriarchal figure, ruling over his family and surroundings, supported by the power of the state, coping with the problems posed by exercise of authority, paradigmatic of Jewish existence in Israel, while Joseph, the "Galus Jew" at the opposite end of the spectrum, without any resources or status, must struggle daily for survival, positioned at the lowest possible rung of Egyptian society.

Thus, it is quite possible to view the three stories of *Vayeshev* as separate episodes, each following the other in sequence as individual units in the saga of Jacob's household.

However, the Torah does seem to imply that this is not the case and that there is a connection between the stories of Judah and Joseph. The episode of Judah and Tamar is introduced by the Torah with the remark that the story of Judah is contemporaneous with *mekhirat Yosef*. Since the time frame of the story stretches over a few years, chronology alone is not the reason for the juxtaposition of the two narratives or the sandwiching of the Judah story between the two acts of the Joseph drama. In addition, it should also be pointed out that Ibn Ezra and others are of the opinion that the events actually transpired at a later time, not at the time of Joseph's sale. Therefore, it seems evident that the Torah is not implying a chronological connection between the two events, but a thematic one. Rather than being two separate episodes occurring to two siblings, they are an intertwined story, one shedding light on the other. Simply put, the Judah and Tamar relationship is a sub-plot to the main story, interesting in itself, but also shedding light on the dynamics involved in the big story.

This last point must be emphasized; I am not claiming, as have some of the commentators, that the sale of Joseph caused the relocation of Judah and set into motion the chain of events which resulted in the ensuing troubles, assuming a causal rather than thematic connection. Our claim is that there are indeed thematic affinities between the two episodes and that our understanding of the one will enhance our appreciation of the other as well.

Let us begin with the Tamar episode. The cardinal sin in these happenings is not the sexual licentiousness of the parties involved, but the treatment of Tamar. Both Judah and his sons treat her as an object to be used (or abused) for their own benefit and pleasure, refusing to relate to her as a human being worthy of respect and recognition as such, whose needs, emotional and other, must be taken into account. Initially manifesting itself in the crude and boorish behavior of Er and Onan, it is true of their father as well.

Er and Onan treat Tamar as a sex object. Desiring of sexual pleasure, they are unwilling to assume the attendant responsibility of parenthood, nor do they take into account the needs of Tamar, yearning to realize herself as a mother. Their egotism can only view other human beings as means for serving their own needs, and cannot recognize their value or autonomy.

This approach, though, does not originate with them, for it is characteristic of their father as well. Judah's response to the deaths of his two sons is to force upon Tamar a waiting period of years, without consulting her or attempting to understand her perspective. Tamar is a woman who has lost both husbands, in need of physical and emotional security and stability, disinclined to marry yet a third brother of the same family while not necessarily interested in a solitary existence as a young and wasted widow waiting for a young child to mature at his father's leisure. Tamar may indeed have been willing, as Ruth in a later day, to remain faithful to the house of Judah; that, though, is not of any consequence in evaluating Judah's behavior. The crucial point in this regard is Judah's directing her to do so, fully expecting her to comply with his directive. The contrast between Judah's subordination of Tamar to his needs and the deep feeling of gratitude exhibited by Naomi and Boaz towards Ruth is a clear illustration of the nature of Judah's actions.

Having accepted upon herself to stay at her parents' home and wait out of a sense of commitment and duty, Tamar eventually makes a move to force a confrontation with Judah over the matter, by engaging him in the episode of her harlotry and the subsequent dealings that ensue.

The client-prostitute relationship is, obviously, the extreme form of using a fellow human being for one's own needs, each party utilizing the other for its own purposes. The I-Thou personal relationship has been replaced with the I-It attitude towards others, as the most intimate and private act, born of the union of two souls revealing themselves to each other, is transformed into a business transaction. What was intended and described by the Torah as inner knowledge of a close partner is perverted and corrupted into momentary physical contact with a coincidental, fleeting stranger, without any lasting obligations or responsibilities.

Judah does not understand this, and therefore misunderstands her intentions when she demands his **personal** belongings as collateral. From his business-like perspective, the only reason that someone would insist upon belongings of a highly personal nature is that they are an effective means of assuring payment, since there is a very high likelihood that the debtor will indeed return to redeem them. Tamar, though, is interested in these belongings as expressive of personality and as a vehicle for establishing a personal relationship. She doesn't want money in return for the sexual favor; her desire is for the establishment of a relationship. This is what will legitimize and justify the liaison, not Judah's sending over a fat check. However, Judah in his current state lacks the awareness and understanding to appreciate this; therefore, he attempts to redeem the personal possessions which he gave to Tamar by sending a courier with a more valuable object (from a monetary perspective) to replace them. Since it is all about monetary value and not personal contact, there is no problem in having a courier deliver the goat, as long as the price is right. That he himself should come in person and further the relationship never occurs to Judah.

However, the harlot is nowhere to be seen, and the people tell his messenger that there **never** was a prostitute. Understood in a deeper sense, they are absolutely right; Tamar was not attempting to compromise or entrap Judah so that she could force him to release or marry her, and therefore acting as a harlot for an evening, only to return to conventional life afterwards; from her point of view, the meeting between her and Judah was meant to serve as the beginning of a relationship, and therefore even then it wasn't harlotry. Indeed, if we look closely at the verses, they never say that Tamar dressed or acted as a harlot, only that in Judah's eyes she appeared as such (39:15).

Judah's response upon hearing that the harlot couldn't be found is revealing. He instructs his companion to set aside the intended payment "so that we shouldn't lose face." It is not the disappointment or the obligation towards the individual which concerns him, but the fact that "it's bad for the business."

The climax is reached at her trial. Here, too, Judah's approach is determined by his perspective, the basis of condemnation being her violation of the family's dignity. Tamar, though, responds by once more reiterating his personal commitment to her. She produces his personal belongings, emphasizing that to the person whose personality is embedded within these objects, who has been willing to reveal and hand them over to her and with whom she was, and is, willing to establish a deep loving relationship, she is pregnant and obligated. *Hazal* underscore and champion this quality of Tamar by stating that, had Judah not admitted his involvement, she would never had betrayed him, even at the cost of death. That is the degree of responsibility towards fellow human beings and the level of commitment towards their needs, even if they have betrayed her, which *Hazal* attribute to Tamar.

The dramatic display of Judah's insignia and other private belongings, accompanied by Tamar's impassioned plea that Judah recognize his obligations to others and establish personal I-Thou relationships with them, is the climatic point in the clash between the two differing perspectives of Judah and Tamar, and it achieves the desired effect. Judah undergoes a transformation, recognizes the truth of her words and embraces the relationship.

At this point, after having focused the issue of chapter thirty-eight (Judah and Tamar) on the interpersonal relationship and the treatment of others, we can readily understand the connection between this and the episode of the sale of Joseph which precedes it. Here, too, Judah's behavior is based upon his inability to treat others as independent, autonomous human beings, deserving to be treated as subjects, worthy of respect and relationship, and not as a means to his ends. The sale of a human being as an object is the utter nullification of the human element within him, transforming him from a subject to an object.

The original plan of the other brothers to murder Joseph by throwing him into the pit, while morally heinous, did not treat him as an object. In this regard, the brothers were more respectful of Joseph than Judah. They viewed him as an enemy towards whom they felt a need to express their feelings of hatred and jealousy; such feelings recognize and respect the uniquely human qualities of the rival, even as they attempt to harm him. Judah, by contrast, treats Joseph as problem which has to be disposed of. He does not want to exhibit feelings of hatred towards Joseph, nor does he want to force upon himself the need to take a morally committing position. His goal is to remove Joseph from the scene without having to dirty his fingers in the process. He prefers banal, seemingly non-committal evil over emotional involvement, his perspective being the legal rather than the human aspect of the issue.

This quality of Judah stands in sharp contrast with that of Joseph. The act of rebuking his brothers (37:2), while not a popular one, reveals concern for them as human beings whose moral and religious state are important to him. Lest we think that Joseph displays such an attitude only when it is convenient for him, his behavior in respect to Potiphar's wife should dispel any such thoughts. Though much easier to succumb to her temptations or to attempt other methods of avoiding her, Joseph bases his refusal upon the moral betrayal and breach of trust of the master as a trusting fellow human being.

Thus, the *parasha* compares and contrasts the attitudes of Judah and Joseph to other persons, using the backdrop of the Judah and Tamar episode to illuminate this point and to tell us about Judah's repentance – so full and complete that it will lead to the future king of Israel through the union of the offspring of Judah and Tamar with Ruth the Moabite, whose altruism follows and complements that of Tamar.

Judah and Tamar – A Story Within a Story?

by Rav Elchanan Samet

I. JOSEPH – A STORY COMPOSED OF SEVERAL STORIES

Parashat Vayeshev is the beginning of the longest story in all of the Torah: the story of Joseph and his brothers, which continues until the end of the book of Genesis. This lengthy narrative is clearly divided into several literary sub-units, each with its own subject and its own literary style, as expressed in all of the parameters of the biblical story. How, then, does the story of Joseph and his brothers represent a single story? Only in one dimension: in the continually developing plot that stretches from the beginning of our *parasha* to the end of the book. We cannot join this story in the middle, because each small literary sub-unit is built on those parts of the plot that preceded it, and unfamiliarity with them will make it impossible for us to understand what is going on. This smaller story must be treated as the basic unit, with its own message, and we must delve into its analysis and probe its message just as we have done with every story until now. On the other hand, the student of this section now has a new task repentance seeking the subject of the greater story in which all of these smaller units are placed like a mosaic.

This *shiur* will address what appears to be an independent narrative "island" within the greater story of Joseph. The story of Judah and Tamar in chapter thirty-eight follows the first literary unit in the greater story – chapter thirty-seven, which is a dramatic opening, containing the thematic foundation for the entire story of Joseph and his brothers. But chapter thirty-eight cuts short the continuity of the narrative by presenting an independent story that is unrelated to what happens either prior to it or thereafter. This *shiur* shall focus on the meaning of the story of Judah and Tamar itself, and on how it serves as a necessary complement to the story of Joseph and his brothers.

II. FIRST SECTION: THE BIRTH OF JUDAH'S THREE SONS (V. 1–5)

The story opens with a formal opening formulation – "And it was, at that time," the likes of which we find also in chapters twenty-one and twenty-two, which may hint at the proximity in time to what was previously narrated.

The first action that takes place in the story is that "Judah went down from his brothers and went in to a man from Adullam, named Ḥira." The significance of this "going down" is, first and foremost, geographical: Judah descended from Ḥevron, which sits atop the Judean Mountains, to the region of the hills lying between the Judean plain and the mountains.

The text does not explain why Judah went down from his brothers. He interacts with the Canaanite environment in several ways: he pitches his tent in the vicinity of the Canaanite city of Adullam, close to Ḥira – his Adullamite friend; he is also a work partner of this friend (v. 12); he marries a woman who is "the daughter of a Canaanite man named Shua" whom he saw "there" in Adullam, and it turns out that Tamar herself is also a local Canaanite woman.[1] Three sons are born to

---

1. What is the meaning of all of this? Were the daughters of Canaan not loathsome to the forefathers (Gen. 28:8)? This difficulty prompts several of the sages, starting from the *Targum Yonatan* and the *Targum Onkelos*, to conclude that neither the daughter of Shua nor Tamar were Canaanite in origin, and that Jacob's other sons likewise did not marry Canaanite women.

   The literal text seems to point in the direction adopted by R. Neḥemia in *Bereshit Raba* (84:21): Jacob's sons were no longer required to exercise such stringency in the matter of marrying wives from their extended family in Haran, which had been observed strictly by Abraham and Isaac. The difference here is related to the difference

Judah from the daughter of Shua, and the pace of the narrative would suggest that they are born in close succession. The names of these sons all hint at what will happen to them in the future.

III. SECOND SECTION: THE DEATH OF ER AND ONAN, AND TAMAR'S EXPULSION TO THE HOUSE OF HER FATHER (V. 6–11)

The borders of this section are determined, interestingly enough, by the movements of the secondary, passive character here: Tamar. At the beginning of the section (v. 6), Judah brings her into his home as a wife for Er, his firstborn, and at its conclusion (v. 11) he sends her back to her father's house.

Er appears to die because of his sin (the nature of which is not made clear in the text) a short time after marrying Tamar. Judah commands Onan, his second son, to fulfill his duty of levirate marriage to Tamar in order to establish continuity for his brother, who died without children. It therefore appears that this institution of levirate marriage (*yibum*) existed among Israelites and the nations even before the giving of the Torah. This, indeed, is Ramban's conclusion (Ramban on 38:8).

Like many customs similar to that of levirate marriage that have prevailed in the world until today, the situation described in our story does not match the Torah's commandment in several details:

1. Although from Judah's words (both to Onan and to Tamar) it would seem that it is the brother who will marry her, from Tamar's deed and from Judah's reaction to it ("She has been more righteous than I, because I did not give her to Shelah, my son") we learn that where *yibum* could not be performed by a brother, it could be performed by the father. (Nevertheless, in this instance, "he did not know her again," for in this case there was indeed a brother, but Judah had not allowed him to fulfill his duty.)

---

in the circumstances of their marriages: Isaac and Jacob were lone individuals; had they married local Canaanite women, they may have ended up assimilating into their Canaanite families. Jacob's family, in contrast, was by this stage already a large clan, and any woman that a son of Jacob would marry would become part of this family.

II. It appears that the woman requiring *yibum* could under no circumstances be permitted to marry outside of the family of her deceased husband.

III. The status of a woman requiring *yibum* was similar to that of a married woman, and if she prostituted herself she was punished with death. According to Torah law, in contrast, this woman is subject to a prohibition – "The wife of the deceased shall not be married to an outsider" – which is not included in the laws of forbidden sexual relations and their punishments.

Onan refuses to fulfill his obligation of *yibum* because he knows that "the seed [that will be born from Tamar] will not be his"; the child will be considered the descendant of his deceased brother. What he does in order to prevent Tamar from becoming pregnant – although unknown to Judah – is clearly evil in the eyes of God, and he, too, dies.

Now Tamar should be married, through *yibum*, to Shelah, who is still too young to marry, and she must therefore wait until he matures. This is indeed what Judah tells her, but the text testifies that this was not his real intention: "For he said, 'Lest he [Shelah], too, die – like his brothers.'" In effect, Judah sentences Tamar to a lifetime of *"aginut"* (a status whereby a woman is legally unable to remarry) without saying so openly. On what basis does Judah fear this outcome? There can be no doubt that he believed that Shelah would be in danger of his life were he to marry her, given her history with his two brothers. A *Beraita* (*Yevamot* 64b) seems to justify his fear: "If a woman is married to the first – and he dies, then to the second son – and he dies, she shall not be married to the third." The woman is referred to as an *"isha katlanit,"* a "deadly woman" who has a record of bringing death to her husbands, and therefore she is not to be permitted to marry again. At the time of our story this was not yet the firmly established practice, for had it been so, Judah simply could have told Tamar why he really had no wish for her to marry his third son. In any event, this was Judah's motive: the fear that Tamar was a "deadly woman."

What does the text tell us about this fear of Judah, and about his deed (or lack thereof) resulting from it? The answer is clear: it was not Tamar who caused the death of Judah's first two sons; rather, the Torah says explicitly that each of them died because of his own sins. Although

Judah had no knowledge of his sons' sins, by preventing Tamar from marrying Shelah he was not acting properly and honestly. He eventually admits this himself: "She has been more righteous than I, for I did not give her to Shelah, my son." In other words, "I should have given her to Shelah, my son, without suspecting her of being a 'deadly woman.'" Even when he says this, Judah still has no idea of the true reason for his sons' deaths, but it is clear from the story that the suspicion of Tamar being a "deadly woman" had been unfounded, for Judah was embarrassed to admit to it at the time that this suspicion guided his actions, and he regretted it afterwards. The Torah likewise testifies that this suspicion was groundless, for Er and Onan clearly died because of their own sins.

IV. SIXTH SECTION: TAMAR'S "TRIAL" (V. 24–26)

Let us skip to verses 24–26. Once Tamar's pregnancy becomes noticeable, "It was told to Judah, saying: Tamar, your daughter-in-law, has prostituted herself." This instance of "it was told" balances the previous instance of the expression in our story (v. 13): "And it was told to Tamar, saying: Behold, your father-in-law is going up to Timna to shear his sheep." The consequences of this "telling" lead to the outcome and the "telling" described here.

Judah pronounces her judgment, and Tamar is taken out to be burned. Now comes her great moment, the moment to which all of her actions have been directed. The signs of Judah's identity – the seal, the cord and the staff – are sent to Judah as proof that he is the father of Tamar's unborn child. Tamar has not "prostituted herself," but rather has arranged her own levirate marriage; she has become pregnant not from harlotry, but rather from the person who prevented her *yibum* because of his unfounded and unjustified fears.

Judah justifies Tamar's actions and confesses openly to his unjust treatment of her. The section concludes with the words "and he knew her no more." The literal meaning is that he had no further relations with her, since, in a case where there exists a brother of the deceased, *yibum* was not usually practiced by the father. Tamar has lost the possibility of marrying Shelah, and she will not be married to Judah, either; she has gained only the twins that she is carrying. Judah's seal, cord and staff are within her, though they have been returned to him.

V. SEVENTH SECTION: BIRTH OF THE TWINS (V. 27–30)

Twice in the book of Genesis we find a description of the birth of twins. Both instances of birth are preceded by a period of longing for motherhood that has not yet been fulfilled: in Rebecca's case because of her barrenness, and in Tamar's case because of the death of her two husbands and Judah's consequent mistreatment of her.

The birth of twins expresses a bursting forth of fertility that comes to compensate for the lack of children until that time – and, in both instances, also for the fact that no further children will be born.

The struggle between the twin brothers in our story concerning who was born first is most reminiscent of the struggle between Jacob and Esau at their birth. But there, the battle began **after** the birth, and it was decided only much later on, when Jacob fought against the "man" (the angel of Esau). In our story, the battle is miraculously decided while the twins are still in the womb, with the child claiming to be the firstborn bursting first from his mother's womb, thereby acquiring the natural firstborn rights. This bursting forth saves both his mother and the Israelite nation as a whole much indecision and controversy.

VI. STRUCTURE AND SIGNIFICANCE OF THE STORY

The story is divided fairly clearly into seven sections. The fourth section (v. 16–18) is of highlighted importance: here the fateful encounter between Tamar and Judah takes place, an encounter that concludes with, "He gave [them] to her, and he came to her, and she became pregnant by him." The importance of this section is recognizable not only in the decisive incident that takes place, but also in the fact that this is the only real encounter between Judah and Tamar where there is a dialogue between them. In both of the other places where they are to be found together (in the second section and in the sixth, which – as we shall see – actually correspond to one another), there is no dialogue, but rather only monologue, and the speech in each of these two cases precedes a parting of their ways. In verse 11 of the second section, Judah speaks to Tamar, and she obeys silently and parts from his family. In verse 25 of the sixth section, Tamar speaks to Judah (via a messenger), and his reaction (which is not conveyed to her), "She has been more righteous than I," immediately leads to "and he knew her no more."

The fourth section is therefore the "central axis" of the story, dividing it into two halves. This section serves as the "central axis" in precisely
the manner that we have defined the concept on a number of occasions:
the events of the first half of the story are aimed at bringing about this
fateful encounter between Judah and Tamar; the events of the second
half result from that encounter, and the encounter itself represents the
most dramatic and important event in the story – a turning point in the
development of the plot.

We may depict the structure of the story as follows:

1. (v. 1–5) Birth of Judah's three sons
2. (v. 6–11) Deaths of Er and Onan without children, Tamar sent
   away
3. (v. 12–14) Preparations for Tamar's encounter with Judah
4. (v. 16–18) The fateful encounter
5. (v. 19–23) Tamar's return to previous situation
6. (v. 24–26) Tamar's "trial," cancellation of her death sentence
7. (v. 27–30) Birth of the twins

There are clear parallels between each pair of sections surrounding the
central axis.

The correspondence between sections one and seven seems clear
enough – in one case, three sons are born to Judah in quick succession;
in the other case, two are born to him together. But the essential parallel between them turns out to be inverse: two of Judah's three sons are
destined to die, and the names of all three hint at unpleasant things
associated with them. The twins born at the end of the story, in contrast,
will live: they come as replacements for Er and Onan, and their names –
Peretz and Zerah – have only positive connotations.

The correspondence between sections two and six likewise seems
clear: in both sections there is death that comes as a punishment for
various sins. In section two it is Judah's two sons who die by the hand
of heaven as punishment for their sins, while poor Tamar is sent away
from Judah's house as a troubled, childless widow who is blamed for the
deaths of her husbands. In section six, Tamar is accused of prostitution

and is sentenced to death, together with the twins in her womb. But here, again, the parallel is obviously inverse – from every angle. The sins of Er and Onan are genuine sins, and therefore they pay with their lives. Tamar's "sin" is fictitious and therefore her life is saved. Another inverse parallel concerns Judah's attitude towards Tamar: in section two he sends her away so that when Shelah matures she can be given to him as a wife, but in truth he has no intention of allowing this. In section six, Judah admits that he has wronged Tamar in this respect – "She has been more righteous than I, for I did not give her to Shelah, my son." This admission by Judah also represents the evaporation of the suspicion that it was Tamar who caused the deaths of her husbands, for it is now clear with absolute certainty that Tamar is not a "deadly woman," but rather – on the contrary – one who brings new life to the world, and is establishing the seed of the house of Judah.

The parallel between sections three and five is quite clearly inverse:

> Section 3: (v. 14) "And she removed the garments of her widowhood from upon her, and covered herself with a veil..."

> Section 5: (v. 19) "And she removed her veil from upon her and wore the garments of her widowhood..."

In both cases, Tamar misleads Judah by wearing clothing that is inappropriate to her at that time.

Now we must clarify what the subject of the story is. It seems that we may take, as the definition of the subject, an expression taken from the story itself (38:5): it is a story about establishing seed. Countering the threat of seed being cut off and the destruction of an important branch of Jacob's household (namely, that of Judah), our story comes to teach how the obstacles were overcome, and Judah's seed was, finally, established.

In the background, almost from the beginning of the story to the end, stands *yibum* as a legal, social and religious institution. This fits in well with the subject of the story, for *yibum* is the means here for dealing with the danger of a person being cut off from his family without leaving children.

The scale for evaluating both characters and actions in our story is the same: to what extent do they promote or hinder the realization of the goal – establishment of seed for the family of Judah? What brings upon Judah's family this chain of disasters and the question mark that hangs over its continued existence? There is one sin that is explicit in the text – the sin of Onan: instead of fulfilling his duty of levirate marriage to Tamar in order to establish his brother's seed, he destroys his seed "so as not to give seed to his brother," and for this reason God punishes him with death.

Even Judah himself, while not knowing the reason for his sons' deaths, becomes a partner, to some extent, in this sin of failing to establish seed: because of a false suspicion, he sends his daughter-in-law Tamar away to her father's house and prevents the *yibum* from taking place through Shelah. This deed is both cruel and unjust towards Tamar, and also represents the halting of the process of establishing seed for his family. Judah's punishment – measure for measure – is that his wife dies; a person who leaves a woman in her status of widowhood needlessly is punished by becoming a widower himself.

Tamar is the only character who is elevated above all of the other characters in the story as someone who fights for her motherhood in the house of Judah, a struggle that also involves the rehabilitation of this household through establishing its seed. Through her intricately planned and clever actions she causes Judah, against his will, to establish the seed of his family and to establish seed also for his sons, who died childless. This, too, is part of Judah's punishment: he is forced to do in a most unrespectable way what he was obligated to do in a respectable way.

Divine providence was with Tamar in all that she did: she was afforded a rare combination of circumstances, which could be exploited only in the most cunning way to bring about her pregnancy through Judah. Tamar's actions are successful at all stages – starting with the fact that Judah is fooled by her disguise, then the fact that she falls pregnant immediately, and culminating in her life (and that of her fetuses) being saved. But the greatest success of all awaits us at the end of the story: the birth of the twins – a bursting forth of the blessing of seed, removing the question mark that had hovered over Judah's household.

This meaning of the story likewise arises from the analysis of its structure, as explained above. Section four represents the "central axis" not because it contains the interpersonal encounter between Judah and Tamar, but rather because it contains the crux of the story's message: here the seed of Judah's house is established.

The inverse parallel between sections two and four [six?], as discussed above, comes to teach us that the failure to establish seed brings punishment and destruction upon the sinners, while she who established seed – even though it was achieved by means of an extreme and dangerous cunning, which brought Tamar's life into terrible danger – was ultimately saved, and her righteousness publicly recognized. Moreover, the person who prevented Tamar from establishing Judah's seed in section two found himself a partner, against his will, in establishing seed with her, and publicly acknowledges this in section six. She who was banished from Judah's house as a "deadly woman" eventually merits recognition as a wife and mother who brings forth life. The contrast between these two sections also illuminates the contrast between sections one and seven. Only the parallel between sections three and five, which is technically inverse, truly reflects their essential equivalence: both describe Tamar's success in all of her attempts to mislead Judah.

VII. JUDAH IN ADULLAM AS CORRESPONDING TO JOSEPH IN EGYPT

Let us now turn our attention to the way in which this story fits in with its literary context – the story about Joseph and his brothers, which surrounds it on both sides. The book of Genesis is the "book of the generations" of the human race, at the center of which we find the story of the generations of the select individuals and their battle to establish their seed. To these select individuals, continuity is not merely a matter of biology; rather, it is their life's mission – a central objective, requiring perseverance until victory is attained. The biological continuity of the chosen branches is not taken for granted. Because of their great value, their existence requires a real fight. Only on the fringes, among those who are not selected, do existence and continuity come easily.

The story of Joseph and his brothers is therefore a story of "the generations of Jacob" at the second stage of his life – the story of the struggle for the establishment of the third generation of Jacob's family. But in contrast to other stories of "generations" in Genesis, here the threat to continuity is not objective: neither the barrenness of the woman in question, nor a flood, nor danger from a threatening relative. The threat in the story of Joseph is internal. The structure of the family, with the mistakes in its management and various sins in its operations, bring about the great rift described at the end of chapter thirty-seven – at the end of the story's first section. As a result of the terrible rift in the family, two main branches separate from it:

> And it happened, at that time, that **Judah went down** from his brothers... (38:1)

> **And Joseph was taken down** to Egypt, and he was bought by Potiphar, chamberlain of Pharaoh... (39:1)

These two "descents" seem to be linked: Judah's descent from his brothers comes as the result of Joseph being taken down to Egypt, Jacob's mourning for Joseph and the arguments between the brothers. At this point, the story focuses on these two branches, that have been become severed from Jacob's household: first, the branch of Judah and his "generations" for some twenty years, during which time Judah is separated from his family; and thereafter the branch of Joseph and his generations for exactly the same twenty years, during which he, too, is separated from the family.

The story of Judah and Tamar describes the threat to the continuity of Judah's family and the victory over this threat through the establishment of his seed in the merit of Tamar. In the description of Joseph's servitude in Egypt and his descent into the dungeon there, our attention is drawn mainly to his bitter personal fate. But this is not the main point of a story whose subject is the struggle for the establishment of seed in Jacob's family. As a slave in Egypt, Joseph is prevented from establishing a family! At the center of the story of Joseph as a slave in Egypt (chapter thirty-nine) is the failure of Potiphar's wife to seduce him. The temptation offered by a woman to a man also stands as the central axis of the previous story, in chapter thirty-eight (except there it is successful). What is the difference between these two acts of temptation? Tamar tempts Judah to turn to her in order to establish seed for his family, and therefore her actions are justified; Judah himself has no criticism because of the positive results of her actions. The temptation of Potiphar's wife, in contrast, is a tragic illustration of Joseph's situation as someone who is unable to establish his seed. For it is not for the purposes of establishing seed that Potiphar's wife approaches him, but rather as a means of sexual entertainment. It is to Joseph's great credit that he withstood the temptation, believing that the day would come when he would be able to establish his seed in a proper way.

With Joseph's incarceration for an unlimited period of time, it appears that any hope of seed being established from this branch of Jacob's family is now lost. But hidden divine providence brings about events in such a way that Joseph is removed from the dungeon and becomes viceroy to the King of Egypt. The climax of his ascent to greatness begins in a verse that seems quite unrelated:

> And he gave him Osnat, daughter of Poti Phera, priest of On, as a wife. (41:35)

Joseph finally marries a wife legally, thus laying the foundation for the establishment of a family. The tangible climax of the story is located near its conclusion:

> And two sons were born to Joseph before the years of famine...
> And Joseph named the firstborn Menashe... and the second one he called Ephraim, for God has made me fruitful in the land of my affliction. (41:50–52)

This conclusion of the story of Joseph parallels the conclusion of the story of Judah and Tamar. At the end of these twenty years during which Judah and Joseph "descended" from their family and during which the continuity of each of them faced a real threat, they both eventually establish their seed, with two sons born to each – an expression of fertility. Peretz and Zerah, and Menashe and Ephraim, are of more or less the same ages, and it is they who bear the message of victory in the battle to establish "generations" for the household of Jacob.

The Prince and the Prison

by Rav Chanoch Waxman

I.

Joseph was a highly successful prisoner. Almost immediately upon land-ing in jail, Joseph managed to "find favor" in the eyes of the minister of prisons (Gen. 39:21). Shortly afterwards, the minister appointed him head prisoner and Joseph's career was back on track.

> And the officer of the prison gave over to Joseph's hand all the prisoners that were in the prison; and whatever was done there, he was the doer of it. The keeper of the prison saw nothing of that which was under his hand … (39:22–23)

While Pharaoh's minister, the officer of the prisons, remained nominally in charge, Joseph constituted the real power behind the penitentiary throne. He made the decisions, ran things on a daily basis and, in the language of the Torah, did whatever was done. While no doubt this constitutes a coveted position amongst the prison population, we may wonder how glorious a job it really is. What exactly does an assistant warden in an ancient Egyptian jail do?

Jail is not the first place where Joseph rose to prominence. Before prison, Joseph had done some time in the house of Potiphar. Before his entanglement with Potiphar's wife, Joseph's career had progressed along the servant fast track. He quickly found a position in the house of Potiphar (39:2), bypassing the more common slave occupation of field hand, a short and nasty existence consisting of back-breaking hard labor. He "found favor" in his master's eyes (39:4), and just a few short verses after Potiphar purchases him, Potiphar appoints Joseph as head servant/slave. He places everything he has in "the hand" of Joseph and leaves him completely in charge (39:4–5). Like the officer of the prisons later on, Potiphar is now oblivious to the goings on in his domain.

> And he left all that he had in Joseph's hand and he knew nothing of that which he had except for the bread which he ate... (39:6)

As in the prison later on, Joseph constitutes the real power in the house and fields of Potiphar. As the headman, the *"charge d'affaires"* of Potiphar, Joseph does all that needs doing. Except for the slightly mysterious bread, Joseph wields total control.

To outline this logically, the "headman" parallel that emerges from the sketch above consists of three fundamental components. In both the house of Potiphar and in prison, we can note "finding favor" in the eyes of the ruling authority (39:4; 39:21), the "placing" of authority into the "hand" of Joseph (39:4, 6; 39:22), and the oblivious, know-nothing attitude of the real chief (39:6; 39:23). In addition, we can add a fourth element. In both cases, the Torah informs us that Joseph was successful, and attributes his success to God's assistance (39:3; 39:23).

Given the tight parallel above between Joseph's two headman positions, we should pay very careful attention to a set of crucial differences between the two stories. In the first, Joseph serves a man of great importance in the Egyptian kingdom. He acts as assistant to Pharaoh's captain of the guard (*sar hatabaḥim*), a man defined as *"seris Par'oh,"* a chamberlain of Pharaoh (39:1). He is in charge of Potiphar's entire estate (39:4–5), works in Potiphar's house, and is even privileged with private access to the lady of the house (39:7–11). In contrast, in the second story, Joseph is no more than the headman of an ancient Near Eastern jail, a miserable pit (40:15). He serves no important minister, inhabits no luxurious offices and enjoys no company except that of his fellow prisoners. His kingdom is a prison and his subjects are the wretched and condemned. Joseph has fallen fast and hard.

But if, in fact, God "is with" Joseph both in the house of Potiphar and in prison (39:3, 21, 23), why has God done this to him? What mysterious divine imperative propels Joseph downwards?

Rather than resorting to the obvious answers, let us complicate things a bit. Joseph plays the role of headman not twice, but in fact three times in *Parashat Vayeshev*. *Parashat Vayeshev* opens with another story of Joseph's success and meteoric rise to headman. Joseph is special to his father. Jacob elevates Joseph above his brothers and gives him a long-sleeved coat (37:3), a garment worn by the children of kings (II Sam. 13:18). Furthermore, Joseph enjoys special access to his father. While his brothers are away with the sheep in Shekhem, Joseph remains home with his father (37:12–13, Ramban on 37:3).

Finally, Joseph serves as Jacob's supervisory agent. Jacob sends Joseph to check on his brothers and the sheep out in the fields of Shekhem (37:14). While Jacob might not have asked for the slanderous reports (*dibatam ra'a*) brought home by Joseph about his brothers (37:2), the surprise is the slander, not the report. Joseph, as the preferred son, acts as supervisor and *charge d'affaires*. As befits his role as second-in-command, he reports to the chief. Needless to say, Joseph's dreams reflect his headman role and, together with his coat and his supervisory role, constitute the cause of his brothers' animosity.

If so, *Parashat Vayeshev* turns out to possess an interesting structure. Joseph starts out as the assistant to Jacob, the headman of the family fated to form God's chosen nation and to realize the blessings of Abraham. But he falls fast and falls hard. We next find him as headman in Potiphar's house, albeit in exile, but in a position of power, prominence and prestige.

But even this is not to be. Joseph descends again, this time to prison. In stage three of the headman structure, we find Joseph supervising a prison. He is far from his family, far from blessing, and far from his dreams.

Once again, all of this is part of God's plan. But then again, there are infinite ways that God could have arranged Joseph's eventual control over Egypt. Why this way? Why the threefold headman structure for

Parashat Vayeshev? In other words, what is the meaning and message of Joseph's descent?

II.

Parashat Vayeshev initiates a crucial turn in the book of Genesis. While Jacob still appears in the *parasha* and is present until near the very end of the book, the storyline is no longer about the forefathers. Rather, the remainder of the book concerns itself primarily with the story of Joseph and his brothers. Along with this change of characters comes a crucial shift in symbols and themes. For example, most of the action in the second part of Genesis (12:1–36:43) has revolved around the issues of covenant, inheritance and blessings. Much of the story is about God's promises and the mysterious process of choosing an heir to the blessings. As of the beginning of *Parashat Vayeshev*, these themes more or less vanish. While covenant and blessings may sometimes crop up as hidden themes, God never appears to make promises and never chooses the next generation. Needless to say, all eleven of Jacob's children become the inheritors of the blessings. None of them is spurned, replaced or expelled.

To put all of this together, the story of the forefathers, the story of covenant formation and transmission, comes to an end at the beginning of *Parashat Vayeshev*. The remainder of the book of Genesis (37:2–50:26) concerns itself not so much with formation but with realization. The story of Joseph and his brothers, which constitutes the remainder of the book, details the descent to Egypt and the beginning of the realization of the Covenant between the Pieces – sojourning and slavery (15:13). Everything in the rest of Genesis connects to Egypt and the twisted path for getting there.

At first glance, *Parashat Vayeshev* seems to contain a striking exception to our newly established rule. Chapter thirty-eight serves up the strange story of Judah and Tamar. While Judah's family problems are quite interesting, we may wonder about the connection to the theme of the third part of Genesis. What do Judah's neglect of Tamar (38:1–11), Tamar's playing the prostitute (38:12–23), and the birth of Judah's sons Peretz and Zerah (38:24–30) have to do with Egypt and the theme of covenant realization?

This can easily be rephrased as a question about the structure of *Parashat Vayeshev*. Earlier I argued that Joseph occupies the role of "number-one man" three times in *Parashat Vayeshev*. He serves as supervisor, first in his father's house, later in Potiphar's house, and finally in prison. By working along these lines, *Parashat Vayeshev* can be grouped into three distinct units, each telling the story of Joseph and the outcome of his headman role. Mapping it out yields the following:

> Unit One (37:1–36) – Joseph in his father's house; the termination of his position through the sale of Joseph by his brothers; the banishment of Joseph.
>> [??? (38:1–30) – The story of Judah and Tamar.]

> Unit Two (39:1–39:20) – Joseph in the house of Potiphar– the termination of his position through his entanglement with Potiphar's wife; the banishment of Joseph.

> Unit Three (39:21–40:23) – Joseph in prison; the failed termination and yet foreshadowing of the eventual termination of Joseph's position through his encounter with the officers of Pharaoh and their dreams.

We really should not need the brackets and question marks above to make the obvious point. The story of Judah and Tamar just doesn't seem to fit into *Parashat Vayeshev*. Why is it here?

III.

Before trying to get a better grasp on the structure of *Parashat Vayeshev*, let us consider the end of *Parashat Vayishlaḥ* and the transition to *Vayeshev*. *Parashat Vayishlaḥ* ends with a long section detailing the descendants of Esau (36:1–43). As if this were not mysterious enough, the last subsection of "*Toledot Esav*" (36:31–43) lists the kings who ruled in Edom. We may be inclined to dismiss the inclusion of these sections in the Torah as an example of a phenomenon that may be termed "witnessing." God has promised Abraham that he shall be the "father of many nations" (*av hamon goyim*) and that "kings shall come from you" (17:5–6). While the special covenant of Brit Mila, including "the land that you dwell in" (17:8), will remain the unique possession of one line of Abraham's descendants, other lines will achieve nationhood, control territory and be ruled by kings. Consequently, the Torah includes "*Toledot Esav*" and its line of kings. The Torah bears witness to the accomplishment of God's promise.

But there seems to be more to it than this. The list of kings begins with the statement, "These are the kings who ruled in Edom before a king ruled over the children of Israel" (36:31). The mention of the kings of Edom seems to bear some connection to the existence of royalty and kingship in Israel. Moreover, the beginning of *Parashat Vayeshev* also seems to take up the topic of kingship in Israel. Part of the action involves Jacob giving Joseph a *ktonet passim* as a symbol of his love (37:3). But this is not an innocuous symbol. As pointed out earlier, a long-sleeved coat is a royal garment, worn by the children of kings of Israel. Finally, we have the dreams. When Joseph reports his dream of bowing sheaves to his brothers (37:6–7), they reply as follows:

> Shall you indeed be king (*hamelokh timlokh*) over us? Shall you indeed have dominion over us? (37:8)

Joseph's brothers resent him not just for his privileged status in their father's house. They resent his pretensions to leadership and future royalty.

If so, it appears that the seam between *Parashat Vayishlah* and *Parashat Vayeshev*, the transition between the second part of the book (12:1–36:43) and the third part of the book (37:1–50:26), consists of the symbols of royalty and the topics of leadership and kingship. This is no accident. As pointed out previously, the thematic shift consists of a move from the stage of covenant transaction and transmission to a stage of fulfillment and realization. This means that the future is no longer the inchoate destiny of a single individual. The future now belongs to a group, a nascent nation. Already now, there exists a group, bound up concretely with the historical reality of the unfolding divine plan. But every group that functions in the real world, that navigates the stormy seas of history, requires leaders. By no surprise, the topic of leadership becomes paramount in the book of Genesis. By no surprise, the topic is formulated in the symbolism of kingship, foreshadowing the future of the family's descendants, the nation of Israel.

All of this should help us with the structure of *Vayeshev*. In keeping with the theme of leadership and kingship, the stories are primarily about Joseph and Judah, the two once and future leaders. Joseph attempts to rule in the house of Jacob and later does rule during the family's time in Egypt. In parallel, Judah leads during the sale of Joseph, and later on, during the famine and confrontation with the Egyptian viceroy. These leadership roles foreshadow much of the future history of Israel. The house of David descends from Judah (Gen. 38:29; Ruth 4:18–22); the line of Yerovam, the rebel king of the secessionist tribes, descends from Joseph (1 Kings 11:26); and Saul, the first king of Israel, descends from Benjamin (1 Sam. 9:1–2), Rachel's other child.

In this light, the inclusion of the story of Judah and Tamar in the *parasha* need no longer disturb us. The story ends with the birth of Peretz (38:27–34), a variation on the younger replacing the older theme prevalent in the book of Genesis. The infant manages to burst out first, despite the fact that his brother had already stuck out his hand. While the older-younger motif no longer signals replacement and expulsion from the covenant, in its modified form here in the third part of Genesis, it signals distinction and the line of leadership. Just as Peretz replaces Zerah, so too Judah occupies a central role in the narrative, thereby "replacing" Reuben and telegraphing his leadership role.

IV.

Let us try to move from the level of textual space and literary markers to the level of character. After all, the story of Judah and Tamar is not just about devoting time to Judah and noting the unusual birth of Peretz. It is also, and primarily, about the character of Judah.

The central action of the story revolves around Judah's treatment of Tamar. Oblivious to the evil nature of his sons Er and Onan, and hence to the real cause of their deaths, Judah attributes their deaths to his daughter-in-law Tamar (38:6–11). She is bad luck. Consequently, Judah decides not to fulfill his legal and moral duty of commanding his remaining son Shelah to marry Tamar (38:11). Judah operates from the perspective that nothing could possibly be amiss in his own house. His sons could not possibly have been struck down by God, and he is certainly justified in banishing the "bad luck" woman from his family.

But Tamar does not accept Judah's decision. She disguises herself as a harlot, contracts a deal with the unknowing Judah and, pregnant with Judah's child, disappears from the crossroads, returning to her life as a young widow (38:13–19).

In the climax of the story, Judah learns that Tamar is pregnant. Without even the slightest hesitation, he pronounces the death penalty (38:24). At the very last minute, upon being taken out to be burnt, Tamar sends Judah his cord, seal and staff that she had received in her guise of harlot as guarantee of payment. She is pregnant by the man who owns these items (38:25). Judah pronounces judgment one more time and spares Tamar's life.

> And Judah recognized [*vayaker Yehuda*], and he said: She is more righteous than I; for I have not given her to Shelah my son. (38:26)

This time Judah passes judgment not on Tamar but on himself. Whereas previously Judah had assumed his own righteousness and the righteousness of his sons, here Judah realizes that his actions have not been justified nor his sons righteous. If he has been with Tamar and still remains alive, than she is not "bad luck" and he is guilty. His sons died of their own sins and he has neglected his duty. The bubble of self-righteousness has burst.

In making his pronouncement, Judah displays the virtue of humility. As Rashi points out (on 38:25), Tamar did not publicly disclose to whom the stick and signet belonged. By sending an apparently private message to Judah, she allowed him the possibility of covering up. He could have avoided the public humiliation of reversing his judgment and admitting he consorted with "harlots." He could have continued to play the role of righteous patriarch and avoided confessing the neglect and tricking of his daughter-in-law, as well as any public acknowledgement of his own sons' evil. Instead, Judah admits.

This behavior marks a radical shift for Judah. As outlined above, previously Judah had acted arrogantly, condemning Tamar rather than his sons and sentencing her without hesitation. Similarly, he previously had been concerned with his public image, sending his friend the Adullamite to make payment to the harlot, and expressing concern "lest it be

for a shame" (38:20–23) when she could not be found and his possessions retrieved. Now, though, he exhibits humility in place of ego, and
acknowledgement of others in place of image.

All of this fits well with our previous interpretation of the story as
one linked to leadership, marking Judah as monarchial material. *Parashat
HaMelekh*, the section of Deuteronomy that defines the criteria and rules
for the king, lists but one fundamental character issue. Buried amidst
the warnings about too many wives, too much gold and the requirement to maintain a personal copy of the Torah, we are informed of the
purpose of all this:

> … that his heart not be lifted up above his brothers … so that he
> may prolong the days of his kingdom, he and his sons in the midst
> of Israel. (Deut. 17:20)

Leadership and kingship are about and depend upon the virtue of
humility.

V.

Before closing, let us return to our point of origin. Earlier on, I argued for
reading *Parashat Vayeshev* as possessing a tripartite structure of "headman" stories. Consequently, I raised questions regarding the meaning
of Joseph's descent and the insertion of the Judah and Tamar story in
an otherwise cohesive structure. Reading *Parashat Vayeshev* as also concerned with marking the leaders/kings and as interested in emphasizing
the leadership criterion of humility helped resolve the inclusion of the
Judah and Tamar story. With this in hand, let us turn back to Joseph and
the problem of his descent.

Does Joseph possess the virtue of humility necessary for leadership and royalty? A quick review of the first headman story should
determine the answer.

Joseph is the favored son. Whether due to virtue and ability, his
being almost the youngest, or his being the firstborn of the beloved
Rachel, Jacob loves Joseph more than he loves his other sons (37:3).
The brothers resent it. They resent the favoritism and its future implications. They hate Joseph and cannot even speak peaceably to him. But

what is Joseph's attitude to the family dynamic? While the text gives us no explicit information, we may glean quite a bit by reading between the lines. At the very least, he seems to feel no qualms about speaking ill of his brothers to their father (37:2), a move which seems to reinforce his claim to superiority. He is above them, sits in judgment upon them and reports on them.

Moreover, immediately after informing us of the brothers' resentment of Joseph's status and their hatred of him, the Torah tells us about Joseph's dreams (37:5–10). Despite the obvious implications of the dreams and the fact that his brothers are already not talking to him, Joseph insists on telling his dreams to his brothers. He grandly proclaims, "Hear this dream that I have dreamed" (37:6). Even after the brothers chastise him for his royal pretensions (37:8), Joseph does not desist. When he dreams again, this time not just of bundles of straw bowing down to him, but of the entire cosmos prostrated before him, he immediately informs his brothers (37:9). In sum, Joseph naively glories in his position and visions. Without regard to his brothers' response, he acts the prince, certain of his position and convinced of his destiny. He is not humble.

To rephrase this in the language of Deuteronomy, Joseph's heart **is** elevated above his brothers. It is almost no surprise that his brothers see the dreamer coming (37:19), strip him of his royal coat (37:23) and defiantly pronounce, "See now what will become of his dreams" (37:20).

If so, this may be the meaning of the descent pattern in *Parashat Vayeshev*. In structuring this pattern, both the *parasha* and divine providence provide an ironic comment on Joseph's pretensions. Joseph viewed himself as a prince, a ruler now and in the future. He prides himself on his talent, his position and his destiny. But how the mighty have fallen. Yes, he is a headman. Yes, he is a ruler – but not of his family, and not of the future nation of Israel. He who elevated his heart above his brothers rules not even the house of Potiphar. He rules only a prison.

But there is more to it than this. I would argue that this very pattern of descent, the providential mocking of his pretensions and pride, effects a change in Joseph. Let us take a look at the bare-bones but significant characterizations of Joseph in the second and third headman stories.

In protesting the advances of Potiphar's wife, Joseph manages to refer to the fact that "there is none greater in the house than me" (39:9), twice mentions the fact that everything has been entrusted to his control (39:8–9), and once refers to his master's ignorance. While this is all part of a profession of loyalty on Joseph's part (39:8–9), Joseph is acutely aware of his status and position. He then tumbles once again.

The final headman story, Joseph's ruling of the prison, presents a different picture. Although the disgraced ministers of Pharaoh have been placed in Joseph's hands along with all of the other prisoners (39:22; 40:4), the Torah describes Joseph as "serving them" (40:4). He inquires after their welfare and sad moods (40:5). He serves, rather than rules, those placed in his charge.

Finally, this new humility may also be discerned in Joseph's offer to interpret their dreams. He ascribes the power of interpretation to God (40:8). While this may not seem surprising to us, it is shocking in the context of ancient Egypt, a land abounding in sorcerers and magicians. Even Joseph himself lauds his sorcerer's powers when playing the Egyptian viceroy for his brothers (44:15). Lauding his magical powers would certainly have gotten him out of the pit much faster. Needless to say, the "officer of drink" forgets the powerless youth and his humble request for help (40:23).

In sum, we have here the same humble Joseph who, when ascribed the power of dream interpretation by Pharaoh, responds that it is God and not he who possesses answers (41:16). We have here the very same Joseph who later humbly tells his brothers that it was all God's plan, that his entire position in Egypt exists for the sake of saving lives and providing for his family (44:5–8). We have here someone suitable for leadership, who acts with humility, whose heart is with his brothers.

Parashat Miketz

Joseph: Dreamer and Interpreter

by Rav Tamir Granot

I. THE PROBLEM WITH THE SOLUTION OF PHARAOH'S DREAMS

When Joseph is brought for an audience with Pharaoh, the Egyptian king receives him thus: "I have heard it said of you that you understand a dream to interpret it." – And indeed, Joseph's interpretation is accepted by Pharaoh as genuine. But Joseph will not accept the compliment: "It is not me! God will give Pharaoh a favorable answer." In other words, the answer is not in my hands; it is not by my own merit. Nevertheless, the story itself proves that Joseph's gift of interpreting dreams cannot be attributed solely to divine assistance. The interpretation has its own internal logic and is suited to the dream – both in the case of the ministers and in the case of Pharaoh. Although Joseph, in his modesty, attributes the entire answer to God, we must assume that this is a general religious statement about God helping him. He does not mean that God reveals Himself to him *ad hoc*, supplying him with the answer in each instance.

If we agree with the assertion that Joseph interprets dreams using his special insight, then two major questions arise:

1. What clues does he use to interpret Pharaoh's dream?
2. How does Pharaoh know that Joseph's interpretation was correct?

The early commentators address these questions, but we are not left with any satisfactory answer. Some opinions assume a super-human gift. Another opinion asserts that Pharaoh dreamed the interpretation along with the dream, but then forgot it. He was immediately reminded of it when Joseph offered his interpretation, and hence Pharaoh knew that this was the correct one. We cannot rule out this possibility, but from an exegetical point of view it is better not to rely on hypotheses that have no basis in the text.

I believe that the correct exegetical working assumption is that the Torah is telling us how Joseph solved the dreams, and it is the task of every Torah scholar to reveal that which is still hidden. In the present instance, the assumption is reinforced by the fact that the Torah elaborates at great length in its description of the dreams. This detail is obviously not meant for the sake of literary ornamentation; rather, it allows us to follow the process of interpretation.

II. REPETITION OF THE DREAMS

Repetition in a narrative generally appears where the development of events is described once by the text itself, and then again by one or more characters involved in the story. In our present case, the text describes Pharaoh's dreams three times:

1. Objective description – of the text itself
2. Description by Pharaoh – here we must decide what the purpose of the repetition is, and which point of view it reflects.
3. Description by Joseph – for the purpose of interpretation. Here Joseph connects elements of the dream to parts of his interpretation, and therefore the repetition is a necessity. In any event, since this is not a word-for-word repetition, we shall pay attention to this version as well.

The focus of our discussion is on the repetition by Pharaoh, because it is entirely redundant. The Torah could simply have recorded that "Pharaoh told his dreams to Joseph" – and left it at that. Alternatively, it could have omitted the description of the dreams in the beginning, and structured the incident differently: "And it was, after two years, that Pharaoh dreamed dreams. He awoke in the morning and called all the magicians of Egypt…," and then, "Pharaoh told them to Joseph, and he said: In my dream, behold…" – and only here provided a full description of the dreams. The repetitive description in full is unquestionably superfluous, and requires explanation.

Let us compare the three descriptions with a view to discovering their differences.

First dream:
Torah's description (41:1): "…Behold, he stood at the river. (2) And behold, from the river there rose seven cows – of beautiful appearance [מראה] and fat, and they grazed in the reed grass. (3) And behold, another seven cows arose after them from the river, of bad appearance and thin, and they stood by the other cows upon the bank of the river. (4) And the cows of bad appearance and thin consumed the seven cows of good appearance and fat."

Pharaoh's description: (17) "…Behold, I was standing upon the bank of the river, (18) and behold, from the river there arose seven cows, fat and of good – visage [תואר], and they grazed in the reed grass. (19) And behold, another seven cows arose after them – wretched and of very bad visage and thin; I had never seen any so bad in all of the land of Egypt. (20) And the cows that were thin and bad consumed the original seven healthy cows. (21) And when they had eaten them one could not see that they had eaten them, for their appearance was as bad as it had been at the start."

Joseph's description: (26) "The seven good cows are seven years, and the seven good sheaves are seven years; it is the same dream. (27) And the seven thin, bad cows that arose after them are seven years, and the seven empty sheaves blasted by the east wind are seven years of famine… (31) And the plenty shall not be remembered in the land because of that famine afterwards, for it will be very severe."

Second dream:

Torah's description: (5) "And behold, seven ears of corn arose on the same stalk – healthy and good. (6) And behold, seven ears that were thin and blasted by the east wind sprang up after them. (7) And the seven thin ears swallowed up the seven ears that were healthy and full."

Pharaoh's description: (22) "...Behold, seven ears of corn arose on the same stalk, full and good. (23) And behold, seven ears – withered, thin, and blasted by the east wind – sprang up after them. (24) And the thin ears swallowed up the seven GOOD ears..."

Joseph's description: (32) "And as to the twofold recurrence of the dream to Pharaoh – it is because the thing has been established by God, and God will hasten to perform it."

We see two types of differences. Those indicated in bold involve the use of synonymous words to describe the fat or thin cows and ears of corn. They do not involve any real difference in the essence of the dream. A different set of discrepancies involves real additions. We must gauge the importance of each of these individually:

"They stood next to the other cows on the bank of the river" – this appears only in the Torah's description.

"I had never seen any so bad in all of the land of Egypt" – this appears only in Pharaoh's version.

"When they had eaten them up one could not see that they had eaten them, for their appearance was as bad as it had been at the start" – only in Pharaoh's version.

It appears that a distinction should be drawn between the first two additions and the third. The first two apparently reflect the objectivity (in the case of the first) or subjectivity (in the case of the second) of the description. The Torah notes the proximity of the two sets of cows, while Pharaoh seems to omit this detail because it seems obvious, or because he forgets it in his excitement. Pharaoh adds a comment about the cows so as to express the powerful impression that their appearance made on him. Clearly, there is no room for an expression such as this in the first description, since from an objective point of view it adds nothing.

But the third difference belongs to a different category: this is a fact; not mere impression. Either Pharaoh actually saw in his dream that one could not know that they had eaten them, or he did not see this, or he saw something else. Whichever the case may be, the Torah makes no mention of this in the objective description. Why does Pharaoh add this fact? Does the strong impression created by the dream cause him to elaborate based on his own imagination? What is the significance of this?

As to the disparities in the descriptions of the cows and the ears of corn, it would seem that these, too, reflect the difference between an objective reporting of facts, and the subjective impressions of Pharaoh, who experiences the dreams.

Joseph's quotations from the dreams generally follow Pharaoh's description, for Joseph does not know what Pharaoh really dreamed. Therefore, his interpretation employs the expressions "good," "empty," "bad," and "blasted by the east wind," all echoing Pharaoh's terminology.

But, as we have explained, the focus is on the additions that Pharaoh makes, which have no parallel in the original version, and especially the comment, "When they had eaten them up, one could not know that they had eaten them, for their appearance was as bad as it had been at the start." Does Joseph know that Pharaoh adds this on his own? This is a critical question. If Joseph knows only the dream as recounted by Pharaoh but not the original dream, he can interpret only what he is told. And then, if the dream has prophetical status and it reveals the future, perhaps the interpretation of Pharaoh's dream is mistaken?

Before answering this question, let us address another critical point in Joseph's answer. Joseph is asked to interpret Pharaoh's dream. In fact, he does much more. His interpretation concludes with the words, "And concerning the twofold recurrence of the dream to Pharaoh – it is because the thing has been established by God, and God will hasten to perform it." Here we would expect Joseph to stop talking – but he goes on, proposing a plan to accumulate a fifth of all produce throughout the seven years of plenty, so as to solve the problem of the famine. He seems to go far beyond interpreting the dream: "And now, let Pharaoh seek out an insightful and wise man, and appoint him over the land of Egypt…" This proposal would seem to bespeak no small measure of arrogance on the part of a prisoner who has been summoned before the king, and who brazenly proposes that he himself undertake the task of advising Pharaoh! How does Joseph have the temerity to talk in this way?

We may regard this as the expert plotting of a man who prepares his listener and gives him precisely the message that he wants him to hear. In other words, Joseph prepares the role for himself, and Pharaoh's response is exactly as expected: "There is none so insightful and wise as you." Alternatively, we may regard Joseph's suggestion as an expression of genuine concern for the welfare of the kingdom. But I believe that neither of these explanations is sufficient. Attention should be paid to the fact that Joseph's operative suggestions actually negate his interpretation of the dream. He tells Pharaoh, "The plenty in the land will not be known because of that famine afterwards, for it will be extremely severe." But if the Egyptians follow Joseph's instructions, "The land will not be destroyed by famine"; on the contrary, the plenty will be known and recognized even during the years of famine, for the accumulation and storage of food will make it possible to eat even during the lean years.

III. SOLUTION TO THE SOLUTION

This problem, I believe, is the key to the crux of the story and the answers to all of our previous questions. Let us systematically analyze the progression of Joseph's interpretation:

The methodology of the solution is: "As to the twofold recurrence of the dream to Pharaoh – it is because the thing has been established by God, and God will hasten to perform it." The two dreams do not require two interpretations, but rather share the same one. The same message is conveyed twice, to show the reliability of its details.

The cows and the ears of corn are symbols. One represents the plant kingdom, the other – the animal kingdom; both connote abundance. Leanness, of course, means the opposite. This part of the dream appears quite simple. The symbols are transparent; their interpretation does not require any special wisdom. Joseph then interprets the number of cows and ears of corn as symbolizing units of time – just as he did in the dreams of Pharaoh's ministers (three vine tendrils = three days). This element of the dream is likewise reasonably intelligible; even the magicians could guess at its meaning.

Joseph then addresses the addition inserted by Pharaoh: "They were eaten up but **one could not tell** [*lo noda*] that they had been eaten," Joseph declares, "The plenty in the land **will not be known** [*lo yivada*] because of that famine afterwards…" It is interesting that this part of the dream is interpreted without any direct quotation of Pharaoh's words.

Now let us pay attention to the way in which the message is conveyed by Joseph: "The plenty in the land will not be known because of the famine afterwards, for it will be extremely severe. And as to the twofold recurrence of the dream to Pharaoh – it is because the thing has been established by God, and God will hasten to perform it. Now, let Pharaoh seek out an insightful and wise man, and appoint him over the land of Egypt" (31–33).

After interpreting Pharaoh's addition, he establishes the principle of the recurrence of the dream as evidence of its reliability, and then he moves immediately on to the stage of advising. Here, I believe, his brilliance is revealed. Verse 31, explaining the addition, is defined by the principle of the repetition of the dream. Pharaoh, in his description, does not repeat a second time the matter of "they were eaten up…"; he adds this only at the end of the first dream. The other details are repeated with precision and at length. Joseph hints here to Pharaoh, "I know that this was an addition of your own invention; you did not dream it. I am interpreting your addition in order that you will understand that it is a symbol of your own anxiety concerning the famine and its results. But right away I will propose to you a way of overcoming this anxiety." In other words, our questions are explained by each other. Joseph advises Pharaoh as to how to alleviate the suffering of the famine by means of exploiting the plenty. He does not negate the fact that the dream is symbolic of a divine decree which is destined to be fulfilled. But he does address the dimension of Pharaoh's personal anxiety and despair, by proposing a practical solution. Joseph's wisdom is revealed in the fact that he is able to locate the objective kernel of the dream and free it of its subjective wrapping. The subjective dimension of "their appearance was as bad as it had been at the start" is the omen for a catastrophic future. If the famine is so severe that it will seem as though the years of plenty never existed, then real devastation awaits Egypt. But in truth, in the dream which He revealed to Pharaoh, God decreed only famine. The despair is Pharaoh's own invention. How the Egyptians will deal with the famine and what its effects will be – these matters have not been decreed, and therefore it may be possible to find ways of coping. Joseph, in his wisdom, senses that Pharaoh has incorporated his personal impression into his description, for he notes that this detail in the dream was not repeated – i.e., it was not a vision like the other visions which Pharaoh repeated with such precision.

If we go back to our original questions, it appears that we already have the answers. The textual repetition of the dream by Pharaoh is essential because the discrepancy between the original dream and Pharaoh's recounting holds the key to the proposal of a solution, in which Joseph's wisdom is revealed. Joseph understood what was really troubling Pharaoh. Pharaoh knew, of course, that the dream contained symbols of abundance and of famine, but did not know if this was a decree of destruction; he did not know if he would be able to deal with it. And it was specifically because Joseph grasped this that Pharaoh recognized his abilities.

Why is Pharaoh struck with terror; why does he believe that the decree of famine is absolute, that it will bring about annihilation, while Joseph immediately understands that the famine is something that can be dealt with? I believe that this reflects more than just the personality structure of each of the two characters involved. Rather, Joseph's view is an expression of a "Jewish" way of handling a harsh reality, while Pharaoh's view is the expression of a pagan consciousness.

Pharaoh lives within a deterministic consciousness. If something has been decreed, there is nothing to be done – certainly not on the level of practical action. Reality weighs down on us, and all we can do is recognize it. Joseph presents Pharaoh with the Jewish alternative: the reality is admittedly harsh, but it should be perceived not as a disaster, but rather as a mission and responsibility. The famine is a fact, but the task of leadership is to find ways of dealing with the suffering that it is likely to cause. This is precisely the spirit of Joseph's proposal, and it is for this purpose that he is appointed. Thus, when Pharaoh says, "Is there

any man like this, with the spirit of God within him?" he refers especially to the particularly Jewish spirit of God by virtue of which Joseph
knew the correct solution.

IV. UNDERSTANDING JOSEPH'S TURNING POINT

An examination of the development of the story reveals that its turning
point is the stage where Joseph turns into the "interpreter of dreams,"
and thus his status is "upgraded" – to the point where ultimately, at the
end of this process, he is appointed second-in-command to the King of
Egypt. The event in which the crux of this "turning point" takes place is
the interpretation of Pharaoh's dreams. Until this point, Joseph has not
been a personality who determines his own path and is active within
the events; rather, events have acted upon him. He is "a dreamer." He is
dispatched by his father, he is cast into a pit, he is sold, he is appointed
head of Potiphar's household, he is drawn towards sin and then thrown
again into a dungeon. It is only when he proposes to Pharaoh's ministers that he will interpret their dreams that the beginning of a change
makes itself felt. The transition from passivity to activity in his relationship to dreams – from dreamer to interpreter – is likewise reflected in
a transition from passivity to activity in his relationship to reality: from
"determined" to "determiner." Joseph, who has been pushed around at
the mercy of his environment, now becomes its director.

Joseph dreamed his dreams within a "fate" consciousness – in a
certain sense – as a seer of the divine future. In other words, reality is
deterministic, dictated; all that is destined to be is set down in advance,
and now it is revealed to me in a dream. When he awakens from the
dream, he runs to tell his brothers about what will come to be – and this,
understandably, angers them. Joseph fails to ask himself the correct questions: "What is this telling me? What is the dream charging me to do?
With which mission is it entrusting me?" This was his mistake and his sin.

The prophet – in complete contrast to the pagan fortune-teller
(diviner, magician, etc.) – does not reveal the future in order to say "what
will be," but rather in order that we will know what we must do in relation
to it. We may say of the prophets of Israel that they prophesy in order
that their prophecies will not be fulfilled. The threat of punishment is
always a call to repentance, which in turn will nullify the punishment.

The moment when Joseph understands that his quasi-prophetic ability is not meant to give him a personal advantage, or just to bring him success, but rather assigns him a mission – everything is open to change. Therefore, the turning point is the stage where Joseph ceases to act as a dreamer of the future, or a diviner, and starts acting as a "prophet."

Joseph did not know the significance of his own dreams. But now he hears from Pharaoh's mouth a dream that contains the same motifs – ears of corn, two groups of ears of corn – and a crazy image of the lean ones swallowing up the fat ones. Is this not my own dream? he asks himself. Is this not my dream, in which my older brothers' sheaves bow down to my own?

Then he understands: the first dream showed me that a day would come when my brothers would need my sheaves. Now, God is showing me – me and not Pharaoh – how this might come about. Therefore, Joseph knew how to interpret the dream, while no one else could possibly have known – because Pharaoh's dream was meant for him all along. Joseph needed no further revelation in order to understand the significance of Pharaoh's dream. It was already there. His wisdom stood him in good stead, and showed him how to connect the dreams.

Joseph thinks: "If until now I did not know how their sheaves would bow down to my sheaf, now God has shown it to me: the land is destined to be struck with famine. Severe famine. My forefathers, Abraham and Isaac, came down to Egypt at times of severe famine – as others must also have done – relying on the abundance of Egypt. If I am in Egypt, I will be in the right place to provide their sheaves – but how? By ensuring that there will be sheaves in Egypt; by ensuring that I will be the person responsible for the Egyptian economy." Hence, Joseph's proposal to Pharaoh has dual significance. For Pharaoh, it reveals the mistake in his story – which, as we have explained, is the key to its solution. The mistake in Pharaoh's story is understood by Joseph as a window, beckoning him to enter. The place where Pharaoh is helpless – that is where I am able to act. The proposal of setting aside a fifth of all the produce, and the heart of this proposal – "Now, let Pharaoh seek out a man who is insightful and wise, and appoint him over the land of Egypt..." – is directed towards a single purpose: for Pharaoh to appoint him to carry out the project. Joseph's audaciousness is surprising, but it has a religious foundation: If I have come this far, if Pharaoh needs me, then there must be something to it. God does not perform miracles for nothing. And indeed, Joseph is appointed by Pharaoh to oversee the implementation of the project. Pharaoh believes that he has thereby found a solution to his own internal problem as King of Egypt, but Joseph knows that he is thereby embarking on the mission that God has given him; a mission whose purpose ultimately concerns not Egypt but rather the household of Jacob.

The Intractable Question: Why Did Joseph Not Send Word to His Father?

by Rav Yoel Bin-Nun

I. INTRODUCTION – RAMBAN'S QUESTION

Seven hundred years ago, Ramban posed a difficult question, one which continues to puzzle whoever studies the book of Genesis:

> How is it that Joseph, after living many years in Egypt, having attained a high and influential position in the house of an important Egyptian official, did not send his father even one message to inform him [that he was alive] and comfort him? Egypt is only six days' travel from Ḥevron, and respect for his father would have justified even a year's journey!... [It would] have been a grave sin to torment his father by leaving him in mourning and bereavement for himself and for Simeon; even if he wanted to hurt his brothers a little, how could he not feel pity for his aged father? (Ramban on 42:9)

Ramban's own astonishing answer to his question is that Joseph's goal was to guarantee the fulfillment of his dreams. Even after the first dream had been realized, he intensified the deception in order to fulfill the second dream: he did everything in its proper time in order to fulfill the dreams, for he knew they would be fulfilled perfectly.

Abarbanel (on ch. 41, question 4) poses the following blunt question:

> Why did Joseph hide his identity from his brothers and speak harshly to them? It is criminal to be as vengeful and recriminating as a serpent!…How is it that as his brothers were starving and far from home, having left their families and small children and, above all, his aged, worried and suffering father waiting for them, did he not show compassion, but rather intensified the anguish by arresting Simeon?

Rabbi Yitzhak Arama (*Akedat Yitzhak* 29, ques. 9; see also Abarbanel on ch. 41, ques. 6) also finds Ramban's solution puzzling.

> What did he stand to gain by having his dreams fulfilled? Even had there been some advantage, that would not have justified sinning toward his father! And as for the dreams, let the Giver of dreams provide their solutions. It seems very foolish to strive to fulfill dreams, as the fulfillment does not depend on the dreamer's will.

To answer these objections, Professor Nechama Leibowitz, *zt"l*, believes that dreams can indeed be acted upon. She cites as proof Gideon, who hears a Midianite tell a dream, and acts upon it (Judges 7:13–14), as well as the Babylonian exiles (Ezra ch. 1), who did not wait for the seventy years of Jeremiah's prophecy to pass, but returned on their own, beforehand (see her *Studies on Sefer Bereishit*, p. 327).

In my opinion, Professor Leibowitz is mistaken. There are two differences between her examples and the case at hand, both of which are mentioned as well by R. Yitzhak Arama. First, neither Gideon nor the Babylonian exiles committed a grave offense in following their dreams. Their dreams did not contradict honoring parents, and certainly did not call on them to cause others grief. Second, the Torah itself clearly differentiates dreams from prophecy:

Let the prophet who has a dream tell his dream;
> And [let the prophet] who bears My word speak My word truthfully;
> What is straw to wheat? The Lord has spoken. (Jer. 23:38)

The Talmud explains:

> Rabbi Yoḥanan said in the name of Rabbi Shimon bar Yoḥai: Just as wheat cannot exist without chaff, there cannot be a dream without false elements.
>
> Rabbi Berekhia said: Although a dream may be partially fulfilled, it will not be fulfilled in its entirety. How do we know this? From Joseph, as it is written: "The sun [representing Joseph's father], the moon [his mother], and eleven stars [are bowing down to me]," and at the time, his mother was no longer alive. (*Berakhot* 55a)

It is dangerous to confuse the different levels to the point where every inspired man is considered to be a prophet or seer; we could never clearly perceive the word of God. We need not deny the existence of great visionaries – or underrate their importance – even when we affirm that they are, after all, not prophets.

The Torah distinguishes Joseph's dreams from the prophetic dreams of Abraham, Isaac, and Jacob. The patriarchs' dreams appear as pathways to divine revelation. In the Covenant between the Pieces (*Berit bein HaBetarim*), Abraham first sleeps and has a vision, and then receives God's word (16:12–13, 17–18). Jacob has a dream in which he sees a ladder and angels, and then God speaks to him. In Joseph's dreams, however, there is no outward prophecy or divine revelation. Even in Joseph's solving of dreams, there is only a general feeling of prophecy:

> Solutions come from God; please tell me [your dreams]. (40:8)

> Not I [but] God will answer for Pharaoh's well-being. (41:16)

Only after completing his explanation does Joseph become more confident:

> God is committed to doing this, and God will do it quickly. (41:39)

Significantly, Joseph uses God's universal name *"Elokim,"* and not the Tetragrammaton or *Kel Shakai*, names God uses when He reveals Himself to Israel.

For all the parallels the Midrash draws between Jacob and Joseph (*Bereshit Raba* 84:6), the Torah clearly differentiates the dreams of one from those of the other. This distinction draws a dividing line between the degree of revelation shown to the patriarchs on the one hand, and to Joseph and his brothers on the other.

Clearly, Joseph's dreams are prophetic, and not mere nonsense. However, they are a form of ruah hakodesh (holy inspiration), rather than *nevua* (prophecy; see Maimonides' *Guide for the Perplexed* II:45, where he specifically mentions Joseph as being on the "second level" of prophecy; see also the *Akedat Yitzhak* ad loc.). Jacob himself provides the appropriate response to Joseph's dreams:

> His father was angry at him and said: "What is this dream you dreamt? Shall I and your mother and brothers come and bow down to you?" ... but his father awaited it. (Gen. 37:11)

R. Levi adds:

> He [Jacob] took pen in hand and wrote down on what date, at what time, and at what place. (*Bereshit Raba* 84:11)

Dreams like this are precisely the kind of experience about which the *Akedat Yitzhak* writes, "Let the Giver of dreams provide their solution." These dreams are not granted in order to be put into action by the dreamer. Together with the sheer experience of prophecy, these dreams grant us the power to wait. A dream which comes true without our active involvement is one that we can acknowledge, after the fact, as a prophetic dream. Only an outright prophecy, such as God's word to Gideon, should lead to action without first waiting. Certainly, only an outright prophecy can suspend a commandment, and only as a temporary measure (*Mishneh Torah*, Yesodei HaTorah ch. 9); it is unthinkable that a dream, the outcome of which is still uncertain, should suspend the fulfillment of a commandment even temporarily. Nevertheless, it is clear that Ramban considers these dreams to be full-fledged prophecies. This position is diametrically opposed to that of the Talmud (*Berakhot* 55a).

Even if we accept Ramban's position on this point, his explanation of Joseph's behavior is untenable. The first dream was fulfilled when the brothers arrived in Egypt the first time.

> Joseph was the ruler of the land; it was he who provided for all the inhabitants. Joseph's brothers came and bowed to the ground before him. (42:26)

There were ten brothers then, excluding Benjamin, who was at home. They had come to obtain grain – the sheaves in the dream.

The second dream is fulfilled when they bring Benjamin and meet with Joseph at his palace for a meal, honoring him and offering him gifts:

> Joseph came home, and they brought him the presents they had with them to his house, and bowed down to him. (43:26)

After all eleven stars had bowed down to Joseph in his own right, as second to the king of Egypt, without any direct connection to the grain, their father's turn comes:

> He greeted them and said: "Is your old father, whom you mentioned, at peace? Is he still alive?" They said: "Your servant our father is at peace; he is still alive." They bent down and bowed. (43:27–28)

This painful scene, in which Joseph's brothers prostrate themselves before him in their father's name, and refer to him as "your servant our father," is the fulfillment of the second dream, in which the sun and the moon bow down to Joseph. The entire family (other than his mother, who was no longer alive) has bowed down to Joseph, albeit indirectly – in Jacob's case – and without realizing the full significance of their actions.

This scene will repeat itself when Judah begs for Benjamin's safety and refers to Jacob four times as "your servant our father" (44:14, 24, 27, 30–31). It must be noted at this point that Joseph arranged this episode in order to keep Benjamin in Egypt (since he could not foretell how Judah would react) **after** the second dream had been completely fulfilled. The dreams had all come true before Jacob's arrival in Egypt, including the dream in which Jacob bows down to his son. In fact, he does not physically bow to Joseph even when they are reunited in Egypt; none of the commentators suggests that he did.

The Torah does tell us that when Jacob was on his deathbed, Joseph came to see him, and "Israel bowed at the head of the bed" (47:31). But it is not clear whether his bowing is before Joseph or before God (*Megilla* 16b, *Sifrei Devarim* 6) – the simple reading suggests the latter – and certainly, his bowing does not come about through Joseph's initiative. It is precisely the verse cited by Ramban in support of his contention which actually contradicts his theory:

> Joseph recognized his brothers, but they did not recognize him. He remembered the dreams he dreamt and told them: "You are spies." (42:8–9)

> It is clear that only at this point does Joseph remember his dreams, as he suddenly realizes that the first dream has been fulfilled. (Rashi on 42:9)

Since Joseph remembers his dreams only when his brothers arrive in Egypt, why did he not send word to Jacob before that? As ruler of Egypt, it was certainly within his capacity to do so.

Ramban answers that the ten brothers' bowing down at the first meeting was not the realization of the first dream, as the eleventh brother had not yet bowed down to him. Joseph's first dream, however, does not specify the number of brothers making sheaves! Benjamin could not have been in the fields with them at the time, as he was eight years younger than Joseph and hence only nine years old.

Thus, even in a dream Joseph could not have seen Benjamin working in the fields. Even if we accept Ramban's assertion that these dreams are prophetic, we may not distort the content of the dreams. The second dream is never completely fulfilled, as Jacob himself did not bow down to Joseph, nor did Rachel, who had not been alive for many years. The family's economic dependence on Joseph cannot be considered a literal fulfillment of the sheaves' bowing down before him.

Ramban himself apparently realized the difficulties inherent in attempting to coordinate the story of the goblet with the dreams. He therefore proposes a second motive for Joseph's actions at this point:

> The second affair, which he caused by means of the goblet, was not intended to trouble them. Joseph was afraid that they hated Benjamin, or were jealous of their father's love for him as they had been jealous of [Joseph]...Perhaps Benjamin had realized that they had harmed Joseph and this had led to acrimony between them. Joseph did not want Benjamin to go with them lest they harm him, until he had verified their love for him. (Ramban on 42:9)

Abarbanel agrees:

> Even after Joseph tested his brothers by accusing them of espionage, he was still not certain whether they loved Benjamin or whether they still hated Rachel's children, so he focused on Benjamin to see whether they would try to save him. (Abarbanel on ch. 42, questions 4, 6)

This second solution is no less problematic than the first. First of all, we cannot avoid the feeling that the exegetes are attempting to explain away what seems to be an accidental outcome as a preconceived plan of events. The Torah itself indicates that Joseph simply had wanted to keep Benjamin behind, after their brothers had gone home. Possibly he feared that they would harm Benjamin at some point, as Ramban suggests, or he may have wished to reveal his identity to Benjamin alone and discuss with him plans for bringing Jacob to Egypt. He may even have intended to force Jacob to come to Egypt by holding Benjamin hostage. It might be that he simply wanted to hear from Benjamin all that had transpired since he was sold. He may have wanted Benjamin's cooperation in establishing the tribes of Rachel as a separate entity. But it seems utterly far-fetched that Joseph planned the affair of the goblet so that Judah would intervene and offer to be enslaved instead of Benjamin, forcing Joseph into an emotional situation in which, losing his self-control, he would finally reveal his identity.

All of this indeed came about, but none of it was premeditated. Joseph could not have intended to test his brothers' attitude toward Benjamin. What would he have done if, as was quite possible, they had accepted the situation as God's will, as punishment for their sin, and left Benjamin with him as they had left Simeon? Would this have proven either that they were not sorry for what they had done to Joseph or that they did not love Benjamin? Does submission to the power of a tyrant prove anything? When Abraham agreed that Sara be taken by Abimelekh, did that mean he did not love her? She herself did not object to this unpleasant means of survival in a strange land (12:10; see Ramban and *Ha'amek Davar* ad loc.).

At no point in Judah's long speech is there any mention of the brothers' feelings toward each other or toward Benjamin. Judah's expressed concern is with his "old father" whom they left behind, and who interested the ruler so much. Jacob is Judah's last resort, and Judah plays it for all it is worth, hinting all the while at Joseph's responsibility for any outcome.

Can we be sure that, had Judah not committed himself to his father under penalty of "eternal guilt," that this outburst would have occurred? It can certainly be taken as a sign of repentance in general. But it was not evoked by any feeling of love or pity toward Benjamin or Joseph, but rather by a feeling of responsibility to his father.

There are two explicit references in our story to the brothers' attitude toward Joseph. The first is during their first visit to Egypt; the second is after Jacob's death.

Joseph hears his brothers express regret at their behavior towards

him, when they had only just arrived in Egypt. This regret is coupled with
the realization that all that is befalling them is a result of that behavior:

> They said to each other: This is our fault, because of our brother;
> we saw his suffering when he cried out to us and we did not listen;
> that is why this misfortune came upon us. (42:21)

Joseph restrains himself at this point, apparently with some difficulty,
and maintains his deception. At no later time does he acquire any new
insights into their character. This confession was elicited freely without
any pressure whatsoever; they never imagined he could understand
them "because the interpreter was between them."

After Jacob's death, the brothers return to Joseph fearing retribution. Their motivations for lying to him in their father's name are
explicit – "Joseph might wish to harm us" (50:15).

Most commentators believe that they then lie and invent the story
of Jacob's deathbed charge, in order to save their lives (Rashi on 50:16;
Ramban on 45:27). Their bowing to Joseph at this point, knowing who
he is, may be considered the final fulfillment of the dreams.

In our attempt to understand Joseph's motivation for waiting so
many years, and then deceiving his brothers, we have ruled out the desire
for forcing the dreams to come true – as "dreams come to us without
our consent" – and certainly do not justify torturing old and suffering
parents. Furthermore, as we saw earlier, Joseph remembers his dreams
only when his brothers appear before him in Egypt.

Testing their regret could also not have been the reason, as he
had already heard them express repentance in his presence. He revealed
himself later only because he heard of his father's suffering. True, the
brothers, especially Judah, were found to be repentant. This was, indeed,
part of a master plan. But the plan was devised not in Joseph's court, but
in a higher domain:

> The brothers were occupied with selling Joseph, Joseph was
> occupied with mourning and fasting, Reuben was occupied with
> mourning and fasting, Jacob was occupied with mourning and

fasting, and God was occupied with creating the light of the Messiah. (*Bereshit Raba* 85:4)

When Joseph does follow his own initiative and asks the chief cupbearer to intercede before Pharaoh on his behalf, he spends two more years languishing in prison.

In summary, I believe that our question outweighs all of its proposed solutions.

II. A NEW APPROACH

I would like to propose a solution which accounts for many perplexing aspects of the story.

Our entire outlook on this story changes if we accept the fact that Joseph did not know that his brothers had fooled his father with the coat, the blood, and the lie that Joseph had been devoured by wild animals. Such thoughts never occurred to him! Hence it was Joseph who spent thirteen years of slavery in Egypt and the following years of greatness wondering: "Where is my father? Why has no one come to look for me?"

All of the factors are now reversed, when seen from Joseph's point of view. Egypt is, after all, close to Canaan, and Jacob was a rich, important and influential man, with international familial and political connections. The Midianites or Ishmaelites who brought Joseph to Egypt were his cousins; is it possible that no one from that caravan could be located in all those years? Ishmael, Medan and Midian were all children of Abraham; even after they had migrated to eastern lands, they certainly could be located. Jacob had manpower enough to marshal herds and flocks as a gift for Esau; surely he had manpower to search for Joseph. We know that Jacob does not search for his son, as he thinks Joseph is dead, but Joseph has no way of knowing this.

Joseph's wonder at his father's silence is joined by a terrible sense of anxiety which grows stronger over the years, as seasons and years pass by and no one comes. Joseph's anguish centers on his father: the voice inside him asking "where is my father?" is joined by another harsh voice – "Why did my father send me to my brothers that day? Why did they strip off my coat the moment I arrived and throw me in the pit?

Didn't he know how dangerous Simeon and Levi are, especially since I
had brought him negative reports about them? What did my brothers
tell him when they returned? Can he really have had no idea at all of
what they had done?"

The voices resound and intertwine, eliciting alternating waves
of fear and helplessness, of anger and hatred. Being thrown into the pit,
the kidnapping to Egypt, slavery – a few months would be enough to
drive him mad – and no one ever comes.

Finally, a quiet acceptance of his fate replaced the anguish. His
brothers must have succeeded in convincing Jacob, and he had been
disowned. Leah must have convinced Jacob that his vain and arrogant
son, who dreamt of ruling over them all, had to be disposed of before
he destroyed the household. Had Abraham not consented to Sara's
insistence that he expel Ishmael, despite his love for Ishmael? Had not
God Himself sanctioned this? Had not Esau lost his birthright? And
had not Isaac capitulated to Rebecca in choosing one son over another?
Perhaps God Himself had told Jacob that Joseph had sinned and had
to be expelled.

Thirteen years of torment brought in their wake a quiet acceptance of his fate. He would live according to his father's traditions but
apart from his home. He would not sin against God even though He had
rejected him; he would not be seduced by his master's wife. Years later,
when Joseph rides in the viceroy's chariot, when he shaves his beard and
stands before Pharaoh, it is clear to him that God must have decreed
that his life would be lived separately from his family.

Joseph gives expression to this feeling expression in the name he
gives his eldest son, born of an Egyptian wife:

He called him Menashe, because "God has made me forget
[*nashani*] all my labor and my father's house." (41:51)

To forget his father's house! Joseph is more subdued when his second
son is born:

[He named him] Ephraim, because "God has made me fruitful
[*hifrani*] in the land of my suffering." (41:52)

III. THE BROTHERS ARRIVE

Joseph's entire world is built on the misconception that his father has renounced him, while Jacob's world is destroyed by the misconception that Joseph is dead. Joseph's world is shaken when his brothers stand before him, not knowing who he is, and bow down to him. At that moment, he must question the new reality he has created for himself; "he remembers the dreams he dreamt about them" and he is thrown back into the past.

Stalling for time, he begins a line of inquiry – and action – which is geared to one end: to find out why his father had rejected him, if at all. He aims to keep Benjamin behind, so that his maternal brother can tell him all that has transpired. After the conversation with Benjamin, he will be able to decide whether to remain silent or to speak out.

All of Joseph's actions from this point onward – including arresting Simeon – are directed towards this goal. He wanted both to get information (could Simeon have been interrogated in prison?) and to force Jacob to send Benjamin to Egypt. The cup was planted in his sack not to test Judah – how could he have predicted his older brother's outburst? – but just the opposite. Joseph assumed that the brothers would not be able to save Benjamin, and that this would be his means of keeping Benjamin with him, ostensibly as his prisoner.

This was Joseph's plan to find out what had happened and how to deal with it.

Judah's response was an attempt to obtain Benjamin's release by appealing for mercy for his aged father. In so doing, he tells Joseph – totally unintentionally – exactly what Joseph wanted so desperately to hear, thereby freeing him, and eventually Jacob, from their mutual errors.

> Your servant our father said to us:
> > You know that my wife bore me two sons.
> > One has left me; I said he was devoured and I have not seen him since.
> > [If] you take this son too and tragedy befalls him, you will bring my old age down to *She'ol* in agony. (44:24–30)

Joseph needs to hear no more. He finally realizes the naked truth: No one has cut him off at all! Not Leah, not his brothers and, least of all, his father. He has not been forgotten!

> Joseph could no longer restrain himself before all who were stand-
> ing before him, and cried:
>> "Have every one leave me!" ...
>> and he cried out loud ...
>> and he told his brothers:
>> "I am Joseph; is my father still alive?" (45:1–3)

Does he live? Is he yet my father, who loves me and has not forgotten me? Is it possible?

Each of the players in our scene had a plan, and pursued that plan. But the plan which was finally revealed was a higher plan, geared at bringing Jacob's family to Egypt and creating the Jewish people.

All of the "forgetting" is revealed to have been a tragic mistake. Jacob symbolically acknowledges the divine plan when, even though he is blind, he knows that he must take his hand off the head of Menashe (whose name connotes forgetting) and place it on the head of Ephraim (whose name connotes fruitfulness).

The misunderstanding, however, does have its results. Not Joseph, but his two sons, will replace him in the list of twelve tribes.

> And now, your two sons born to you in the land of Egypt before
> I came to you in Egypt are mine; Ephraim and Menashe, like
> Reuben and Simeon, belong to me. (48:5)

The ten tribes who were exiled and not heard from since (see the dis-
pute in *Sanhedrin* 110b–111a about whether they will return), the division of the Israelite kingdom into two, all of the "forgetting" of our ancient forefather – are but illusions. All of what we consider reality is revealed as secondary to the divine plan – "Our father is still alive."

IV. THE TORAH'S VIEWPOINT

If we look at the text and the text alone, this conclusion is well-nigh unavoidable. This interpretation is directly based on Judah's words, paraphrasing his father: "I said he was devoured and I have not seen him since." Now we see why these words caused Joseph to break down and reveal himself – for he learned for the first time that his father was deceived; his father did not reject him! Now we understand why Joseph names his son Menashe, "forgetting." Only this interpretation is free of the assumption that Joseph meticulously planned exactly what transpired, while the Torah itself presents the climax as a total surprise to all who were involved in it.

This explanation is also mandated by the historical paradigm, as it is presented in the Torah's view of Jewish history:

> Is Ephraim My cherished son, the child I played with, that when I speak of him, I should be reminded of him? But My insides pine for him; I will be compassionate toward him, says the Lord. (Jer. ch. 31)

Jewish history reverberates until our times with questions of forgetfulness and dispossession (see especially Jer. ch. 3, 31) – and, on the other hand, the discovery of errors and repentance.

"Twelve brothers are we" – not one is missing! If one seems missing, it is only an illusion, a tragic misconception which will, at the correct time, be revealed.

And finally, only this explanation merges with the Jewish mystical tradition, which differentiates between the revealed and the hidden, between the best-laid plans of even the purest of men and the plans of Providence, and weaves even failings and misunderstandings into the light of the Redemption, bringing all twelve tribes together at last.

The Meaning of Joseph's Estrangement

by Rav Yaakov Medan

Iwould like to critique the theory offered by Rav Yoel Bin-Nun
to explain why Joseph did not contact his father, and to offer an alternate explanation.

I. CRITIQUE OF RAV BIN-NUN'S THEORY

I find untenable Rav Bin-Nun's thesis that Joseph suspected that his
father had rejected him and had approved of the brothers' actions. Joseph
knew that he was, after all, his father's favorite son, and that his father
had made him the striped coat. He also knew that his father had loved
Rachel more than his other wives. Above all, would a man like Jacob
behave so deceitfully, sending Joseph to his brothers on the false pretext
of ascertaining their well-being, intending in fact that they sell him as a
slave? Is there a son who would suspect his father of such a deed? This
assumption is totally unrealistic.

It also remains unclear why Joseph, surprised that his father did
not seek him out, came to harbor the kind of suspicions attributed to
him by R. Bin-Nun. How could he be certain that his father knew of
the sale, but refrained from searching for him? Why did it not occur
to him that his father regarded him as dead? To this day, a person who

disappears without a trace is presumed dead. Why should we assume that Joseph did not believe that the brothers were lying to his father? It was precisely because the brothers did not habitually report their actions to their father that Joseph found it necessary to tell his father all of their misdeeds (37:2).

In addition, R. Bin-Nun claims that Joseph's stubborn silence was broken upon hearing Judah report Jacob's words: "He was surely devoured and I have not seen him since" (44:28). Joseph realized at this point that his father had not deserted him. However, according to the simplest reading of the text, Joseph's resistance broke down when Judah offered himself as a slave instead of Benjamin:

> ... Therefore, please let your servant remain as a slave to my lord instead of the boy, and let the boy go back with his brothers. For how can I go back to my father unless the boy is with me? Let me not see to the sorrow that would overcome my father! ... Joseph could no longer restrain himself. (44:32–45:1)

R. Bin-Nun claims that Joseph's feelings of rejection by his family are the foundation for the naming of his first born "Menashe," meaning, "God has made me forget my hardship and my father's home" (*nashani* = made me forget).

In my opinion, the meaning of the verse is different. "My hardship" (*amali*) is to be understood as follows (see Ibn Ezra on Gen. 6:13): "God has made me forget completely my hardship and the **hardship** of my parental home." Joseph does not offer thanks to God for having made him forget his parental home, but rather offers thanks for enabling him to forget his tribulations in his father's house. It is only after Joseph rises to the throne that he is able to make sense of his suffering in the two previous episodes, in prison ("*amali*") and in his father's house ("*beit avi*").

II. AN ALTERNATIVE EXPLANATION

Abarbanel offers the following explanation for Joseph's not contacting his father while in Egypt:

> Even after Joseph tested his brothers by accusing them of espio-

nage, he was still not certain whether they loved Benjamin or whether they still hated Rachel's children, so he focused on Benjamin to see whether they would try to save him. (Abarbanel on ch. 42, questions 4 & 6)

Joseph's behavior is part of an overall scheme to test the brothers and provide them with an opportunity to repent fully for selling him into slavery. The sin of Joseph's brothers in selling him is not one of the milder misdeeds of the book of Genesis. This sin – selling a free man into slavery – is considered in the Torah and Prophets (Ex. 21:16; 20:13; Deut. 27:7; Joel ch. 4; Amos 2:6–10; and many more) as one of the most severe sins that can be committed. It is comparable to the sin of Cain and the sins of the generation of the Flood, the generation of the Tower of Babel, and the people of Sodom. It is only natural that the punishments meted out to Cain, to the generation of the Flood and to the people of Sodom should be replaced here by the repentance of Joseph's brothers. This repentance is one of the foundations upon which all of Genesis rests – together with the punishment of sinners – and it should not be presented as an insignificant detail related only in connection with Joseph's mistake. The story of the brothers' repentance is equal in weight and importance to the story of the Flood and the overturning of Sodom – if not greater than them.

Reuben and Judah were vying for the family leadership, Jacob having effectively ceased playing the leadership role (see for example 34:5; 34:13–14; 35:22; 43:5). After Simeon and Levi are excluded from the race for leadership, the struggle continues between Reuben and Judah. It finds expression in their argument as to Joseph's fate (37:22, 26–27), in the recognition of the sin of his sale (42:22 vs. 44:16), in the assumption of responsibility for Benjamin in Egypt (42:37 vs. 43:8–9) and in additional verses in the Torah.

Reuben and Judah were each engaged in a process of penitence for similar sins – Reuben for having slept with his father's wife (as appears from the simple textual reading); Judah for having lain, albeit unknowingly, with his son's wife. It seems clear that their individual repentance is also part of the leadership struggle.

At first glance, there seems to be no connection between Reuben's sin with his father's wife or Judah's sin with his son's wife and the selling of Joseph. This, however, is misleading. According to the simple reading of the text, Reuben's intention when committing his sin was to inherit his father's leadership role during his father's lifetime, like Absalom who slept with David's concubine. His attempt to rescue Joseph and Joseph's dreams of royalty (37:20) are part of his repentance for his sin with Bilha.

The proximity of the story of Judah and Tamar to the selling of Joseph indicates a connection as well. The chain of disasters that strike Judah, the loss of his wife and two sons, is apparently a punishment for selling Joseph. Reuben later advances the strange suggestion that Jacob kill his two sons, should he fail to return Benjamin from Egypt (42:37). It would seem that he was influenced by the punishment Judah had received for selling Joseph – the death of his two sons. This terrible punishment for a terrible sin is branded into Reuben's consciousness. Reuben is ready to receive the same punishment if he deserts Benjamin in Egypt.

Initially, Judah did not imagine that his sons died due to his sin, believing instead that "Tamar's fate is that her husband will die" (*Yevamot* 34; see also Gen. 38:11). Finally, Judah realizes that Tamar was in the right and he admits, "She is more righteous than I" (38:26). Only at this stage did he realize that she was not destined to have her husbands die, but rather that it was his destiny to lose his sons. The sin was his. From this recognition he rebuilds his shattered home.

The process of repentance accompanies the brothers wherever they go. When the Egyptian viceroy commands them to bring Benjamin, the second son of Rachel, the brothers are immediately reminded of the sale of Joseph. The two contenders – Reuben and Judah – respond in character. Reuben sees only the punishment for the crime, and he does not suggest any means of rectification.

And Reuben answered them: "Did I not tell you, Do not sin against the child; but you did not listen, and now his blood is being avenged" (42:22).

Judah acknowledges his sin, but also suggests a positive path of repentance for the evil done. He is not satisfied with sackcloth and fasting, which are merely expressions of mourning and acceptance of the verdict.

And they tore their clothes ... And Judah said, "What shall we say to my lord? What shall we speak? Or how shall we clear ourselves? God has revealed the sin of your servants; we have become my lord's slaves." (44:13–17)

Further on, Judah suggests firm action:

Let your servant stay instead of the boy as a slave to my lord and let the boy go up with his brothers. (44:33)

From Judah's speech, it is apparent that when he said, "God has revealed the sin of your servants," he was not confessing to stealing the cup. He considered the whole episode of the stolen goblet as a fabrication. Otherwise, there is no sense in his recounting of Benjamin's journey to Egypt, nor in his suggesting that he replace Benjamin. Rather, "God has revealed the **sin** of your servants" undoubtedly refers to the selling of Joseph.

Similarly, Judah's words to his father, "If I bring him not to you and set him before you, then I shall have **sinned** to you for all days" (43:9), indicate his understanding of the connection between Joseph's being brought down to Egypt and Benjamin being brought down to Egypt. Benjamin's abandonment in Egypt would be a continuation of his grievous sin of selling Joseph. Otherwise, how can we understand what sin he is referring to and why he should be punished if Benjamin is taken forcibly? We must therefore view the necessity of bringing Benjamin down to Egypt as a consequence of the sin. For Judah, protecting Benjamin at all costs is the atonement demanded for the selling of Joseph. In offering their respective propositions, Reuben and Judah remain faithful to their personalities: Reuben through acceptance of the punishment, and Judah through confrontation with the sin itself.

III. JOSEPH'S MOTIVATIONS

We have attempted, then, to prove that all of the brothers' actions – and particularly those of the two leaders, Reuben and Judah – are influenced and dictated by the sin of selling Joseph and the need to atone for it. Our impression is that the ultimate structure of the family and the fate of the brothers depend on their repentance being accepted. Joseph knows this, and regards himself as a partner in this process – both because of his close (passive) connection with the sin, and because of his constant feeling, especially because of his dreams, that he is responsible for the future of Jacob's family.

Perhaps Joseph was troubled by the brothers' terrible sin and the prospects for the future of Jacob's household no less than he was concerned for his own personal fate. From the time he is sold, he begins to build – along with his own personal life – the process of reunification of the family. It is preferable that this reunification not be forced upon the brothers, but rather that it be brought about through good will and love. If Joseph would send a messenger to his father, letting him know that he was still alive, Jacob would admittedly have redeemed him from Egypt and restored him to the family as a free person, but he would still be hated by his brothers, the sons of Leah, and there would be no guarantee that they would not make further attempts to rid themselves of him. Joseph did not want such a situation; he wanted a reunification based on the brothers' regret for their sin and arising from their complete repentance.

Joseph had commanded his brothers to bring Benjamin to Egypt. When the brothers actually brought Benjamin to Egypt, despite the danger, in order to redeem Simeon and to buy food, Joseph, who was unaware of Judah's assumption of guardianship and its importance, presumably saw the brothers' action as yet another failure to meet the test and challenge that he had set before them.

Joseph cries three times. The first two times he cries in private, and then restrains himself. The third time he breaks down totally and cries, openly and without control. R. Bin-Nun cites the third episode as proof that Joseph was taken by surprise by the developments, and therefore concludes that this outcome had not been planned by Joseph. However, R. Bin-Nun ignores the obvious connection between the three instances. Let us examine these three episodes.

A. **First Tears:**
The brothers are subjected to an intensive interrogation during three days of imprisonment, inducing them to repent for their sin and accept the punishment and suffering, with Reuben in the lead:

On the third day, Joseph said to them, "Do this and you shall live, for I am a God-fearing man. If you are honest men, let one of you brothers be held in your place of detention, while the rest of you go and take home rations for your starving households; but you must bring me your youngest brother, that your words may be verified and that you may not die." And they did accordingly.

They said to one another, "Alas, we are being punished on account of our brother [Joseph], because we looked on at his anguish, yet paid no heed as he pleaded with us. That is why this distress has come upon us."

Then Reuben spoke up and said to them, "Did I not tell you, Do not sin against the child; but you did not listen, and now his blood is being avenged."

They did not know that Joseph understood, for there was an interpreter between him and them. He turned away from them, and wept. But he came back to them and spoke to them; and he took Simeon from among them and had him bound before their eyes. (42:18–24)

We have previously defined this kind of repentance as "Reuben's repentance," a repentance which involves submission and acceptance of the verdict, but lacks a program for improvement and change. Joseph is prepared to accept his brothers' confession and their submission. He witnesses the beginning of the ten brothers' reconnection to the sons of Rachel, and he cries (42:24). But this is not sufficient for him. He requires a fuller, deeper repentance.

B. Second Tears

Joseph expected that the brothers would return to him empty-handed, placing themselves in danger by explaining to him that they had decided not to endanger Benjamin for the sake of Simeon and were willing to suffer the shame of hunger. This is what would have happened, had Jacob had his way. Thus Joseph was disappointed when it became clear to him that the brothers had brought Benjamin in order to redeem Simeon, despite the danger to their youngest brother.

> Looking about, he saw his brother Benjamin, his mother's son, and asked, "Is this your youngest brother of whom you spoke to me?" And he went on, "May God be gracious to you, my boy."
> With that, Joseph hurried out, for he was overcome with feeling toward his brother and was on the verge of tears; he went into a room and wept there. (43:29–30)

Joseph is still unaware of Judah's assumption of responsibility for Benjamin. His mercy is aroused when he realizes that his younger brother's fate is to be no better than his own – Joseph views Benjamin's being brought to Egypt as a recurrence of his own sale. True, in this case it is brought on by hunger and is not the outcome of jealousy or hatred. Nonetheless, this was not the total repentance that was expected in the wake of the confessions he had heard from the brothers and Reuben previously.

The verse tells us that Joseph feels compassion towards Benjamin, and weeps in private. Joseph believes that Judah, the man who had proposed his sale, had prevailed over Reuben, the man who had tried to save him. This is the only possible explanation of Joseph's crying over Benjamin, his tears being tears of mercy for Benjamin and not tears of happiness at the event of their meeting. Why else should the exiled brother, who had spent a third of his life in prison, have pitied his thirty-year old brother, who had remained with his father and raised a large family?

c. Third Tears

Joseph decided to test his brothers once more. This time, however, the test would be more difficult. He makes his brothers jealous of Benjamin in the same way that they had once been jealous of him. He displays more outward affection for Benjamin than for them and increases his portion five times over, as well as giving him a striped coat (and five other garments [43:34]). He also attempts to arouse the brothers' hatred towards Benjamin for having stolen his goblet, an act that re-implicated them for the crime of espionage. Joseph's aim is to test their reaction to the prospect of Benjamin's permanent enslavement in Egypt.

The brothers rend their garments (parallel to Joseph's torn coat). Judah says, "God has revealed the sin of your servants," and then offers himself into permanent slavery as atonement for his lifelong sin towards his father:

> Judah approached him and said: "…Now your servant has pledged himself for the boy to my father, saying, If I do not bring him back to you, I shall have sinned to my father for all days. Therefore, please let your servant remain as a slave to my lord instead of the boy, and let the boy go back with his brothers. For how can I go back to my father unless the boy is with me? Let me not be witness to the woe that would overtake my father."
>
> Joseph could no longer control himself before all his attendants, and he cried out, "Have everyone withdraw from me!" So there was no one else about when Joseph made himself known to his brothers. His sobs were so loud that the Egyptians could hear, and so the news reached Pharaoh's palace. (44:32–45:2)

At this point, Joseph is convinced of their total repentance. Judah's act combines two kinds of repentance. The first form of repentance is that required by the early mystics (foremost, Rabbi Eliezer of Worms, author of the *Sefer Rokeaḥ*), whereby penance must counterbalance the crime. Judah, in a torn garment as a permanent slave in Egypt, is in the exact position he had placed Joseph. Secondly, we have the repentance as defined by Rambam:

> What is complete repentance? When a person is confronted with the opportunity to repeat his sin but restrains himself because of repentance, and not because of fear or weakness.(*Mishneh Torah*, Hilkhot Teshuva 2:1)

Judah is now prepared to give his life to save Benjamin. Joseph comes to realize his mistake in crying for pity over Benjamin. He understands that Benjamin's being brought down to Egypt was not the result of the brothers' disdain for Benjamin but rather the result of Judah's becoming Benjamin's guarantor. Judah's repentance, including his attempt to amend the past, is a continuation and completion of Reuben's atonement.

Joseph's weeping for the third time is a continuation of his weeping the first time, when Reuben submitted to the divine punishment.

When the repentance is complete, Joseph is no longer capable of restraining himself, and he weeps openly. At this stage, the brothers' repentance for selling Joseph into slavery is complete, and Joseph can reveal himself to them.

(This presentation of Rav Medan's ideas is abridged from a much longer article in Megadim, vol. 2.)

RAV BIN-NUN RESPONDS:

After carefully reading Rav Medan's detailed arguments, I nevertheless maintain that my presentation of the events is the correct one.

There is clearly a process of repentance and rectification on the part of Joseph's brothers, and this is our guide to understanding the affair. But all of this is God's plan, not Joseph's. All of R. Medan's evidence proving a process of repentance is correct; but there is no reason to credit Joseph with this.

At the end of Genesis (50:15–21) we find the brothers, after Jacob's death, prostrating themselves before Joseph and offering themselves as slaves. This indicates that their prior repentance had not been complete, and they did not regard Joseph as having orchestrated (and accepted) their repentance earlier. Thus, the challenge of repentance offered to the brothers regarding Benjamin is a challenge issuing from God. Joseph himself was forever acting according to natural, human considerations, as I explained.

It should be noted that R. Medan gives an extremely contrived interpretation of the verse explaining Menashe's name, "For God has forced me to forget all my tribulations and my father's house." The verse seemingly coheres with my explanation. He also totally ignores the significance of Judah's quotation of Jacob's words, "You have known that my wife bore me two; one departed from me and I said he was surely devoured." There is no proof that Joseph's inability to restrain his tears was due solely to Judah's final words and not to Judah's speech as a whole.

Reuben and Judah

by Rabbanit Sharon Rimon

I. INTRODUCTION

Our *parashot* deal with Jacob's sons and the relationships between them –
specifically, the issue of leadership. In 1 Chronicles, chapter five, the
subject is summarized in the following words:

> The sons of Reuben, the firstborn of Israel – for he was the first-
> born, but when he defiled his father's bed his birthright was given
> to the children of Joseph, son of Israel, but not the actual first-
> born status; for Judah prevailed over his brothers, and dominion
> emerged from him, but the birthright was given to Joseph.

These verses describe the birthright being taken from Reuben and
transferred to Joseph and Judah. Joseph is given the birthright in terms
of inheritance (i.e., the double portion usually given to the firstborn),
while Judah is given leadership.

Why are these firstborn privileges taken from Reuben? According to verse 1, it is because of the episode of Bilha that the birthright is
given to Joseph. But why is leadership bestowed upon Judah? Here the
reason is different: "For Judah prevailed over his brothers, and dominion
emerged from him." Judah acquired leadership quite naturally from his

brothers. The transfer of leadership from Reuben to Judah was not the result of Reuben's sin with Bilha, but rather a reflection of Judah's greater suitability for leadership than Reuben.[1]

Let us examine two incidents that demonstrate the respective leadership of Judah and of Reuben, and try to understand the leadership style of each of them – or the differences between them. This may help us to understand why "Judah prevailed over his brothers" and was bequeathed the leadership role.

II. THE SALE OF JOSEPH (GEN. 37:18–30)

When the brothers conspire to kill Joseph, how do the two "leaders," Judah and Reuben, respond? While Judah offers no response at this stage, Reuben hears of the plan and immediately tries to save Joseph. Were it not for his immediate intervention, Joseph would have been killed there and then. However, the verse also covertly conveys another message. It starts with the words "Reuben heard [of it]." From here we deduce that Reuben was not really a participant in the discussion among the brothers. He stands on the sidelines and hears them talking. This would indicate the possibility that there was a certain distance, or lack of partnership, between Reuben and his brothers.

The brothers seek to kill Joseph, and Reuben tells them: "Let us not take his life." Do the brothers listen to him? In the next verse there is no response on the part of the brothers, but rather another utterance by Reuben. This tells us that the brothers did not listen to him, and therefore Reuben was forced to speak again in an attempt to persuade them to adopt a different plan. He tries to persuade them that killing Joseph will be regarded as a sin on their part, and proposes an alternative: instead of killing Joseph with their own hands, they should cast him into a pit.

Reuben's suggestion here represents a different approach from the one that he proposed before. Now, he seemingly agrees with the brothers, agreeing with their idea of killing Joseph, but suggesting that it be done in a "cleaner" way: Joseph will die by himself, in the pit. The

---

1. As Rashi comments ad loc: "Even if Reuben had not defiled Jacob's bed and the birthright had not been taken from him, Judah would still be the best suited to rule."

brothers will thereby achieve two objectives. On the one hand, Joseph will be dead. On the other hand, they will not be directly responsible for the death; they will not have killed him with their own hands, but rather will have caused his death indirectly, and this will not be considered spilling blood.

Reuben's true intention was to save Joseph from the pit, as the Torah testifies. But because the brothers do not listen to him and he is unsuccessful in standing up to them to prevent outright murder, he is forced to make an indirect proposal. He seemingly accepts their position, agrees to their plan, but suggests a "better" alternative in the hope that they will find it acceptable. They accept Reuben's suggestion – but attention should be paid to the fact that the brothers do not respond verbally to Reuben. Even the text omits noting, "His brothers listened to him," or, "They cast him into the pit as Reuben had said." There is no utterance that expresses any attention on the part of the brothers to his words.

The brothers sit down to eat bread, and when the Ishmaelites appear, Judah says: "What profit is it if we kill our brother?" From these words it is clear that the brothers are still intending to kill Joseph! Reuben was unsuccessful in deterring them from this plan. The brothers were not prepared to hear him and Reuben was not strong enough to stand up to them. He folded and, at least outwardly, accepted their position – that they should kill Joseph – but suggested a "cleaner" way of doing so. Therefore, when the brothers cast Joseph into the pit and sit down to eat bread, they are still expecting Joseph to die.

The story could develop in a number of different directions: It is possible that the brothers would have left Joseph to die in the pit; Reuben would have saved him without their knowledge, and then perhaps there would have been another struggle with the brothers trying to kill Joseph. Or perhaps the brothers would have waited close to the pit to see him die, not allowing Reuben to save him. Then, either Joseph would have died in the pit, or the brothers would have ensured his death, by either direct or indirect means.

However, the story ends differently, in the wake of Judah's intervention. Let us examine Judah's words, and his relationship with his brothers:

A. Judah sits with his brothers to eat bread. His suggestion to them is also prefaced with the words, "Judah said to his brothers…" Clearly, he is part of the group; he is not an outsider. This fact stands out against the background of the relations between Reuben and the brothers. At the beginning of the story the brothers "said to each other…come, let us kill him" – they are unanimous in their intention;[2] Reuben is not party to their discussion, but rather hears from the sidelines and intervenes: "Reuben heard of it, and [sought to] save him from their hand." Now, too, with the brothers sitting together to eat, Reuben is not with them – as we shall see from the continuation of the story.

B. Judah speaks in the first person; he includes himself together with them: "What profit is it if **we kill** our brother and **we cover** his blood? Come, **let us sell** him to the Ishmaelites, and **let our hand** not be upon him, for he is **our brother, our flesh.**" Reuben, in contrast, spoke in the second person: "Do not spill [*al tishpekhu*] blood; cast [*hashlikhu*] him into the pit…but do not lay [*al tishleḥu*] a hand upon him." Reuben does not count include himself within the company of the brothers.

C. The content of his words: Judah starts by asking, "What profit is it if we kill our brother." Rashi explains: "'What profit' – i.e., what monetary gain." Ibn Ezra: "What benefit." According to both commentators, Judah tells his brothers that they will gain nothing by killing Joseph. Afterwards, he suggests: "Come, let us sell him to the Ishmaelites." Having clarified to them that there will be no profit from killing Joseph, he presents a profitable solution: selling him. This will earn them real money.

Judah's suggestion is shocking: he is relating to the killing or selling of his brother in terms of monetary profit and loss! Seemingly, if it were more profitable to kill Joseph, then that is what he would advocate! But after mentioning the consideration of profit, he also invokes the moral consideration: "Let our hand not be upon him, for he is our brother, our flesh."

---

2. Judah's participation is also problematic; he sides with the brothers when they seek to kill Joseph!

Why does Judah mention this moral concern only at the end? According to the order of his speech, one might think that the consideration of profit is of greater importance to him, and therefore he mentions it first. However, we may also understand this differently: Judah seeks to persuade his brothers. Therefore he does not start by preaching to them, for this will likely cause them to distance themselves from him and to close their ears and their hearts to his argument. Rather, he starts with an argument that they will be prepared to hear. Hence, he starts by presenting the "profit" consideration, and only afterwards introduces the moral issue. Thus he succeeds in persuading the brothers to accept his plan.

Reuben, in contrast, starts with the moral case. While this testifies to his significant moral stand, it may be that his choice to approach the situation from this angle is what caused the brothers to close their ears. Later on, in order to save Joseph, Reuben is forced to backtrack, as it were, from his moral stand and to agree to the idea of killing Joseph, suggesting only that it be done in an indirect way. This withdrawal from a moral stand is dishonorable, and the brothers do not identify with his words.

In order to persuade people it is not sufficient to hold a meaningful and just position; one has to know how to present one's case in such a way as to enter people's hearts, without arousing opposition. Judah was successful in this; Reuben failed.

d. Finally, close attention to Judah's words reveals an interesting phenomenon: twice, in referring to Joseph, he mentions the word *"aḥenu"* – our brother. This word appears both at the beginning of his speech, as he presents the "profit" argument, and at the end, when he speaks of the moral issue. From the outset he creates the sense that they are talking about "our brother." This feeling is further reinforced when he says, "For he is our brother, our flesh." Judah introduces into his words an emotion that has so far not featured, and it touches the brothers' hearts.

The word "brother" (*aḥ*) appears four times in the two verses that record Judah's words. Twice it is used to describe the relations between Judah and his brothers, and twice Judah refers to Joseph as "our brother." It would seem that fraternity is one of the important motifs in Judah's behavior and speech. This, apparently, is one of the most influential factors in persuading his brothers. The sense of Judah's partnership with them causes the brothers to listen to him, and the fact that he includes Joseph within this partnership, calling him "our brother," leads them to see Joseph in a different light: he is not their enemy, but their brother.

According to the above, it would seem that the fact that Judah starts his speech with the profit motive is matter of tactics rather than one of principle. The profit motive is not Judah's primary concern, but he uses it as a means to persuade the brothers.

Reuben, in contrast, does not address the sense of fraternity at all. He does not call Joseph "our brother." Just as he is removed from the other brothers, so he is removed from Joseph. While his words about saving him are moral, they are devoid of emotion. And his words fail to enter his brothers' hearts.

The result is clear – Judah's words are accepted by the brothers, and the Torah takes pains to emphasize this: "His brothers listened to him." Against the background of this emphasis, the failure of the brothers to listen to Reuben stands out all the more starkly.

In any event, the fact that Reuben was not with the brothers during the meal testifies to his severance from them. Reuben, as we have already seen, is not one of the group; he does not regard himself as being included together with the rest of the brothers. He is not party to their discussions, nor to their meals together. While this situation does have its advantages – he is not party to their evil counsel – his distance from the brothers is a factor in their not accepting his words.

The fact that Reuben is not together with his brothers at this critical time is most revealing. If Reuben sees that his brothers seek to kill Joseph, he knows that he has not succeeded in deterring them and they still want Joseph dead, how can he leave the scene at such a fateful moment? At any second something could happen that would change everything! Admittedly, he intends to save Joseph – but if he would take real responsibility for his brother's fate, he would sit with the brothers and take part in their discussion, in order to avoid a rekindling of violent intent, in order to avoid any undesirable development that may harm Joseph. Reuben's absence at these critical moments testifies to the fact that he does not follow his fraternal responsibility to the end. Ultimately, when Reuben comes to the pit and discovers that Joseph is gone, he tears his clothes and suffers great remorse – but over what? Over himself: "And as for me – where shall I go?"

What do the brothers reply to Reuben? According to the text, the brothers offer no response to Reuben's anguish. They do not respond to his pain. The next verse already describes the ruse: they will dip Joseph's coat into blood, and send it to their father. The brothers prepare an alibi to absolve themselves of responsibility. Admittedly, the brothers are engaging in an act that matches Reuben's line of thought: Reuben now has no idea how he is to approach his father, how he can take responsibility for the act. The brothers do something that will relieve Reuben – and all of them – of responsibility. But the text does not describe any explicit reaction by the brothers to Reuben's words. It is as if they are saying to him, "Is that what you're worried about? That's no problem. We can easily absolve you of all responsibility for what happened."

III. DESCENT TO EGYPT

Several years later, when the brothers come to Egypt to buy food and Joseph – as the second-to-the-king – subjects them to unusual trials and demands, we read of a discussion among the brothers recalling the sale:

> They said to one another: But we are guilty for our brother, for we saw his torment, when he begged us and we did not listen; therefore this trouble has come upon us.
>
> And Reuben answered them, saying: Did I not speak to you, saying: Do not sin against the boy – but you did not listen, and now his blood is required. (42:21–22)

Once again we are witness to a conversation among the brothers, with the expression "they said to one another" recalling their earlier conspiracy to kill Joseph, which was introduced with the same words. In both cases the brothers "say to one another," and in both cases Reuben is an onlooker; he is not party to the discussion, and he offers a comment from the outside.

In recalling the sale of Joseph, the brothers describe the event in emotional language: they mention Joseph's pleading and their own cruelty towards him. It seems that they view this as the most serious aspect of the crime, as Ramban explains:

> "They regard their own cruelty as deserving of greater punishment than the sale, for their brother – their own flesh – was begging and pleading with them, but they had no mercy…"

The text takes pains to emphasize, in the brothers' words, "We are guilty for **our brother.**" It was Judah who had inculcated in them the feeling that Joseph was their brother, and that it was therefore proper for them to have mercy on him. Now, as they recall the event many years later, their attitude towards the event is still colored by Judah's view of it: He is our brother, our flesh, and we did not have pity on him. Although we did not kill him, we sinned towards him.

Reuben's reaction is interesting. Firstly, he is removed from the company of the brothers: "Reuben answered them"; he is not party to the preceding communal breast-beating. The brothers feel guilty for their cruelty towards Joseph, and Reuben does not share in this sense of guilt (after all, he tried to save Joseph, and he had no part in the sale!). Rather, he stands apart and tells them: "I told you so!" A person who makes such a statement has no empathy for what the other person is going through; all he wants is to have it on record that he was right. Once again, the chasm separating Reuben from the other brothers is revealed.

Once again, Reuben emphasizes the spilling of blood as a sin that hovers over the brothers, and once again he makes no reference to any emotional connection to Joseph. The brothers echo Judah's stance – "He is our brother" – while Reuben repeats his own previous position – "Do not spill blood."

Another significant aspect to Reuben's words is the fact that he himself declares, "You did not listen." This serves to reinforce our understanding that at first Reuben had tried to prevent the killing of Joseph, and only after he was ignored did he suggest that Joseph be cast into the pit.[3] Here Reuben explicitly states that the brothers did not listen

---

3. See Ramban and Abarbanel on Gen. 37:22.

to him, and this highlights the difference between himself and Judah, concerning whom we read: "His brothers listened."

IV. THE GUARANTEE TO BRING BENJAMIN HOME

The brothers return home from Egypt and describe to their father how the Egyptian ruler treated them, with his demand that they bring Benjamin with them the next time they go. When Jacob refuses, Reuben responds immediately to his father's words in an attempt to persuade him:

> Reuben spoke to his father, saying: Slay my two sons if I do not bring him to you; give him into my hand and I shall return him to you.

Reuben meant to persuade Jacob to send Benjamin, but his words have the opposite effect. Before Reuben spoke up, Jacob merely expressed sorrow and his reservations. Now, he refuses explicitly to allow Benjamin to go: "He said: My son shall not go down with you." Reuben's offer has brought about a hardening of Jacob's stance, instead of a softening. Later on, however, Judah succeeds in persuading his father to send Benjamin with them. Why is this so? Does Jacob not trust Reuben? Or is Reuben's timing perhaps not propitious? Perhaps it is his suggestion itself that is problematic?

Perhaps Reuben's timing was wrong. The brothers have just returned, with a fearful account of what they endured in Egypt. Jacob has not yet had time to digest what has happened and to think logically. This is not the time to pressure him; he should be left alone to calm down and to consider his options. In addition, the brothers have just brought food from Egypt, and so Jacob is in no hurry to send Benjamin. When all of the food is finished he will understand that there is no choice, and he will agree to send him. Hence, it is possible that Jacob agrees to Judah's offer (43:3–5) while refusing Reuben's offer simply because of their respective timing. This, too, is an important quality: to know when to say something to a person so that he will accept the message rather than opposing it.

However, is Reuben's offer rejected only because of its timing? His offer contains two problematic aspects. What does he mean by offering that his own two sons be slain? Is this supposed to calm and comfort Jacob; will this help him? As Rashi comments:

> He did not accept Reuben's words. He said: What a foolish first-born son. He suggests that his own sons be slain – as if they are only his children, and not my grandchildren!

What Reuben means, obviously, is to make an oath – typically undertaken "by the life of" a close relative – the intention being to promise that he will do everything in his power to fulfill his oath because he does not want his own sons to die. But even with the best of intentions, one has to know how to say something in such a way that it will be accepted by the listener.[4] The very idea of suggestion that his sons be slain is most peculiar, but for Jacob it touches an especially sensitive nerve. He is suffering in his bereavement: Joseph is gone, Simeon is gone, he is worried about Benjamin; is the idea that his grandsons, too, might die the best that Reuben can offer him?!

In addition, Reuben presents his case in the negative, "Slay my two sons," instead of focusing on the positive aspect of his commitment. If he would say: "Give him into my hand and I shall return him to you," and only afterwards utter his oath, the whole proposal would sound better. If he would first emphasize his commitment to bringing Benjamin home, perhaps Jacob would accept it. But Reuben starts off by first emphasizing the negative, the worst-case scenario that will come about if Benjamin does not return.

---

4. As noted in several *midrashim*. *Bereshit Raba*, 91:9: "Rabbi said: He is a foolish firstborn. Are they your sons but not mine? How can you say such a thing?!"; *Avot DeRabbi Natan*: "He who asks an improper question and provides an impertinent answer – this is Reuben. As it is written, 'Slay my two sons...' Was Jacob then a murderer? One who asks a pertinent question and answers properly – this is Judah, as it is written: 'Judah said to his father, Israel: Send the boy with me...I shall be surety for him; you may require him from my hand.'"; *Bereshit Raba* 98: "When someone used to utter a well-thought statement before Rabbi Tarfon, he used to say: 'Excellent!' And when someone used to say something worthless, he would say: 'My son shall not go down with you.'"

Thus, Reuben states his oath with good intentions; he means to promise his father that he will make every effort to return Benjamin safely. But the timing of his proposal, along with the over-the-top style that serves only to highlight the danger, deter Jacob even more strongly: "My son shall not go down with you."

When all of the food that they brought from Egypt is used up, Jacob asks his sons to go back to Egypt and bring more. Since Jacob's categorical refusal to allow Benjamin to go to Egypt, no one has dared to raise the subject for further discussion. The brothers make no mention of going back to Egypt. Only when Jacob himself initiates the move does Judah use the opportunity to explain the situation to Jacob in the clearest possible terms: he emphasizes twice, at the beginning of his speech and at the end, that "the man" – the Egyptian viceroy – told them, "You shall not see my face unless your brother is with you." In other words, there is no possibility of going to Egypt without Benjamin. Judah continues and presents Jacob with two choices. If you send Benjamin – we shall go down and bring food; if you do not send him, we shall not go down, and – obviously – there will be no food. Judah presents the situation clearly, objectively and unemotionally; he leaves the decision to Jacob: "You decide," he is telling him, "the responsibility is yours alone."

Jacob responds with sorrow and despair: Why have you done this to me? The utterance is not productive, nor does it answer directly the choice presented by Judah. Jacob is well aware that he has no choice, and he must decide, but the choice hurts him, and his response is one of pain rather than one of logic. The brothers attempt to rationalize what occurred: we did not tell him our story of our own initiative, and we could not have guessed that the man would want us to bring Benjamin. There was no logic to it!

But Jacob was not asking a logical question that required an answer; he was expressing profound anguish. Judah understands this, and he makes no attempt to answer the question; he gets back to the point – the matter of going down to Egypt:

> Judah said to Israel, his father: Send the boy with me, that we may arise and go and that we may live and not die, both we and you, and our children.

> I shall be his surety; from my hand you may require him.
> If I do not bring him to you and present him before you, I will
> have sinned to you forever.
>
> Had we not tarried, we would now have returned a sec-
> ond time. (44:10)

Once again, Judah presents the two possibilities. If Jacob sends Benjamin – "we will live"; if not – we will all die. He emphasizes "we, and you, and our children," as if to tell Jacob, "Weigh the two alternatives: the certain death of all of us, versus the possibility of something happening to Benjamin."

"I shall be surety for him; from my hand my you require him" – these words parallel those previously spoken by Reuben. Judah, too, undertakes to be personally responsible for returning Benjamin safely. But the style of his proposal is different. Firstly, he begins with the positive aspect of the oath: "I shall be his surety; from my hand you may require him" – I promise to be responsible for his return. Then Judah presents the negative aspect: should he not succeed in bringing Benjamin back, "I will have sinned to you forever." While Reuben's oath is more powerful – he swears by the life of his sons, demonstrating his absolute readiness to accept responsibility – we have already seen that his formulation is tasteless and especially inappropriate when talking to Jacob.

Jacob agrees to accept Judah's words – both because of the timing (there is no food left and he now has little choice; he understands this alone), and because Judah presents the alternatives very clearly, forcing Jacob to recognize that this is what he must do. In addition, Judah's style of speech is also more convincing than Reuben's was: he first presents the positive aspect of the oath, and only afterwards the negative aspect. The style of his oath is also better suited to his audience: he does not raise the specter of further bereavement, as Reuben did, but rather assumes a very heavy personal responsibility, acceptance of guilt even in the World to Come.

Despite all of this, it is clear that Jacob's agreement is not wholehearted:

A. He introduces his speech with the sense of no alternative: "If that is the case, then…"

B. At first Jacob makes no mention of Benjamin; rather, he mentions other things that the brothers should take with them. The brothers are undoubtedly waiting tensely to hear whether Jacob agrees for Benjamin to go or not, but only at the end does he say: "And take your brother." Clearly, it is difficult for him to say the words; he does so only because he must.

C. Finally, after all of this, he says: "As for myself – if I am bereaved, then I shall be bereaved." This is an expression of great anxiety, perhaps even despair.

D. Attention should be paid to the fact that Jacob does not address Judah, his interlocutor. He offers no thanks to him for offering to bear full responsibility; he fails even to respond to his words. He addresses all of the brothers collectively: "Israel their father said to them…" Likewise, Jacob does not send Benjamin with Judah, but rather with all of the brothers: "And take your brother." The fact that Jacob ignores Judah's words in his response shows that he does not accept them wholeheartedly.

And so, in order for the brothers to go back to Egypt in order to bring food, Jacob is forced, against his will, to send Benjamin along. Both Reuben and Judah have tried to persuade him: Reuben's words cause him to adopt an even more defensive stance, while Judah's words lead him to send Benjamin – even if it is really for lack of choice. Judah is more convincing, both because of his sense of timing and because of his style of persuasion.

Admittedly, Jacob does not explicitly place Benjamin in Judah's hands, and from this we may deduce that the responsibility to bring him home rests upon all of the brothers, including Reuben. But later on in the story we see that it is indeed Judah who assumes personal responsibility for him. When the brothers go back to Egypt, we do not read that Benjamin went specifically with Judah, but rather that all of them went down together. When Joseph's messenger pursues them and tells them that they are suspected of having stolen his royal goblet, they all answer him together. No specific brother takes the lead, conducting the negotiations with the Egyptian. All are equal in stature. At first, they are so certain that none of them is the thief, that they go so far as to propose the death sentence for the thief, while all the rest of them will be servants. The Egyptian does not agree to this idea; rather, he wants only the thief as his servant. While the verse records no response on the part of the brothers to this proposal, it seems that they were in agreement, and therefore they allow him to search through their belongings.

The agreement with the Egyptian had admittedly been that only the "thief" would be a servant, but all of the brothers assume responsibility here, and return together with Benjamin to Egypt. They do not abandon him, and certainly show no anger towards him for stealing the goblet. Rather, they all proceed together to Egypt, all sharing the same distress. Against this background, the next verse is interesting:

> Judah and his brothers came to the house of Joseph, and he was still there, and they fell before him to the ground. (44:14)

Judah comes at the head of the brothers. Here it is clear that he is the leader. Indeed, further on, it is Judah who speaks with Joseph, on behalf of all of them:

> Joseph said to them: What is this deed that you have done? Did you not know that a man such as I can certainly divine?
> And Judah said: What can we say to my master; what shall we speak, how shall we justify ourselves? God has found out the sin of your servants; behold, we are servants to my master – both we and he in whose hand the goblet was found. (44:15–16)

Attention should be paid to the fact that Judah speaks in the plural. He speaks on behalf of all of the brothers, as their accepted leader, and he presents Joseph with the same proposal that the brothers previously offered to his messenger: not only Benjamin will be a servant, but all of them. Seemingly, this is acceptable to all of the brothers. Indeed, they themselves proposed it from the start. But since then they agreed to the deal proposed by the messenger – that only the thief will be a servant. Why, then, now that the thief has been found, are they not prepared to see only him imprisoned? Why do they return to the original proposal – that they all suffer punishment?

Perhaps the reason is that when they agreed to the messenger's proposal, they were certain that none of them was the thief. Now that the goblet has been found with one of them, it seems that they are not prepared to accept this prospect at all.

But perhaps there is a different reason. If one of the other brothers were to have been imprisoned, they would have agreed that he would remain as a servant in Egypt, while the rest of them returned home. But since the matter concerns Benjamin, they will not do this. They know how important it is to Jacob that Benjamin return. Jacob sent Benjamin with them on the responsibility of all of them, not only Judah – as we saw above. Therefore they all feel responsible, and are all prepared to commit themselves to servitude together with Benjamin.

But the "Egyptian" does not agree. It is not fair to imprison all of the brothers because of a theft committed by only one. The guarantee of the brothers is being put to a very tough test. What are the brothers to do now that the Egyptian ruler insists on imprisoning only Benjamin, not allowing them to be imprisoned together with him?

It is at this moment that Judah is revealed in all of his power:

> Judah approached him and said: Please, my lord, I pray you, let your servant speak a word in my lord's ear, and let your anger not burn against your servant, for you are like Pharaoh. (44:18)

Judah focuses not on being punished for Benjamin not returning, but rather on his father's suffering. On the basis of the guarantee that he gave for Benjamin, Judah makes an astounding offer: he alone will be imprisoned, and Benjamin will go up to his home, together with all of the brothers.

Seemingly, the Egyptian viceroy should not accept this offer, for it is not logical to punish a different brother while freeing the "thief" – even if the thief is dearly beloved by his father! However, since the viceroy is Joseph, this proposal finds favor in his eyes, and it is this that causes him to reveal his identity to this brothers.

In Judah's words, Joseph detects the power of his leadership, based upon the strong fraternity that prevails among all the brothers, leading Judah – and all of them, following his example – to be guarantors for Benjamin's welfare and the welfare of their father. The guarantee is so powerful that Judah is prepared to pay a very heavy personal price in order that Benjamin may return to his father.

Various aspects of Judah's leadership are revealed here: First, it is he who assumes responsibility for Benjamin, even though his father never appointed him to be personally responsible. Second, he is responsible for the atmosphere of fraternity among the brothers, leading all of them to feel that there is no possibility of leaving Benjamin behind in Egypt. Third, he is ready to pay a heavy personal price – to be imprisoned, in order to save his father anguish.

Once again, we see that Judah has the special gift of saying the right words at the right time, causing his listeners to accept what he is saying. Although Judah has no idea that it is Joseph who stands before them, he manages to find the words that touch the most sensitive part of him.

Thus, Judah's approach to Joseph, as representative of the brothers, expresses his leadership in the clearest possible way. In the wake of this encounter, it appears, Judah became the clear leader of the brothers – in the eyes of Jacob, too, as we find later on when Jacob prepares to go down to Egypt, and sends Judah before him:

> He sent Judah before him to Joseph, to show the way before him to Goshen, and they came to the land of Goshen. (46:28)

Finally, when Jacob blesses his sons, he praises Judah and bestows upon him the blessing of leadership:

> Judah, it is you whom your brothers will praise; your hand is upon the neck of your enemies; your father's children shall bow down to you. A lion's whelp is Judah; from the prey, my son, you have risen up. He bowed, he crouched like a lion and as a lioness – who shall rouse him up? The staff shall not depart from Judah, nor a ruler from between his feet, until the coming of Shilo, and the nations shall obey him. (49:8–10)

Reuben is the eldest of the brothers, and as the firstborn he holds a position of responsibility towards what happens in the family. His intentions are good, but essentially he is unsuited to leadership, and therefore his brothers do not listen to him. Therefore, leadership is given over to Judah, who is a more natural leader.

Parashat Vayigash

Judah's Plea and Its Audiences

by Rav Chanoch Waxman

I. JUDAH AND ABRAHAM

Like his great-grandfather Abraham who had pleaded with God, Judah approaches his master and pleads.

> And Judah came near and said: Please my master, let your servant speak a word in my master's ears and please do not be angry. (44:18)

Just as Abraham "came near" (*vayigash*) (18:23), so too Judah comes near (*vayigash*) (44:18). Just as Abraham addressed his pleas and prayers to his master (18:27, 30–32), so too Judah speaks to his "master" (44:18–20). Finally, in another echo of Abraham's prayer, Judah prefaces his plea with the hope that his daring to speak will not arouse his master's anger (18:30, 32; 44:18).

Admittedly, the "Prayer of Abraham" (18:23–33) and the "Plea of Judah" (44:18–34) constitute fundamentally different events. In the former story, Abraham pleads with the Master of the Universe. In the latter story, Judah pleads with no more the master of the Egyptian granary. Yet at the same time, they are united by more than just the stylistic markers of servant-master prayer noted above. In both cases, the "prayer" involves pleading for the sparing of the condemned. Just as Abraham pleads for the sparing of Sodom, so too, Judah pleads for the sparing of Benjamin.

Moreover, the method is the same. Abraham's prayer tactic consists of defining a guiltless group, some number of righteous men in Sodom, and linking their fate to the fate of the guilty. By dint of God's mercy upon the innocent, the guilty should also be spared. Judah employs an identical method. He defines Jacob as undeserving of death, which would result from Benjamin's slavery. Jacob has already suffered enough. This is somehow supposed to lead to the sparing of Benjamin. A quick sketch of the highlights of Judah's plea should confirm this point.

Judah begins with a recap of the first conversation between the brothers and the Egyptian (44:18–23), in which he elaborates on the previously unmentioned death of Benjamin's brother, the death of Benjamin's mother and his father's unique love for Benjamin (44:20; see also 42:13). It turns out that the brothers had told the Egyptian viceroy that "the lad cannot leave his father: for if he should leave his father he would die" (44:22). Even if this "death" predicted by Judah in the recap of the original conversation refers to that of Benjamin (Rashi, Ramban), and not to the death of Jacob (Rashbam), Judah has already made his point. Jacob has suffered enough and deserves to suffer no more.

In the second section of his speech, his recounting of the conversation between Jacob and his sons during their interlude in Canaan (44:24–29), Judah emphasizes Jacob's suffering again. In addition, he warns of the certainty of Jacob's death upon losing Benjamin. Judah has Jacob refer to the fact that "his wife" bore him only two sons, and one has already been torn to death. If this last son will be taken, "You will send my white head down to *She'ol* in sorrow," a clear reference to Jacob's death (44:27–29).

Finally, in the last section of his plea, his summary and conclusion (44:30–34), Judah makes explicit what had previously been perhaps merely implicit. The soul of the father is tied up with the soul of the son (44:30). Consequently:

> ... when he sees that the boy is not with us, he will die, and your servant will have sent ... our father in grief down to *She'ol*. (44:31)

In sum, in the case of Abraham, the guilty people of Sodom, and God, Abraham sought to introduce a fourth actor and thereby spare the guilty. So too Judah, in pleading with the Egyptian, seeks to introduce a fourth player, the innocent, long-suffering and ancient Jacob. By linking the guilty Benjamin to the innocent Jacob, he hopes to persuade the master to act with mercy.

In fact, we should realize that it is not just mercy that Judah seeks. He also seeks justice. Abraham's tactic allowed him to challenge God. He brazenly challenged God not to "slay the righteous with the wicked," for after all, "shall not the judge of all the earth do right?" (18:25). Similarly, Judah implicitly presses the Egyptian for justice. The Egyptian should not slay Jacob the righteous as part of his quest to enslave the guilty.

The parallel to the prayer of Abraham, the tripartite structure of Judah's plea and the mercy-justice content outlined above should make us realize that part of Judah's plea seems not to belong. At the very end of his plea, deep into his conclusion, after warning of his father's death, Judah states the following:

> For your servant has pledged himself for the lad [*arav et hana'ar*] from my father and said: If I do not bring him to you, then I shall have sinned to my father forever. (44:32)

Judah continues on to offer himself as slave in place of Benjamin (44:33) and concludes his speech with a confession of inability:

> For how can I go up to my father and not have the lad with me? Lest I see the evil that shall come upon my father. (44:34)

Judah seems to segue from a servant-master plea for mercy and justice, involving the coupling of the fates of the innocent and guilty, to something else altogether. He offers a substitution of himself for Benjamin (44:33). This new approach is bracketed on either side by Judah's discussion of his personal relationship with his father (44:32, 34). He cannot sin to his father; he cannot bear to see his father's pain and suffering.

This problem of a sense of disjunction, of a shift in theme and

465

approach, can be rephrased in far sharper fashion. The second plea of Judah, "Substitution and Confession" (44:32–34), appears unnecessary. If Judah has already carefully structured a classic mercy-justice linkage plea and has successfully made the case for the sparing of Benjamin for Jacob's sake, why offer substitution? Why describe his promises to his father and his personal pain? At the very least, he should wait for a "no" from the viceroy before trying a new tack. Moreover, the material connected to Judah and Jacob's relationship seems wholly irrelevant. What possible interest could the Egyptian viceroy have in the promise Judah had made to his father, or in Judah's personal concern for his father's suffering?

II. THE SUBSTITUTION SHIFT

Both Ramban and Abarbanel relate to the shift in Judah's plea noted above. According to Ramban (commentary on 44:18–19), although Judah does embark on a systematic effort to arouse the mercy of the Egyptian viceroy, he never expects to achieve more than substitution. The offer of substitution is necessary, and the shift is not a shift. Since Ramban does not comment extensively on the inclusion of the Judah's guarantee and anguish, which bracket the substitution offer, we must turn to Abarbanel to complete the picture. In Abarbanel's account, Judah ends with his anguish as part and parcel of his effort to arouse the mercy of his audience. He portrays himself, as well as his father, as deserving of mercy. He includes mention of the guarantee he gave his father in order to explain why it is that he (as opposed to any of the other brothers) has stepped forward to plead. In sum, both the offer of substitution and the inclusion of the Judah-Jacob relationship can be integrated into the general theme of a mercy-justice plea.

While this can be made to work, it nevertheless seems insufficient. The claim that Judah never expects to achieve anything more than substitution fails to give sufficient importance to the parallel of his plea with that of Abraham. The parallel seems to imply that linkage of the innocent and the guilty constitutes a valid argument.

Furthermore, the request for mercy and the offer of enslavement seem mutually contradictory. If Judah intends to capitalize on the sympathies of the viceroy for his commitment and relationship to his father, why offer to spend his life as a slave? Can he truly expect the viceroy to believe that enslaving the wrong man constitutes an act of mercy?

Moreover, as Ramban and Abarbanel themselves recognize, reading the text afresh always leaves us with a sense of surprise. Judah's offer of substitution strikes us as unplanned, a last minute addition, akin to the irrational flailing of a drowning man. It is not part of any premeditated plea for mercy and justice. On the contrary, it seems to be a spontaneous outburst, a desperate and almost illogical act of despair. Judah cannot bear to leave Benjamin behind. In light of the awful possibility, he is willing to try anything.

The language of the text seems to support this last point. In the first section of Judah's plea (44:18–23), the terms "master" (*adon*), "servant" (*eved*) and "father" (*av*) comprise a conceptual triangle, each appearing five times. This fits with the notion of a servant-master prayer, revolving around the fate of the innocent father. Judah's final words, the third section of his speech containing his offer of substitution and confession (44:30–34), also include a conceptual triangle delineated by three terms. But they are not the same terms. The term "youth" (*na'ar*) replaces the term "master," and along with "servant" (*eved*) and "father" (*av*) appears six times. This telegraphs that Judah's plea is no longer about arousing the master's mercy and sense of justice. Rather, everything is driven by this horrifying combination of the youth, slavery and his father, the terrible triangle that threatens to engulf Judah.

If so, we are left with two alternatives. We can adopt the approach of Ramban and Abarbanel and explain away the shift. Either their specific answers, or others, can be utilized to integrate Judah's closing words into the overarching structure of his plea. We can reject the premise of the problem. Alternatively, in a second approach hinted at above, we can accept the premise of the problem. Judah's speech does in fact undergo a mutation midway through. While he begins in purposeful and deliberate fashion, he ends in a crescendo of emotion, baring his despair to the Egyptian. He cannot bear the thought of returning to his father without the boy. Even a lifetime of slavery is preferable to letting down his father.

III. WHO'S LISTENING

The analysis of Judah's plea presented above rests upon a simple and crucial premise. Everything assumes that Judah addresses Tzafnat Pa'aneaḥ, the Egyptian noble who serves as second-in-command of Egypt and governs the economy. Of course, Judah does in fact address the Egyptian viceroy. However, unbeknownst to Judah, he also addresses the man behind the Egyptian mask, his brother Joseph. His words penetrate beyond the persona, to the real person entombed within. A proper and complete analysis of Judah's talk must take into account not only the intended audience of the talk, the Egyptian, but also the unintended audience, the brother beneath.

Shifting to Joseph's perspective puts a highly different cast on the problematic section, "Substitution and Confession" (44:32–34), discussed above. It is immediately after Judah's offer of substitution and his expressions of personal responsibility and concern for his father that Joseph reveals himself. It is Judah's final words, his cry of "How can I go up to my father and not have the lad with me?" and his lament of "Lest I see the evil that shall come upon my father" (44:34) that pave the way for Joseph's shocking revelation (45:1–3). While Judah might have intended to stir the soul and arouse the mercy of the Egyptian, his words have stirred an altogether different soul.

> And Joseph could no longer restrain himself before all that stood by him; and he cried out, "Have everyone taken out from me." And no man stood by him when Joseph made himself known to his brethren. And Joseph wept aloud… (45:1–2)

No doubt, the intended, planned and "standard" portions of Judah's speech play a causal role in Joseph's revelation. Judah frames the story of the suffering father and his impending death to arouse the mercy even of a manipulative Egyptian governor. Surely the plea possesses the power to stir the heart of the very son whom the father pines for. But this is only part of the cause of Joseph's unmasking.

When Joseph hears Judah expressing concern for Jacob and responsibility for Benjamin, he hears the words he didn't hear twenty years earlier. We can never know for certain whether Joseph overheard his brothers' plotting, upon Judah's suggestion, to sell him. Nevertheless, the quick textual progression from the stripping of the coat and the tossing of Joseph into the waterless pit (37:23–24), to the brothers' callous sitting down to share a meal and intra-dinner plotting (37:25–27), certainly implies geographic proximity. The brothers' later confession of guilt due to ignoring Joseph's pleading for mercy and begging for his life (42:21) further reinforces the assumption of proximity. Joseph's plaintive calls from the pit were met by nothing but the sounds of munching and money-making (37:25–28).

As pointed out previously, throughout the latter parts of his plea, Judah emphasizes the unique relationship of Jacob with Rachel, as well as the privileged status of her children. When Judah quotes Jacob, the latter refers to "my wife," a singular term, as if Rachel had been his only wife (44:27). Jacob still pines for Joseph (44:28), possesses a bond of souls with Benjamin (44:30) and will certainly die if stripped of Benjamin (44:29, 31). Judah not only accepts and respects this situation, but out of love and duty feels obligated to mortgage his very freedom to maintain it.

To put all of this together, when Joseph hears Judah's offer of substitution and confession, he hears the reversal of the exact family dynamic that had led to his slavery in Egypt. Instead of callous disregard and resentment of Jacob's choice of favorites, Joseph hears respect, duty, caring and self-sacrifice. In place of hatred of Joseph, he finds brotherly regard for Benjamin and his role.

But even this is only partial. By repeatedly returning his brothers their money and demanding Benjamin in return, Joseph recreated the circumstances of his own sale. When Judah refuses to leave Benjamin behind in Egypt in exchange for the grain and money, he refuses to repeat the sale of Joseph, the favored son of Rachel. In fact, when Joseph hears Judah's offer of substitution, he realizes that Judah is not just refraining from committing the same crime again, but is reversing the original situation. Whereas before, Judah had counseled to sell Joseph, a son of Rachel, into slavery (37:26–28), he now counsels selling himself into the very same slavery, instead of Rachel's son.

In sum, it is precisely Judah's offer of self-sacrifice and his expressions of responsibility, anguish and caring that complete the reversal of

Joseph's youth. It is precisely the section of "Substitution and Confession" that shatters Joseph's Egyptian front and prompts his revelation. The section constitutes not a problematic digression from a carefully crafted servant-master plea for mercy and justice aimed at an Egyptian noble, but rather the exact words necessary to draw out the brother underneath.

But this seems problematic. Judah possesses no clue that the Egyptian and Joseph are one and the same. He is dumbstruck upon learning the real identity of the governor. How does he manage to say exactly the right thing?

We may be inclined to write this off to coincidence, the random interplay of the free will of human beings. Unable to control himself, to maintain the molded form of a defense attorney crafting a closing argument, Judah shifts from his mercy-justice plea to an offer of substitution and a baring of his soul. His outburst, the breaking of his mask, is met by an equal outburst, the breaking of Joseph's mask.

Alternatively, we may, and probably should, assign this all to divine providence. Right after revealing himself to his brothers, Joseph repeatedly states that it was really God who had sent him to Egypt, to eventually provide sustenance for his family (45:5, 7). He even goes so far as to claim that "... It was not you that sent me here but God" (45:8). This is not apologetics, but rather part of the mysterious mix of human free will and divine providence present throughout the story of Joseph and his brothers.

So too the shift in Judah's speech. On the surface, Judah speaks to an Egyptian and either concludes as planned, or, as argued here, shifts to a new offer and almost unwillingly bares his soul. But underneath the surface, something altogether different is going on. Joseph constitutes the real audience and God plays a role in choosing Judah's words. In some mysterious fashion, God helps Judah to shift, to bare his soul and reveal the concealed. This is God's plan, and it helps Joseph to reveal the concealed. This divine intervention allows Joseph and his brothers to reconcile.

IV. JUDAH'S TRANSFORMATION

Before closing, I would like to discuss a third audience present at Judah's plea. As Abarbanel hints at the end of his discussion of Judah's speech, the address is not only directed at both the Egyptian and Joseph, but also at the reader of the story, the critical viewer interested in the saga and character development of Judah. Abarbanel makes this point by claiming that Judah must offer himself up for enslavement, must offer substitution, in order to suffer measure-for-measure punishment, or perhaps atone, for recommending the sale of Joseph.

Earlier on, I claimed that the second audience, Joseph behind the mask, is already aware of Judah's culpability, the reversal and his repentance. Nevertheless, Abarbanel is fundamentally correct. Only the third audience, the reader, possesses all of the pieces of the puzzle necessary to string together the story of Judah's character.

This can best be realized by noting that all of the key stories involving Judah throughout *Vayeshev*, *Miketz* and *Vayigash* are linked together by a series of terms and literary symbols.

Judah first rises to prominence in the story of the sale. He formulates the plan (37:26–27). Shortly afterwards, the brothers cover their tracks by tricking Jacob. They dip Joseph's coat in blood and "send" the coat to their father (37:31–32). They ask him to "please acknowledge" (*haker na*), is this the coat of Joseph or not (37:32)? Jacob indeed does recognize and acknowledge (*vayakirah*), concluding that Joseph has been torn to shreds (37:33). These very terms reappear in the next chapter, the story of Judah and Tamar. Just as Tamar is being taken out to be burnt, she "sends" to her father-in-law and asks him to "please acknowledge" (*haker na*), to identify, to whom the stick, seal and cord belong (38:25). Like his father previously, Judah does indeed recognize and acknowledge (*vayaker*), concluding that Tamar is more righteous than he (38:26).

Just as the first and second Judah stories are linguistically linked, so too the second Judah story connects with the remaining Judah stories. In making the deal with the prostitute, Judah transfers his staff, seal and cord as a pledge (*eravon*), a guarantee of future payment. This root and symbol reappears in the two remaining Judah stories. In arguing for Jacob to allow Benjamin to accompany the brothers to Egypt, Judah pledges his word and very self. He tells his father, "I will be guarantee [*a'arvenu*]" and "from my hand you may demand him" (43:9). Finally, this Hebrew root (*a-r-v*, ע.ר.ב.) surfaces one last time in the fourth Judah story, the narrative of Judah's plea. It constitutes the key term in Judah's offer of substitution. Judah opens his offer with the statement that he has pledged himself for the boy (*arav et ha-na'ar* [44:32]).

Mapping this out yields the following:

> Judah and Joseph (the sale of Joseph, 37:26–36) – "sending," "recognizing";

> Judah and Tamar (38:17–30) – "pledge-guarantee" and "sending," "recognizing";

> Judah and Jacob (43:1–10) – "pledge-guarantee";

> Judah and Joseph (Judah's plea, 44:30–34) – "pledge-guarantee."

The resulting A-B-A-B-B literary pattern, which portrays the gradual move from "sending" and "recognizing" to the symbol of "pledge-guarantee" (signifying commitment and responsibility), constitutes far more than literary artistry. In fact, it seems to mark a crucial transformation in the character of Judah.

In suggesting and executing the sale of Joseph, Judah behaves in a highly inappropriate fashion. Since there is "no profit in killing our brother and covering his blood," he advises selling Joseph instead. After all, Joseph is their brother, their own flesh and blood (37:26–27). At this point, Judah possesses a very poor sense of brotherhood and family responsibility. He acts cruelly, without regard for the suffering of Joseph or the feelings of his father. He is arrogant, wholly removed from the effects of his actions on the souls of others. His sphere of interest consists of no more than the twenty silver pieces received in exchange for his brother. The act of sending the coat to Jacob and demanding that he recognize it captures and symbolizes the character and behavior of Judah.

In the Judah and Tamar story, Judah is subjected to a bit of his own medicine. Just as Judah once sent to his father Joseph's coat and demanded Jacob's painful acknowledgement of Joseph's death, now he himself receives the objects and acknowledges. He engages in the undoubtedly painful acknowledgement of having consorted with a harlot, of having neglected his familial responsibility to his daughter-in-law, of the evil of his sons and of having arrogantly and presumptuously passed judgment upon his daughter-in-law. In sum, he moves from a realm of haughtiness, arrogance and neglect of responsibility to a realm of humility, caring and responsibility. To rephrase, he moves from the world of the symbols of his own "sending" and demanding "recognizing" to an existential world defined by his admission and marked by the symbols of "guarantee-pledge." The categories of humility, caring and responsibility now constitute the core of his character.

The last two stories confirm this point. Utilizing the transformed symbol of "guarantee-pledge," Judah offers his very self to his father and assumes responsibility for his family's survival, his brother's safety and his father's heart and life (43:8–10, 14). By no accident, the term is monetary. Judah mortgages himself, as he had once sold off Joseph.

By now the point should be obvious. The pattern reaches its crescendo in the final Judah story, in the final section of Judah's plea, what we have termed "Substitution and Confession." Judah's newfound character of humility, concern, caring and responsibility leads him to volunteer to substitute himself for Benjamin. It leads him to undo the crucial sin of his earlier self. Without concern for himself or his personal destiny, he accepts upon himself a lifetime of slavery.

If so, we have arrived at a third role for Judah's finale. The verses of "Substitution and Confession" are not just about persuading the Egyptian, or, through the mystery of divine providence, provoking Joseph's revelation. They are also aimed at the reader, reminding us who Judah has been and who he has now become.

Judah vs. Tamar as Background to Judah vs. Joseph

by Rav Yonatan Grossman

I. JUDAH'S DILEMMA

Our *parasha* is the climax of the conflict between Joseph and his brothers. When Judah stands before Joseph, attempting to persuade the viceroy to allow Benjamin to return to his father, he is revealed as a figure of outstanding character.

We cannot know with certainty whether Judah believed his younger brother's claim that he had not stolen the goblet. On the one hand, the goblet had been found in Benjamin's sack – seemingly ample evidence that Benjamin had taken it. On the other hand, Joseph had previously hidden something in the brothers' provisions: their money, payment for the grain that they had purchased. On the two occasions of the brothers' descent to Egypt, Joseph had returned their payment to them. The first time we are told:

> And Joseph commanded that their vessels be filled with grain, and that each man's money be returned to his sack. (42:25)

This money was discovered by the brothers when they stopped at their lodging place (42:27–28). Joseph repeated this strange ritual and hid their money once again on their second descent to Egypt:

> Fill the sacks of these men with food, as much as they can carry, and place each man's money at the mouth of his sack. (44:1)

No further mention is made of this second concealment of money, and it is difficult to understand what Joseph hoped to achieve by repeating this tactic a second time.

On the first occasion, we learn of the brothers' fear upon discovering the money hidden in their sacks. The tactic serves, to some degree, to further the plot. When Joseph invites the brothers to his house, they are reminded once again of the money hidden in their sacks, and they fear that they are about to be punished on account of it (43:18).

But we hear nothing after the second concealment, not even any mention of the brothers discovering the money. What, then, is the significance of Joseph hiding their money the second time?

Notably, the concealment of the money is particularly emphasized in the case of Benjamin's sack:

> And my goblet, the silver goblet, shall you place in the mouth of the sack of the youngest one, with the money for his corn. (44:2)

This instruction is given immediately after the previous one – "and place each man's money at the mouth of his sack," such that it is already clear that Benjamin's money will be returned to him. Nevertheless, Joseph repeats the command to conceal the money together with the goblet in Benjamin's sack, thereby giving special emphasis to it.

The question of when the brothers discovered that their money had been returned to them seems to have a fairly simple answer. When "the man who oversaw Joseph's house" reaches the brothers and challenges them with his claim that they have stolen the goblet, the search through their belongings begins. Here the text emphasizes that the man searched in all of the sacks, for he began with that of the eldest and proceeded until he reached Benjamin.

We may reasonably assume that the search for the goblet was not restricted to a cursory inspection of the men's clothing and food, but rather included a thorough search of every corner of their sacks. At this stage, it seems, the brothers must have noticed that their money had been returned to them. To their surprise, the Egyptian makes no comment. But in Benjamin's sack, together with the money, he finds the goblet.

Ramban (commentary on 44:1) understands from this fact that, on this occasion, Joseph returned their money to them openly, even notifying them of it:

> "And place each man's money at the mouth of his sack" – with their knowledge, for [the servant] said to them: "My master knows that he treated you unjustly the first time, and wants to make it up to you." For if he had done as the first time, [returning their money] without their knowledge, they would have had an excuse concerning the goblet – that the same thing had happened in that instance as had happened concerning their money. But [this time] it was with their knowledge, and they were aware of the money just as they were aware of their load, for they recognized that he had given them as much as they could carry.

To Ramban's view, if the money had been hidden without the brothers' knowledge again on the second occasion, they would have had a claim against the Egyptian viceroy: it was not they who were responsible for the theft, but rather someone else who had slipped something into their sacks without their knowledge, like the hidden money. Ramban himself discusses the opposite view and explains why we may nevertheless posit that the money was hidden without their knowledge. In my opinion, the text suggests that the money was hidden without their knowledge. Joseph commands "the man who oversaw his house" to conceal the money, and he does not declare it to the brothers.

This, then, appears to represent the function of the concealed money. Joseph wants to confuse the brothers. On the one hand, he presents Benjamin as a thief; on the other hand, he "arms" the brothers with the understanding and feeling that Benjamin may well be innocent. Just as their money suddenly turned up in their sacks, so could the goblet have been planted there.

Our original question – whether Judah believed that Benjamin was innocent – remains difficult to answer. The goblet was indeed found in his sack, but the money had been found there too – as well as in the sacks of Judah and all the other brothers!

II. JUDAH AND TAMAR

Judah's suggestion, despite his doubts, that he replace Benjamin as Joseph's slave, is among the most noble moments in the Tanach. It is fitting, however, as Judah played a main role in the brothers' campaign against Joseph. It was he who suggested that Joseph be sold as a slave to Egypt (rather than killing him, or leaving him to his fate in the pit, as Reuben suggested); it was he who succeeded in convincing Jacob to allow Benjamin to go down to Egypt together with his brothers (unlike Reuben, who could not convince their father). And so it is he who now stands before Joseph, with tremendous self-sacrifice, offering himself as a servant instead of Benjamin.

At the same time, there is another story which, to my mind, appears to make a more important contribution to our understanding of Judah's actions in this situation – the story of Judah and Tamar. The significance of this story in the continuum of the saga of Joseph and his brothers has often been questioned. Why does the Torah record this story immediately after the sale of Joseph? We assume that the story of Judah and Tamar is presented as a sort of reaction to what preceded it; namely, the sale of Joseph. *Ḥazal* already noted literary similarities between the two narratives: "Please recognize," the brothers declare, presenting Joseph's blood-drenched coat to Jacob, and "Please recognize," declares Tamar, presenting Judah with the items that he had left in her safekeeping. However, we can also see how the story of Judah and Tamar serves as background to the encounter between Judah and Joseph in our *parasha*.

This idea arises from an analysis of the general structure of the story of Joseph and his brothers. We are used to seeking and analyzing the structure of a limited literary unit, but sometimes the Torah weaves a string of stories into a single unified structure, such that each of the component narratives must be read in light of its place in the general structure. Thus, the story of Joseph and his brothers follows a chiastic form:

A. Jacob with all of his sons in Canaan (seventeen years)
  B. Chapter 38: Judah and Tamar / chapters 39–41: Joseph in Potiphar's house, in prison, and in the royal palace
    C. First descent of the brothers to Egypt
    C1. Second descent of the brothers to Egypt
  B1. Judah "approaches" Joseph and causes him to reveal his identity
A1. Jacob with all of his sons in Egypt (seventeen years)

The beginning and conclusion of the story each describe a period of seventeen years during which Joseph lives with his family and with his father – first (A) in Canaan, and ultimately (A2) in Egypt. At the heart of this literary structure (C and C1), we read of two descents by Joseph's brothers to Egypt. There are many points of comparison between these two descents, and the second should be read against the backdrop of the first, so as to appreciate the development that takes place among Joseph's brothers. Obviously, all of this lies beyond the scope of our present discussion.

The structure outlined above has far-reaching implications for our understanding of the story of Joseph and his brothers, as well as of the structure of the family (especially the complex relationship that exists between the two "firstborns," each of whom aspires to leadership). But we shall focus here only on the somewhat surprising middle parallel – B and B1.

In B, the two central figures – Judah and Joseph – take center stage separately: there is Judah's grappling with the story of Tamar, and Joseph's grappling with his situation in Egypt. The way in which these two brothers address the challenges that face them teaches us much about their respective characters. Judah, in the story of Tamar, first falls and then mends his ways, in contrast to Joseph, who does not fall. Judah's failure lies in his fear of allowing his youngest son to marry Tamar, and in his insensitive treatment of her: "Remain a widow in your father's house" (38:11). Needless to say, this ruling is merely a preparation for the second ruling issued by Judah concerning Tamar in this story: "Bring her out and let her be burned!" (38:24). However, Tamar – in her wisdom – causes Judah to retract this decree and to mend his ways: "She has been more righteous than I, because I did not give her to Shelah my son" (38:26).

From this perspective, Judah takes the stage as a penitent, a *"ba'al teshuva,"* a characterization used by Ḥazal in connection with Judah's descendant, King David (*Moed Katan* 16b; *Avoda Zara* 5a). In complete contrast, Joseph – while admittedly also engaged in repairing his relationship with his brothers – does not fail when tempted by Potiphar's wife. Joseph is not the prototype of the penitent, but rather of the righteous person (*Tzaddik*) who does not fail.

The process which each of these figures undergoes individually climaxes in their encounter with each other. The structure of the story presents Judah's process of *teshuva* as the backdrop to his self-sacrifice when standing before Joseph, and the trials and tribulations experienced by Joseph in Egypt as the backdrop to his posture before his brothers – a posture that has changed dramatically. Far from the boy who would report his brothers to his father, Joseph has become a figure who perceives even his brothers' terrible act of selling him as a slave as being part of the divine plan concerning their family, and as playing a part in the unfolding of history as guided by God's hand.

The other party in this encounter – Judah – has also undergone an important process of development from the beginning of his story, with the death of his wife Bat Shua and the death of his two sons (Er and Onan), to its conclusion, when he "receives" a new wife (Tamar) and two sons (Peretz and Zeraḥ); from his original insensitivity to Tamar's plight to his open declaration, "She has been more righteous than I."

This story, then, is presented as a literary backdrop to the encounter between Judah and Joseph, not only because of the chiastic structure outlined above, but also because of the perfect analogy between the two images.

In the story of Judah and Tamar, Judah refrains from giving his third son, Shelah, to Tamar, out of fear that he too will die, like his brothers, and he will have no children left from his wife, Bat Shua. In the encounter between Judah and Joseph, Judah describes an identical situation in relation to Jacob, his father:

> And your servant, my father, said to us: You know that my wife
> bore me two sons. One went out from me, and I said, "He has
> surely been torn apart." And I never saw him since. If you take

this one, too, from me and some calamity befalls him, you shall bring down my gray hairs with sorrow to *She'ol*. (44:27–29)

Jacob, too, fears for the life of his youngest son, lest he die like his elder brother, and therefore he resists handing him over to his brothers when they are ready to return to Egypt. It should be kept in mind that Jacob himself describes Benjamin as the third son who is to be taken from him: "You have bereaved me of my children: Joseph is gone, and Simeon is gone, and you will take Benjamin – all of this has befallen me" (42:36). In exactly the same way, Judah felt that Er was gone, Onan was gone, and therefore he had to be especially careful with his third son.

In fact, since Jacob's words are uttered here by Judah, we are almost justified in positing that Judah's outcry: "If you take this one, too, from me and some calamity befalls him," also describes his own situation, in his long-distant deliberation as to whether to allow Shelah to marry Tamar.

The identification of Judah with his father Jacob is complete. Judah himself has experienced the feelings of Jacob, fearing for the life of his youngest son. It is specifically Judah who realizes his mistake, recovers, and repairs his ways. Only he musters the necessary courage and resourcefulness before his father and persuades him to allow Benjamin to go with him to Egypt.

In this context, we reach the literary motif that is common to both images, Judah vs. Tamar on the one hand, and Judah vs. Joseph on the other. In both cases, Judah gives a pledge. This pledge eventually remains with Tamar, and it is only by means of it that she is able to convince Judah of his mistake in judging her so hastily. In his speech to Joseph, again Judah emphasizes his pledge:

> For your servant was surety for the boy to my father, saying: If I fail to bring him to you, I will have sinned to my father forever. (44:32)

In the story of Tamar, Judah gives her his personal effects, demonstrating his personal pledge and commitment. In the story of the descent to Egypt, Judah makes himself a surety for Benjamin – again, obviously, the surety represents his personal commitment to his brother's safety.

At the same time, though, if we follow the events surrounding the surety in both these stories, we discover an important difference between them. In the story of Judah and Tamar, we expect that Judah will assume responsibility for Tamar's fate and nullify the impossible situation created by his previous decree: "Remain a widow in your father's house." Tamar's loneliness bothers Judah's conscience, for he – as the head of the family – has driven her into this difficult situation by his refusal to let her marry Shelah.

In contrast, in his readiness to serve as surety for Benjamin and in his self-sacrifice in proposing himself as a slave in Egypt in his brother's place, Judah is acting in a manner beyond what is expected of him. Here he could easily declare, with a clear conscience, that the responsibility for the fate of Benjamin – who appears doomed to a terribly lonely future in Egypt – rests with the younger brother who stole the goblet. Here Judah could stand silently and watch while Benjamin was led away into slavery; I am not convinced that we could accuse him of any wrongdoing.

But this is not what Judah chooses to do. Out of remarkable filial sensitivity, knowing that his father would prefer his brother's return to his own, he suggests that Benjamin's servitude be exchanged for his own.

Returning to the matter of the money returned in the brothers' sacks, we note that in both instances, there is a problem of payment for something, but they are opposites of one another. Judah sends by the hand of his Adullamite neighbor a kid goat as payment for the "prostitute on the road," but the man cannot find her. Ultimately, Judah never pays anything at all to Tamar, whom he "considered a prostitute, for she had covered her face" (38:15).

In Judah's encounter with Joseph, there is a problem surrounding payment, but in the opposite sense. The brothers do not succeed in paying Joseph – whom they believe to be the Egyptian viceroy – for the grain that they receive from him. Their money is returned to them time after time. Thus, the two characters who "hide" from Judah – Tamar and Joseph – both resist accepting payment for their service to him (and the brothers). The implication of this situation is that, as a result, something of much greater importance – the "surety" – is slated to remain in their hands: Judah's personal effects remain with Tamar, and now Judah himself is about to remain as a slave to the Egyptian viceroy.

I believe that it is the lack of acceptance of payment by the two characters "hiding" from Judah that ultimately leads him to realize his important inner strengths. It is as though Tamar and Joseph hint to him: You cannot solve the conflict that faces you with money. Beneath the surface here lies a more significant conflict, and you are required to demonstrate self-sacrifice in order to solve it. Indeed, in both cases Judah does display great inner strength, declaring in one case, "She has been more righteous than I," and in the other – "Let your servant remain instead of the boy as a servant to my master."

Thus, the story of Judah and Tamar stands as a double background to Judah's speech to Joseph in our *parasha*. On the one hand, it highlights Judah's identification with Jacob, the identification of fathers who have lost children and who fear for the fate of their remaining son. On the other hand, it also highlights Judah's special quality of putting himself on the line for others: correcting the wrong that he did to Tamar, and illuminating the darkness of Egypt with his great selflessness on behalf of his younger brother.

The Twilight Years

by Rav Ezra Bick

In *Parashat Vayigash*, there is an exact point where Jacob is finally transformed, almost "reborn," as it were. The verse states "*Vatehi ruah Yaakov avihem*" – the spirit of Jacob their father was revived. This is clearly and dramatically indicated not merely by the plain meaning of the verse, but by the startling juxtaposition of the names of the chief actor in this verse with the following one:

> …the spirit of **Jacob** their father was revived.
> **Israel** said: It is much; my son Joseph is alive – I shall go and see him before I die. (45:27)

The significance of the sudden change in Jacob's name is irresistible, and nearly all commentators who remarked on it interpret it to mean that Jacob's personality was transformed, with the name Jacob referring to a lower, diminished level, and the name Israel signifying the higher, inspired manifestation of Jacob, not merely the individual with his personal problems, but the **forefather**, the protagonist of Jewish history, the divinely inspired manifestation of Jewish destiny itself.

In light of this, it is noteworthy that the Torah does not continue to refer to Jacob as Israel, and in fact there is a rather sudden reversion to the name Jacob:

> **Israel** travelled with all that was his, and he came to Be'er Sheva, and he sacrificed sacrifices to the father of his father Isaac.
> And God said to **Israel** in a vision of night, and He said: **Jacob Jacob**, and he said: I am here.
> He said: Do not fear to descend to Egypt, for I will make you a great nation there.
> And **Jacob** rose from Be'er Sheva, and the children of Israel bore **Jacob** their father and their infants and wives on the wagons which Pharaoh had sent to bear him. (46:1–5)

Israel begins the journey and reaches Be'er Sheva; from there **Jacob** continues the rest of the way to Egypt. What has taken place in Be'er Sheva? God appears to **Israel**, and speaks to him, calling him **Jacob**. It seems almost as though God has taken Jacob down a peg, changing his name back to the old one, the one he bore the entire time that Joseph had been missing. What is taking place here?

Ramban (commentary on 46:2) explains that God calls Jacob by the name Jacob to tell him that this descent to Egypt is the beginning of the exile. The name Israel means "for you have struggled with God and man and **have prevailed**," and in Egypt he will "be in the house of bondage until God will raise him, for now the exile begins for him." The obvious problem with this explanation is that the slavery does not begin immediately, but Ramban has, I think, warded off this critique by stating that the "exile begins **for him**." For Jacob, or rather for Israel, to have to go to Egypt after settling in *Eretz Yisrael*, and after having built his house there (*"vayeshev Yaakov be'eretz megurei aviv"*) is exile, in a sense that it is not for his children (who, as Ramban points out, are called *"Benei Yisrael"* in the very same verse where Jacob is called Jacob).

The Netziv has a similar interpretation. He disagrees with Ramban concerning the appropriateness of the name Israel in exile – on the contrary, the Netziv argues that this name is especially relevant to exile, as there will be need there to struggle with God and man in order to survive. He ascribes the name change more to the personal life of Jacob,

Jewish people is **helplessness** and subjugation, and the redemption as well will be one in which they are passive and are saved by the mighty hand and the outstretched arm of God. *Parashat Vayigash* sets the stage by "retiring" Jacob (as well as Judah) and placing the house of Jacob in the position they will suffer for the next several hundred years – dependency and passivity, subject to forces beyond their control, ultimately to the force of the revealed arm of God. Hence the final verse of the *parasha* – "Israel dwelled in the land of Egypt in the land of Goshen and they settled in it, and they grew and multiplied very much." For the first time, we meet an entity called Israel (which is clearly not Jacob in this verse). Historically, we have passed from individual history to national history, to that of the group.

There is still a delayed role for Jacob to play, seventeen years after he descends to Egypt, and that is the giving of the blessings. These are not about the sojourn in Egypt and do not effect it; they are about the distant future. But it is Jacob's final role as forefather, as the greatest of the forefathers, and not surprisingly, he will be consistently called Israel in *Parashat Vayḥi*.

Tzafnat Pa'aneaḥ – Prince of Egypt

by Rav Yair Kahn

I. JOSEPH'S PUZZLING POLICY

The story of Joseph and his brothers is more than fascinating family drama. Based on the principle of *ma'aseh avot siman labanim* (the actions of the fathers are a sign for the children), it profoundly impacts the way Jacob's family will develop into *Knesset Yisrael*. According to our sages (*Sukka* 52a), the imprint of the Joseph story will still be felt in the Messianic era.

However, the Torah's detailed documentation of Joseph's financial policy in governing Egypt is perplexing. Only peripherally connected to the story of Joseph and his brothers, expressing the preferential treatment they received, it seems superfluous. The section begins:

> And Joseph sustained his father and his brothers and his father's entire household, bread per child. And there was no bread in the entire land, for the famine was very harsh and the land of Egypt and the land of Canaan languished due to the famine. (47:12–13)

The section concludes:

> And as for the people, he removed them to the cities, from one

end of the border of Egypt to the other end ... And Israel dwelt in
the land of Egypt, in the land of Goshen; and they took possession
therein, and were fruitful, and multiplied exceedingly. (47:21, 27)

According to our sages, Joseph acted this way so that his brothers should
not feel like exiles; all of the inhabitants of Egypt lived in "exile." However, this message does not justify the detailed account of the negotiations with the people of Egypt.

What then does this section teach us? Further, what lesson
should we learn from how Joseph treats the Egyptians? Should a leader
take advantage of natural disasters to enslave a nation? Does his policy
correspond to Torah values? Surely proper behavior demands that one
follows HaShem's ways, who "opens His hands and satisfies every living
thing with favor" (Ps. 145:16)?

To decipher the meaning of this section, we must consider the
complexities of Joseph's position as viceroy of Egypt. By revisiting the
appointment of Joseph, we can understand his present behavior.

II. JOSEPH'S RISE TO POWER

After deciphering Pharaoh's dreams, Joseph concludes, "Now let Pharaoh look for a clever and wise man and set him over the land of Egypt"
(41:33). Ramban comments: "And Joseph said all this so that they should
choose him." Ramban's interpretation is consistent with his thesis that
Joseph's actions were part of a plan to ensure that his dreams were realized (Ramban on 42:9). However, a sensitive reading may lead us to a
different conclusion.

When the butler mentions Joseph to Pharaoh, he refers to him as
a *"na'ar eved Ivri,"* a young Hebrew slave. Rashi notes that this description was intended to disqualify Joseph for any royal position; Joseph
was young and inexperienced. He was a slave, not suitable material for
royalty. Moreover, he was a Hebrew in a racially prejudiced atmosphere
in which Egyptians refused to eat together with Hebrews. In addition,
this Hebrew slave was a prison inmate, convicted of attempting to rape
the wife of an important Egyptian minister!

It is also noteworthy that Joseph never presented himself as wise,
the quality required for the position he suggested Pharaoh establish. He

attributed his ability to decipher dreams to HaShem and denied any personal insight. In a surprising move, Pharaoh identifies Joseph's spiritual ability with wisdom. He turns to Joseph and says, "Since God has shown you all this, there is none as clever and wise as you. You shall be over my house, and according to your word shall all my people be ruled" (41:40–41). It is therefore difficult to accept Ramban's assertion that Joseph's suggestion to appoint a clever and wise man was a manipulative ploy to advance his own candidacy. It is far more likely that Joseph simply wanted to be freed from prison so that he could return to his father.

How was Joseph's appointment received by members of Pharaoh's court? What did Pharaoh's wise men think of the decision to place a Hebrew slave-prisoner in charge of Egypt? To anyone even mildly versed in human nature, the answer should be clear. The Torah, however, offers us only a subtle hint. After Joseph deciphered the dream, the Torah informs us: "And it was good in the eyes of Pharaoh and the eyes of all his servants" (41:37). However, the decision to appoint Joseph was that of Pharaoh alone. From this point on, the members of Pharaoh's court seem to disappear, as Pharaoh unilaterally wields his authority: "And Pharaoh said unto Joseph: 'Behold, I have set you over all the land of Egypt'" (41:41). Pharaoh removed his signet ring from his hand and put it upon Joseph's hand; he had Joseph dressed in royal garments and had him ride on the royal chariot. It is Pharaoh alone who places Joseph over all of Egypt.

Finally, Pharaoh makes a royal oath: "I am Pharaoh, and without you shall no man lift up his hand or his foot in all the land of Egypt!" Why was it necessary for Pharaoh to take an oath? Why did he hand over his ring and have Joseph ride the royal chariot (reminiscent of the power Haman craved for)? Perhaps the Torah is trying to hint that members of Pharaoh's court were less than thrilled with the appointment of the Hebrew slave.

It is noteworthy that, despite his liberal decision to appoint a Hebrew prisoner to a position of great power, Pharaoh insisted on changing Joseph's identity. Joseph received an Egyptian name and was given an Egyptian wife of high social standing. He transforms overnight into a member of Egyptian nobility. We can assume that his "dark" past was a closely guarded secret. Had the masses known that Tzafnat Pa'aneah was a Hebrew, wouldn't Jacob or the brothers have heard? If Joseph originally entertained thoughts of returning to his father, after his royal appointment, those plans were put on ice. (In fact, this may answer Ramban's famous question – why didn't Joseph contact home once he was freed from prison?[1])

Joseph indeed played his role well. As a powerful Egyptian prince, he managed to forget his troubles: "And Joseph named his firstborn Menashe, for 'God has enabled me to forget all my labor and the entire household of my father'" (41:51). Despite all of his power and success, however, late at night he was acutely aware that he was still confined to a foreign land: "And he named the second Ephraim, for 'God multiplied me in the land of my oppression'" (41:52). Although Joseph was one of the most famous people in Egypt, he was forced to hide his past. Despite being one of the most powerful people in the land, he was quite vulnerable.

With the passing of the seven years of plenty and the arrival of the seven years of famine, Joseph's position was strengthened. Now all of Egypt was dependent on him. All went well until his brothers arrived. When Joseph could no longer control himself and wished to reveal his true identity to his brothers, he removed everyone from the room. Did he do so only to avoid embarrassing his brothers? Perhaps he was desperately trying to keep his identity hidden from the Egyptian people. Despite his efforts, the news traveled and was heard all over Egypt. At that point, however, Joseph had proven his loyalty to Egypt. His position was safe, and the revelation of his past did nothing to tarnish his stature.

III. THE LAND OF GOSHEN

Pharaoh, in an additional display of liberal tendencies, invited Joseph's family to Egypt and offered them "the good of the land of Egypt" (45:18). According to Rashi, this refers to the land of Goshen. This interpretation is quite difficult, however. Consider how carefully Joseph acted upon the arrival of his family. He met his father and brothers in Goshen, and took only his father and some of his brothers to the capitol city to meet

---

1.   See the above articles by Rav Yoel Bin-Nun and Rav Yaakov Medan on this subject.

Pharaoh. Before they went to meet Pharaoh, Joseph told his brothers what he would tell Pharaoh and how they should respond:

> And Joseph said to his brothers and his father's household, "I will go up and inform Pharaoh and I will say to him: 'My brothers and my father's household from the land of Canaan have come to me. The men are shepherds, for men of flock they have been from their youth till now, and they have brought their sheep and cattle and all their possessions.' And you will say: 'Your servants were men of flock from our youth till now, we and our ancestors.'" (46:31–34)

Why did Joseph prepare a speech for his brothers, and why does the Torah trouble to inform us of this detail? Joseph himself explained his motive: "In order that you shall dwell in the land of Goshen, for shepherds are an abomination to Egypt." If Pharaoh had already invited Joseph's family to Goshen, why would this manipulation have been necessary?

Let's take a closer look at Pharaoh's invitation: "And take your father and your household and come to me" (45:18). In other words, Pharaoh invited Joseph's family to the Egyptian capital – to join the royal court. Joseph took pains to thwart that plan and to ensure that his father's household remained in Goshen, far away from Pharaoh's court. It is instructive that Joseph told his brothers that he would say to Pharaoh, "My brothers and my father's house, who were in the land of Canaan, **have come to me**" (46:31). But what he actually said to Pharaoh was that they had arrived from Canaan and **were currently in Goshen** (47:1). Joseph could not tell Pharaoh that they had come to him, contrary to Pharaoh's explicit invitation. It was only after the brothers delivered to Pharaoh the speech that Joseph had prepared for them, saying that they were shepherds (considered an abomination in Egypt), that Pharaoh conceded: "And Pharaoh spoke to Joseph saying: 'Your father and your brother have come to you'" (47:6). Only at this point did Pharaoh offer them Goshen, which was also considered the "good of the land of Egypt" (47:7).

Pharaoh intended to invite Jacob and his family to his court.

Even after the change of plan, Pharaoh considered the family of Jacob as Egyptian nobility, as evidenced by his offer that Joseph's brothers serve as ministers in charge of Pharaoh's own flock. Joseph had to act manipulatively to prevent this from occurring. It is likely that Joseph was concerned with the continued development of the family as a covenantal community. He wanted to avert the threat of assimilation in a situation in which they would be forced to change their names and dress and act as Egyptians in Pharaoh's court. The alternative – that they would openly retain their traditions in Pharaoh's court – would have been totally unacceptable and might have undermined Joseph's status.

We have attempted to demonstrate the complexities of Joseph's position in Egypt. He was one of the most powerful and most popular people in the land, but it was really Tzafnat Pa'aneah, the prince of Egypt, who was popular and powerful. After proving his loyalty to Egypt, he was considered an Egyptian prince even after his secret was revealed. But Joseph the Hebrew had no power at all. How does this impact upon Joseph's economic policy?

IV. YOU HAVE GIVEN US LIFE

Joseph's economic policy troubles us because it doesn't reflect ethical values of charity and compassion which we would expect from a descendant of Abraham. At first glance, it seems that Pharaoh gave Joseph a free hand in dealing with the famine. Why, then, did Joseph capitalize on the hunger of the Egyptians to turn them into slaves? Moreover, why did the Egyptians react so favorably to Joseph when he did so? "And they said: 'You have given us life'" (47:25).

These questions troubled the midrash:

> It says: "He that withholds grain, the people shall curse him; but blessing shall be upon the head of him that sells it" [Prov. 11:26]. "He that withholds grain the people shall curse him" – this is Pharaoh. "But blessing shall be upon the head of him that sells it" – this is Joseph. "The people shall curse him" – this is Pharaoh, who hid the wheat during the years of famine and the creatures were cursing him. But Joseph sustained the world during the years of famine, like this shepherd who leads his flock. (*Bereshit Raba*)

The midrash softens the judgment regarding Joseph's policy by contrasting it with the harsh measures taken by Pharaoh, but this midrash seems to have no biblical basis. The Torah describes Pharaoh as passive, giving Joseph almost absolute freedom. Is there any hint in the Torah that Pharaoh hid grain? Moreover, what would be the motivation for such a policy? Even if Pharaoh was an evil despot, why would he want to see his subjects die of starvation? Finally, would this really solve our problem? Is all that we expect from Joseph that he act with less cruelty than an evil ruler?

I believe that the midrash is based on a nuanced reading of the following verses:

> And the seven years of famine began, as Joseph had said; and there was famine in all lands, but in all the land of Egypt there was bread. And all the land of Egypt was famished, and the people cried to Pharaoh for bread; and Pharaoh said unto all the Egyptians: "Go unto Joseph; do what he says to you." (41:54–55)

There is bread in the land of Egypt, and yet the people are famished! It is only when they cry to Pharaoh out of starvation that they are sent to Joseph. Pharaoh knew that the famine had started. Why didn't he have Joseph open the warehouses immediately? Moreover, when the people cried to Pharaoh in desperation, why didn't he calm them to prevent panic? Why didn't he inform them that Egypt was prepared for the disaster and that no one would starve? Why didn't he show leadership and gain the adoration of the masses by ordering Joseph to feed the people?

According to the midrash, the people cried out in starvation because initially Pharaoh hid the grain. It is unlikely that this was done out of sadistic cruelty, but rather as a strategy aimed at taking advantage of the famine to solidify his control over the people. He hid the grain and brought the people to their knees. He showed them no compassion, but rather sent them to Joseph, who was meant to implement the plan.

Joseph was trapped. Should he continue to starve the people and force them into submission? How can he watch as hundreds die, until the people are ready to forfeit their freedom? On the other hand, can he betray Pharaoh his patron and simply open the warehouses of grain?

Joseph chose to implement Pharaoh's plan, but in a more humane way. He refused to cause human suffering. He opened the warehouses immediately in exchange for a price. After the people's money was gone, Joseph sold the grain for cattle. After Pharaoh gained control of all the cattle, Joseph bought the people themselves – but as serfs with reasonable terms, not as slaves (Ramban on 47:19). The people realized that there was something quite extraordinary about Joseph's behavior and therefore exclaimed, "You have given us life."

Apparently, Joseph managed to escape the trap unscathed. Not only did he prove his loyalty to Pharaoh, he gained the adoration of the people as well. Ultimately, however, Joseph did take advantage to enslave a starving nation. Although we now have insight into what might have motivated such a policy, it is problematic, and will return to haunt *Benei Yisrael* in the future.

Parashat Vayḥi

Jacob's Blessing to Joseph

by Rav Yehuda Rock

I. INTRODUCTION

In this *shiur* we shall examine various aspects of Jacob's words to Joseph
in their second encounter in the *parasha*. We shall also broaden our discussion of one particular expression – with which the commentators
have grappled, and for which we shall propose a new interpretation – to
shed light on a more general picture.

Jacob and Joseph meet three times in this week's *parasha*. In their
first encounter (Gen. 47:29–31), Jacob calls to Joseph and asks him to
bury him in Canaan, rather than in Egypt. At their third encounter (ch.
49), Joseph is present together with all of Jacob's other sons, each receiving a blessing from their father. We shall focus on the second meeting,
as recorded in chapter forty-eight.

Joseph initiates the second meeting with Jacob, upon hearing of
his father's illness. First, Jacob addresses Joseph, in verses 3–7; thereafter,
when Jacob sees Ephraim and Menashe, who have accompanied Joseph,
he blesses them, and then concludes with parting words to Joseph. We
shall pay special attention to Jacob's first speech to Joseph at this meeting:

> Jacob said to Joseph: The Almighty God appeared to me in Luz, in
> the land of Canaan, and blessed me. And He said to me: Behold, I

shall make you fruitful and multiply you, and I shall make of you
a community of peoples, and I shall give this land to your descendants after you, as an everlasting possession. And now, your two
sons, who were born to you in the land of Egypt, before I came to
you in Egypt – they are mine; Ephraim and Menashe shall be for
me like Reuben and like Simeon. And those born of you whom
you shall bear after them, shall be yours; they shall be named after
their brethren in their inheritance. As for me – when I came from
Padan Aram, my Rachel died in the land of Canaan, on the way,
with a little distance before you come to Efrat. And I buried her
there, on the way of Efrat, which is Bethlehem. (48:3–7)

Jacob's monologue here comprises three parts:

A. Mention of the blessing of "the Almighty God" (*Kel Shakai*) to
Jacob (v. 3–4)
B. Status bestowed on Ephraim and Menashe like that of Jacob's
sons for the purposes of inheritance (v. 5–6)
C. Mention of the death and burial of Rachel (v. 7)

Let us examine the significance of each part, and the connections
between all of them.

II. GOD'S BLESSINGS AND THE FIRSTBORN
PORTION OF THE INHERITANCE

The significance of giving Ephraim and Menashe equal status to Jacob's
sons is clear: Jacob is giving Joseph the portion of the firstborn, i.e., a
double portion of his inheritance. This is stated explicitly, in the book
of Chronicles: "Reuben … for he was the firstborn, but when he violated
his father's bed his birthright was given to the sons of Joseph, son of
Israel … and the birthright to Joseph" (I Chron. 5:1–2).

The Torah connects parts A and B in Jacob's speech with the word
"ve'ata" – "and now." In other words, the doubling of Joseph's portion (B)
is somehow based upon God's blessing to Jacob (A).

Rashi explains homiletically that the connection lies in the fact
that in God's blessing to Jacob he is told, "I shall make of you a commu-

nity of peoples"; from the seeming redundancy (*"kehal amim"*) Jacob deduced that after this blessing was given to him, another two tribes were destined to be added: one was Benjamin, and Jacob now sees to the addition of the twelfth tribe by turning Joseph into two tribes. A similar explanation is offered by Ibn Ezra in the name of R. Sa'adia Gaon, but they draw their conclusion not from the expression *"kehal amim,"* but rather the multiplicity that is inherent in the expression, "Behold, I shall make you fruitful," where the minimal fulfillment here is two descendants.

Rashbam explains the connection between God's blessing to Jacob and the double-portion awarded to Joseph with the following simple, clear words: "In other words, since the Holy One, blessed be He, gave me the land of Canaan, I am entitled to make you the firstborn for the purposes of taking a portion equal to that of two tribes; thus, your two sons will receive the same as Reuben and Simeon." In other words, God's blessing to Jacob is the basis of his authority to divide the land as he sees fit.

As noted, Jacob makes mention here of the blessing given to him by God at Beit El, when he returned from Padan Aram. A comparison between the language of the blessing here and the blessing as it was given (35:9–12), shows that Jacob is paraphrasing God's words, rather than quoting them exactly. Nevertheless, there is a clear parallel between the elements in both places, and the changes are linguistic rather than substantive – except for one expression, which Jacob adds here, which is found nowhere in God's original promise. This expression is *"ahuzat olam"* – "an eternal possession."

The word *"ahuza"* means a fixed acquisition in one's possession; it is used especially in contexts referring to an acquisition that is bequeathed (see Lev. ch. 25). The expression *"ahuzat olam"* here is taken from God's promise to Abraham, at the time of his circumcision (17:1–8). This promise, too, was given in the name of "the Almighty God," and contains similar elements and language to those appearing in God's promise to Jacob, although it is more elaborate. When Isaac conveys this blessing to Jacob, as he dispatches him to Padan Aram, he makes no mention of the *"ahuzat olam."* And, as noted, in God's blessing to Jacob this expression is similarly omitted. But Jacob, it seems, knew of the language of the blessing that Abraham had received; it was apparently passed down from generation to generation. He perceived great significance in the words "*aḥuzat olam*," understanding it as representing a fundamental characteristic of the blessing and relevant to the blessing that he himself had received, even though these words were not mentioned in his own blessing. The reason that Jacob regarded this expression as so important was that it meant that the land was given to him as an inherited acquisition held in his possession, such that he could bequeath it further as he saw fit. (Apparently, this view was also the basis for Jacob's desire, many years previously, to receive the blessing of Isaac – which Jacob expected to be the blessing of "the Almighty God." Since Isaac had received the land as an "eternal possession," Isaac was authorized to bequeath it in his blessing to whomever he chose.) For this reason, Jacob adds this expression now, in order to emphasize that by virtue of God's blessing to him, he is authorized to bequeath to Joseph a double portion of the land.

Ibn Ezra, too (ad loc.), offers a similar explanation to that of Rashbam, and seems to note Jacob's emphasis on the "eternal possession":

> What seems correct in my eyes is that he said, "God told me that the land of Canaan would belong to my descendants as an eternal possession; I now give you a double portion in the inheritance of the land, and Ephraim and Menashe will receive their portion in the land just as Reuben and Simeon will…"

In this context it should be noted that the halakha as set down in the Torah is that a person bequeathing his estate cannot transfer the birthright (the double portion due to the firstborn) from one son to another. This is stated explicitly in Deuteronomy: "If a man has two wives – one more beloved and the other less so – and the beloved wife and the less beloved wife bear him sons, and the firstborn belongs to the less beloved – then on the day when he bequeaths to his sons, he cannot assign the son of the beloved wife the firstborn in place of the son of the less beloved wife, who is [actually] the firstborn" (21:15–16). This law is apparently not fundamental to the definition of the concept of the birthright, but rather a specific law that the Torah sets down for future generations.

This law was not adhered to in Jacob's time; rather, it became halakha when the Torah was given.[1]

III. THE DEATH AND BURIAL OF RACHEL

Let us now turn our attention to the third element in Jacob's words to Joseph: the mention of the death and burial of Rachel. Why does Jacob mention this here?

R. Sa'adia Gaon (quoted by Ibn Ezra), who, as noted, explains that Jacob understood that the accounting of Ephraim and Menashe as independent tribes was necessarily entailed by God's blessing to him, now accordingly explains that the mention of Rachel's death likewise fits in with Jacob's claim: since after he received the blessing only Benjamin had been born, and Rachel had died and could no longer bear children, the additional son had to come from an accounting of grandsons as sons. But aside from the problem that this entire idea seems far removed from the literal intention of the text, this interpretation also fails to explain why Jacob also mentions Rachel's **burial** here. It would also seem logical that, according to this interpretation, Jacob should mention Rachel's death along with God's blessing to him, before jumping to the conclusion that Ephraim and Menashe should be considered as independent tribes in their own right.

Other commentators (Rashi, Ibn Ezra and Ramban) maintain that Jacob is apologizing here to Joseph and explaining why he did not bury Rachel, Joseph's mother, in the burial place of his fathers, in the Cave of Makhpela – the place where he asks Joseph to bury him. (The commentators are divided as to the actual reason why Jacob did not bury Rachel in the Cave of Makhpela; see Ramban ad loc.) The difficulty with this interpretation is that it would seem to require Jacob to

---

1. It is possible that the Torah introduces this law as a lesson learned from Jacob, whose tendency to show preference towards Joseph had started already in Joseph's youth, and eventually led to the entire family moving to Egypt. As the Talmud teaches in *Shabbat* 10b: "Raba bar Maḥasia quoted Rav Ḥamma bar Guria, who taught in the name of Rav: A person should never treat one child of his children differently from the others, for it was on account of the weight of two *sela* of fine wool, which Jacob gave Joseph over and above his other children, that his brothers were jealous of him, and this eventually led to our forefathers going down to Egypt."

mention Rachel's death and burial not here, but rather previously – in the first encounter between Jacob and Joseph in the *parasha*, when Jacob asks Joseph to bury him in the burial place of his forefathers. Rashbam attempts to resolve this difficulty by explaining that although Jacob's motivation in his words is to apologize for not having buried Rachel in the Cave, he offers these words here because of the associative connection with God's blessing to him. Rachel had died on that same journey as they traveled from Beit El, where Jacob had received the blessing that he now recalls. Nevertheless, in view of this interpretation of his words, their proper place and context would still seem to be in juxtaposition to Jacob's request for his own burial.

It appears, then, that the significance of Jacob's mention of Rachel's death and burial here must be explained in an altogether different way. Jacob is describing Rachel undergoing a process of transgression and punishment: her sin in stealing the *terafim*, tools for divination, as well as other actions, and repentance that began with abandonment of her sin as part of the preparations for the ascent to Beit El, and concluded with her death, when she called her son *Ben-Oni*.[2]

In *Parashat Vayishlaḥ*, after Rachel's death and her burial, we are told: "Jacob placed a monument over her grave – it is the monument of Rachel's grave to this day" (35:20). Why did he place a monument there? And why does the Torah take the trouble to emphasize the fact that the monument continues to stand there?

Rachel's death took place on the way, following their departure from Beit El. In Beit El, immediately after God's blessing to Jacob, we are told: "Jacob placed a monument at the place where He had spoken to him, a monument of stone" (35:14). There seems to be a connection between the two monuments.

Apparently, Rachel's sins gave rise to the thought – among Joseph's brothers, and perhaps in Jacob's own mind – that perhaps Rachel and her sons had no place in Israel. Just as in previous generations there had been brothers who were rejected and excluded from the covenant

---

2. See our shiur on *Parashat Vayetzeh* (available online at http://www.vbm-torah. org/archive/parsha67/07–67vayetze.htm) and Daf Kesher, Shemot 5758, vol. 635, "*LiDemuta Shel Rachel.*"

with God and inheritance of the land, so it was possible that Rachel and her children should similarly be rejected. It seems that Joseph's brothers regarded Rachel's sins as a justification – if not the actual motivation – for their sale of Joseph. (We infer this from the fact that when Joseph seeks to recreate for the brothers the same situation in relation to Benjamin that they had previously faced in relation to Joseph, he chooses to create a suspicion that Benjamin stole his royal goblet used for divining.) It seems that Jacob viewed the situation as follows: Rachel had not been punished so long as they were living outside of the land of Canaan, but rather died only as they entered the land, and only after she had lived to see the altar of atonement at Beit El, where God blessed Jacob and promised him the land. Jacob declares, as it were: The same divine providence that blessed me and gave the land of Canaan to me, also postponed Rachel's death until after she entered the land, stood at Beit El, and had the opportunity to repent. This told him that her place, and the place of her children, was in the land. Indeed, the Torah confirms this message by emphasizing the continued existence of the monument there.

Jacob repeats this message in our *parasha*, in his words to Joseph. As a continuation of his earlier words, in which Jacob emphasizes his rights with regard to the land and the extra right of Joseph in the land, he mentions Rachel's death and her burial, as if to say that divine providence itself had shown that Rachel's place – and the place of Joseph, Rachel's son – was in the land.

It seems that the emphasis on "as for me" at the beginning of the verse should be viewed in the same light: I, Jacob, owner of the "eternal possession" in the land, bearer of the authority to bequeath the land and the birthright in the land, chose to bury Rachel at the place where she died, as a statement that the place of her death was significant and not coincidental: what it meant was that you, Joseph, are entitled to inherit in the land.

Ultimately, Rachel – who, by virtue of her repentance for her sins, merited an inheritance in the land – became a symbol for her children, who were destined to repent and thereby to be returned to their land: "So says God: there is reward for your endeavor, says God…and there is hope for your future, says God, and the children shall return to their borders. I have surely heard Ephraim bemoaning himself... bring me back and I shall return, for You are the Lord my God. For after I returned, I was turned away, I repented; after I was instructed, I struck upon my thigh... Return, O virgin Israel, return to these, your cities."

Jacob's Blessing

by Rav Tamir Granot

I. INTRODUCTION

At the center of this week's *parasha* we find the blessings that Jacob
bestows – first upon Ephraim and Menashe, and then on the rest of his
children, followed immediately by the description of Jacob's death and
burial. We may view Jacob's blessing as a sort of epilogue, in which he
summarizes and also looks to the future of his children and the tribes
that will descend from them.

The Torah refers to Jacob's speeches here as "blessings": "This is
what their father told them, and he blessed them – each according to his
blessing, he blessed them," and they do indeed give the impression of
being blessings. But the concept of "blessing" is itself somewhat opaque.
A blessing can be a wish or prayer. On the other hand, it may also be a
sort of division of inheritance or roles. Another possibility is to perceive
Jacob's words here as a prophecy or divinely-inspired vision. Indeed, at
the outset Jacob says: "Gather yourselves and I shall tell you what will
befall you at the end of days."

In this *shiur*, I would like to examine the content of Jacob's blessings, in an attempt to answer the question of their status and intention.

II. THE BLESSING TO EPHRAIM AND MENASHE

Jacob's first blessings are to Ephraim and Menashe. These are apparently meant to be regarded as part of the blessings to the tribes. It should be remembered that later, Jacob also blesses Joseph. The blessing to Ephraim and Menashe here is not a replacement for, or at the expense of, a blessing to their father. The crux of their blessing "upgrades" their status to that of the tribes: "Ephraim and Menashe shall be unto me like Reuben and Simeon." Joseph's sons attain equal status to that of Jacob's sons. The *de facto* significance of this decision by Jacob is a double-portion in the inheritance for Joseph. This leads many commentators to conclude that Joseph receives here the inheritance of a firstborn, since the law of the firstborn is that he receives a double inheritance: "To give him double of all that is in his possession, for he represents the beginning of his strength…" If this explanation is correct, then Joseph is in fact being indirectly "appointed" as firstborn by Jacob. If Joseph is indeed chosen as the firstborn, we must inquire as to the status of the other brothers – including those who should receive the birthright on the basis of the order of their birth and others who may be considered worthy of the birthright by virtue of their abilities.

III. THE BLESSINGS TO THE TRIBES

Let us now move on to the blessing to the tribes. We may point to a few different types of blessings. Reuben, Simeon, and Levi are apparently rejected. In their place, Judah and Joseph are chosen. Two tribes (the middle tribes in the blessings, Dan and Gad) are granted military might, while four tribes (Zebulun, Issachar, Asher and Naphtali) receive material blessings. In the middle of the blessings we find the verse "For Your salvation I wait, God," and the description of Benjamin as a wolf concludes the blessings.

Placing Judah on one side and Joseph on the other, both "chosen," according to their blessings, we see that the blessings are in fact arranged chiastically, as follows:

A. Chosen tribe – Judah
  B. Material blessings – Issachar and Zebulun
    C. Military blessing – Dan

D. Pinnacle – "For Your salvation I wait, God"
C1. Military blessing – Gad
B1. Material blessings – Asher and Naphtali
A1. Chosen tribe – Joseph

In this format, the "arms" of this unit are arranged facing each other in symmetrical form: outer framework reflecting outer framework; internal facing internal, etc. In the center we find the climax, the pinnacle. Jacob's blessings, as we may see, are built around this structure. On the outskirts we find the introduction – addressing the tribes that are rejected – and Jacob's words to Benjamin at the end, who is also described as possessing military prowess, but is not part of the framework.

It seems that Benjamin's removal and exclusion from the complex pyramidal structure is of significance, for at least two possible reasons:

The tribe of Benjamin, during the period of the Judges, was cast out by the tribes of Israel, and nearly lost any hope of continuity (episode of the concubine in Giva). It is possible that Benjamin's removal from the structure of the blessings hints at his future removal from the nation of Israel.

During a later period, Benjamin became absorbed or annexed into the tribe of Judah, and its independent tribal status was no longer recognizable.

It is possibly for these two reasons that Benjamin's blessing is mentioned as an addendum to the main body of blessings rather than as part of them.

Regarding the reproached, disqualified tribes, Reuben is Jacob's biological firstborn son. His rejection for this status arises from his sin with Bilha. The next sons in line are Simeon and Levi, but they, too, are rejected – because of their sin involving Shekhem. This rejection is not presented by Jacob only as punishment, but also as the result of their unsuitability for the leadership entailed by the birthright, as evidenced by their sin. Reuben is "great dignity and great power; unstable as water…" Due to this trait he is unworthy of leadership. Simeon and Levi have instruments of cruelty for swords; their anger is strong and their fury fierce; hence they, too, are unworthy. The obvious answer is to move on to Judah, and we shall expand on this below.

As we have demonstrated, there are tribes that are blessed with abundance in their inheritance, while others are blessed with military success. The blessings match what we know about the development and history of the tribes of Israel: Issachar, Zebulun, Naphtali, and Asher received blessed portions in the valley region, the Galilee, the coastal plain and the fertile valley of the North. Dan and Gad settled the border towns and were required to protect the borders of Israel. The future indeed bore out Jacob's blessings.

The mirror arrangement also emphasizes the parallels between them. Issachar and Zebulun, sons of Leah, are blessed with abundance and, correspondingly, so are Naphtali and Asher – a son of Bilha and a son of Zilpa. Gad, son of Zilpa, is blessed with military success, and so is Dan – son of Bilha. Thus, the blessings of material abundance and military power are divided equally between the sons of the maidservants, one each, and two correspondingly for each couple. The rest of the blessings of abundance are given to the two remaining sons of Leah. Here we would expect to find a symmetric balance with the sons of Rachel, but we know that Rachel has only two sons, and Benjamin is rejected (or at least left out). We do admittedly find a blessing of abundance being given to Joseph, who – as discussed – is blessed as two tribes, Ephraim and Menashe, and he indeed receives two portions. The blessing of abundance comes through prominently in the words, "blessings of the heavens above; blessings of the deep crouching below; blessings of the breasts and of the womb…"

Thus, the symmetrical chiastic structure creates a parallel that is not only structural but also symbolizes the logic of the division of blessings, which are equally distributed among the tribes, the children of the matriarchs and the children of the maidservants. The reason for this division will be addressed below.

Finally, recognizing the structure of the blessings allows us to understand Jacob's call/prayer. When we read the blessings in a continuous, linear way, the prayer "For Your salvation I wait, God" follows immediately after the blessing to Dan, and it is somewhat difficult to understand its purpose. Many commentators have proposed that since Jacob envisioned Dan engaged in war, he called for his salvation. This hypothesis may be correct, but we may add to it. First of all, the prayer for salvation is located between the two blessings dealing with war, and is linked to both – the blessing to Gad and the blessing to Dan. In addition, since this verse represents the center and pinnacle of the entire chapter, we may say that it belongs to the chapter as a whole and is directed towards the blessings of all of the tribes. At the same time, by virtue of its central location, it creates the symmetry and parallel between the various blessings.

IV. LEADERSHIP

Let us now move on to the most critical aspect of the blessings: the selection of leadership. What makes it so difficult to understand Jacob's intentions in this regard is that it appears, in fact, that he chooses twice – i.e., he does not decide. Expressions of chosenness are found in the blessings of both Judah and Joseph:

> Judah: "It is you whom your brothers shall praise"; "Your father's children shall bow down before you"; "The staff shall not depart from Judah, nor a lawmaker from between his feet" ...

> Joseph: "From the hand of the Mighty One of Jacob, from there the shepherd, the stone of Israel"; "The crown of the head of he who was separated from his brothers."

On the basis of the general pattern, it seems that this represents a deliberate continuation of the idea we mentioned previously: Jacob intends to scatter the centers of power. We shall return to this answer, but first let us examine some others.

We know that *Ḥazal* and our tradition speak of two ideal models of leadership: *"Mashiaḥ ben Yosef"* and *"Mashiaḥ ben David."* There are two models of leadership because Mashiaḥ, after all, is a king – i.e., a leader – and there are two classic forms of such leadership. *"Mashiaḥ ben Yosef"* deals with the material problems, while *"Mashiaḥ ben David"* is responsible for spiritual leadership. In other words, *Ḥazal* noted that Joseph and Judah represent two forms of leadership, which will find expression in lofty manifestations of humanity. Is there a hint of this idea to be found in Jacob's blessing?

Let us first examine the question on the basis of different representations in Tanach itself. The first source is from Psalms, end of chapter seventy-eight:

He brought them to His holy border; to this mountain, acquired by His right hand. He drove out nations before them and apportioned them an inheritance by line, and caused the tribes of Israel to dwell in their tents. But they tested and rebelled against the Supreme God, and did not observe His statutes... God heard and was very angry, and greatly abhorred Israel. So He abandoned the Tabernacle of Shilo, the tent where He dwelled among men... He abhorred the tent of Joseph, and did not choose the tribe of Ephraim. He chose the tribe of Judah; the mountain of Zion, which He loved. And He built His Sanctuary like the high heavens, like the earth which He established forever. (Ps. 78:54–69)

This chapter is a historical review with a religious-moral message. We shall focus here on its presentation of God's relationship with the chosen tribes. The psalmist draws a parallel between the process whereby Shilo was abandoned and Zion chosen, and the process of rejecting Joseph and choosing Judah. The significance is far-reaching – just as the selection of Shilo was temporary and came to an end, so the choice of Joseph is temporary and transient. And just as we have here a clear historical trend moving from the earlier Shilo to the later Temple, so the selection of Joseph is chronologically earlier, and he is then rejected in the face of the selection of Judah. According to this insight offered by the book of Psalms, then, the choice is indeed double: there is a period in history where Joseph is chosen, and afterwards Judah is chosen.

The next source is from Chronicles:

And the children of Reuben – the firstborn of Israel, for he was the firstborn, but when he defiled his father's couch his birthright was given to the children of Joseph, son of Israel, but the firstborn status was not attributed to him. For Judah arose over his brothers, and the ruler came from him, although the birthright belonged to Joseph. (5:1-2)

These verses give a precise clarification as to the division of roles and status. Reuben is the firstborn according to natural right. By defiling his father's bed (exactly the same expression used by Jacob) he causes his birthright to be given to the sons of Joseph. Here, too, there is an explicit reference to Jacob's words: "Like Reuben and Simeon they shall be for me." Now the verse goes on to clarify the division of roles between Judah and Joseph. Judah "arises" or "prevails" over his brothers ("Your father's children shall bow down before you"), and "The ruler came from him" (strength and power of his reign) – but the birthright belongs to Joseph. We can easily understand this description on the basis of the Ibn Ezra, who explains that only Joseph was still worthy of the birthright, for only he was actually a *"peter rehem"* – the actual firstborn of a womb (Rachel's). Therefore the birthright is given to him when it is taken from Reuben. The formal expression of the birthright is a double portion – and indeed, Joseph receives a double portion instead of Reuben. The leadership, in the sense of power and kingship, is given to Judah. These verses in Chronicles display attention to the problem of understanding Jacob's choice, and they provide a precise solution: a distinction must be drawn between the birthright which carries rights (given to Joseph) and the legacy of leadership (given to Judah).

I will propose another idea, continuing in the direction of the verses from Chronicles, and based on a comparison between the blessing that Jacob gives and the one that he received from Isaac. We have addressed in the past the three sets of blessings that Jacob receives, and noted that only the second and the third were meant to express his chosenness over Esau. Here there is a clear distinction between the intentions of Isaac and those of Jacob. Isaac, in his second blessing, establishes that the "blessing of Abraham" – i.e., the divine choice, with its obligations and privileges – will belong to Jacob alone. Jacob is chosen; Esau is rejected. Jacob, on the other hand, blesses his children with the desire that all will be part of the divine choice, and the blessing is distributed among all of them. The strategy of dividing up the blessings among the tribes is meant to preserve all of them within the divine blessing and promise. Each receives a part of it, according to what he deserves.

We cannot say whether Jacob understood this from the start; it is certainly not clear that the brothers did. I believe that the great conflict between Joseph and his brothers arose from the fear that whoever would not be chosen would be rejected. Perhaps Jacob's preference and special love for Joseph was interpreted by the brothers as a threat to their very existence as part of the family or the nation chosen by God. They certainly did not know what we, with the benefit of hindsight, do: that the family as a whole became the founding structure for *Am Yisrael* – the nation of Israel – for all the children of Jacob were chosen, but not all the children of Abraham or of Isaac, his forefathers.

If the brothers contemplated their family experience, they saw the fate of Ishmael and of Esau, and feared that the same would happen to them. It seems that Jacob understood the secret of the establishment of the nation, which is the sum total of all of the various elements within the family, with no rejection. Only his action for the sake of the unity of the family – as expressed also in the division of the blessing – facilitated the co-existence of all of the tribes as part of the promise to *Am Yisrael*.

The most difficult question concerns the choice of leadership. The division of assets does not necessarily create the impression of preference or rejection. But leadership that is given to one of the children may be interpreted by the others as a sign of their rejection. How did Jacob counteract this impression? What did he do so that his decision concerning the leadership would not cause problems in the family relations?

It seems that the answer can be found by looking at the blessings given to Judah and Joseph and comparing them to Isaac's blessings to Jacob. As explained, we refer here only to the blessing given to Jacob disguised as Esau – a blessing meant to bestow the birthright, but not containing any decision as to the choice of leadership.

	Material abundance	Rulership
Isaac's blessing to Jacob	May God give you of the dew of heaven and the fatness of the earth; and much corn and wine.	May peoples serve you and nations bow down to you; may you rule over your brethren, and may your mother's sons bow down to you.
Blessing to Judah	Binding his foal to the vine and his ass's colt to the choice vine, he washes his garments in wine, and his clothes in the blood of grapes.	Judah – your brothers shall praise you, your hand shall be upon the neck of your enemies, your father's children will bow down to you; "the peoples shall obey him"
Blessing to Joseph	By the God of your father, who will help you, and by the Almighty, who will bless you – blessings of the heavens above, blessings of the deep that crouches beneath, blessings of the breasts and of the womb. The blessings of your father prevail over the blessings of my ancestors…	

I believe that this parallel offers us a better understanding of Jacob's intentions. Jacob is conveying the blessing that was given to him, as the firstborn, to his children. This blessing, once again, does not reflect any desire to reject any of them. Jacob is faced with two firstborn sons: the firstborn of Leah, and the firstborn of Rachel. Leah's firstborn is Judah – since Reuben, Simeon, and Levi are all disqualified; Rachel's firstborn is Joseph. The unity of the family depends on a division of the blessing such that all receive something and all are dependent upon each other. There is no advantage to having power to reign if there is no economic abundance, and the fruits of abundance cannot be enjoyed and utilized property without a strong and wise leadership.

But, as we saw above, Jacob does not make the division arbitrarily, just to maintain fairness and unity. The division of the blessing is directed towards the prominent traits and talents of the sons themselves. Each receives a blessing in the sphere in which he has proved himself to be particularly capable. Judah, who has proved his leadership with respect to the brothers and towards Joseph, in presenting them and standing before him, receives the gift of leadership. And indeed, the kingship of Israel is the eternal dynasty of David. Joseph, who has proved his abilities on the material level, in his economic organizational ability, receives the blessing of material abundance. Indeed, the portions of Ephraim and Menashe are large and fertile, while the majority of the portion of Judah is desert, its principal yield being wine (the region of the mountains of Judah is full of vineyards). And even when Joseph attained royalty, it was temporary and generally unsuccessful.

This leads us to the distinction drawn by *Ḥazal*, as borne out by later generations, between *"Mashiaḥ ben Yosef,"* whose responsibility extends to the material dimension, and *"Mashiaḥ ben David,"* whose kingdom is one of divine justice – an eternal kingship.

Clearly, Jacob's blessing contains an element of prophecy – for the inheritances that the tribes received and their future ultimately bore out Jacob's words – at least so far as we are familiar with the history. Indeed, at the "end of days" – in later times – the tribes of Israel experienced what Jacob predicted or prophesied for them. But according to our interpretation, the immense importance of Jacob's blessing lies in the distribution of the various elements of blessing among the tribes so as to preserve the unity of the family: to award each and every tribe some special quality, while preserving the balance between the different forces. Thanks to Jacob's blessing, the tribes all remained "the tribes of God" – the nation of Israel.

Joseph – From Exile to Redemption

by Rabbanit Sharon Rimon

I. THE DEATH OF JACOB AND THE DEATH OF JOSEPH

Although the *parasha* gets its name from the opening word, *"Vayḥi"* – denoting life – the *parasha* actually describes the death of two people: Jacob and Joseph.

It begins with a description of Jacob's preparations, knowing that he is about to die. He commands Joseph to bury him in Canaan; he declares that Ephraim and Menashe will have special status as sons deserving of an inheritance; he blesses all of his children, and commands all of them to bury him in the Cave of Makhpela. The text then describes his death, the mourning that follows, and the funeral procession. Then there is a conversation between Joseph and his brothers, straightening out the affairs between them. It then ends with Joseph's parting words to his brothers and his death.

If we compare the two descriptions of death – that of Jacob and that of Joseph – we find a considerable degree of similarity. Admittedly, the description in Jacob's case is far more detailed, but the same central elements appear in both:

Dwelling in Egypt:

> Jacob : "And Israel dwelled in the land of Egypt" (47:27)
>
> Joseph: "And Joseph dwelled in Egypt – he and his father's household" (50:22)

Noting of the length of life:

> Jacob: "And Jacob's lifetime, the years of his life, were a hundred and forty-seven years" (47:25)
>
> Joseph: "And Joseph lived a hundred and ten years" (50:22)

Mention of the redemption:

> Jacob: "And Israel said to Joseph: Behold, I am going to die, but God will be with you and restore you to the land of your forefathers" (48:21)
>
> Joseph: "And Joseph said to his brothers: I am going to die, but God will surely remember you and bring you up from this land to the land which He promised to Abraham, to Isaac, and to Jacob" (50:24)

Command concerning burial in the land:

> Jacob: "Place your hand under my thigh, and act towards me with kindness and truth: do not bury me in Egypt. Let me lie with my ancestors; you shall carry me from Egypt and bury me in their burial place. And he said: Swear to me; and he swore to him" (47:29–31)
>
> "Bury me with my ancestors at the cave which is in the field of Ephron, the Ḥittite" (49:29–32)
>
> Joseph: "And Joseph caused Benei Yisrael to swear, saying... And you shall take up my bones from here" (50:25)

The death:

> Jacob: "And he gathered his legs to his bed, and he expired, and was gathered to his people" (49:33)

> Joseph: "And Joseph died, aged a hundred and ten" (50:26)

Embalming:

> Jacob: "And the physicians embalmed Israel" (50:2)

> Joseph: "And they embalmed him" (50:26)

Burial:

> Jacob: "And Joseph went up to bury his father … and his sons carried him to the land of Canaan, and they buried him in the cave of the field of Makhpela" (50:7–13)

> Joseph: "And placed him in a casket in Egypt" (50:26)

Both Jacob and Joseph know that there will be redemption from Egypt, and both command their descendants to bury them in **Canaan**. However, there are two important differences between them: Jacob does not tell all of his sons that there will be redemption; he tells only Joseph. Joseph, on the other hand, tells all of his brothers. Second, Jacob's body is brought to Canaan for burial, while Joseph's body remains, for the meantime, in a casket in Egypt.

Why is Joseph's body left, for the meantime, in Egypt? Why does he not command his sons to bury him right away, as his father did, instead commanding them to take up his bones only when they are redeemed from Egypt? And why is it specifically Joseph who tells the brothers about the future redemption, rather than Jacob? These questions will serve as the basis for this *shiur*.

II. WHEN DOES THE EXILE BEGIN?

A further question that arises in the wake of Joseph's speech is why he feels the need to tell his brothers that "God will surely remember you and bring you up from this land." Are they not currently free to get up and leave? Are they already subjugated now, during Joseph's lifetime?

This question is further reinforced by the fact that when *Benei Yisrael* want to go and bury Jacob, they need to first seek Pharaoh's approval. Joseph, the second-to-the-king, must ask permission from the king to go and bury his own father! Moreover, he does not dare to present his request directly; he appeals via "Pharaoh's house." Pharaoh indeed agrees immediately, but the manner of the request is most surprising. We have the sense that Joseph's position is not as high and mighty as we had imagined. In a certain sense, he is subjugated, enslaved to Pharaoh.

In addition, when Jacob's funeral procession sets off, the Torah tells us: "They left their children, their flocks and cattle in the land of Goshen." This verse is strongly reminiscent of the interactions between Moses and Pharaoh several generations later:

> And Moses and Aaron were brought back to Pharaoh, and he said to them: Go, serve the Lord your God. Who exactly is going? And Moses said: We shall go with our youth and with our elderly; with our sons and with our daughters, with our flocks and our cattle we shall go, for we have a festival unto God. (Ex. 10:8–9)

This theme returns in the context of the plague of darkness:

> And Pharaoh called to Moses and he said: Go, worship the Lord. Let only your flocks and your cattle remain; let your children, too, go with you. (10:24)

When *Benei Yisrael* are subjugated in Egypt, Pharaoh does not allow them to leave with their children and with their flocks and cattle. So long as they leave their children and their livestock behind, they will still have a connection with Egypt and will have to return there.

When Jacob's sons go to bury him in Canaan, they leave their children behind, along with their animals. These are the anchor ensuring their return – and indeed, the sons return to Egypt.

In light of the above, we might sense that the Egyptian exile has already begun, and perhaps *Benei Yisrael* have already been subjugated. However, there is an important difference that should be noted between the episodes. In the book of Exodus, Pharaoh insists that only the men will go, while Moses insists that everyone must go. In contrast, in *Parashat Vayḥi*, the brothers leave their children and their livestock in Egypt voluntarily. No one tells them to do so. They leave them behind because Egypt is their home; they have every intention of returning there. This is not real subjugation, but it represents the beginning of the Egyptian exile, for they have become so entrenched in Egypt that they cannot imagine leaving.

Joseph sees this reality – the way in which *Benei Yisrael* are "taking root" in Egypt – and he senses that this is the beginning of a long-term exile. Joseph is the "dreamer of dreams." Although this earned him much scorn from his brothers, this quality is of profound significance. Joseph is a man of vision. He has the ability to read the present and to sense the future. He sees how the family is settling down in Egypt (and perhaps also senses the attitude of the Egyptians towards the foreigners in their midst) and he feels that this situation is not going to solve itself easily. Already now, he discerns the early signs of exile and subjugation.

III. THE PROMISE OF REDEMPTION – "GOD WILL SURELY REMEMBER YOU"

In perceiving the situation and its significance, Joseph understands that divine intervention will be needed to bring this exile to its conclusion, and therefore he tells his brothers, "God will surely remember you." Joseph anticipates the exile, but even before it begins he foresees the future redemption, and before his death he leaves the nation with this vision.

However, it is not Joseph who "invents" the vision of exile and the redemption from it. It is Jacob who discovers this secret, expressing it in the words, "God will be with you, and will restore you to the land of your forefathers" (48:21). Jacob had received this prophecy several years previously, on his journey down to Egypt to see his long-lost son Joseph:

God said to Israel, in a night vision, and He said: Jacob, Jacob. And he said: Here I am. And He said: I am the Almighty, the God of your father. Do not be afraid of going down to Egypt, for I shall make you into a great nation there. I shall go down with you to Egypt, and I shall surely also bring you up, and Joseph will put his hand upon your eyes. (46:2–4)

Prior to his death, Jacob conveys to Joseph the promise of redemption, and it is Joseph who will transmit it further, to his brothers.

Years later, when the time of redemption arrives, Moses is sent to *Benei Yisrael* with the following message:

Go, gather the elders of Israel, and say to them: The Lord God of your forefathers appeared to me – the God of Abraham, Isaac and Jacob – saying: I have surely remembered [*pakod pakadeti*] you, and that which is done to you in Egypt. (Ex. 3:16)

God tells Moses that when he tells this to the elders of Israel, they will listen to him. Why will they listen to him? The Midrash explains:

"He [Moses] said to them [the elders]: Thus said the Holy One, blessed be He: I have surely remembered you." *Benei Yisrael* had a sign: any redeemer that would come with this sign – "*pakod pakadeti*" – would be known to them as a true redeemer, for thus Joseph had told them: "God will surely remember you" [Gen. 50:24]. Since he mentioned the words "*pakod pakadeti*," immediately "the people believed" [Ex. 4:31]. (*Midrash Tanḥuma* [Buber] *Shemot* 21)

The expression "*pakod pakadeti*," which Moses uses in order to convince the elders of Israel to listen to him, is the same language that was used by Joseph when speaking to his brothers. It was Joseph who had planted in the hearts of *Benei Yisrael* the hope of redemption, by telling them twice "*pakod yifkod*."

This hope, originally inspired by Joseph, had echoed in the ears of *Benei Yisrael*, subjugated in Egypt. Joseph's words had been passed from the mouth of one suffering slave to the ear of another; from father to son, throughout the years of crushing slavery, maintaining the hope that one day they would be redeemed.

But Jacob himself had foreseen the redemption. Why, then, did Jacob not tell his sons himself? Why did he choose to leave the momentous role of promising an eventual redemption specifically to Joseph? Possibly, Jacob passed away at a time when *Benei Yisrael* were still not so entrenched in Egypt, and therefore it was not yet appropriate to prophesize about a redemption from there. Therefore, he revealed this only to Joseph, and when Joseph was about to die he decided that the time was right to make the matter known.

However, it is possible that there was also a deeper reason; that it was specifically Joseph's words that would have to accompany *Benei Yisrael* over the course of the long and difficult Egyptian exile. It was specifically Joseph's words that echoed in their ears all this time, and specifically his words that came to represent redemption.

IV. "YOU SHALL TAKE UP MY BONES"

Furthermore, Joseph is not buried in Canaan, as Jacob was. Rather, his bones are kept in a casket in Egypt. Joseph could have commanded his brothers to bury him in the land of Israel – as Jacob had commanded his sons. And had there been any concern that Pharaoh would not agree to this, he could have arranged it with Pharaoh in advance. However, Joseph chooses to command his brothers to take up his bones together with them when they leave Egypt, at the time of their redemption. When *Benei Yisrael* leave Egypt, the Torah emphasizes the fact that Moses fulfills Joseph's last will, and takes his bones:

> And Moses took the bones of Joseph with him, for he had made *Benei Yisrael* swear, saying: God will surely remember you, and you shall take up my bones from here with you. (Ex. 13:19)

The Torah says nothing about the bones of the other brothers, although it would seem reasonable to assume that they, too, were brought up from Egypt. The Torah records only Joseph's command, and the fact that *Benei Yisrael* fulfill his wish. Apparently, then, the taking up of Joseph's bones is a matter of great importance. Why is this so?

When Joseph commands his brothers to take up his bones, he binds this together with the matter of redemption: "God will surely remember you, and you shall take up my bones with you from here." The taking up of Joseph's bones, then, is closely bound up with the redemption, as the Midrash explains:

> The time for Israel's redemption arrived... and Moses walked about the city for three days and three nights to find Joseph's casket, for they could not leave Egypt without Joseph. Why? For so he had made them swear, prior to his death, as it is written [Gen. ch. 50], "Joseph made *Benei Yisrael* swear, saying..."
>
> When he [Moses] had become extremely weary, he was met by a certain Segula... [1] She said to him, Come with me and I will show you where he is. She led him to a stream, and said: In this place the magicians and wizards made a casket of five-hundred talents, and cast it into the stream. And so they said to Pharaoh: Do you want this nation never to leave here? Here are the bones of Joseph. If they never find them, they will not be able to leave.
>
> Right away Moses stood at the edge of the stream and said: Joseph, Joseph! You know how you promised to Israel [Gen. ch. 50], "God will surely remember you!" Give honor to the God of Israel, and do not hold back the redemption of Israel!... Ask for mercy from your Creator and rise up from the depths. Immediately, Joseph's casket began to rise up from the depths, like a single reed. Moses took it and placed it upon his shoulder..."
> (*Devarim Raba* 11:7)

Joseph's bones continue to accompany *Benei Yisrael* on their journeys through the desert, and afterwards during the years of conquest and division of the land. Only after the process of redemption is complete, after the death of Joshua, do we find a description of the burial of Joseph:

And the bones of Joseph, which *Benei Yisrael* had brought up

---

1. In other midrashim, he is met by Seraḥ, daughter of Asher.

from Egypt, they buried in Shekhem, in the portion of the field
which Jacob had purchased from the sons of Ḥamor, the father of
Shekhem, for a hundred *kesita*, and they became an inheritance
for the children of Joseph. (Josh. 24:32)

Joseph is not buried in Canaan immediately after he dies. Rather, his
bones remain with *Benei Yisrael* in exile, and they accompany *Benei Yisrael*
throughout the process of redemption. What is the significance of this?

V. REPAIRING THE SALE OF JOSEPH

This may be viewed as a repair ("*tikkun*") for the sale of Joseph. Joseph
had been sold by his brothers in Shekhem, and that is the beginning of
the story of the Egyptian exile. The redemption from Egypt is bound up
with a repair for the sin of selling Joseph, and therefore it also involves
the return of Joseph (or at least his bones), specifically by the brothers,
and specifically to Shekhem, from where he was sold, as described in
the midrash:

> So said the Holy One, blessed be He, to the tribes: You sold
> Joseph; now restore his bones to their place.
> A different interpretation: Joseph said to them – I swear to
> you that from the place from which you kidnapped me, to there
> you shall return me. And so *Benei Yisrael* did: "And the bones of
> Joseph, which *Benei Yisrael* had brought up from Egypt, they bur-
> ied in Shekhem." (*Bereshit Raba* [Theodore-Albeck, ed.], *Parasha*
> 85, s.v. "*vayered Yehuda*")

According to this understanding, the Egyptian exile was a result of (or
punishment for) the sale of Joseph.

VI. JOSEPH AND THE PROCESS OF
EXILE AND REDEMPTION

Let us now consider a deeper significance to the fact that Joseph accompanies the process of redemption from Egypt. Joseph arrives in Egypt
ahead of his brothers, and he unwittingly prepares the ground for their
move. It is thereby he who causes them to come down to Egypt and who

facilitates their settling there. It is he who gives them the land of Goshen and ensures that they will stay there instead of going back to Canaan!

Similarly, it is Joseph who initiates the process of redemption: when he feels that *Benei Yisrael* are putting down roots in Egypt, even before their subjugation, he prophesizes *"pakod yifkod,"* and commands them to take his bones with them when they are eventually redeemed. Thus, he paves the way for their redemption.

The book of Genesis does not end with the descent to Egypt and the settling there that represents the beginning of the exile. Rather, it ends with the story of two burials, which express the hope for redemption. One story is the procession of *Benei Yisrael* to Canaan, to bury their father Jacob. The burial of Jacob in the land of Israel concludes the stories of the patriarchs, all of whom were buried in the land of Israel.

The burial of the patriarchs in the land of Israel represents a powerful and significant hold on Canaan by *Benei Yisrael*. While Jacob dies in Egypt, he insists that his children bury him in Canaan, thereby continuing their powerful connection with the land, the land of their forefathers, the place where their forefathers are buried.

The second story is about the burial of Joseph. We do not read the end of this story here, only its beginning. Joseph does want to be buried in the land, but he asks not to be buried there now; rather, he will remain with *Benei Yisrael* in Egypt, and his will that his bones be buried in Canaan represents part of the hope for redemption. When they are redeemed, they will fulfill Joseph's command and take his bones up for burial in the land.

The burial of Jacob in the land of Israel, and the oath to bury Joseph in the land in the future, together represent a heavy anchor that draws them back to the land, with the promise that redemption will arrive and take them back.

Let us now return to Joseph. Joseph is the one who initiates the process of the descent to Egypt, and he is the one who initiates the process of their redemption from there. There seems to be special significance to the fact that it is Joseph who accompanies *Benei Yisrael* in the processes of exile and redemption (through his bones and his prophetic words). It is Joseph's essence that must accompany the nation through these formative experiences. Why is this so? What is Joseph's special essence?

VII. JOSEPH'S STRENGTHS

Joseph has two principal characteristics, and both are of great importance for the existence of *Am Yisrael* in exile as well as in preparation for their redemption. First, as we saw in *Parashat Vayeshev*, Joseph has a special ability to deal with difficult situations; he manages to emerge from them strengthened. He is sold as a slave to Egypt, but immediately succeeds in attaining a respected position in Potiphar's house. He is then cast into jail, but manages once again to achieve recognition of his special qualities, and he is once again promoted to an important position. He is then taken from the prison to become second to the king.

The ability to deal with difficult situations and to rise from those depths to even greater heights is an ability of great importance for *Am Yisrael* in order to not only survive in exile, but to emerge from exile strengthened and with greater powers.

Second, throughout his own personal exile in Egypt, Joseph manages to maintain his identity. He never denies or hides his origins, nor is he ashamed of his heritage. Therefore, everyone knows that he is a Hebrew. Potiphar's wife refers to him thus: "See, he has brought us a Hebrew man, to make a mockery of us … the Hebrew slave, whom you brought to us to make a mockery of us, came to me" (Gen. 39:14, 17). Similarly, the royal butler mentions him to Pharaoh as follows: "There was with us a Hebrew lad, a slave to the officer of the guard…" (41:12). Even when he becomes second to Pharaoh, Joseph continues to maintain his Hebrew identity: "They placed [bread] for him [Joseph] separately, and for them [the brothers] separately, and the Egyptians eating with him – separately, for the Egyptians could not eat bread with the Hebrews, for it was an abomination for the Egyptians" (Gen. 43:32). Despite the fact that his stubborn maintenance of his identity as a Hebrew creates a distance between him and the Egyptians, he does not capitulate.

Joseph's preservation of his Hebrew identity finds expression not only in the title "Hebrew" (*Ivri*), but also in the fact that he always takes care to mention that God helps him. The episode of Potiphar's wife proves that Joseph does not succumb to Egyptian culture; rather, he continues to maintain the moral standards that he learned in his father's house. When *Benei Yisrael* were mired in the Egyptian exile, they needed Joseph's image to accompany them so that they would be able to get through the experience intact, to remain worthy of redemption from their exile, and to be able to emerge strengthened. The image of Joseph – who himself lived in exile for many years, and grappled with it – is the image that *Benei Yisrael* keep in mind as they deal with their own exile experience. Joseph, who had experienced difficult situations and had emerged from them successfully, prepares *Benei Yisrael* for their exile and prophesizes that they will emerge from it; that there will be a redemption.

Joseph's Tears

Adapted from a lecture by
Rav Aharon Lichtenstein

At the center of the drama played out over the final third of the book of Genesis, we find the tangled web of relationships in Jacob's household. The Torah presents Joseph, "the distinguished of his brothers" (49:26), amid the divisiveness that characterizes the household, with all of the suspicion and tension that crackles in the often poisonous atmosphere. The Midrash (*Midrash Tanhuma, Vayigash* 3), in its picturesque language, portrays the confrontation between the brothers and Joseph as one between a lion and an ox.

Like a thread running through all of the acts and scenes of this multi-faceted tragedy, there is one rather surprising motif. We follow the progress of the mighty battle waged by an innocent young man against a cabal of brothers motivated by their fear and their judgmental attitude, by rejection and suspicion. Throughout all of this, we find an unexpected element that reflects the development of the drama and leaves its mark on the events themselves: *bekhi*, weeping.

Its presence is felt throughout the narrative; it is manifest at certain critical junctures, either as a reaction or as an impetus. Yet its appearances are not symmetrical. The brothers, in general, do not weep. They are a group of practical men, men of action, who plan, execute and improvise; they are devoid of romantic visions and stormy emotions. Other than Benjamin, the son of his father's old age, all of the brothers are occupied, as shepherds, with settling the world, building (as Ḥazal emphasized) the infrastructure for the future nation of Israel. The brothers devote themselves conscientiously and consistently to their tasks, big or small, with no tendency towards drama or sentimentality.

Even at their most difficult, terror-filled moments, they keep their wits about them and try to plan ahead; where necessary, they scheme and plot. Even after Jacob's death, they hatch a scheme (50:15–17) to protect themselves from Joseph's supposed wrath. Even at that hour of dread, the brothers do not cross the Rubicon that lies between supplication and tears. In this critical encounter, as in others, the brothers do not weep.

It is not only in the heat of the moment that the brothers eschew tears; even in the aftermath of their actions, they do not weep. Immediately after throwing Joseph into the pit "they sat down to eat bread" (37:25). Seforno notes:

> They did not regard any of this as a misfortune or an obstacle preventing them from having their meal – as would have been proper for righteous people such as they after causing a misfortune. In comparison, concerning the Israelites – after they annihilate the tribe of Benjamin – we read: "They sat until the evening before God, and they lifted their voices, and they wept a great weeping, and they said: 'Why, Lord God of Israel, has this happened in Israel?'" (Judges 21:2–3)

There is no such weeping in the case of Joseph's brothers. Their attitude is altogether pragmatic, practical, unsentimental. Even the suffering of their father does not move them to tears:

> Jacob rent his garments and he placed sackcloth upon his loins, and he mourned for his son for many days; and all of his sons and all of his daughters arose to comfort him, but he refused to be

comforted, and he said: "For I shall go down to my son, mourning, to the netherworld." And his father wept for him. (37:34–35)

Here the *Or HaHayyim* notes the seeming redundancy and comments:

When Jacob heard his [own] words, he wept for him all over again. Here the Torah specifically says "his father [wept for him]," so as to exclude "all of his sons and all of his daughters," since only his father wept at the mention of him.

On the other hand, on no less than eight occasions, Joseph gives expression to his emotions, and his tears flow freely. Let us briefly review these instances:

The first instance is where the brothers appear before Joseph and he hears them talking. The Torah narrates: "He turned away from them and wept" (42:24).

The second instance is where Benjamin finally appears before Joseph: "He felt compassion towards his brother, and he wanted to weep; so he entered his chamber, and wept there" (43:30).

The third instance is in the most dramatic encounter between Joseph and his brothers: "He gave his voice to weeping, and the Egyptians and the house of Pharaoh heard" (45:2).

Following this outburst, Joseph reveals his identity and tells his brothers all that has happened to him in Egypt. Towards the end of this encounter, we read: "He fell upon the neck of Benjamin, his brother, and he wept; and Benjamin wept upon his neck. And he kissed all of his brothers and he wept upon them" (45:14–15).

The next instance is the encounter between Joseph and Jacob: "Joseph made ready his chariot and he went up to Goshen to meet Israel his father; and he presented himself to him, and he fell upon his neck; and he wept upon his neck a good while" (46:29).

Finally, we have a three-fold weeping following the death of Jacob, in the final chapter of this dramatic story. First, there is the immediate reaction to the death: "Jacob...expired and was gathered to his people. And Joseph fell upon his father's face and wept upon him and kissed him" (49:33–50:1). Later, there is weeping not only by Joseph, but by the entire Egyptian nation: "The Egyptians wept for him for seventy days" (50:3). This is a public demonstration of mourning, in contrast to Joseph's personal weeping. The final instance of weeping is a return to the personal, intimate realm: "Joseph's brothers saw that their father had died, and they said: 'Perhaps Joseph will hate us, and will repay us for all the evil we did to him.' So they sent word urgently to Joseph, saying, 'Your father did command before he died, saying: Please forgive the sin of your brothers…'" – and Joseph's reaction: "And Joseph wept as they spoke to him" (50:15–17).

Thus, the narrative as a whole is linked by a chain of weeping, in changing circumstances, at different times, in varying contexts. A more detailed examination of each instance leads us to draw two general conclusions regarding this abundance of tears.

First, the weeping has no uniform, monolithic motivation or manifestation. It is a profound and diverse expression, in terms of both its inherent nature and its roots. There can be tears of sorrow, joy, mourning, celebration, collapse, excitement, helplessness, courage, supplication, despair, guilt, self-rebuke or repentance. In fact, as we examine each instance individually, we discover that – as we might have expected of such a sensitive personality – Joseph's weeping is not all of a kind. It changes and transforms itself according to the circumstances.

Second, as fitting for such a drama, every instance of weeping that occurs has its own significance. At the same time, though, each represents a link in a chain which is continuous and progressive. We are able to trace the development from one station to the next, each reflecting the playing out of the true and central drama – which is internal.

Before addressing the various instances of weeping and the circumstances surrounding them, we must first consider those instances in which Joseph refrains from crying. Here it quickly becomes apparent that at the most bitter and difficult times, Joseph ceases to be the dreamy romantic – garbed in a striped coat and curling his hair – whom we encounter at the beginning of the story. He remains calm, deals with the situation, and rises above it, demonstrating a most impressive survival instinct.

Even at the bitterest moment in his life, when he is cast by his own brothers into a pit infested – as the sages (*Shabbat* 22a) describe it – with snakes and scorpions, he demonstrates restraint. In the original account, we do not find even the mildest word of protest. Only later on do we discover that Joseph does indeed attempt to avert his fate, with no success, as the brothers say: "We saw his anguish when he pleaded with us, but we did not listen" (42:21). Nevertheless, while the Torah refers to pleading, it does not mention tears.

Joseph is sold to a caravan of Ishmaelites, but he does not weep. Instead of wallowing in self-pity at his bitter fate, he transforms himself from someone who cannot find his way – from someone who just the day before had wandered through the fields while seeking his brothers (37:15–17) – into a capable and accomplished manager in the house of Potiphar.

When he is unjustly thrown into prison, Joseph again refrains from weeping. Once again, he demonstrates an amazing ability to adapt and survive. By virtue of his impressive practical abilities, Joseph attains a position whereby "everything that he did, God would cause to succeed" (39:23). Even when Joseph is left to rot in jail, abandoned and betrayed by Pharaoh's butler, he still does not weep.

Admittedly, in many of the episodes that we have just enumerated, Joseph is the passive object of actions taken by others; hence, perhaps, his fortitude is not all that relevant to our discussion. Nevertheless, even if in these situations we regard him as merely a passive victim, his innermost reaction – reflecting much of the calm acceptance which he has nurtured and which he maintains – represents an achievement that is entirely his own. It reflects his openness to the ups and downs of reality, and the development of a personal, psychological ability to deal with them.

It is not his own peril that moves Joseph to tears. His weeping begins where the drama intensifies, where Joseph finds himself in an encounter that is less dangerous, but of far greater significance: the renewed encounter with his brothers. The mutually contradictory inclinations, the mixed (and sometimes conflicting) emotions – it is these that affect Joseph so profoundly.

The period during which Joseph is completely cut off from his brothers lasts longer than two decades. During this time, he emerges as a firm, determined, energetic leader, the embodiment of pragmatism and achievement. He probably harbors, in the depths of his heart, some long-ing for his father's house and its spiritual climate. He must feel nostalgia for its teachings and values, its sources and its atmosphere; beyond his nostalgic memories, Joseph must feel real concern for his father's wel-fare and his state of mind. Still, none of this manages to topple the wall of equanimity and the screen of distraction. The sense of distance, the sense of physical and existential severance that he feels, is expressed in the names that Joseph gives to his sons. First is Menashe, "For God has caused me to forget [*nashani*] all my toil and all of my father's house" (41:51). The name of his second son, Ephraim – "for God has caused me to be fruitful [*hifrani*] in the land of my affliction" (v. 52) – expresses conspicuous contentment alongside genuine feeling.

Under these circumstances – severance from homeland and fam-ily; occupation with steering an empire through its challenges; building his household and family; a day-to-day reality of impressive achievement; a sense of strength and power that provide enormous satisfaction – there is no one and nothing that causes Joseph to weep. For the same reason, he is not required to restrain himself from weeping.

It is only when he comes face to face with his brothers again that he wants and needs to weep. On some occasions, when Joseph is unable to hold himself back, his tears burst forth. In these encounters, all of the feelings that have been suppressed and submerged rise up again. All that has been forgotten floods back into his consciousness. In place of the comforting thought that "God has caused me to forget," he is hit with the impact of memory: "Joseph remembered the dreams which he had dreamt about them" (42:9). Joseph remembers not only the dreams, but also everything that came with them, the atmosphere within which they had appeared, and the chain of events they brought in their wake.

This encounter opens a Pandora's box. Joseph is waging a battle not only with his brothers, but also with himself, with his past, present and future. As he wrestles with his own demons, there open before him those gates which the sages (*Berakhot* 32b) teach are never locked: the gates of tears. The great Irish writer W.B. Yeats said that "We make out of the quarrel with others, rhetoric, but of the quarrel with ourselves, poetry." The world of poetry, he maintains, is the pure, refined world of emotion – a world in which weeping, whether external or internal, is granted a place of honor. This world is something Joseph cannot escape. When Joseph hears his brothers admit their guilt, "He turned away from them and wept" (42:21–24).

This is the first instance of weeping in the entire narrative. What is its meaning? Rashi explains: "Because he heard that they were contrite." In his view, it is the brothers' remorse as human beings, and their acknowledgment that God is exacting punishment of them, measure for measure, that brings Joseph back to his existential and religious roots. Suddenly, the embers which had burned so low – the connection to his brothers, his home, his past – are reignited. A spark of empathy and fraternity, perhaps even of love, is kindled inside him, reconnecting him with his past. This represents a seismic tremor, shaking up and undermining the Egyptian reality within which Joseph is now firmly rooted.

Seforno adopts a different interpretation: "He wept upon perceiving their anguish." Joseph's weeping is not related to his personal, human, existential or religious aspirations; rather, it is simply a matter of compassion towards his brothers. Indeed, the burden is an onerous one. The brothers' past deeds have left a deep scar in Joseph's heart, affecting him in the present and destined to influence him in the future. Is that old hatred – "They hated him even more, for his dreams and for his words" (37:8) – no longer in his brothers' hearts? Or perhaps that old cruelty and abusiveness – captured in Jacob's words, "The archers attacked him and shot at him and loathed him" (49:23) – still lurk in their character? Joseph, too, for his part, has yet to bring closure to his struggle. In the very same verse, he shows himself to be an astute and quick-witted adversary, detaining Simeon and complicating the brothers' mission in every possible way. Still, what Seforno means is that, as the saying goes, blood is thicker than water; when he sees his brothers suffering, he is moved to tears.

His weeping here expresses compassion. It bespeaks Joseph's desire to be reunited with his brothers immediately, and it is quite understandable. Yet, while inside him an emotional storm is brewing, Joseph is not prepared – perhaps even unable – to vent it. "He turned away from them and wept." At this stage, he is not prepared to lower even slightly the screen of deception – not only before his brothers, but even in his own mind. This is not a simple matter. With regard to others,

Joseph can, with the slightest of movements, continue to conceal the evidence. However, he cannot hide the truth from himself. He might have said to his conscience, echoing King David's words to God: "Where can I hide from Your spirit? From Your presence, where can I flee?" (Ps. 139:7). Facing his brothers, he comes back to himself: "He returned to them and spoke to them, and he took Simeon from among them and imprisoned him in their presence" (42:24); but for himself, once the genie has escaped from the bottle, there is no hope of stuffing it back inside. "He turned away from them" – I imagine that this is meant not only outwardly, so that they will not notice, but also as an indication that at this stage Joseph lacks the courage, at the moment of his weeping, to look at them directly, openly and honestly. Such is the situation for now, but it will change.

Indeed, the change is not long in coming. Within a few months, the supply of food taken back to Jacob is finished. The brothers then return to Egypt, this time accompanied by Benjamin, and here Joseph cries for the second time. This instance is similar to the previous one in terms of its roots – the confrontation with the past, the renewed connection with the family – but very different in its intensity. For Joseph, this is not only a reunion with Benjamin, his beloved brother, but an encounter fraught with the cumulative effect of all that has happened since his first weeping. The meeting with the other brothers is climactic in its own right; the meeting with Benjamin is a crisis of a different order.

As the child of his father's old age, who occupies a marginal position in the group, Benjamin is a unique character. However, there is more to his distinctness than his age, as Ramban boldly points out. Noting Jacob's words to his sons (as recounted by Judah [44:27]): "You know that my wife bore me two," Ramban questions: "Were there [only] two? Did his wives not bear him twelve sons?" He explains:

> The reason [for this statement] is that Jacob willingly married only Rachel. Therefore he says, "My wife bore me" – meaning: there were born to me, of the woman who was my wife by my own will, only two; and I invested my love in them as though

they were my only children, while the rest were, in my eyes, like children of concubines.

Benjamin, then, is special in his own right. Obviously, in relation to Joseph, his status is unique for two reasons. First, not only is he Joseph's full brother, but his very existence is bound up with their mother. Benjamin embodies the price that Rachel and Joseph pay for him, for Rachel dies in giving birth to him. Second, Benjamin is the only one of all the brothers who has played no part in the terrible plot. For this reason, too, the reunion between Joseph and Benjamin is an intensely emotional one.

This is reflected in the verses. Seforno, as noted above, asserts that Joseph's weeping in the first encounter arises from his observation of their anguish, but the verse there gives no indication of this. Here, on the other hand, it is stated explicitly: "Joseph hastened, for he felt compassion towards his brother, and he wanted to weep; so he entered his chamber and wept there" (43:30). The element of compassion, the inner, emotional bond that contrasts so starkly with the royal role that Joseph plays in Egypt, rises up all at once, and with great power. This is expressed and emphasized, in relation to the weeping, in the auxiliary verb: "He wanted [*vayevakesh*] to weep."

The Hebrew root *b-k-sh* (.ש.ק.ב) has three fixed meanings in the Torah. One expresses searching, as Joseph says: "I seek [*mevakesh*] my brothers" (37:16); similarly, Saul seeks his father's donkeys (1 Sam. 9:3). This "I" does not express any special personal feeling; rather, it is a purely technical search. In its second meaning, this root refers to a request that one addresses to another. Queen Esther tells Ahasuerus "my wish and my request [*bakashati*]" (Esther 5:7). The third meaning of this root is "will," not just the will that expresses one's desire, but rather will that involves an effort at actualization; this is the clear meaning earlier in Esther, when the plot of the would-be assassins Bigthan and Teresh is uncovered: "They desired [*vayevakshu*] to lay hands upon King Ahasuerus" (Esther 2:21). Sometimes, these various meanings are interwoven, as in the verse, "I make one wish of God; it is that which I request [*avakesh*]" (Ps. 27:4) – in the sense of seeking, requesting and willing.

It seems reasonable to assume that here the term "*vayevakesh*" means an effort, a will and an aspiration. The tears do not flow of their own accord; Joseph actively seeks to weep. In his first encounter with his brothers, Joseph wanted to restrain himself, but was unable to; here, he seeks to weep: that is what is psychologically and emotionally appropriate. Joseph is entirely accepting of his weeping here; he merely seeks the proper opportunity and setting to carry it out, so "he entered his chamber."

The first and second encounters differ also with regard to the location where Joseph weeps. At the first encounter, Joseph does nothing more than turn his face aside, while he remains standing in his place. The second is different. Here, he moves from one spot to another, as Rashi explains: "He distanced himself from them so that they would not see him weeping." He heads from the vestibule to the hall. The move expresses more than just a physical, geographical transition from one place to another. It is a transition from one level of existence to an entirely different one; from the external world to the inner world, the world of home. There is a strong focus here on the inner workings of man, especially in tragic circumstances.

Elizabethan theater in England featured two stages. First, there was a vestibule, an outer room, an external stage, where public events would take place – the "rhetoric," to employ Yeats' term. Then there was an inner, more intimate stage, where man's tragic struggles would be played out, in the form of the drama taking place within the hero himself. When Shakespeare's Juliet declares, "My dismal scene I needs must act alone" (*Romeo and Juliet*, Act IV, Scene iii), she passes from the outer stage to the inner one. Her declaration accompanies her transition. "He entered his chamber," then, is the "dismal scene" that Joseph "needs must act alone." Here, in the inner chamber, he gives expression to his tragic conflict, to his explosion of emotion. This can happen only in the inner chamber, where there is no need to conceal or hide. Concerning God Himself, the prophet says, "My soul weeps in secret" (Jer. 13:17). The Talmud (*Ḥagiga* 5b) asks, "Does God then weep?" The verse is explained by means of a distinction between the "outer chamber" and the "inner chamber." In His "inner chamber," even God cries, as it were.

In Joseph's inner chamber, the weeping busts forth with such intensity that, when he emerges, he must recompose himself: "He washed his face and he emerged, and he restrained himself, and he said: Bring bread"

(43:31). When he weeps the first time, Joseph has no need to wash his face. Here, the washing of the face is more than a physical act. Joseph must compose himself and rearrange his official mask; when he leaves the chamber, his face washed and his demeanor composed, he is once again Tzafnat Pa'aneah (41:45), the Revealer of Secrets, viceroy over Egypt.

The difference is expressed in another slight difference: "He restrained himself" (*vayitapak*). This insertion is critical for an understanding of Joseph's situation in Egypt. It is a stark contrast to what happens later on, when Joseph reveals himself to his brothers. There, the text introduces his revelation with the words, "Joseph was unable to restrain himself" (45:1). Here, "he restrained himself." As I understand it, this "restraint" is different from the sort that is mentioned in other contexts. For example, when, after parading Mordekhai through the streets of Shushan on the king's horse, "Haman restrained himself, and he came to his house" (Esther 5:10), it denotes refraining from expressing outwardly the anger that one feels inside. It is neither seemly nor proper for a man of Haman's standing to appear to be angry, to look as though he has lost his self-control. He is in control of himself, and all the more so of his surroundings, and therefore he restrains himself. This restraint has nothing to do with inner, spiritual or existential turmoil. Isaiah also speaks of restraint when it comes to God: "Will You restrain Yourself for these things, God; will You be silent?" (64:12). This is a variation on the question posed by the prophets in many different contexts, concerning the question of theodicy on the national level. It does not reflect an internal struggle, so to speak, of God.

In Joseph's case, I believe, the restraint has a completely different meaning. The transition here from restraint to its absence is of far greater significance. When Joseph reveals his identity, we read:

> Joseph could not restrain himself before all those who stood before him, and he called out: "Take every person from my presence!" So no one stood with him when Joseph revealed himself to his brothers. He gave his voice to weeping, and the Egyptians and the house of Pharaoh heard. (45:9–11)

Until now, Joseph's weeping has been conducted in secret. First he "turned away" to weep, then he "entered his chamber" to weep. Now he no longer cries alone, in solitude. His weeping is full-voiced and public: "He gave his voice to weeping." His tears over his brothers reach all the way to Pharaoh's house; his weeping is heard throughout the land of Egypt.

What is the nature and significance of this weeping, "When Joseph revealed himself to his brothers"? I believe that on one level, at the beginning, Joseph cries out of sheer emotion, heightened by the drama of the occasion, combining great joy with sadness. In another sense, Joseph's weeping here expresses a sort of release. Freed of the yoke of his public position, Joseph transforms the outer chamber to an inner chamber; he is master of an emotional domain that contains both. Rashbam explains:

Until now, he has performed all of his actions by virtue of being inwardly restrained, as it says above, "He restrained himself."

This expression – "he restrained himself" – is mentioned only once, but Rashbam seeks to draw a broad, all-encompassing conclusion from it. He views the lone example as a prototype, reflecting Joseph's state of being and demeanor throughout this narrative.

I am strongly inclined to adopt Rashbam's interpretation. As discussed above, I perceive Joseph's restraint as fundamentally different from Haman's restraint or, *lehavdil*, the restraint that Isaiah perceives in God. Joseph's "restraint" reflects an existential struggle, a conflict of identity. It speaks to the chasm between his inner being and his external appearance, all the more so because the external appearance is not merely play-acting and reflects a genuine aspect of Joseph's existence in Egypt. Politically, his success is meteoric; economically, too, he prospers. He serves as both foreign minister and finance minister. He has an Egyptian wife, and his children grow up like any other aristocratic Egyptians. Joseph is well-integrated in the top tier of Egyptian society; he most likely also finds himself participating in its culture and absorbing its values. All of this is one facet of his identity.

At the same time, Joseph constantly carries within himself a mental picture of his father's house and his Hebrew identity. This consciousness is given startling depiction in a midrash which, notwithstanding its extreme imagery, expresses the sages' view of Joseph. The text tells us that Joseph imprisons Simeon in the other brothers' presence; in the midrash (*Bereshit Raba* 91:8), Rabbi Yitzḥak states: "'In their presence,' he imprisoned him; but when they left, he gave him food and drink, bathed him and oiled him." Outwardly, Joseph presents himself as a harsh ruler, the master of the house and sovereign of the country. In his heart of hearts, though – whether out of fraternal love or out of compassion – he does not suffice with providing food for his brother, but actually serves him; not only does he bring him food and drink, but he "bathes him and oils him"! Such is the extent of the contrast between the inscrutable ruler who locks up Simeon and the brother who serves Simeon, tending to him as would a common slave.

Indeed, an enormous chasm separates these two identities. It is precisely the intensity of the contrast that reflects Joseph's feelings and the reality of his life. Here, of course, his "restraint" is that point of contact and equilibrium between his Jewish aspiration, his inner, spiritual and existential purpose, and the external appearance with which he plays out his role in the "outer chamber" – which also seeps inward and smolders within him. The compassion and the weeping that accompanies it are essentially connected to his inner, Hebrew identity; this part of his being desires to be merciful and needs to weep. The world of Judaism is full of love and compassion. Jews are defined as "merciful ones, descendants of merciful ones" (*Ketubot* 8b), while scholars have noted the death-fixation of Egyptian culture.

The mercy that is aroused along with the tears has a connection to Joseph's father's house. There, he was neither ruler nor sovereign nor master. In his father's house, Joseph was simply a boy. It reminds me of a letter a good friend sent me upon the death of my mother, *z"l*:

> When Rav Kook's mother passed away, he cried bitterly. Someone approached him and asked: "Rabbi – we all understand your pain and sorrow, but [why do you weep] to such an extent?" Rav Kook answered, "She was the only one who called me '*mein kind*,' my child."

Such was the case for Joseph. His Jewish identity is expressed, inter alia, through weeping, while his "restraint" must hold back, and sometimes even suppress, those mixed feelings that jostle for position in his consciousness. His is a situation of equilibrium between two worlds, and here Joseph seeks his innermost identity.

Ultimately, his personal history comes out. From this point onwards, while he continues to rule over all of Egypt, his Hebrew identity is overt and publicly known: Pharaoh's house knows, and the Egyptians know. Even Joseph's two Egyptian sons, whose very names recall the severance from home, will be brought to Jacob, their grandfather. This represents their transition from the Egyptian culture of their birth and education to the house of their father's father, where they are brought under the wings of the Divine Presence.

Joseph's encounter with Benjamin serves as a catalyst; it spreads, deepens and overtakes the entire scene. Nevertheless, at the moment of Joseph's revelation, the essence of his weeping is not altogether clear. According to the literal text, only Benjamin and Joseph weep, while the other brothers do not: "He fell upon the neck of Benjamin, his brother, and wept; and Benjamin wept upon his neck" (45:14). From Joseph's perspective, the weeping that begins with Benjamin continues when he faces the rest of his brothers: "He kissed all of his brothers and he wept upon them" (45:15). We hear nothing of their weeping. For Joseph, however, this is an event of immense significance. The excitement and emotion, the need to restrain himself up until this point, the inner conflict – all of this has been transformed into a sigh of relief, accompanied with great joy.

Still, there is another, darker element that is interwoven. This should have been Joseph's greatest hour; it is the realization of his dream. He has dreamt of having everyone dependent upon him – and now this dream has become reality! Joseph believes that at this encounter his brothers will be filled with joy. He removes the mask from his face – but he is suddenly taken aback. Instead of having his brothers plead before him, he pleads before them: "Please [*na*] come near me" (45:4). The word "*na*" always indicates pleading. What is he begging for? Is this moment not meant to be the high point of Joseph's life, the instant when all of his hopes and dreams are literally realized?

Let us look at Joseph's message for Jacob:

Hurry and go up to my father, and tell him: "So says your son, Joseph, 'God has made me lord over all of Egypt. Come down to me; do not delay. You shall dwell in the land of Goshen, and you shall be near to me – you and your children and your children's children, and your flocks and your herds, and all that is yours, and I will support you there.'" (45:9–11)

His message is clear: I will bring; I will support; I will nourish; I will lead. I will treat you as though I am one of you – but you will all be dependent upon me.

At this moment it becomes clear to Joseph the terrible price he has paid for his success, for his integration into Egyptian culture, for all of his restraint. Joseph stands alone. Even once he has decided to emerge from his isolation, to put an end to his alienation, those around him remain alienated from him. It is only now that Joseph discovers what he has sacrificed in exchange for the power that he has accumulated, for being the ruler over all of Egypt, for presuming to be the one to feed, nourish, command and sustain.

This tone, so tragic for Joseph, finds further expression later on. After Jacob's death, Joseph cries once more: "Joseph fell upon his father's face and wept upon him and kissed him" (50:1). Understandably, he is filled with sorrow over the death of his father, but why is he the only one weeping? Where are all of his brothers?

It seems that what separates Joseph at this point is not the grief over Jacob's passing, but the guilt over his separation. It is not only the two decades of silence; even the seventeen years during which Jacob lives in Goshen are years in which Joseph is preoccupied with matters of state. Apparently, his weeping with Benjamin does not put an end to his restraint. Admittedly, the center of gravity has shifted. The man who now cries is no longer Tzafnat Pa'aneaḥ, viceroy of Egypt, with a tenuous tie to Jewish culture. Rather, it is Joseph, who stands firmly and squarely within Jewish culture. Still, the connection with Egypt prevails in his home; he is the master of Pharaoh's house. Joseph is still involved in Egyptian life and culture. It is this connection that finds expression later on, in Egypt's seventy days of weeping. Is the nation really so touched by the death of Jacob? This is not an inner, genuine weeping, but rather an external show, part of an official ritual. In the first chapter of The Waning of the Middle Ages, the historian Johan Huizinga describes medieval society as characterized by the need to weep the loudest, to spill the most tears. Egypt is no different.

It is after the burial that Joseph stands at the most difficult climax of the story. All of the fear that has accompanied him, the abyss that has opened between him and his brothers – all of this now confronts him in his final scene of weeping, when confronted with the imaginary story that his brothers concoct:

> When Joseph's brothers saw that their father had died, they said: "Perhaps Joseph will hate us and repay us for all the evil we did to him!"
>
> So they sent word urgently to Joseph, saying: "Your father commanded before he died, saying: 'So shall you say to Joseph, "I pray you, please forgive the sin of your brothers and their iniquity, for they caused evil to you."' And now, please forgive the sin of the servants of your father's God."
>
> And Joseph wept as they spoke to him.

It is clear why Joseph cries: what more could he have done for them in order to gain their faith, their affection, and their trust? Joseph has removed his mask; he has returned to his roots. He has revealed himself, wept aloud, brought together the torn shreds of their fraternity. What else can he do? Despite all of this, Joseph's brothers continue to regard him with suspicion, and fear that he will take revenge. Is this the level of brotherly love they award him? Admittedly, they have moved away from their starting point of "They hated him even more," but the same primal distrust remains.

At this moment, Joseph discovers the limits of raw power. He discovers the extent to which the human connection, the personal connection, the family connection, hold far more value and importance than does power – both for the person himself and for all those around him. Ultimately, power finds expression in dependence. When all is said and done, who is dependent upon whom? Are Joseph's brothers dependent upon him – the master, the lord, the ruler, the viceroy – or is he perhaps dependent upon them, yearning for their acceptance, desiring their closeness?

Many years later, Joseph again faces the limits of power: "Joseph said to his brothers: I am dying" (50:24). In death, all power disappears as though it had never existed; everything is lost. He continues, "But God will surely remember you": you belong to the land of Israel; you belong to the Jewish faith; you belong to our father's household. You belong to him, you represent him, while I remain on the outside. Bring me in, Joseph asks (v. 25): "God will surely remember you, and you shall carry up my bones from here."

Who will bring up the bones of the brothers to the land of Israel? The text, it seems, has no need to address this question; someone will take care of it. However, there is no one who will willingly, of his own initiative, bring up the bones of Joseph; he must bind his brothers by an oath. Joseph remains attached to his mask, the mask of his life.

Here the secret is revealed. It is this that causes Joseph to weep in the beginning, and it is for the same reason that he cries in the end. He weeps over the weakness inherent in power, over the terrible price that he has paid for it. His dreams have indeed been realized, on some level, but the tragedy remains just as real. The torn shreds of the family have not been made completely whole.

When will the shreds be made whole? Only a few hundred years later, with someone who appears on the stage of Jewish history as an infant crying in a basket among the bulrushes. It is he who seeks the bones of Joseph and, in the midst of the exodus, takes the trouble to bring them up for burial in Israel. It is only when they leave Egypt, only when they leave the territory where Joseph had been lord and ruler, and only through renewed weeping, that Joseph succeeds – that history succeeds – in sewing the pieces back together.

The story of Joseph's weeping is a stirring tragedy, full of lessons, brimming with spiritual, psychological, and social significance. His weeping conveys the inner reality of a person who allows himself to lower all of the barriers with which a person tends to surround himself. By weeping, Joseph allows his inner self to break through and to rise up.

We, too, surround ourselves with barriers, preserving and protecting our individuality and independence, our inner reality; we, too, live in a state of perpetual restraint. We must learn from Joseph how to overcome our restraint and allow the spiritual essence within us to have its say.

Contributors

Rav Amnon Bazak serves as a *Ram* in Yeshivat Har Etzion and teaches Tanach at Herzog College and at the SKA Beit Midrash for Women in Migdal Oz. He authored the two-volume *Nekudat Petiḥa* – short studies in *peshuto shel mikra*, and *Makbilot Nifgashot*, on literary parallels in the book of Samuel.

Rav Yaakov Beasley graduated Yeshiva University with a degree in Tanach and Jewish Education. He has taught Tanach in schools and programs in and around Jerusalem for the past 15 years.

Rav Joshua Berman studied at Yeshivat Har Etzion and received his doctorate in Tanach from Bar-Ilan University. He teaches Tanach at Bar-Ilan and Herzog College. He is the author of several books, including *The Temple: Its Symbolism and Meaning Then and Now*, and *Created Equal: How the Bible Broke with Ancient Political Thought*.

Rav Ezra Bick teaches Talmud and Jewish philosophy at Yeshivat Har Etzion, and is the Director of the Israel Koschitzky Virtual Beit Midrash. He is the author of *In His Mercy: Understanding the Thirteen Midot*.

Rav Yoel Bin-Nun studied at Yeshivat Merkaz HaRav and Yeshivat Har Etzion, where he was among the founders. He was Rosh Yeshiva of Yeshivat HaKibbutz HaDati, and currently teaches Bible and Jewish Philosophy in Herzog College.

Rav Mordechai Breuer *zt"l* taught at Yeshivat Har Etzion for over thirty years, where he trained a generation of younger scholars. He was the originator of the method of biblical interpretation known as *"shitat habeḥinot."* He authored two volumes of *Pirkei Moadot* (1986). Two volumes of his articles on Genesis (*Pirkei Bereshit*) appeared after his death, as well as a volume on the book of Isaiah.

Rav Yonatan Grossman studied at Yeshivat Har Etzion and received a doctorate in Bible from Bar-Ilan University. He has taught at Yeshivat Har Etzion since 1998 and currently teaches Bible at Bar-Ilan University and Herzog College.

Rav Tamir Granot studied at Yeshivat Har Etzion and earned a doctorate in Jewish Philosophy from Bar-Ilan University. He teaches Talmud and Jewish Philosophy at Herzog College and other colleges, and is the author of a VBM series on Jewish thought and the Holocaust.

Rav Michael Hattin teaches Ḥumash and Prophets at the Pardes Institute of Jewish Studies. He holds a professional degree in architecture from the University of Toronto and did his rabbinical studies at Yeshivat Har Etzion.

Rav Yair Kahn is head of the Overseas Students Program and has been a *Ram* at Yeshivat Har Etzion since 1987. Rav Kahn is the editor of the *Shiurei Hagrid* series.

Rav Menachem Leibtag headed the Overseas Program at Yeshivat Har Etzion for over a decade. He initiated the Tanach Study Center, a comprehensive program for the study of Tanach on the Internet. He teaches Tanach at Yeshivat Har Etzion, Midreshet Lindenbaum and Yeshivat Sha'alvim.

Rav Aharon Lichtenstein is senior Rosh Yeshiva of Yeshivat Har Etzion, and the author of numerous works on Jewish philosophy and Talmud.

Rav Mosheh Lichtenstein is Rosh Yeshiva of Yeshivat Har Etzion. He holds a degree in English Literature from Hebrew University, and is the author of *Moses: Envoy of God, Envoy of His People.*

Rav Yaakov Medan is Rosh Yeshiva at Yeshivat Har Etzion. He serves as a *Ram* for fourth-year students at the yeshiva, and teaches Tanach and Jewish Thought at Herzog College.

Rabbanit Sharon Rimon holds a master's degree in Bible from Matan Institute and Baltimore University. She teaches Tanach at the Women's Beit Midrash in Efrat.

Rav Yehuda Rock received his *semikha* from Rav Aharon Lichtenstein שליט״א. He has taught in the Otniel *hesder* yeshiva, and was Rosh Kollel at the Boca Raton Community Kollel. He is the author of *Eved HaMelekh* on Tzitzit and *tekhelet.* yrock20@gmail.com

Rav Reuven Taragin earned an MA in Jewish History and Education at Touro College (Israel). He is the Dean of the Overseas Students at Yeshivat HaKotel, and has taught at Yeshivat Har Etzion, Nishmat and Be'er Miriam.

Rav Elchanan Samet has taught at Yeshivat Birkat Moshe (Maale Adumim) and currently is a senior lecturer at Herzog Teacher's College. He is the author of two series of studies in *parashat hashavua* as well as *Pirkei Eliyahu, Pirkei Elisha,* and *Yad LaRambam.*

Rav Chanoch Waxman received *semikha* from Yeshiva University and holds Master's degrees in Jewish and General Philosophy. He has taught at Matan in Jerusalem and been the Rosh Kollel of the Torah Mitzion Kollel in Chicago. He currently teaches at Yeshivat HaMivtar and Yeshivat Har Etzion.

The fonts used in this book are from the Arno family

Maggid Books
The best of contemporary Jewish thought from
Koren Publishers Jerusalem